KU-102-917

Tom Biddle
07316 564 592

EUROPEAN BUSINESS

This lively and accessible textbook examines the increasing impact of the European Union on the European business environment, addressing the core challenges facing enterprises in the formative years of the new millennium. By focusing on the links between the processes of globalisation and regional economic regeneration, the authors offer a unique insight into European policy.

In addition to dealing with conventional EU policy areas such as European Monetary Union (EMU) and competition policy, the book also covers important topics and issues which are often excluded from other texts on EU policy and business. Key features include:

- a detailed synopsis of the evolution of the EU and its institutions, and the development of the European business environment
- an in-depth examination of the impact of European policy on business strategy in crucial areas such as the environment, energy, transport, small and medium-sized enterprises and the information society
- a reappraisal of enterprise and policy maker responses to the challenges imposed by globalisation to secure European competitiveness in the twenty-first century
- well structured chapters providing an excellent balance of contemporary issues combined with boxed features, mini-cases and illustrative figures and diagrams

With exceptional coverage of the relevant topics and a highly up-to-date approach, *European Business* is essential reading for students of international business, European business strategy and policy, and European economics.

Debra Johnson is Principal Lecturer at Hull Business School, University of Lincolnshire and Humberside. **Colin Turner** is Principal Lecturer in European Business Strategy at Huddersfield University Business School. They have both published widely in the field of European integration.

EUROPEAN BUSINESS

Policy challenges for the new commercial environment

DEBRA JOHNSON
and COLIN TURNER

LONDON

AND NEW YORK

First published 2000 by Routledge
11 New Fetter Lane, London EC4P 4EE

Simultaneously published in the USA and Canada
by Routledge
29 West 35th Street, New York, NY 10001

Reprinted 2001

Routledge is an imprint of the Taylor & Francis Group

© 2000 Debra Johnson and Colin Turner

Typeset in Plantin and Rockwell by
Keystroke, Jacaranda Lodge, Wolverhampton
Printed and bound in Great Britain by
TJ International Ltd, Padstow, Cornwall

All rights reserved. No part of this book may be reprinted or
reproduced or utilised in any form or by any electronic, mechanical,
or other means, now known or hereafter invented, including
photocopying and recording, or in any information storage or
retrieval system, without permission in writing from the publishers.

British Library Cataloguing in Publication Data
A catalogue record for this book is available from the British Library

Library of Congress Cataloging in Publication Data
Johnson, Debra.
   European business : policy challenges for the new commercial
environment / Debra Johnson and Colin Turner.
      p. cm.
   Includes bibliographical references and index.
   1. European Union countries—Commercial policy. 2. Industrial
policy–European Union countries. 3. European Union countries–
Economic policy. 4. Business enterprises–European Union
countries. 5. European Union countries–Economic integration.
6. Competition, International. I. Turner, Colin, 1967–
II. Title.
   HF1531.J64 2000
   338.94–dc21   99–29676
            CIP

ISBN 0–415–22024–6 (hbk)
ISBN 0–415–22025–4 (pbk)

CONTENTS

FIGURES

TABLES

BOXES

CASE STUDIES

PREFACE

There are many books available on the European Union and its policies so why write another one? Our experience in teaching European integration to a wide range of business students is that, excellent as many of these books are, the majority of them are written for political scientists or economists and therefore do not link policies to their impact on the business environment or to individual enterprises. After failing every year to find a book which exactly suited our needs, we decided to write one ourselves. This volume is the result of our efforts and, although inevitably far from perfect, we believe we have moved a considerable way towards presenting a more business-centred approach to European policy. Our main target is business but in the same way as existing books on European integration are useful for business students in helping them to understand the process of policy formation and the underlying socio-economic rationale for policy, so we believe that this volume can also add another dimension to EU policy for political scientists and economists.

The book is also timely. It was written after the negotiation of the Amsterdam Treaty (but before the ratification process was complete) and is one of the first books to reflect the outcome of the Treaty negotiations. In addition, as economic and monetary union is realised, we believe that it is even more important for businesses to take the European policy dimension into account in their planning. This applies not only to members of the Eurozone but also to enterprises from the EU members remaining outside the Eurozone in its initial stages and to companies from third countries.

Our primary aim is to set the development and establishment of policy within the context of the business environment and to foster greater awareness of how European policy interacts with business. Accordingly common themes permeate the chapters. The book was written during a period when economic liberalism and its reliance on the beneficial effects of competition had become the dominant policy paradigm. Market access, deregulation and liberalisation therefore appear in various guises in most, if not all, of the chapters.

EU policy is not formed in a vacuum and reflects pressures from three inter-related levels – the national, the European and the global. Therefore, in several instances, the chapters reflect the pressures on EU policy coming from member states and how different national approaches influence European policy. Increasingly, however, it is global factors which are having a major impact on the business environment. As liberalisation advances into new areas of the international arena and technological changes facilitate more effective and efficient communication and transactions, so the global economy is becoming more and more interdependent and wielding a greater influence on the determination of EU policy. The impact of growing global interdependence on policy determination at EU level is a theme which runs through many chapters.

The book opens with a chapter on the theory and practice of integration. In particular, it examines various processes which have resulted in greater integration at European level.

The intention is to approach integration from a business perspective and to highlight the interaction between the process of integration and its impact on the business environment. Subsequent chapters on individual policies pick up this interaction in relation to individual policy issues. However, integration at European level is becoming increasingly intertwined with the effects of growing global interdependence. These themes are also highlighted in Chapter 1. The literature on globalisation seems to be expanding exponentially and the word 'globalisation' is used extensively throughout the text. The chapter discusses different interpretations of the forces at work in the international environment and sets out scenarios regarding the potential evolution of these forces, relating them to their impact both on regional integration and on the business environment. Later chapters highlight these themes in a more applied form.

The second chapter is intended to supply a historical and institutional context for the individual policy chapters which follow. European integration generally and individual policy initiatives did not emerge out of thin air but arose from a specific set of economic and political circumstances. Chapter 2 therefore traces the evolution of European integration to the conclusion of the Amsterdam Treaty. The second part of the chapter highlights the functions of the main European institutions with a particular emphasis on identifying points in the policy making process which are accessible and open to business lobbying. Although lobbying is important, it is also important for all businesses in Europe to appreciate the rationale for EU policy and how the EU works.

The next fifteen chapters discuss individual EU policy areas. The policies were selected on the basis of their importance for business. We acknowledge that it could be argued that other policies should have been included but we have also striven to include issues which, although the subject of much contemporary debate about the business environment, are frequently excluded from books on EU policy. The chapters on policies relating to small and medium enterprises and to the information society fall into this category. We have also included a generic chapter on trans-European networks which have become a major plank of EU policy but which are often ignored in many books, apart from the occasional aside about transport infrastructure. Other chapters are more predictable in their inclusion.

The concluding chapter of the book pulls together a number of the themes of the preceding chapters, enabling us to put forward tentative conclusions about the role and influence of European integration on the business environment and of its interaction with international trends.

The intention in writing individual chapters was not to present an exhaustive description of individual policies (as well as being a lengthy process, it would also be extremely tedious for the reader). Rather we have aimed to highlight key themes in the contemporary debate about individual policies. For example, the chapter on labour market policy reflects the flexibility debate and the chapter on environment policy looks at the cost versus ecological modernism debate. In other words, we have endeavoured to ensure that the text of chapters reflects the broad sweep of policies and the ideas and themes surrounding them: more detailed analysis of individual policies is confined to boxes, a device which is also used to present case studies relating to the impact of policy changes on individual sectors or companies. An added benefit of this more thematic approach is that, although more recent data will become available, the book itself will not date as quickly as it might otherwise have done.

A degree of cross-referencing of chapters is included: this highlights common themes across chapters and encourages the reader to consider and appreciate linkages between policies. Each chapter finishes with a summary of key points and suggestions for further reading. The latter have been kept deliberately short: the literature on EU policy is vast and growing and exhaustive lists can discourage students. We also encourage students to consult key policy documents directly, many of which are now available in full text form on the Internet, and have included references to them in the suggested reading.

The reader is the best judge of the extent to which we have achieved our original aims and attained an appropriate balance within and between chapters.

Debra Johnson and Colin Turner
Hull and Huddersfield, September 1998

ABBREVIATIONS

ACP	Africa Caribbean Pacific
APEC	Asia Pacific Economic Co-operation Forum
bcm	Billion cubic metres
CAP	Common Agricultural Policy
CCP	Common Commercial Policy
CBI	Confederation of British Industry
CEE	Central and Eastern Europe
CEFIC	European Chemical Industry Federation
CEFTA	Cental European Free Trade Area
CET	Common External Tariff
CFI	Court of First Instance
CFSP	Common foreign and security policy
CHP	Combined heat and power
CI	Community Initiative
CIS	Commonwealth of Independent States
CMEA	Council for Mutual Economic Assistance
CoR	Committee of the Regions
Coreper	Committee of Permanent Representatives
CO_2	Carbon dioxide
CRS	Computer reservation system
CTP	Common transport policy
DG	Directorate-General
EAGGF	European Agricultural Guidance and Guarantee Fund
EAP	Environmental Action Programme
EBRD	European Bank for Reconstruction and Development
EC	European Community; electronic commerce
ECB	European Central Bank
ECJ	European Court of Justice
ECSC	European Coal and Steel Community
ECT	Energy Charter Treaty
ECU	European Currency Unit
EdF	Electricité de France
EDI	Electronic data interchange
EEA	European Economic Area
EEC	European Economic Community
EFTA	European Free Trade Area
EIA	European Infrastructure Agency
EIB	European Investment Bank
EIF	European Investment Fund
EMAs	Euro-Mediterranean Association Agreements

EMI	European Monetary Institute
EMP	Euro-Mediterranean Partnership
EMS	European Monetary System
EMU	Economic and monetary union
ENSR	European Network for SME Research
EP	European Parliament
EPC	European Political Co-operation
ERDF	European Regional Development Fund
ERM	Exchange Rate Mechanism
ESB	Electricity Supply Board
ESC	Economic and Social Committee
ESCB	European System of Central Banks
ESF	European Social Fund
ESI	Electricity supply industry
ETNO	European Telecommunication Network Operator
ETSI	European Telecommunications Standards Institute
EU	European Union
Euratom	European Atomic Energy Community
FDI	Foreign direct investment
FIFG	Financial Instrument for Fisheries Guidance
FSU	Former Soviet Union
FTA	Free trade area
G8	Group of Eight States (Canada, France, Germany, Italy, Japan, Russia, the United Kingdom, the United States)
GATS	General Agreement on Trade in Services
GATT	General Agreement on Tariffs and Trade
GCC	Gulf Cooperation Council
GDP	Gross Domestic Product
GHG	Greenhouse gas
GNP	Gross National Product
GSP	Generalised System of Preferences
HDTV	High definition television
ICT	Information and communication technology
IEM	Internal energy market
IGC	Intergovernmental conference
ILO	International Labour Organisation
IMP	Integrated Mediterranean Programme
IMPACT	Information Market Policy Actions
IPCC	International Panel on Climate Change
ISDN	Integrated services digital network
IT	Information technology
ITU	International Telecommunications Union
LNG	Liquefied natural gas
LSE	Large scale enterprise
MAS	Market Access Strategy
M&A	Mergers and acquisitions
MEP	Member of the European Parliament
MEIP	Market economy investor principle
MFA	Multifibre Arrangement
MFN	Most Favoured Nation
MNC	Multi-national corporation
MNE	Multi-national enterprise

MoU	Memorandum of Understanding
Mtoe	Million tons of oil equivalent
NAFTA	North American Free Trade Area
NATO	North Atlantic Treaty Organisation
NCPI	New Commercial Policy Instrument
NegTPA	Negotiated third party access
NH_3	Ammonia
NTA	New Transatlantic Agenda
OECD	Organisation for Economic Co-operation and Development
OEEC	Organisation for European Economic Cooperation
OPEC	Organisation of Petroleum Exporting Countries
PC	Personal computer
PHARE	Poland and Hungary: aid for the reconstruction of economies
PPP	Public private partnership
PPS	Purchasing power standard
PSO	Public service obligation
PTO	Public telecommunication operator
QMV	Qualified majority voting
REC	Regional electricity company
regTPA	Regulated third party access
SAP	Social Action Programme
SBM	Single buyer model
SEA	Single European Act
SEM	Single European Market
SIM	Single insurance market
SLIM	Simpler legislation for the internal market
SME	Small and medium enterprise
SPD	Single Programming Document
TABD	Transatlantic Business Dialogue
TACIS	Technical Assistance Commonwealth of Independent States
TARGET	Trans-European Real-time Settlement Express Transfer
TBR	Trade Barriers Regulation
TENs	Trans-European networks
TEP	Transatlantic Economic Partnership
TEU	Treaty on Economic Union
TNC	Transnational corporation
TPA	Third party access
TRIMS	Trade-related investment measures
TRIPS	Trade-related intellectual property measures
UCPTE	Union for the Co-ordination of Production and Transport of Electric Power
UNCTAD	United Nations Commission for Trade and Development
UNFCCC	United Nations Framework Convention for Climate Change
UNICE	European employers organisation
USSR	Union of Soviet Socialist Republics
VER	Voluntary Export Restraint
VOC	Volatile organic compound
WEU	Western European Union
WIPO	World Intellectual Property Organisation
WTD	Working Time Directive
WTO	World Trade Organisation

1

THE EVOLVING EUROPEAN
BUSINESS ENVIRONMENT

European business, by which we mean all enterprises located within the fifteen states of the European Union (EU), whether indigenously owned or not, is undergoing a period of substantial challenge and change. The essence of this challenge stems from changes in the European business environment at three levels:

- the national level where the discretionary actions of policy makers are increasingly constrained by European integration and the internationalisation of markets;
- the European level where previously fragmented markets are being integrated into a single unit;
- the international level where freer global trade is stimulating greater international interdependence.

It is in the light of these changes that policies to enhance the performance of European business within national, European and global markets are developed. As a result of this interdependence, policy formulation increasingly takes into account policies and developments elsewhere in the international economy. Policy makers thus more and more regard their role as aiding the creation of a climate in which European business can flourish: commercial success itself comes directly from the strategies and decisions of enterprises and not from the actions of policy makers who are essentially facilitators.

The initial sections of this chapter are concerned with the challenges posed by freer trade and interaction for the existing models of economic management within European states. However, the core focus is upon an exploration of the two main forces facing European business – the internal and external pressures towards integration. Consequently, the chapter explores the nature and commercial implications of the process of European integration. This is followed by an examination of the more diluted integration represented by the trend towards globalisation. It is important for the reader to understand at this juncture that it is these primary forces to which many of the policies examined within this text are responding.

THE CHANGING EUROPEAN BUSINESS MODEL

As the European business environment changes, so the basis of policy measures alters or at the very least comes under challenge. The EU provides a theatre for two potentially conflicting socio-economic models – Continental and Anglo-Saxon capitalism. These differing perspectives, and their consequent legacy for respective commercial cultures, have frequently led to disputes about policy developments at both trans-national and supranational levels. Such conflicts have been most evident in areas such as social and industrial policy.

The social model of capitalism

The social market model, which in its various guises has been the norm in Continental Europe's post-war commercial environment, is based upon an assumption that society is best served when its stakeholders (that is, employers, employees and the general population) agree how best to run an economy. Although the market is accepted as the primary means of allocating resources, it is underpinned by a series of consensual structures orchestrated by the state to ensure that the interests of the assorted stakeholders are accounted for. In its present form, the key characteristics of this model include:

- co-operation and partnership within industrial structures;
- a financial system that complements the above objectives;
- a generous social welfare system;
- a comprehensive education and training system;
- a decentralised political system;
- a series of independent government agencies;
- a consensual economic policy;
- a large number of medium sized enterprises;
- an active industrial policy.

The above is, of necessity, a simplification of reality: EU states in practice operate variants of this model. For example, the Scandinavian model has larger elements of social regulation than many countries and France has a highly centralised political system. Currently, many states are re-examining the appropriateness of the social market model in view of demographic changes, financial constraints on public budgets and the limits imposed on many EU states to operate this model effectively as a consequence of international market forces. This latter point underlines that this form of capitalism was closely associated with Keynesian economic management which increasingly fell out of favour during the late 1970s and early 1980s. Overall, many EU states are seeking to alter the social market model by incorporating elements of the more market-centred approach of Anglo-Saxon capitalism.

The Anglo-Saxon model

The Anglo-Saxon model of capitalism places a stronger emphasis upon capital and lower levels of state involvement within the economy. This accepts more explicitly the primacy of market forces and the private sector in resource allocation. This system is most typified by the UK who, under the politico-economic ideology of Thatcherism, strengthened the role of markets through privatisation and wholesale liberalisation. This bred the central notion of establishing a business friendly environment via macro-economic stability (in which low inflation was the primary objective), supply side liberalisation and enhanced economic freedom. In this context, business performance is judged by share value and profit and not by some broader notion of social obligation. This form of capitalism places emphasis upon commercial efficiency as the deliverer of economic, and ultimately social, success.

Changes within the business environment are creating a more hybrid, arguably more homogenous, form of capitalism within many European states. States are increasingly developing policies that reflect the traditional social market model watered down by the freer market approach of the Anglo-Saxon model as global/international markets start to impose constraints on policy options. This change has been compounded by an, albeit gradual, political shift away from active intervention which many regard as failing to deliver its promises. In addition, the view is gaining ground that the lack of commercial discipline upon and flexibility within firms resulting from the consensual system has helped undermine the performance of European enterprises. Changes, even diluted ones, are therefore regarded as necessary if the social market model is to survive. Consequently, the gradual adoption of features of Anglo-Saxon capitalism (for example by setting explicit profit targets and encouraging shareholder activism and corporate restructuring) are becoming integral to re-defined social market models. In turn, there is limited evidence (for example, by ending the UK social policy opt-out and the adoption of a minimum wage) that the UK's 'New Labour' government accepts elements of the European social market model within its broadly pro-market economic management stance.

Businesses in most parts of Europe broadly accept the European model of capitalism but realise that certain facets of it can impede their success in global markets. If policy is about sustaining Europe's position in the global arena, then policy makers need to establish a form of capitalism that enables European enterprises to achieve this objective. Firms can only be successful if the framework within which they act facilitates such strategies. One opinion views the entire problem as stemming from over-regulation of the European business environment. Or to put it another way, the environment is regulated in such a way that it inhibits the ability of European enterprises to compete successfully on a global scale largely by imposing higher costs upon enterprises. Such problems are not uniform across the EU but they are problems nonetheless.

INTERNAL INFLUENCES ON THE EUROPEAN BUSINESS ENVIRONMENT: THEMES AND FEATURES OF ECONOMIC INTEGRATION

To offer a simple dictionary definition, economic integration is based upon the removal of frontiers which inhibit the movement of goods, services, labour, capital and communication flows between states, regions or any other geographical unit. In the context of the European Union, this is defined as removing the impediments to trade and mobility between the individual units so that the area can eventually be recognised as a single economic unit. This implies that both markets and economic policy measures are integrated to reflect the growing interaction and interdependence between member states. This process is not static and tends to evolve in response to the requirements of enterprises and other commercial and policy actors. This is confirmed by the experience of the European Union which evolved from a customs union into an economic and monetary union via the development of a single market. There is no inevitability about such trends which are often a pragmatic response to the needs of economic actors as they exploit opportunities created by the removal of discrimination. Economic integration also implies the sustenance of some degree of discrimination by these member states *vis-à-vis* the rest of the world.

Tinbergen (1965), as quoted in Robson (1997) split the process of integration into two distinct aspects. The first is negative integration which refers to the removal of discrimination and restrictions on movement: that is elimination of measures used by states to inhibit the free flow of resources across borders. This contrasts with positive integration which involves the modification of existing instruments and institutions to enable trans-national markets to function more effectively. Negative integration is generally easier to achieve than positive integration.

The process of integration is much more than the simple physical coalescence of formerly disparate units into an integrated system. This is to understate the nature, form and implications of the process. The endgame of the integration process is a unified socio-economic and political body. However, the process of economic integration was not inevitable, or indeed deliberate. It emerged as a consequence of on-going processes within and, increasingly external to, the European economy. The initial themes and concerns of integration arose from the after-effects of two world wars that devastated the European economy (see Chapter 2) and stressed the need to contain conflict. These initial objectives have increasingly been overtaken by a renewed and more potent rationale based upon supporting Europe's commercial position in which consolidation as opposed to fragmentation is regarded as the most effective way of enabling the continent to sustain and enhance its economic and commercial standing in international markets. This is especially important for the many relatively small European states who need to redefine their commercial position within an increasingly internationalised economy.

Thus gradual economic integration is a starting point for the examination of the notion of challenge and change that European enterprises face. It is important to underline that such integration will be pivotal to European business success upon the global stage. Policy therefore seeks to establish fora for integration and policies which complement its consequences in terms of business functioning and operations. These policies are central to the realisation of corporate efficiency across the European economic space which can then be used as a basis for success within global markets.

Table 1.1 and Figure 1.1 highlight the core stages of economic integration: the former highlights core features and the latter indicates the dynamism within the process. There is no hard and fast law that integration starts with a free trade area and inevitably concludes with economic and monetary union (EMU). The speed and depth of the integration is driven and determined by many factors such as the requirements of enterprises, levels of interaction across borders and the political willingness of elites to commit themselves to deeper forms of integration. Integration is therefore a pragmatic affair determined by the requirements of a specific area. In the European Union, integration started with a customs union not with a free trade area as set out in Figure 1.1. Geographical proximity, shared historical experiences, cultural affinities that stimulate commerce, converging levels of economic development and rising levels of intra-industry trade have all combined to stimulate and enhance the integration process in Europe. Other regional blocs have seemingly little desire to move beyond the most diluted form of integration – the free trade area. However, this may alter as states reconsider their economic interests in the light of continuing globalisation.

Table 1.1 highlights the commonly recognised forms of economic integration. Each form implies a differing degree of commitment by states to the integration process and acceptance of the consequences for their freedom of action. Free trade areas generally require little constraint upon national policy actions whereas an EMU implies a considerable loss of policy discretion. Other forms of economic integration lie somewhere in between.

An element of dynamism can operate within the integration process (see Figure 1.1) which results in the spillover of shallower forms of integration into ever deeper integration. This dynamism is frequently born of commercial need: as enterprises exploit the opportunities arising from one form of integration, the need for further freedoms emerges.

Table 1.1 Forms of economic integration

Forms of integration	Characteristics
Free trade area	• loose agreement between participants • little ceding of sovereignty • tariff and quota-free trade between member states • no positive integration • persistence of non-tariff barriers between member states • retention of national tariffs *vis-à-vis* third countries • problems of trade deflection (whereby commodities from third countries enter the FTA via the member state with the lowest tariff) overcome by rules of origin
Customs union	• free trade in goods and services with a common external tariff to overcome problems of trade deflection • some positive integration • more fulsome development of common policies, especially with regard to trade with third countries
Single market	• customs union enhanced by freer mobility of factors of production – notably, labour, capital and services • moves towards more positive integration • fuller development of other common policies, such as competition and regional policy
Economic and monetary union (EMU)	• measures to secure economic unification strengthened via enhanced co-ordination and, possibly, inter-state transfers • more intense positive integration • policy harmonisation to remove the remaining impediments to commodity and factor mobility • severe limits on the independent actions of states • monetary stability as an accompaniment to economic unification achieved via stabilised/fixed exchange rates or a single currency • the range and effects of common policies are more marked, notably with regard to macro-economic policy tools • more fulsome development of centralised supranational power, possibly within a federal context

Internal dynamic processes

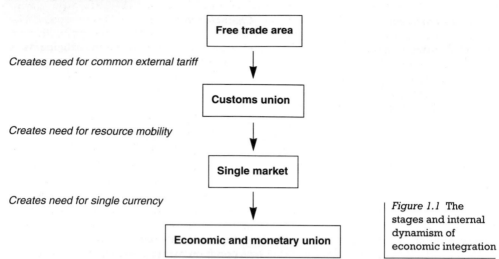

Figure 1.1 The stages and internal dynamism of economic integration

For example, in exploiting the opportunities of a customs union, firms may find they need greater resource mobility to fully realise commercial gains thereby creating pressure for a single market. Within weaker forms of economic integration, states can overcome problems derived from concerns such as trade deflection via rules of origin, thereby removing the motive for a common external tariff and the need to develop a customs union. However, if closer trading links raise a demand for closer co-ordination of other internal policies, this process may be hard to resist.

Consequently, the notion that integration is dynamic and cannot readily be halted is not a foregone conclusion. Where dynamism does exist, it comes more from the daily interactions associated with commercial operations than from the conscious decisions of policy makers. However, there is no certainty about this process as these forces are shaped by other considerations such as the willingness of elites to forgo or to pool more sovereignty within a more broadly defined, deeper economic union.

Economic integration has been traditionally examined within the bounds of static analysis in which the relative benefits and costs of integration are assessed in terms of trade creation and trade diversion. Briefly, the former seeks to derive cost benefits from accessing cheaper resources and commodities within partner countries as opposed to their provision from relatively more expensive indigenous production. The latter seeks to assess how costs are increased as a result of the integration process as resources/commodities from third countries (which are now subject to a common external tariff) are replaced by relatively more expensive production from within the newly formed trading bloc. Such analysis offers an examination of the theoretical gains (through welfare economics) from engaging in integration but is often divorced from the process via which gains are realised. The static nature of such analysis does not lend itself to the dynamic nature of the integration process. As a process, integration is osmotic in nature, born of the adaptation strategies of actors to events within the political, economic and social sphere within which they operate and which brings them into closer proximity with other actors in their own and related spheres.

The process of integration is complemented by a series of policy events which formalise the interactions and emerging interdependencies within the integrating unit. These policy events are best explained as a decision which often, via the legal, political or economic system, directly affects the actions and interests of operators. A classic example is provided by the Single European Market (SEM) and its effects upon the strategies of bodies involved in the operation and development of the European economic space. The evolution of integration in Europe is littered with such events which have gradually over time pushed integration in Europe. The development of integration in this domain is in part explained by spillover where the establishment of one policy born of the integration process develops over time into a justification for further policy initiatives. Accordingly, integration from this perspective is the result of a series of events which are reflected in assorted policy initiatives which push towards deeper integration.

Examining integration as a consecutive series of policy events underplays the deeper processes at work. Such policy events are often formal statements of these underlying processes. There is no inevitability that the development of one policy will necessitate the development of further policy measures. Policy spillover will only occur if the interactions between operators are of sufficient intensity to warrant its development. This underscores a vital rationale for policy development: that is, its evolution should be pragmatic and respond to the changing needs and requirements of those operators/actors directly affected by it. Policy is a phenomenon that can kick-start such processes but the outcome is very much a micro-phenomenon arising from the individual strategies and actions of each operator. For example, the SEM brought freedom of movement for factors of production but its effects were only as great as the willingness and ability of the individual actors to exploit the opportunities it created. Thus policy events as formal expressions of economic integration are born of the on-going processes which stimulated their initial development.

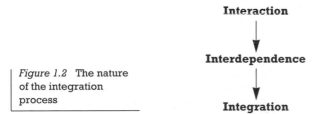

Figure 1.2 The nature of the integration process

The process of integration is formalised within Figure 1.2. The three inter-related phases identified exhibit the following features and characteristics:

Stage one: interactions

Interlinkages and inter-relationships across borders grow to a degree of intensity where the interests of each state become mutually defined, both formally and informally. In terms of the integration process, these links result from the operations of indigenous enterprises in the economies of partner states. Thus the prosperity of the domestic economy starts to exhibit an increasing reliance upon events and processes in other economies. Consequently the intensity of interactions will be determined by phenomena such as intra-union foreign direct investment (FDI), resource movements between member states and trade links.

Stage two: interdependence

The mutuality of interest between actors (stimulated by the intensity of interactions) creates a degree of reliance in which the commercial interests of each party become mutually dependent. The result of such interdependence is a non-zero sum game for the states involved. Economic prosperity is mutually dependent to the extent that any independent action to secure advantages for domestic enterprises over foreign firms is likely to result in a commercial loss for all parties concerned. For example, levels of FDI between states can grow to such an extent that independent action to protect indigenous industry can be mutually damaging to all economies concerned.

Stage three: integration

The result of the process is the establishment of a policy event whereby the mutuality of interests reflected in the process is formalised. Integration need not be fully expressed as a policy event: it may be represented in economic terms by a series of formalised industrial or sectional re-organisations which reflect the preferences of economic operators functioning within the larger economic space. Such integration reflects a response to the increased interactions and interdependence across space and may need to be sanctioned by policy measures or regulatory decisions.

In this context, the integration process reflects decisions made by enterprises and/or public sectors in recognition of interactions and interdependencies. Commercial operators exploiting the changes in their operating environment are a powerful factor driving the process of economic integration. Operators working across borders may find limits upon their preferred level of interaction and may require policy measures which further stimulate the integration process. Any policy measure that does not reflect the desire for increased interaction is unlikely to be a powerful motor within the integration process which requires a political willingness by policy makers to participate and to meet the commitments imposed by policy initiatives.

The emergence of the network economy is an example of the above process in action and will promote integration via the gradual expansion of networking relationships (see below). Networks are tools of trans-national corporate strategy, enterprise value-added, market access and organisational efficiency. Such networks will be enhanced as mobile factors of production become ever more important for enterprise success on an international level and as wealth creation becomes more evidently tied into technology and intellectual investment.

Within the context of the network economy, Wallace (1990) offered a distinction between formal and informal integration which broadly mirrors the above analysis and which seeks to provide a formal statement of how, in practice, integration within the EU is likely to evolve. Informal integration arises from the interaction among market dynamics, technology and communications networks. In short, the development of informal integration is due to the practicalities of economics and commerce and not to any conscious political decision. Formal integration is a more pragmatic form of integration that occurs on a case-by-case basis. Generally formal integration acts as a catalyst and facilitates the actions of commercial operators and public administrations and parallels the 'policy and event' analysis offered above. The osmotic tendency to political (formal) integration is driven by processes derived from market behaviour. Such a stance perceives economics and enterprise functioning as the primary drivers behind the processes of integration to which politicians respond via a series of policy measures. Thus political integration is a derivative of broader socio-economic integrative forces.

As economic integration has deepened, so there has been pressure to complement this process via closer political union. Increasingly bigger political units are advocated as necessary to support the development of big business and as a complement to the coalescence of economic units. This is true of sectors where economies of scale are evidently needed for the establishment of a global presence in specified sectors. Laffan (1992) distinguishes between four different aspects of political integration:

- *institutional*: based upon collective decision making;
- *policy*: based upon the transfer of policy developments being transferred to a higher level;
- *attitudinal*: sources of support for the process amongst assorted communities;
- *security*: non-violent inter-state relations.

Such political centralisation is frequently associated with dirigiste economic policies. In part, the desire to develop European champions as a replacement for national champions in the globalising economy to some states offers a commercial rationale for deeper political integration. Business, as a matter of routine, requires a policy (and therefore a political) arena that best complements the needs and requirements of the environment within which they operate.

Policy initiatives that shape the development of the European business environment arise out of this process. The Treaties of Paris and Rome which established the European Coal and Steel Community (ECSC) and the European Economic Community (see Chapter 2) were modest in what they prescribed in terms of necessary policy measures to complement their objectives. However as these foundations have been built upon, so the range and potency of policies developed at a trans-national or supranational level have expanded. This is a response to the need to account for spillovers in terms of resources and the effects of their consumption (for example, pollution), the need to address inter-dependencies in stabilisation policies (for example, the ability of competitive devaluations to distort intra-EU competition) and the need to compensate for the potentially negative side-effects of existing policy to complement further integration (for example, cohesion and convergence policies). It is through these processes that policy starts to have an increasingly influential impact upon the performance of business.

THE BUSINESS ENVIRONMENT AND EUROPEAN INTEGRATION

Businesses have been amongst some of the strongest advocates of European integration, even if they differ about exactly how deep the process should go. Generally, larger enterprises have a stronger preference for deeper integration than small and medium enterprises (SMEs). This may be because the latter tend to operate within a localised market base whereas the former is seeking to exploit the network economy. Clearly integration, as Table 1.2 shows, offers many commercial opportunities and challenges to business. Initially, in a commercial sense, integration is based upon the common values shared by European states, namely the allegiance to capitalism (and all its implications) and the mixed economy. Thus whilst a common commercial culture may still (at least in the short term) be elusive, there is a broad commitment to the market mechanism performing the central role in the allocation of resources within the European business environment. Frequently, this will involve FDI strategies to enable enterprises to exploit both new markets and the opportunities created for the organisation of production.

Businesses require that integration delivers a regulatory, economic, legal and political environment that creates the necessary opportunities, consistency, certainty, clarity and transparency that enables them to operate in the best interests of the European economy. This includes smooth and predictable decision making (see Chapter 2) as well as the opportunities afforded to enterprises by the opening of national markets. Such issues render it important that businesses are aware of where political power lies within the

Table 1.2 Typical business challenges and opportunities from integration

- enhanced value-added from more diverse sourcing opportunities
- greater intensity of competition within domestic markets
- stimulus to product innovation
- greater opportunities within foreign markets
- re-organisation of production and distribution systems on a trans-national basis
- pressure upon costs and prices
- operational efficiencies derived from economies of scale
- exploitation of the international division of labour
- greater price transparency
- rationalisation of product lines
- development of networking relationships
- possible harmonisation of labour conditions
- opportunities for financing business through integrated capital markets

European business environment, especially with regard to decisions that will affect their strategy and commercial performance. Clarity over power structures and sources of policy decisions are essential for business and offer opportunities for access and influence over these political structures. The need to address a number of policy authorities when developing a strategy is both time consuming and costly and is therefore something enterprises wish to avoid. In seeking policy approval for actions/strategies (where required) a 'one-stop shop' is almost always preferred. It is these primary concerns that influence the position of business with regard to European integration. The attainment of such objectives is hindered by fragmentation and a lack of credibility over policy formation and decision making.

Cross-border strategies, notably via the emergence of networking relationships, have been a key factor in the shaping of the process of economic integration by commercial actors. Policies developed at national, supranational and, to an extent, at global levels have worked to support such corporate strategies. Many of these relationships are interactions based upon the emergence of a series of networks to develop positioning within selected markets. This corporate dynamism is a key factor in pushing the integration process. Such developments are symptomatic of the emerging network economy that business has established as a response to the integration process and to the commercial opportunities it affords.

The development of these trans-national networks is designed to offer advantages to enterprises in terms of lower transactions costs when accessing new markets or developing new products. They can also produce efficiencies in terms of the division of labour and other aspects of resource usage. The strength of such networks depends upon the intensity of the links between enterprises which is probably best judged in terms of inter- and intra-firm resource links. It is also important to see these networks as political organisations due to the way in which they are formed (as an arena for firm participation) and to the struggle for resources which is often the raison d'être for their development. Enterprise strategy, in view of the integration process and improved market access, will increasingly be based upon the nature and form of the links that it establishes and to the trans-national networks to which it belongs. In this context, integration arises out of a network of inter- and intra-firm networks across the European space. These can find an expression in trans-national joint ventures, mergers, alliances, subsidiaries and the like. These networks are both a reactive and proactive force in the integration process.

They are a commercial response to the changing economic environment within which enterprises find themselves and which, by its very nature, is an expression of the growing interdependence between states.

Within this context, policy, in its simplest form, becomes a tool to promote, control and harness networks as a complement to the integration process and thus as a means of ensuring Europe's commercial success. Competition, industrial, transport and research and development policies amongst others are some of the clearest expressions of the way in which policy has a direct bearing upon the development of the network economy. This network management role highlights the reactive manner in which policy evolves in the light of corporate strategy: a phenomenon that, to many, offers a rationale for further and deeper integration. This network management role of policy seeks to establish and foster links and to ensure that maximum value-added is derived from them and that activities of enterprises in exploiting these new freedoms do not run counter to the objectives of the regional bloc (for example by establishing trans-national cartels).

Enterprises will seek to use the opportunities created by the process of regional integration to maximise market share, profits or sales. Thus strategy will seek to organise production or inter- and intra-firm trade to attain these objectives. This not only implies the international reallocation of resources but may also change the location of production to ensure the minimisation of tax commitments. In turn, resource allocations by an enterprise may simply be reactive to the strategies of major rivals. The exact response of trans-national corporations (TNCs) to the process of economic integration depends upon the nature of the barriers facing these enterprises. In simplistic terms, enterprises have tended to respond via investment creation or investment diversion. In the former strategy, FDI is stimulated by the need to circumvent barriers created by the development of the regional bloc. This applies to non-EU companies striving to service a market from which they feared they would otherwise be excluded. For EU enterprises, investment diversion is more important as they re-organise production to exploit specialisation and economies of scale. In addition, enterprises exhibit a greater range of motives and investment strategies to meet the challenges and exploit the opportunities created by regional integration. Notably firms can undertake investment designed to:

- protect market share in response to the increased competition stimulated by regional integration;
- re-organise themselves along trans-national lines;
- enhance market share in new and existing markets;
- reflect the competitive advantages of different parts of the economic grouping.

The extent to which regional integration and market integration encourage these investment effects means two changes to industrial structure are anticipated:

- a reduction in horizontal integration as firms eradicate duplication across states and concentrate production in one or two key plants;
- increased vertical integration as firms seek to minimise the transactions costs involved in serving a more integrated market.

The result of these trends is that many firms are undertaking investment strategies that are more offensive than defensive in nature.

In practice, the benefits for business from the development of integration have in part been retarded by the extent of political and economic diversity within Europe. Such problems have limited the coherence of the process and have thereby limited the commercial opportunities from integration. The need to accommodate a full range of interests can seriously impede the realisation of the benefits of integration. Given that it is unlikely that all states will proceed at the same pace towards integration, alternative arrangements are required. This has led to proposals for an 'à la carte' or a 'multi-speed' Europe. In part, this is to ensure that within whatever political framework is established within Europe, the commercial benefits of the process of integration are not dissipated. In addition, graduated membership offers the potential for further benefits and ensures that slower member states do not hinder the realisation of benefits from the moves towards integration by other states. The existence of such flexibility in the arrangements will inevitably hinder the ability of the European economy to allocate resources in a manner that maximises efficiency.

ECONOMIC INTEGRATION AND THE INTERNATIONAL BUSINESS ENVIRONMENT

As the global environment has altered so, as mentioned above, the rationale behind integration has changed to meet the requirements of internationalising markets. Increasingly European integration is evolving to meet the requirements of enterprises within this context and the process of integration is spreading to other parts of the global economy. Other notable regional trade agreements include the North American Free Trade Area (NAFTA) and the closer ties among south-east Asian states.

Although the need to improve Europe's economic performance in relation to its main competitors, Japan and the United States, was a significant factor behind the renewed drive towards European integration in the mid-1980s, the resulting focus on the creation of one 'economic space' paradoxically encouraged a concentration on the dynamics of internal processes, resulting in an almost total neglect of its external impact. However, policy makers, academics, journalists and other commentators simultaneously adopted the word 'globalisation' which is frequently used both to explain the economic ills besetting the advanced industrial economies, such as the return of mass unemployment and the apparent unaffordability of welfare states, and to justify the policy inertia of governments in the face of these ills.

The word 'globalisation' is often used loosely, with some limited agreement on its meaning but with scant consensus on whether the world economy is actually in the process of going global or on what stage it has reached. This creates problems for politicians in developing responses to the undoubted changes that are underway in the world economy. This is not the place to tackle these issues directly, but it is crucial to remember that European integration takes place within a much broader world context and that what happens outside Europe's borders (if in fact these borders still matter, which the pure globalists would deny) has a significant and increasing impact on the formulation of EU policy and on the strategies of European firms.

Trade in goods remains an important, and one of the easier to measure, indicators of economic links between countries. In 1997, the value of world trade in merchandise exports reached $5.3 trillion, representing a 3 per cent increase in value terms over 1996. The strength of the dollar against many major traders resulted in a steep fall in the dollar price of exports for many years, leading to modest increases in trade in value terms but growth of 9.5 per cent in volume terms – the strongest growth rate for many years. Service exports totalled $1.3 trillion, of which approximately 40 per cent was accounted for by exports from EU members.

Increasingly, however, it is insufficient to measure linkages between nations purely in terms of trade. The rapid growth of FDI has both changed the nature of these relationships and the way in which trade relationships should be interpreted. Between 1973–95, the annual global flow of FDI increased 12.5 fold from $25 billion to $315 billion whereas the world exports of goods grew 8.5 times from $575 billion to $4.9 trillion, significantly higher than world output growth but nevertheless two-thirds of the growth rate of FDI. The steady build up of the stock of FDI over this period has resulted in a situation in which the sales of foreign affiliates of multi-national corporations (MNCs) exceed world trade in goods and services ($6.1 trillion in 1995). In 1995, sales by Japanese manufacturers located outside their own base ($427 billion) exceeded total Japanese exports ($410 billion) for the first time. As such, trade statistics alone under-estimate the extent of economic interactions between nations as the output of overseas operations can act as a substitute for exports.

The growth of TNCs and the resulting growth in intra-firm trade means that world trade is currently divided almost equally into three parts:

- intra-firm trade;
- exports of trans-national corporations to non-affiliates;
- trade among national firms.

Although the existence of truly global firms is limited, this breakdown of world trade shows the extent to which trade has become dominated by firms which have an extensive presence in a number of countries. Table 1.3 takes this a stage further, demonstrating that each of the world's top 500 firms had total sales greater than the gross national product (GNP) of Kenya, the country which ranked seventy-third on the World Bank's GNP rankings. The sales of General Motors, the company with the world's largest sales, are broadly similar to the GNPs of Turkey and Thailand, twenty-third and twenty-fourth respectively in the World Bank's GNP rankings. At least sixty countries have GNPs less than the sales of Sun Company, the 500th company in Fortune's Global 500, and at least eighty-three have GNPs below the fiftieth company on the list. These statistics partially explain why many MNCs are now regarded as major economic units in their own right and why the regulation of such entities can prove problematic, particularly with the extra-territorial problems which their multinationality entails. It is the influence of such companies and the growth of FDI which, together with the emergence of technological

Table 1.3 Ranking of countries and companies by GNP and total sales ($ billion)

	GNP/sales	Rank[1]		GNP/sales	Rank[1]
United States	7,443	1	Mitsui	143	3
Japan	5,149	2	South Africa	132	28
Germany	2,364	3	Mitsubishi	129	4
Korea	483	11	Royal Dutch Shell	128	5
Russia	356	15	Unilever	49	35
Belgium	267	19	Algeria	44	48
Indonesia	213	22	Tokyo Electric Power Inc.	43	46
General Motors	178	1	Bulgaria	9.9	68
Turkey	178	23	Costa Rica	9.1	72
Thailand	178	24	Sun Company	9	500
Ford	153	2	Kenya	8.7	73

Source: World Bank and Fortune Global 500
Note [1] Rankings for countries based on World Bank Development Indicators (1996 GNP); rankings for companies derived from Fortune Global 500 (1997 sales)

advances which facilitate cross-border communications and the development of capital mobility and international financial markets, are feeding the globalisation debate.

THE EMERGENCE OF THE CONCEPT OF GLOBALISATION

There are many strands to the concept of globalisation but the unifying theme is one of interdependence, a phenomenon which has allegedly arisen because of the successive removal of obstacles to the movement of factors of production, resulting initially in the blurring of national boundaries and ultimately in the creation of what Ohmae (1994) called 'the borderless world'. Concepts of globalisation have arisen from a mixture of positive and negative factors which came together to challenge the certainties which had prevailed in the advanced industrial world since the end of the Second World War. The Keynesian consensus, for example, had given rise to the expectation that national governments could successfully control and manage national economies. In other words, the state could control markets. The economic crisis of the 1970s, resulting from the collapse of the Bretton Woods system and the 1973 oil price hike, both emphasised the growing interdependence of the world economy and administered a sharp shock to the belief in governments' powers over markets. These fears were intensified by the accelerating trend towards de-industrialisation in the advanced economies: this shift towards the service sector and away from traditional sources of wealth generation undermined long held beliefs about the origins of wealth and raised fears about the emergence of competition from low cost production centres in the developing world.

The more positive factors stem from the liberalisation and deregulation of trade in goods which later spread to financial markets and other services. The impact of this deregulation was maximised by technological developments which revolutionised communications both within firms and between firms and their suppliers and customers. The outcome of these trends is international capital mobility, the integration of business activities worldwide and the search for strategic alliances and the development of global networks, again within and between firms, to ensure survival and growth in an increasingly competitive marketplace. Such developments, so the argument goes, will ultimately spill over into the transfer of dominant cultures, facilitating the emergence of the global product. In this world, market forces come to dominate not only economic life but also political life as national governments find it increasingly difficult to exercise any real control over what happens within their borders. Latterly, the end of the Cold War has marked the ideological defeat of Communism and the victory of capitalism, leading commentators like Fukuyama to talk of the 'end of history' which, in this case, can be translated into the inevitability of the dominance of market forces.

From the corporate standpoint, such forces result in the intensification of competition, within both domestic and export markets, requiring increasingly rapid adjustments to changes in business operating environments. Responses and strategies can vary but the forces alluded to above, according to the globalisation model, encourage the growth of the truly stateless enterprise which plans according to the dictates of the market and regards national borders as an increasing irrelevance. The characteristics of such strategies include a global conception of markets and a striving for critical mass, or size, as both a defensive and offensive response to intensified competition. A typical strategy would be a renewed search for agreements, alliances and joint ventures – the growth of networks and network economies. These links both help companies share the burdens of a range of costs and confer upon them valuable 'insider' status in markets outside their home base.

Table 1.4 sets out the typical challenges and opportunities facing larger firms under the 'ideal type' globalisation model, challenges to which firms have already started to respond

Table 1.4 Typical business challenges and opportunities from 'ideal type' globalisation

- intensification of competition in domestic and non-domestic markets with pressure on prices, costs, efficiency and innovation
- emergence over time of a global view of products and markets
- tendency to focus on core activities and rationalise product lines
- intensification of search for offensive and defensive networks, agreements and alliances to enter markets quickly, to share burdens of research and development, to gain access to partner's knowledge of markets and technology and to broaden access to skills and finance
- efforts to achieve critical mass to meet challenges of competition
- possible regulatory confusion originating from multiple regulation or from a regulation vacuum arising from insufficient supranational co-operation
- cross-border links arising from direct investment, technology transfer and capital flows as well as from trade
- specific regional and cultural differences need to be taken into account

and which parallel the challenges and opportunities enumerated in Table 1.2 in relation to business challenges and opportunities from integration. This parallelism arises because, at one level, integration and globalisation represent similar processes, both being about forming fragmented, separate markets into one consolidated 'economic space'. Both scenarios involve intensified competition with all the attendant effects of downward pressure on costs and prices. However, the process is both more extensive and profound at the European level where a majority of member states are moving ahead with the creation of a single European currency, thereby requiring a more immediate and far reaching response from firms.

This concept of globalisation results in a totally interdependent world economy in which market forces dominate and national borders become increasingly meaningless to the corporate sector. This outcome creates dilemmas for the traditional sources of economic regulation and governance – the nation state. Globalising trends remove from them the means to regulate markets and they are faced with the question of whether to attempt to regain some of their, by now illusory, sovereignty by recreating or participating in regulatory mechanisms on a more supranational level. The alternative is a return to the old protectionist option. This no longer seems fully viable given that many of the modern technological developments in communication are immune from its effects and that the prevailing economic philosophy is neo-liberal and supportive of the free rein of market forces which globalisation represents.

THE GLOBALISATION BACKLASH

'Globalisation' entered common parlance from the mid-1980s onwards but its use has caught on quickly, raising many questions about its implications and latterly about whether the claims for it are exaggerated. Indeed, there are signs of a backlash against 'ideal type' globalisation. Hirst and Thompson (1996) argue that much of the case against globalisation and the ungovernability of world markets is overstated. According to them, the existence of genuine multi-national corporations, borderless firms as outlined above, is relatively rare. Most firms are trans-national, based in one member state and trading in a variety of countries. The world economy itself is far from global: capital flows and trade and investment are increasingly concentrated in the triad of Europe, North America and East Asia with developing countries becoming more and more marginalised. The triad itself, particularly if it engages in policy co-ordination, has the capability of exerting strong governance pressures over a significant portion of the world economy and, even if its members act separately not as trading blocs, they retain strong powers to influence economic events.

Hirst and Thompson do not deny the existence of some of the trends which have resulted in the development of the globalisation view but interpret them in a different way, arguing that what the world is experiencing is a shift towards an 'inter-national' rather than a global economy. This view acknowledges the growing interconnection between national economies, indeed national economies are the main players in this system, becoming increasingly integrated with each other resulting in strong national special-isations and the international division of labour. Trade remains important but investment links take on an increasingly key role. Despite the tighter links, domestic and international frameworks remain separate for economic policy making purposes and to a relative extent for economic effects. They describe interactions as being of the 'billiard-ball' type: that is, international events do not necessarily directly penetrate the national economy but have an indirect effect through the national policy and processes or work 'automatically' through market forces. Hirst and Thompson also argue that inter-national structures are not new, and that the economic arrangements prevailing from the mid-nineteenth century to the outbreak of the First World War when Britain was the predominant economic power as an earlier economic power were more inter-national than the current situation. The interwar years were ones of protectionism and economic action behind national boundaries. This reaction to the end of British political and economic dominance demon-strates the dangers of assuming that changes in the international economy are inevitable or irreversible – an assumption which often colours pure globalisation views.

Hirst and Thompson are not alone in doubting the inevitability of globalisation. Other commentators are asking questions about the governance of markets and the role of the nation state in the process and, if the state is unable to perform this role, what alternatives to the state are possible. Although detailed conclusions differ, there is far more optimism about the ability of human society to extend an influence over workings of the market than the pure globalisation approach would allow. Some commentators maintain that the nation state can still play a significant role whereas others place more emphasis on regional trading blocs, closer co-ordination between regional trading blocs or the emer-gence of international institutions with a more profound global remit. These various scenarios are examined in more detail below.

IMPLICATIONS OF GROWING ECONOMIC INTERDEPENDENCE: A SCENARIO APPROACH

The above presentation of the conflicting views of the directions and nature of change in the world economy simplify reality for the purposes of making sense of what is happening and for clarifying issues around these trends. This is particularly appropriate for assessing the impact of such trends on the current regulatory régimes facing business and how they may be required to change as a result of these trends. In practice, rather than viewing the two expressed above as alternatives, it is useful to consider them as points on a continuum (see Figure 1.3). The 'ideal type' globalisation model sits at the full integration end of the continuum. This can be regarded as the international equivalent of the 'informal' integration referred to by Wallace in the European context. The key question is the extent to which informal integration acts as a driver for the development of formal integration –

Fragmentation – nation states ←——————→ *Integration at world level – globalisation*

Figure 1.3 Fragmentation–globalisation continuum

that is, the development of governance mechanisms which parallel and respond to informal integration on a world scale. Fragmentation, representing a world in which the nation state remains the dominant economic force and the unit of economic governance, is located at the other end of the continuum. Between integration and fragmentation sit any number of variations, including 'inter-nationalisation' which, with the continuing role for nation states within the framework of increasing economic interdependence, contains elements of both.

The purpose of the continuum is not to set the position of the world economy in concrete. As trends emerge and develop, the economy can move along the continuum in either direction, with varying implications for economic governance and policy making for nation states, the European Union and other regional blocs and international organisations. In order to tease out some of these implications, various scenarios are presented below. These scenarios do not set out what will happen (that is, they are not a forecast) but what could happen, nor are they mutually exclusive – the same elements appear in more than one scenario with perhaps a different interpretation placed on them – or cover all possibilities.

Scenario one: balance between the national and the international

This scenario continues the existing trends of deregulation, privatisation and neo-liberal economics and builds on other aspects of the status quo. According to this philosophy, a systematic return to protectionism is not an option (that is not to say, that individual acts which can be construed as protectionist will not take place) and the role of governments is to promote an environment in which private enterprise can flourish and compete. This approach has increasingly gained ground within member states of the European Union and is also the underlying rationale behind many aspects of EU policy itself (see Chapters 3, 5, 6 and 9 in particular). However, such an approach, although facilitating the emergence of trans-national businesses, does nothing in itself to enable the state to perform the key regulatory roles of transparency, access and fairness. The most likely response to this is for a limited transfer of authority to international bodies such as the World Trade Organisation (WTO) to prevent the worst excesses of market failure making themselves felt. In practice, this has already happened to a certain degree with the inclusion of many non-trade aspects in the Uruguay Round and the growing pressure to include issues like labour policy, competition policy, the environment and investment rules on the agenda for future talks (see Chapter 17).

For many commentators, even if they do not subscribe to the full globalisation view, there is a growing gap between the levels of economic integration (extensive) and political integration (limited) which is enabling the market to gain the upper hand by default as member states hold on to concepts of sovereignty and control which rely on national borders and which are increasingly illusory in a world where independent economic forces are no respecters of political frontiers. For the pure market theorist, there is nothing wrong with this situation: the market will resolve issues of resource allocation and market efficiency much more effectively than politicians. Such a perspective results in an approach to labour market flexibility, for example, which encourages downward movement of wages perhaps bringing short term benefits to the firm but neglecting the advantages of a high skills, high trust approach (see Chapter 13). However, the pure market theorist is out-numbered by those who, whilst acknowledging the broad benefits of competition, also see significant elements of market failure (see Chapter 14 on environmental policy), do not believe it is appropriate to treat all factors of production purely as commodities and see the potential for the public barriers to trade which are removed in the liberalisation process to be replaced by private barriers unless effective measures are taken at the appropriate level. The remaining scenarios look at other possible responses to these concerns.

Scenario two: triad co-operation

Despite talk of globalisation, many of the developments ascribed to it have been dominated by the world's main trading and economic blocs of Europe, North America and Asia in the form of Japan and the countries of East Asia. These three blocs are commonly referred to as the 'triad' and each has been experimenting with their own forms of regional integration, with the European Union both the most ambitious and the most advanced.

Although these blocs compete fiercely with each other, they also, according to the co-operation scenario, recognise their interdependence in terms of trade, finance, technology, investment and strategic alliances and acknowledge their mutual self-interest in ensuring each other's economic well-being through co-operation rather than conflict. Elements of this scenario already exist through the workings of G8 and were highlighted by President Clinton's decision in 1998 to provide finance to help Japan overcome its internal economic crisis. Such co-operation aims at creating a climate of stability and steady growth in which enterprises can flourish and largely takes place outside the framework of established organisations like the WTO. This mode of controlling powerful economic forces poses serious questions for countries outside the triad which are effectively excluded from the magic circle.

Scenario three: triad conflict

This scenario has the same starting premise as scenario two: that is the dominance of the world economy by the three main trading blocs. However, rather than recognising their mutual interests and adopting a co-operative approach, these blocs revert to intense competition, including the re-erection of protective barriers around each other. It was the fear of the emergence of an exclusive Europe within the framework of the single market programme which caused large scale FDI from Japan and other Far Eastern countries in western Europe in the late 1980s in an attempt to get behind possible protective barriers. Fears of a 'Fortress Europe' have proved unfounded and this investment in Europe has, ironically, served to contribute to the globalising trend rather than to act as an antidote to protectionism.

Although trade disagreements and disputes persist, there are no signs as yet of a return to protectionism. The dominance of economic liberalism remains strong throughout the world and the example of the slump of the 1930s, which originated in large part from resurgent protection, is frequently cited as a warning against going down that path. In short, although a return to protectionism cannot be ruled out (history demonstrates that the ideological pendulum can and does swing and a spreading of the impacts of the Asian crisis could provide an interesting test of the extent to which protectionism has been banished), this appears currently to be one of the least probable of the scenarios outlined here.

Scenario four: regional agreements – extending the chain

This scenario is similar to scenario two, except that co-operation takes place on a world-wide basis, and is not exclusive to the triad, and ultimately results in global economic and policy integration. This scenario views regional economic integration as a positive step in the process of globalisation and recognises the proliferation of regional trading agreements which has occurred since the late 1980s. By mid-1998, the WTO reported that it had been informed of almost 180 regional trade arrangements (of which well over half remain active) in which all but three of its 132 members were involved.

In an environment in which global free trade in its widest sense (that is, liberalisation of services, investment as well as trade in goods) is unlikely to take place rapidly within the multilateral framework of the WTO, regional groupings can perform these tasks more efficiently within their own geographical area. Familiarity with the benefits of liberal trading regimes within regions, which are often developed initially as a defence against globalisation by providing a platform from which to confront international competition, will demonstrate the benefits of such systems on a wider scale and the logic of extending openness through the linking of different regional groupings. This optimistic view takes a long term perspective.

There is some evidence of attempts to link economic groupings: the European Union, after developing the European Economic Area which extended much of the Single European Market to the European Free Trade Area (EFTA), absorbed three key members of EFTA within its own framework; it has embarked upon a similar process in Central and Eastern Europe where enlargement is set to take place early in the twenty-first century and is strengthening its links with the countries of the Mediterranean region. Ideas of extending the North American Free Trade Area (NAFTA) into South America, initially to incorporate Chile, and of exploring the possibility of creating a transatlantic free trade area have been raised. However, many regional trading organisations have proved short-lived in the past and are subject to the vagaries of the political and economic cycle. The Asian economic crisis, for example, has resulted in increased reluctance to continue along this path in some areas. Plans for a free trade area for the Americas appear becalmed, a situation intensified by the unpopularity of NAFTA in some US quarters, and the integrating efforts of the Asia Pacific Economic Co-operation Forum (APEC) have reached an impasse. It remains to be seen whether this is a temporary or more permanent phenomenon.

Scenario five: the SEM writ large

Figure 1.2 formalises the processes of the integration process within the context of European integration, stressing the links from interaction through to interdependence and ultimately integration. This model sees integration as a dynamic process in which the functional spillover, which is so central to the neo-functional theory of European integration, plays a key role. This approach to European integration can be transplanted to the international dimension. In the same way as the interdependence created by a customs union led almost inexorably to a common market and has been an important, albeit not the sole, factor in the moves towards a single European currency, so the interdependence created by trade liberalisation and service deregulation is creating pressure for international agreements and rules relating to labour markets, the environment and competition to preserve the integrity of markets and to avoid differential practices from distorting trade.

If this scenario does come to pass, it is unlikely to do so quickly. The European Union has taken over four decades to reach its current state of advanced integration and has done so on the basis of a relatively homogenous group of countries. The challenges of transferring this process to a world level are enormous and the possibility of creating an SEM equivalent must remain far in the future. Nevertheless, the seeds of this process have already been sown with the expansion of the international trading agenda referred to earlier and, if spillover is really effective, the process could gain significant momentum once it is seriously underway.

CONCLUSION

What does all this mean for the European Union and for business? The previous sections demonstrate that beliefs about trends in the world economy and about economic management colour the debate about the most appropriate governance structure at national, European and international level and consequently affect the type of regulation and influence exerted by the political system on the business environment. Adherents of a strong globalisation view would, if they also propounded the superiority of market forces over government intervention in the market, not argue for stronger international policies, except in limited areas. Other globalists would argue for a new approach to regulation of the international economy which subsumed and sub-ordinated national level processes and promoted international measures. Those who acknowledge movements towards 'inter-nationalisation' of the economy but who fall short of accepting the full globalisation thesis would argue that these trends can be contained within a modified version of the existing system with a continuing role for national actors and perhaps an enhanced role for regional and international players.

Regardless of globalising trends, economic liberalism, as manifested in the form of the SEM, has already resulted in a changed role for the state from intervention to regulation. This willing transfer of sovereignty for ideological reasons from state to markets has not been fully balanced by a willingness to transfer power and sovereignty to the European level. Although supportive of the creation of a European market, which is intended to act as the domestic market for EU firms, member states have resisted efforts to transfer parallel powers to a European polity to exercise control over this market. The outcome is a régime which is suitable for performing the role of Tinbergen's negative integration (that is, the removal of obstacles to trade) but which is not necessarily suitable to the demands of positive integration. Similarly, as international liberalisation spreads from trade in goods to trade in services, member states have resisted proposals to accord the Commission the same powers to negotiate on their behalf in service negotiations as it has in trade in goods. Until policy processes catch up with autonomous economic forces which, to a greater or lesser extent, ignore political frontiers, enterprises will be operating in an environment in which the market rather than the state (or supra-regional or inter-national organisation) tends to be sovereign. The theme of how many policy issues which have been previously regarded as a European or a purely national preserve are increasingly being assessed for their international implications is common to many of the following chapters.

KEY POINTS

- **Some convergence has taken place between different models of economic development within Europe as countries struggle to come to terms with demographic changes, financial constraints and the pressures of globalisation.**
- **The objectives of integration have changed. It is a complex process which is increasingly driven by the needs of business. Policy responses at national and EU level can slow down or accelerate the process, depending on the willingness of the politicians to act.**
- **Integration, in turn, results in industrial restructuring as companies seek to position themselves in line with new market realities.**
- **Integration and globalisation are posing serious questions for the governance of markets and are pulling many previously national policy issues onto European and even international agendas.**
- **Although the meaning of globalisation and its implications are open to varying intepretations, global economic interdependence is on the increase.**

SUGGESTED FURTHER READING

Archibugi, D. (1997) *Technology, Globalisation and Economic Performance*, Cambridge University Press.

Archibugi, D. and Michie, J. (1998) *Technology, Trade and Growth: New Perspectives*, Cambridge University Press, 1998.

Boyer, R. and Drache, D. (eds) (1996) *States v. Markets: the Limits of Globalisation*, Routledge.

De Melo, J. and Panagariya, A. (1992) *New Dimensions in Regional Integration*, Cambridge/Centre for Economic Policy Research.

Drucker, P. (1997) 'The Global Economy and the Nation State', *Foreign Affairs*, Sept.–Oct.

Dunning, J. (1993) *The Globalisation of Business: the Challenge of the 1990s*, Routledge.

Hirst, P., and Thompson, G. (1996) *Globalization in Question*, Polity Press.

Jovanovic, M. (1992) *International Economic Integration*, Routledge.

Laffan, B. (1992) *Integration and Co-operation in Europe*, Routledge/University Association of Contemporary European Studies.

Ohmae, K. (1994) *The Borderless World*, Harper Collins.

Pelkmans, J. (1997) European Integration, Longman.

Robson, P. (1997) *The Economics of International Integration*, (fourth edition), Routledge.

Strange, S. (1996) *The Retreat of the State: the Diffusion of Power in the World Economy*, Cambridge University Press.

Thurow, L. (1994) *Head to Head: the Coming Economic Battle among Europe, Japan and America*, Nicholas Brealey Publishing.

Tsoukalis, L. (1997) *The New European Economy Revisited*, Chapter 10, Oxford University Press.

Tsoukalis, L. (1998) *The European Agenda: Issues of Globalisation, Equity and Legitimacy*, Jean Monnet Chair Papers, 98/49, April, European University Institute Florence, (web address: http://www.iue.it/RSC/WP-Texts/tsoukalis.html).

Wallace, W. (ed.) (1990) *The Dynamics of European Integration*, Royal Institute for International Affairs/Pinter.

2

THE EVOLUTION OF THE
EU AND ITS INSTITUTIONS

Given the creation of the Single European Market (SEM), the development of related policies and the introduction of economic and monetary union (EMU), European businesses and, indeed enterprises owned and located primarily outside Europe but with aspirations to penetrate the European market, are increasingly affected by policies and programmes devised at the EU level. Subsequent chapters explore this phenomenon in relation to a range of individual policy areas. These policies belong to a broader context of national, European and international environments which are explored in more theoretical terms in Chapter 1. In order to understand these policies more fully and to identify where business can attempt to influence EU policy outcomes, business needs to be able to fit these policies into their historical and institutional context. This chapter therefore outlines the evolution of the EEC into the EU, highlighting key developments and focuses on the main institutions and actors in the formulation of policy before concluding with preliminary discussion of the main challenges which will face the European Union and its enterprises in the early years of the twenty-first century.

EMERGENCE OF THE EUROPEAN ECONOMIC COMMUNITY (EEC)

The idea of European unity pre-dates the establishment of the EEC by decades if not by centuries. However, it took the devastation of the Second World War to lead to the first pragmatic steps to make this idea a reality. In the immediate post-war era, which coincided with the beginning of the Cold War, Western Europe was preoccupied with economic and political reconstruction, the need to break the cycle of recurrent military conflict and assessment of the security threat from the Communist bloc. This led directly to the formation of the Organisation for European Economic Co-operation (OEEC) which later evolved into the Organisation for Economic Co-operation and Development (OECD); the defence organisation, NATO; the Western European Union (WEU), intended to strengthen European security co-operation and give Europe a stronger voice within NATO; and the Council of Europe which has been assiduous in promoting human rights.

However, the key development in European integration took place in 1951 when Belgium, France, Italy, Luxembourg, the Netherlands and West Germany signed the Treaty of Paris which established the European Coal and Steel Community (ECSC) and which took effect in 1952. On one level, the ECSC was a technocratic organisation intended to rationalise crucial coal and steel markets. However, it represented much more than that. To some, it symbolised the first step in the construction of a European community which would be achieved via the gradual extension of common policies to other activities. Coal and steel were merely the starting point: both products were central to industrial production and their surrender to supranational control made disintegration into military conflict much more difficult. The ECSC, therefore provided a framework for the re-integration of Germany into the European mainstream and, in particular, for Franco-German reconciliation.

BOX 2.1 MILESTONES IN EUROPEAN INTEGRATION

1951	Treaty of Paris establishing the European Coal and Steel Community (ECSC) signed by Belgium, France, Italy, Luxembourg, the Netherlands and West Germany
1952	ECSC starts work under the leadership of Jean Monnet
1955	Messina Conference (Belgium, France, Italy, Luxembourg, the Netherlands and West Germany) agree to establish an intergovernmental committee to develop an appropriate framework to move ahead with integration
1957	Belgium, France, Italy, Luxembourg, the Netherlands and West Germany sign treaties establishing the European Economic Community (the Treaty of Rome) and Euratom (European Atomic Energy Community)
1958	Treaty of Rome comes into effect
1960	Austria, Denmark, Norway, Portugal, Sweden, Switzerland and the United Kingdom establish the European Free Trade Association (EFTA)
1961	Denmark, Ireland and the United Kingdom apply to join the EEC
1962	Norway applies to join the EEC
1963	President De Gaulle of France vetoes British membership of the EEC
1965–6	Empty chair crisis leads to Luxembourg Compromise and retention of national veto
1967	Denmark, Ireland, Norway and the UK make their second EEC membership application and Sweden its first
1967	Treaty merging the three European Communities (ECSC, EEC and Euratom) comes into force
1968	Completion of customs union and establishment of Common External Tariff
1969	Hague meeting of leaders of EC (6) agrees to open membership negotiations with Denmark, Ireland, Norway and the UK. They also discuss completion of the single market, deeper integration and agree to phase in economic and monetary union by 1980
1970	Council agreement to allocate 'own resources' to the EC
1972	Introduction of currency 'snake'
1972	Norway rejects EC membership in a referendum
1973	EC (6) becomes EC (9) with accession of Denmark, Ireland and the UK
1974	Heads of State or Government agree to meet regularly as European Council
1975	UK referendum votes 'yes' to continued EC membership
1975	Greece applies to join EC – accession negotiations start in 1976
1977	Spain and Portugal apply to join EC – accession negotiations begin in 1978
1979	European Monetary System established
1979	First direct elections to the European Parliament

1981	Greece becomes tenth EC member
1982	Greenland votes to leave EC
1985	Jacques Delors becomes President of the European Commission
1985	Commission presents White Paper on the single market
1986	Spain and Portugal become EC members
1987	Single European Act in force
1987	Turkey applies to join the EC
1988	Hanover Council instructs committee chaired by Jacques Delors to present concrete proposals for the creation of EMU. Delors Report presented in 1989
1988	'Delors 1' on reform of the budget, the CAP and the doubling of Structural Funds
1989	Spain joins ERM
1989	Austria applies for EC membership
1990	IGCs on political union and EMU in parallel from December
1990	Stage one of EMU begins
1990	Cyprus and Malta apply to join EC
1990	German re-unification – five eastern länder become part of EC
1990	UK joins the ERM
1991	Sweden applies to join EC
1991	Maastricht Council reaches agreement on draft Treaty on European Union → signing of Treaty on European Union in February 1992
1992	Finland, Switzerland and Norway apply to join EC
1992	In referenda, 50.7 per cent of Danes vote against ratification of TEU and 51 per cent of French vote in favour
1992	Portugal joins ERM and the UK and Italy leave it
1992	EC and EFTA leaders sign agreement establishing the European Economic Area (EEA) but rejected by Switzerland in a referendum
1992	Single Market deadline – majority of programme completed
1993	Second Danish referendum returns 56.8 per cent majority in favour of TEU ratification
1993	Currency crisis results in widening of ERM bands from 2.25 per cent to 15 per cent
1993	Maastricht Treaty (Treaty on European Union) enters into force
1993	White Paper on *Growth, Competitiveness, Employment*
1994	Stage two of EMU begins
1994	EEA Treaty in force minus Switzerland
1994	Hungary and Poland apply to join EU
1995	Austria, Finland and Sweden bring membership of European Union to fifteen
1995	New Commission begins five year term of office under Jacques Santer
1995	Romania, Slovakia, Latvia, Estonia, Lithuania and Bulgaria apply to join EU
1996	Czech Republic and Slovenia apply to become EU members
1996	Intergovernmental conference on review of Maastricht Treaty and preparation for eastern enlargement opens in Turin
1996	Italy rejoins ERM
1996	Dublin Council agrees stability and growth pact for EMU
1997	Amsterdam Council ends IGC and reaches agreement on draft 'Amsterdam Treaty'
1997	'Agenda 2000' sets out Commission Opinions on membership applications, budgetary details until 2006 and principles of proposed CAP and Structural Fund reform
1998	Enlargement negotiations begin with Poland, Hungary, Czech Republic, Estonia, Slovenia and Cyprus

1998	Decision that all EU members bar Denmark, Greece, Sweden and the UK will participate in EMU from 1 January 1999
1999	Third stage of EMU begins on 1 January – the single currency is born
1999	European Commission resigns following report on fraud, mismanagement and nepotism
1999	Amsterdam Treaty enters into force on 1 May

The ECSC was dirigiste in nature and was run by a strong supranational executive body, the High Authority. These characteristics reflected the backgrounds and aspirations of its architects, Jean Monnet and Robert Schumann, who sought a united Europe based on economic unity and strong, centralised supranational institutions. These ambitions were not wholly shared by participants in the 1955 Messina Conference which led directly to the negotiation of the Treaty of Rome establishing the European Economic Community (EEC) and the European Atomic Energy Community (Euratom). Political unity, however, did not figure highly on the agenda: problems within the ECSC and failure to agree the terms of a European Defence Community stymied more ambitious plans for European integration. Rather, the Treaty of Rome stressed economic integration (it did, after all, establish the EEC) and reflected the strong liberal philosophy of Germany and the Benelux countries who sought benefits from the development of a common market but who did not have the same attachment to dirigisme as France.

The Treaty of Rome made a commitment to an 'ever closer union', to economic and social progress 'by common action to eliminate the barriers which divide Europe' and to 'the constant improvement of the living and working conditions of their people'. The predominantly economic nature of the EEC was brought out by Article 2 which stated,

> The Community shall have as its task, by establishing a common market and progressively approximating the economic policies of Member States, to promote throughout the Community, a harmonious development of economic activities, a continuous and balanced expansion, an increase in stability, an accelerated rise in the standard of living and closer relations between the States belonging to it.

Apart from the Common Agricultural Policy, the prevailing philosophy of the Treaty of Rome was laissez-faire rather than interventionist, relying on benefits to materialise through the mechanisms of competition and interdependence – an approach which exactly matched the growing popularity of neo-liberal economics in Europe which started to emerge strongly from the 1980s onwards.

THE TREATY OF ROME TO THE FIRST ENLARGEMENT

The trading credentials of the EEC were initially insufficient to attract the UK. The UK, always somewhat aloof from Europe and valuing its links with the Commonwealth and the US, preferred an arrangement which involved minimal surrender of national sovereignty. This resulted in the creation of the European Free Trade Area (EFTA) in 1960 comprised of the UK, Norway, Sweden, Denmark, Austria, Portugal, Iceland and Switzerland. EFTA provided for the dismantling of tariff barriers among member countries but also enabled members to govern their own trade with non-members. Nevertheless, concerned about the possibility of growing economic and political isolation, the UK re-evaluated its position and applied for EEC membership in 1961. This was followed shortly afterwards by applications from Ireland, Denmark and Norway who sought opportunities to extend the range of their markets. This initiative rapidly came to nought following veto of the British application by French President, Charles de Gaulle in 1963, and again in 1967.

President de Gaulle was at the centre of another controversy which had a more long lasting effect on the process of integration. The ostensible cause was the 1965 attempt by the European Commission to make the EEC self-financing. This was too much for de Gaulle who was very protective of national sovereignty, wary of supranationalism and who, accordingly, strongly resisted what he saw as the aggrandisement of supranational institutions, namely the Commission and the European Parliament which would receive increased budgetary powers under the proposals. Failing to secure the support of other member states against the Commission, de Gaulle responded by withdrawing France from all involvement in EEC affairs – the so-called 'empty chair crisis'. In order to return business to normal, the other member states agreed to a number of concessions in what became known as 'the Luxembourg Compromise'. The most significant element related to the envisaged shift from unanimous voting to qualified majority voting. The Luxembourg Compromise had no legal standing but it established the principle that when matters of national interest were under discussion, every effort should be made to reach a consensus. Failing this, each member state retained a right to veto policy if it adjudged its vital interests were at stake. The outcome was a slowing down of decision making, reduced ambitions and a tendency to lowest common denominator policy formulation.

Although the first decade of the EEC was not without its successes (the customs union was achieved ahead of schedule, for example), the 1969 Hague Summit relaunched the integration process, giving it an ambitious new agenda which included:

- the opening of accession negotiations with the United Kingdom, Ireland, Denmark and Norway – the first three became the first set of new members in 1973. Norway rejected the terms of its membership in a referendum;
- a re-examination of the system of financing the EEC, which resulted in a shift from membership contributions to a system of Community own resources;
- the creation of a system of foreign policy co-operation. European Political Co-operation (EPC) was established shortly thereafter, evolving gradually ever since;
- the introduction of economic and monetary union (EMU) to augment the common market by 1980 as set out in the 1970 Werner Report (see Chapter 16). In fact, the introduction of EMU had to wait almost twenty years beyond the deadline set at the Hague.

POLITICAL STAGNATION AND ECONOMIC SCLEROSIS

Despite the Hague Summit's attempts to give the Community greater momentum, the balance of success and failure was mixed by the late 1970s and early 1980s. On the positive side, the customs union was well established and accompanied by a common commercial policy as laid down in the Treaty. Although there had been some progress on mutual recognition of qualifications and approximation of some laws, there had been relatively little success in moving onto the next stage of integration – the creation of a common market – and many barriers to trade in goods, services, capital and labour remained firmly in place. The institutional structure of the Community and the principle of unanimity in particular were hampering further developments.

At the beginning of the 1980s, the process of European integration appeared becalmed and there was a fear that European competitiveness was falling behind that of the United States and Japan, resulting in 'Eurosclerosis' – a period of lagging growth rates and rising unemployment. From 1979–84, the European Community was dominated by the efforts of the British Prime Minister Mrs Thatcher to achieve a permanent solution to what she viewed as the inequitable budgetary system. The only other policy measure which received any attention was the Common Agricultural Policy, widely perceived to be badly in need of reform. The looming southern enlargement to include Greece (which took place in 1981) and Spain and Portugal (both 1986) also raised alarm bells about the need for political and institutional reform to offset the danger that the increased diversity resulting from the inclusion of three states with different problems to existing members would paralyse decision making in the Community.

RENEWED VITALITY: FROM THE SINGLE EUROPEAN ACT TO THE TREATY ON EUROPEAN UNION

By the mid to late 1980s, a number of factors had come together to boost the integration process. The 1984 Fontainebleau Council reached a settlement on the budget issue and introduced measures to limit the growth of agricultural surpluses, thereby removing some of the obstacles to further development and opening the way for enlargement. In the economic sphere, the old consensus around Keynesian economics was dead, but a new one was emerging around supply side economics – that is, the introduction of a range of policies designed to create an environment in which competition and thus enterprises could flourish and to remove barriers to trade. This approach had its most vocal adherents in the UK, but elements of supply side economics were creeping into contemporary Community policy documents and gaining influence in a number of member states. Of particular importance was the French abandonment of old-style expansionary policy and its embrace of a more liberal approach. At the same time, large European firms were adopting an increasingly supranational perspective and, particularly through the European Roundtable of Industrialists (a lobby of the most influential entrepreneurs in Europe), were adding another powerful voice to the pressure for change.

In 1985, Jacques Delors became President of the European Commission. He was able to pull together and capitalise upon these disparate factors and, together with the Internal Market Commissioner, Lord Cockfield, propose and promote the campaign to finally end the fragmentation of European markets – a major factor in Europe's continuing relatively poor economic performance. This revitalisation of European integration took two forms: the 1985 White Paper *Completing the Internal Market* which identified almost 300 obstacles which needed to be removed to end Europe's market fragmentation and the Single European Act (SEA) which introduced institutional changes to facilitate the implementation of the single market measures (see Chapter 3). In the wave of Euro-enthusiasm which followed, the Community also adopted the Social Charter; pushed through the Merger

BOX 2.2 KEY FEATURES OF THE SINGLE EUROPEAN ACT

The SEA, the first comprehensive revision of the EC treaties, was essentially a response to the need to overhaul the decision making process in the light of the ambitious single market programme and the Iberian enlargement. Its key features were:

1 More qualified majority voting

Article 100A enables the Council of Ministers to adopt most single market legislation by qualified majority voting. In conjunction with the new approach to standards and extensive use of the principle of mutual recognition, Article 100A became a powerful weapon in the implementation of the SEM programme. Tax measures, workers rights and the free movement of people were excluded from the provisions of 100A and remained subject to unanimity.

2 Increased role for the European Parliament

The SEA introduced a new decision making procedure – the co-operation procedure – which applied to most single market legislation, some aspects of social policy, regional funding and research and technology. The co-operation procedure enabled an absolute parliamentary majority to reject a common position adopted by qualified majority voting in the Council of Ministers, in turn, which can only overrule the European Parliament's vote by acting unanimously. Parliament was also given the right to reject by absolute majority the admission of new member states and association agreements negotiated by the Commission.

3 Enhanced Community policy competence

The SEA formalised and clarified the policy competence of the European Community in the areas of environmental policy, research and technology and economic and social cohesion and codified the Community's role in foreign policy co-ordination.

4 Creation of a new court

The SEA established the legal base for the creation of a new court, the Court of First Instance (CFI), which was intended to relieve some of the heavy burden on the European Court of Justice.

Control Regulation – a particularly timely achievement given the wave of mergers and acquisitions which accompanied the single market programme; extended the reach of the SEM to previously excluded sectors like energy and revived the drive towards EMU.

The SEA represents a second, more successful relaunch of the process of European integration. Within a short period of time, the apparent paralysis in European integration had been overcome and the institutional obstacles to the successful adoption of Community level legislation had been removed, giving renewed momentum to the integration project. During this period, both within the SEM framework and through flanking policies (such as competition and social policy), EC activity spread into new areas and a doubling of the size of the Structural Funds, intended in part to offset potential negative regional effects of the SEM, and a significant increase in budgetary resources, signalled the willingness of member states at this stage to support greater integration.

Against this background, it is not surprising that EMU reappeared on the agenda. The 1988 Hanover Council established a committee under the chairmanship of President Delors to identify the specific steps which needed to be taken to introduce EMU. This initiative led directly to the intergovernmental conference (IGC) which resulted in the Treaty on European Union (TEU), commonly known as the 'Maastricht Treaty'. This revitalisation of the Community also gave renewed impetus to further institutional reform and the extension of EC competencies to new areas, the most significant of which was foreign and defence policy. Accordingly, a decision was taken to hold a second IGC on political union to run in parallel with the first.

The TEU, the most radical revision of the treaties to date, set the stage for EMU and extended the competencies of the Community into new areas. It defined itself as marking 'a new stage in the process of creating an ever closer union among the peoples of Europe' and set itself a number of objectives, including:

- the promotion of balanced and sustainable economic and social progress through the creation of an area without frontiers, greater social and economic cohesion and EMU;
- the assertion of identity in the international arena, particularly by the implementation of a common foreign and security policy (CFSP), including a common defence policy;
- greater protection of individual rights through the introduction of Union citizenship (in practice, a more limited version of citizenship than exists in member states);
- closer co-operation on justice and home affairs.

BOX 2.3 KEY FEATURES OF THE MAASTRICHT TREATY

The TEU is frequently compared to a temple supported by three pillars:

Pillar 1: the European Community

The first pillar represents the traditional 'acquis communautaire' and is composed of the customs union, the single market, the Common Agricultural Policy, structural policy, etc. and of new elements such as economic and monetary union and trans-European networks. Policies under the first pillar are governed by Community institutions.

Pillar 2: common foreign and security policy (CFSP)

Pillar 2 specifies that the Union and its member states 'shall define and implement a common foreign and security policy . . . [which] shall include all questions related to the security of the Union, including the eventual framing of a common defence policy' [Articles J1 and J4].

Pillar 3: co-operation in justice and home affairs

The third pillar requires member states to regard a number of justice and home affairs issues as matters of common interest. These include asylum policy, controls on external borders, immigration policy and residence rights of third country nationals, measures to combat drug addiction and international fraud, and customs and police co-operation.

Pillars 2 and 3 are essentially intergovernmental in nature and are dealt with within the Council of Ministers as common policies agreed among independent states and not within the normal framework of Community institutions.

Pillar 1 involves two types of amendments to the founding treaties of the European Communities:

1 Institutional changes:

European Parliament (EP):

- the TEU introduces a further legislative procedure – the co-decision procedure – which builds on the co-operation procedure established by the SEA. Under the co-operation procedure, the Council of Ministers can ignore the EP's wishes provided it acts unanimously. However, the co-decision procedure gives the EP a veto over legislative proposals which cannot be overruled. The TEU brought many of the measures designated as co-operation procedure measures under the co-decision procedures;
- the EP is granted the right to subject an incoming Commission to a vote of approval before its formal appointment;

- the EP to appoint an Ombudsman to receive complaints from citizens about maladministration by Community institutions.

Council of Ministers

- some extension of qualified majority voting.

European Court of Justice

- ECJ given power to impose fines on member states which fail to comply with its judgements or implement Community law.

Committee of Regions

- the Committee of Regions established to provide the Council and Commission with advice on matters of significance for the regions.

2 Policy changes

Community competence is extended in some areas and the Community is awarded new competencies in others.

- EMU: the TEU sets out the timetable, criteria and institutions required for the creation of EMU, the single, most ambitious European integration project to date;
- new policies and policies which previously did not have an explicit treaty base were brought within the scope of the treaties, including consumer protection, development co-operation, public health, trans-European networks, education, culture;
- strengthening of policies areas which were first brought into treaties by the SEA, including environmental policy, research and technological development and social and economic cohesion which was boosted by the creation of the Cohesion Fund which provides funding for environmental and transport TENs projects in the four poorest EU members;
- The incorporation of the principles of the Social Charter into the legal framework of the Community in the form of the Social Agreement and the Social Protocol. Given the UK's decision to opt out from these procedures (see Chapter 13), the Agreement and Protocol were attached to rather than part of the TEU and subject to a unique set of procedures which enabled eleven out of twelve member states to develop social policy without UK participation.

Negotiation of the Treaty was no easy matter. Notwithstanding the Euro-enthusiasm of the late 1980s, radically divergent views on the future of the Community were becoming apparent. Chief among the dissenters from the push towards 'ever closer union' was the UK government. Under the leadership of Mrs Thatcher, the United Kingdom had been highly supportive of the SEM which both reinforced its own supply side agenda and represented the ideal type of Community from the British point of view – an organisation based upon optimising conditions within the marketplace but which does not necessarily require significant formal transfers of power from the nation state to the supranational level. Mrs Thatcher's resignation in 1990, largely caused by internal party divisions over Europe, did not lead to a significant change in the approach of the British government and

John Major, her successor, was able to negotiate opt-outs for the UK from the final stages of EMU and from the Social Agreement and Protocol. The United Kingdom is not alone in its reservations about further integration: Denmark also shares its preference for intergovernmentalism over supranationalism and enthusiasm appeared to be waning more generally for further integration even before the Maastricht negotiations were complete.

The radical step forward in integration which the TEU represented raised fears of loss of national sovereignty and identity and the rise of a European super-state. In order to prevent the Community acquiring too much power and influence at the expense of member states, the TEU also formally introduced the notion of subsidiarity, which stated that:

> In areas which do not fall within its exclusive competence, the Community shall take action, in accordance with the principle of subsidiarity, only if and in so far as the objectives of the proposed action cannot be sufficiently achieved by the Member States and can therefore, by the reason of the scale or effects of the proposed action, be better achieved by the Community. Any action by the Community shall not go beyond what is necessary to achieve the objectives of this Treaty.
>
> (Article 3B of the Treaty on European Union)

The subsidiarity principle was introduced to ensure action was taken at Community level only when it was clear that it was the most appropriate and effective level. The principle is difficult to apply in practice and, despite the development of guidelines to facilitate operationalisation of the subsidiarity principle, can give rise to argument about its implementation. In view of these problems, a Protocol on subsidiarity was attached to the Amsterdam Treaty, stating more precisely what it is and how it should be applied.

THE MAASTRICHT BACKLASH TO AMSTERDAM

In view of these reservations, ratification of the Maastricht Treaty was by no means a foregone conclusion. In July 1992, the Danish population voted against the Treaty in a referendum, technically sinking it forever. However, other member states continued with the ratification process in the expectation that some compromise would be achieved to make Denmark change its mind. Although the Irish population voted 2:1 in favour of the Treaty, ratification troubles rumbled on and the Treaty underwent a challenge in the German constitutional court. Even though it was not required under French law, President Mitterrand of France decided to hold a referendum on the Maastricht issue, believing an overwhelming vote in favour would put integration back on track. However, the referendum campaign became more of a popularity vote on his government, also coinciding with the second European currency crisis in a year, and the outcome was an extremely narrow pro-Maastricht vote. Ratification was able to proceed however, following minor concessions to Denmark who finally voted in favour of the Treaty, allowing it to come into force on 1 November 1993, one year later than planned.

Other factors also took the momentum out of European integration for a while, including:

- the highly ambitious nature of the Maastricht Treaty: Europe's leaders were pushing ahead with integration too quickly for many European citizens, resulting in a lack of popular enthusiasm for, and even distrust of, the European project;
- the very complex, technocratic and incomprehensible nature of the Treaty;
- the end of Soviet hegemony over Central and Eastern Europe which necessitated a rethink of fundamental assumptions about Europe's political geography;

- German reunification which placed a major burden on the German economy, resulting in a greater focus on domestic problems for a time;
- the unfortunate timing of the Maastricht negotiations and ratification with economic recession: support for European integration has always been strongest when the economy is buoyant (early 1960s and late 1980s) and weakest when economic performance is sluggish (late 1970s and early 1980s);
- the currency crises in autumn 1992 and summer 1993;
- the inability of member states, despite their CFSP aspirations, to develop a common approach to the Yugoslav crisis.

In view of these setbacks and reservations, the European Commission which took office under Jacques Santer in 1995 continued the less pro-active, less visible approach to European integration begun during the final years of the Delors Presidency. Nevertheless, there were some significant achievements during this period. Although not fully complete by the deadline of 31 December 1992 and with implementation and enforcement issues outstanding, the SEM had still made significant progress. In addition, the most radical reform of the Common Agricultural Policy to date and a significant overhaul of the Structural Funds took place in 1992. The accession of Austria, Finland and Sweden in 1995 went ahead smoothly, only one full year after the European Economic Area (EEA) agreement, which had given EFTA states access to the SEM, came into force. A relaunch of the Community's relationship with the countries of the Mediterranean took place and the Community grasped the nettle of reassessing its links with Central and Eastern European (CEE) countries and later of preparing them for accession (see Chapter 15). Moreover, despite the apparent improbability at one stage of any member states apart from Luxembourg satisfying the convergence criteria by the deadline, the EMU project became unstoppable and was launched with the participation of eleven out of fifteen member states in January 1999.

Article N of the TEU required the convening of a further IGC in 1996 to review the Maastricht revisions. As 1996 approached, enthusiasm for the IGC was low-key. The agenda for the conference concentrated on three themes:

- bringing the 'Union closer to its citizens', including improvements in visa, asylum and immigration policy; universal access to essential services; the strengthening of environmental policy and improved application of the principle of subsidiarity;
- more effective and democratic institutions, including simplification and clarification of legislative procedures, greater scope for the co-decision procedure, including a wider role for the European Parliament generally; the weighting of votes in the Council of Ministers and an extension of qualified majority voting; a reassessment of the role of national parliaments; greater efficiency in the Commission's operations, including its composition and effectiveness and the possibility of introducing flexibility into the system so that integration does not have to proceed at the pace of the least able or most unwilling. Achievement of these goals, which was patchy, would greatly ease the next big expansion of the Union;
- improvements to the Community's ability to take external action, including refinements of the CFSP and greater coherence in external economic relations.

BOX 2.4: KEY FEATURES OF THE AMSTERDAM TREATY

- Immigration and asylum moved from the third to the first pillar – that is, shifted from intergovernmentalism to incorporation into the European Community.

- Schengen agreement brought into Pillar 1 with derogations for the UK, Ireland and Denmark.
- Anti-discrimination adopted as key Community objective, opening the way for equal opportunity cases on the basis of gender, racial or ethnic origin, religion or belief, disability, age or sexual orientation.
- Employment chapter introduced to the Treaty, giving a higher priority to the fight against unemployment which, nevertheless, remains primarily the responsibility of member states.

Institutional changes

The biggest changes related to strengthening the European Parliament. Difficult political decisions on qualified majority voting and the size of the Commission were delayed until the next IGC which must take place at least one year before EU membership exceeds twenty members to review the composition and operation of institutions.

European Parliament

- Considerable extension of co-decision and virtual disappearance of the co-operation procedure, except for some aspects of EMU;
- Some simplification of the co-decision procedure;
- EP elections to be conducted in line with 'principles common to all member states', thereby opening the way for proportional representation for election to the EP in the UK;
- Parliament to approve the appointment of the President of the Commission;
- Parliament failed to secure extension of assent procedure to cover all international agreements and amendments to the Treaty.

Council of Ministers

- Limited extension of QMV: QMV to apply to all new Treaty provisions but only extended to research framework programme among existing provisions. Unanimity retained for all tax measures.
- Reweighting of votes in the Council: deferred until the next IGC and will be linked to size of the Commission (new weightings will take into account the situations of member states required to give up their second Commissioner).

European Commission

- Upgrading of the Commission President: President gains right to object to appointment of Commissioners and the right to allocate and reshuffle portfolios.
- Number of Commissioners deferred until the next IGC: at the next enlargement, the Commission will consist of one national from each member state, provided agreement is reached on the reweighting of votes.
- The Commission's right of initiative boosted by creation of new areas of EU competence (employment, health); through transfer of power to Community in matters relating to free movement and greater involvement in third pillar matters (now related to police co-operation and criminal matters).

European Court of Justice

- Jurisdiction extended in some areas of third pillar.

Flexibility

Article K.15 allows member states to co-operate more closely, provided the principles of the treaties are respected, a majority of member states are involved; the acquis communitaire is not affected, participation is open to all member states and that this provision is used only as a last resort.

This section of the Treaty formalises the differential practice which had been happening for a number of years (the ERM, the Social Charter followed by the Social Agreement and Social Protocol, EMU, the Schengen Agreement). These clauses are potentially among the most important in the Amsterdam Treaty, although it remains to be seen how much and how they will be used in practice.

The Amsterdam Treaty, the draft of which was agreed at the Amsterdam Council in June 1997, came into force on 1 May 1999. Its ratification proceeded almost without notice and certainly without the controversy which surrounded the Maastricht ratification process: indeed, the normally reluctant Danes endorsed the Treaty without demur in a referendum in May 1998. This is more a symptom of the innocuous nature of the Amsterdam Treaty and the postponement of difficult decisions to the next IGC than of any renewed Euro-enthusiasm. Unlike the TEU, which as a result of EMU posed major questions for Europe's political and economic systems, the Amsterdam Treaty's achievements are more modest and incremental. The most significant developments are the extension of powers of the European Parliament, the inclusion of an Employment Chapter and changes to the third pillar. However, the IGC did not manage, as many had hoped, to extend qualified majority voting; to resolve questions about the size of the Commission; to incorporate the Schengen Agreement into the Treaty without derogations; to extend the Commission's right to negotiate on behalf of the Community in terms of services and intellectual property rights; nor to achieve a significant simplification of the complexities of EU decision making. In short, it left the controversial issues unsolved.

INSTITUTIONS OF THE EUROPEAN UNION

An understanding of European institutions and of their role in decision making is important for business when identifying how to ensure that their views on key policy issues are heard. Businesses can try to influence decision makers directly themselves or through national or European trade associations and can target policy makers at national or at European level, notably the Commission and Parliament. The Council is not amenable to direct lobbying but companies and national interest groups can work to influence the position of their governments in Council negotiations. Several sectors have close and strong ties with the relevant national ministries: for example, national farming lobbies often maintain close links with national agricultural ministries. Once a directive has been passed, the lobbying of national governments will often continue as interested parties try to influence the way it is implemented. Further details of the roles of the four main Community institutions are outlined below.

The European Commission

The European Commission is the public face of the Community and in many ways, it is the glue that holds the Community together. The Commission is also a focus of criticism for those of a more Euro-sceptic persuasion who tend to portray the Commission as a huge monolith, full of faceless bureaucrats circulating endless pieces of paper designed to tie companies and citizens down in a mass of regulation. The reality is more complex: the Commission performs a range of tasks which give it no exact parallel in member states. The Commission:

- is the Community's civil service;
- performs part of the executive function within the tight limits set by the Treaties;
- represents member states in international negotiations;
- acts in a minor capacity as a legislator;
- acts in a quasi-judicial capacity through its role as guardian of the legal framework and as competition policy policeman.

Yet these formal functions do not capture the full role of the Commission which, through its informal role as broker between member states, defends and promotes wider European rather than national interests.

The Commission itself is composed of twenty Commissioners, many of whom are senior politicians in their own state, who are nominated by national governments for a renewable term of five years. France, Germany, Italy, Spain and the United Kingdom supply two Commissioners each and other member states each provide one. Once appointed, the Treaty requires Commissioners to act totally independently: in other words, they must act in the Community interest and not as representatives of their own state. Each Commissioner has a portfolio of responsibilities corresponding to the Commission's areas of competence. Member states, by consensus, also appoint a President of the Commission and following ratification of the Amsterdam Treaty the President's agreement must be obtained to the appointment of the other Commissioners. The Commissioners are supported in their work by the Community's permanent civil service which is sub-divided into twenty-four Directorate Generals and a number of supporting services such as translation, interpreting and the statistical office.

The Commission is charged with being guardian of the treaties and is engaged in policy formulation at all stages and levels: the nature of its involvement varies, ranging from policy broker to legislator itself in certain fields of secondary legislation. More specifically, the Commission performs the following tasks:

- *Initiator of legislation*: the Commission has the sole right to propose legislation under Pillar one of the treaties and has resisted attempts by the European Parliament to gain the right of initiation. This monopoly facilitates the achievement of a coherent and consistent body of legislation. The Council of Ministers can only take decisions based on Commission proposals, although it can and does ask the Commission to draw up proposals;
- *Legislator*: the Commission also has the power to legislate in its own right. Decisions on legislation involving major political issues or points of principle are taken by the Council of Ministers but its work would become bogged down if it was responsible for all decisions. Commission legislation therefore relieves the legislative burden on the Council by dealing with more detailed, technical legislation;
- *Administrator and monitor of EU laws*: the Commission executes and monitors the application of Community law by member states. Failure to implement EU law properly can result in the Commission taking a member state to the Court of Justice under Article 169 of the Treaty of Rome;
- *Representative of the Community in international fora and negotiator of trade agreements*: the Treaty empowers the Commission to act on behalf of the Community in certain aspects of international economic relations upon receipt of a negotiating mandate from the Council of Ministers (see Chapter 17);

- *Manager of the EU's finances*: the Commission draws up the Community's annual draft budget and plays a key role in management of its finances;
- *Broker and mediator*: in addition to bringing forward legislative proposals, the Commission plays a central, albeit informal, role in trying to reconcile differing views of member states on policy issues. This task calls for highly developed diplomatic and political skills and can be made more complex because of divergent views within the Commission itself. For example, a proposal on energy taxes, controversial enough in itself, will receive input from at least three DGs, including XVII (Energy), XI (Environment) and XXI (taxation), each of which approaches the proposal from a different perspective.

Given the Commission's central role in the initiation and formulation of policy, businesses are assiduous in lobbying Brussels. Although the Commission could easily be overwhelmed by the number of interests wishing to gain its ear, particularly since the mushrooming of European interest groups and the siting of public affairs offices in Brussels by many companies and local and regional authorities following the SEM initiative, it remains open to technical policy inputs from specialised interests. Despite criticisms of its size, the number of European civil servants engaged in the development and monitoring of policy is less than those employed in national ministries of medium importance or even within a large regional authority. Indeed, shortages of in-house technical expertise create heavy Commission reliance on specialised committees and working parties made up of member state officials and independent experts. For example, the Auto Oil Programme to reduce vehicle emissions is effectively a partnership between the Commission and the Community's oil and motor industries. This brings needed technical expertise into the policy formation process but also opens the Commission to criticism that it is working according to the narrow agenda of industry rather than to a broader environmental agenda. In addition, consultation of interests can smooth the way for the passage of legislation. The Commission is most open to European-wide groups: these bodies have already achieved a consensus on key issues and relieve the Commission of the danger of being accused of showing preference to one part of the Community over another.

Arguments about reform of the Commission have centred upon reducing the number of Commissioners. The Amsterdam Treaty made no changes in this respect but change will almost certainly occur before the next round of enlargement takes place to prevent the Commission becoming too unwieldy. Internal restructuring of the Commission is also scheduled before the new Commission takes office in 2000 'to ensure an optimum division between conventional portfolios and specific tasks'. In other words, the present system in which a Commissioner's responsibilities are spread over one or more DGs or Commissioners share responsibilities within the same DG will be rationalised.

The Council of Ministers

The Council of Ministers performs elements of executive and legislative functions and remains the most important of the EU's decision making bodies, despite being required to share its legislative powers more equally with the European Parliament since the introduction of the co-decision procedure. Whereas the Commission and the European Parliament are charged with representing European interests, it is in the Council of Ministers that the balance of national interests among member states is worked out and consequently where the big political battles are fought and compromises forged.

The Council itself is composed of ministerial representatives from member states. Its membership is fluid as ministers attend the Council according to the subject under

BOX 2.5 TYPES OF EU LEGISLATION

Regulation

A regulation has general application and is binding and takes effect directly in all member states. The Merger Control Regulation is an example of this.

Directives

Directives are binding in terms of the results and objectives to be achieved but their implementation is dependent upon member states passing legislation in their own national parliaments to implement the Directive. This approach confers upon member states the ability to meet agreed objectives in ways which respect their own traditions and conditions.

Decisions

Decisions are binding upon those to whom they are addressed which can be individual member states or even companies.

Recommendations and opinions

These instruments have no binding legal force.

discussion: agriculture ministers, for example, attend the Agriculture Council whereas transport ministers will be present at Transport Councils. Member states take it in turn to act as President of the Council for a six month period. The Council Presidency sets the agenda, within constraints, for its period of office, co-ordinates the Union's business and, along with the Commission, acts as a broker to find agreement between states at odds with each other. The Presidency, sometimes as part of the 'troika' (the immediate past, present and future Council Presidents), also acts as Council representative in relation to other institutions such as the European Parliament and to third countries.

In addition, at least once during each Presidency, the European Council, which is composed of heads of government or state, meets to debate broader and wide ranging issues surrounding European integration. Although the Council of Ministers was accounted for within the Treaty of Rome, the European Council was formalised in 1974 and was only incorporated into the Treaties under the Single European Act (SEA).

Another less public, but vital part of the Council network is Coreper (the Committee of Permanent Representatives) which is composed of national officials of ambassadorial rank, supported by lower ranking national officials. Coreper carries out much of the preparation for Council meetings and works out the more detailed and technical aspects of legislation, thereby leaving the elected representatives of member states in the Council free to take the more strategic and political decisions.

The history of the Council of Ministers has been dogged by controversies surrounding its voting procedures. The first concerned the debate over qualified majority and unanimous voting. As discussed above, the intention was always to move towards more qualified majority voting (QMV) once the initial transition period was complete but the Luxembourg Compromise put paid to that. The SEA represented the first major increase in QMV which has since been extended further. Without this procedural change, many achievements of the SEM would have been unattainable given the difficulty of gaining the

Table 2.1 Weighting of votes under qualified majority voting

Austria	4	Italy	10
Belgium	5	Luxembourg	2
Denmark	3	Netherlands	5
Finland	3	Portugal	5
France	10	Spain	8
Germany	10	Sweden	4
Greece	5	United Kingdom	10
Ireland	3		

agreement of what were then twelve member states to such a wide range of proposals. Unanimity still prevails in a number of matters, including amendment of the Treaty, enlargement, citizens' rights, taxation, foreign policy and derogations. The second voting issue relates to the allocation of votes within the Council (see Table 2.1 for weightings). A blocking veto normally consists of twenty-six votes, but as a result of a compromise forced by the United Kingdom in 1994, if there are twenty-three votes against a measure it is withdrawn for a period of reflection before it is reintroduced. The weightings have been devised to create a balance between the interests of large and small states but the most recent and approaching enlargements have caused controversy as efforts to raise the number of votes needed to achieve a blocking veto proportionally to the additional number of votes have been resisted by the United Kingdom in particular which has argued for retention of the existing number of votes for the veto in absolute terms.

The feeling of disappointment and even failure that permeated some commentary on the final draft of the Amsterdam Treaty mostly centred around the failure of member states to take decisions on these issues in preparation for the next enlargement, a failure which necessitates the holding of another IGC before enlargement takes place.

BOX 2.6 OTHER EUROPEAN INSTITUTIONS

In addition to the four main European institutions – the European Commission, the Council of Ministers, the European Parliament and the European Court of Justice – there are a number of other institutions which play an important role in the work of the European Union.

The Economic and Social Committee (ESC)

The Economic and Social Committee (ESC) was established by the Treaty of Rome to involve representatives of employers, workers and other interest groups in the creation of the common market and other EU issues. The main role of its 222 members is to draw up opinions on matters referred to it by the Commission and the Council of Ministers. In some cases, consultation is mandatory and in others it is optional but the Council is under no obligation to take heed of its findings.

The Committee of the Regions (CoR)

The Committee of the Regions (CoR) was established as a consultative body by the Maastricht Treaty as, among other things, a partial response to the need to develop ways to uphold the principle of subsidiarity. It is composed of 222 appointed members who are elected officials at local and regional level in their own member state. The role of the CoR is to bring its collective experience of the impact of Community policies at local level to bear on other EU institutions. As such, the CoR must be consulted on matters relating to TENs, public health, education, youth, culture and economic and social cohesion. It can also take the initiative and give its opinion on other issues affecting regions such as agriculture and environmental protection. There is no obligation on other institutions to take heed of CoR opinions.

The Court of Auditors

The Court of Auditors scrutinises the accounts of the European Union to ensure that its spending takes place in line with the Union's budgetary rules and for the purposes for which it was intended. The Court has the power to carry out on-the-spot audits into EU spending wherever it takes place, including programmes managed outside the Community. The Court publishes an annual general report on Community finances and also reports back on individual cases of errors, mismanagement, irregularities, potential fraud and flaws in systems and procedures which allow irregularities to take place.

The European Investment Bank (EIB)

The EIB is the EU's financing arm, providing long term loans for capital investment to promote EU development and integration and works closely with other sources of Community finance such as the Structural and Cohesion Funds. The Bank's annual ECU 20 billion of lending goes towards the promotion of one of the following objectives:
• economic progress in disadvantaged regions;
• construction of trans-European networks;
• the enhancement of industrial competitiveness, integration at a European level and support for SMEs;
• protection of the environment, quality of life and Europe's architectural heritage;
• the achievement of secure energy supplies.
In addition, the Bank lends outside the boundaries of the EU in support of the financial aspects of the Community's co-operation policies.

The European Investment Fund (EIF)

The EIF was set up as a co-operative joint venture between the EIB, the EU and several dozen commercial banks as part of the European Growth initiative. The initial purpose of the EIF was to provide loan guarantees for major infrastructure projects, especially TENs priority projects, and for capital investment by SMEs. Following its June 1996 general meeting, the EIF is able to take a direct equity stake in TENs-related projects but such initiatives will be modest at first.

The Ombudsman

Since the coming into force of the Maastricht Treaty, all European citizens have had the right to apply to the European Ombudsman if they are the victim of maladministration by a Community institution or organisation.

The European Parliament

For a long time disregarded by many commentators as a talking shop of little consequence, the European Parliament (EP) has, particularly since the first set of direct
elections in 1979 which increased its democratic legitimacy, gradually secured an
enhanced role in the EU's policy making process. This transformation has been slow and
incremental and the EP is still a long way from fulfilling the same functions as national
parliaments. However, the EP has been the major beneficiary in terms of subsequent
IGCs (see Boxes 2.2, 2.3 and 2.4). Further reform will be required to accommodate the
next enlargement and will attempt to simplify and enhance the EP's role further, a process
which is helped by Parliament's position as the only supranational institution which is
directly elected by the citizens of Europe.

The European Parliament itself consists of 626 members (MEPs) who are organised
into eight political groups along transnational rather than national lines (see Table 2.2).
Once a month, the Parliament meets in plenary session in Strasbourg. A further week
is set aside for meetings of trans-national political groupings. Two weeks every month,
the EP's committees sit and work in Brussels. In order to expedite Parliament's work
during plenary sessions, there are twenty standing committees of the EP, each of which
specialises in a particular area. In addition, the EP sets up temporary committees to deal
with particular problems or committees of inquiry.

The EP's three basic functions are:

Legislation

After years in which the EP's only right was to be consulted on European legislation, it
gradually gained powers to amend legislation (although this could be overturned by the
Council of Ministers acting unanimously) and now has the power to reject many items of

Table 2.2 Composition of the European Parliament by political grouping and by
member state, 1998

Belgium	25	European Socialists	214
Denmark	16	European People's Party	181
Germany	99	Union for Europe Group	55
Greece	25	Liberal, Democratic and Reformist Party	41
Spain	64	Confederal Group of the European United Left/	
		Nordic Green Left	33
France	87	Green Group	28
Ireland	15	European Radical Alliance	20
Italy	87	Independents for a Europe of Nations	18
Luxembourg	6	Non-attached	36
Netherlands	31		
Austria	21		
Portugal	25		
Finland	16		
Sweden	22		
United Kingdom	87		
Total	626		626

legislation in their entirety. Following ratification of the Amsterdam Treaty, there will be in practice three possible procedures by which the European Parliament engages in the legislative process:

- *The Consultation procedure (one reading)*: the EP's opinion must be obtained before a legislative proposal from the Commission is adopted by the Council. However, there is no obligation upon the Council to act upon Parliament's views which, nevertheless, are supposed to be a factor in the Council's deliberations. The consultation procedure was the dominant procedure in earlier years but has become less important as subsequent Treaty revisions have given the European Parliament greater powers.
- *The co-decision procedure*: the Amsterdam Treaty has both simplified and extended the co-decision procedure to cover areas which previously came within the scope of the co-operation procedure which has been retained only for some aspects of EMU. (Under the co-operation procedure, the EP's rejection of legislation can be overridden by the Council, albeit with difficulty, whereas this is not possible under co-decision). The co-decision procedure moves the European Parliament towards greater parity with the Council of Ministers. Under co-decision, Parliament can prevent the adoption of a proposal if it believes the Council has failed to take its views sufficiently into account. In addition, if Parliament decides to reject a proposal, it cannot be adopted by the Council. If deadlock is looming, a Conciliation Committee of representatives of Parliament, the Council and the Commission will try to resolve differences before the third reading of legislation.
- *The assent procedure*: the European Parliament must give assent for the accession of new member states, association agreements, matters relating to citizenship, the Structural and Cohesion Funds and the tasks and powers of the European Central Bank. The Parliament can block decisions under this procedure but it cannot amend them.

Scrutiny of the executive

Scrutiny of the executive is a key function of democratic parliaments world-wide and the executive is frequently drawn from the legislature itself. However, this is not the case in the European Union and the problems of executing this task are made even more complex by the unusual blurring of executive roles between the Commission and the Council. Scrutiny of the Commission takes many forms, including approval of members of the Commission and the ultimate power of passing a censure motion on the Commission which would lead to its resignation. In relation to the day to day work of the Commission, MEPs receive and examine regular reports from the Commission, submit written or oral questions to it and question Commissioners directly in committees or plenary sessions.

Parliament's powers in relation to the Council of Ministers have been extended through greater use of the co-decision procedure. In addition to directly blocking proposals, the requirement for Parliament's approval of legislation almost certainly affects the way proposals are drafted. At the beginning of its Council presidency, a member state presents its programme to Parliament and accounts for its achievements at the end of its six months in office. The EP President also attends the European Council to present Parliament's views on agenda items and reports back to Parliament on the Council's proceedings.

Budget

Approval of the Community's budget by the European Parliament is needed. Its power to amend the budget is restricted to non-compulsory items within certain expenditure limits. Compulsory expenditure applies mostly to agriculture, traditionally the largest item of EU expenditure but declining as a share of total expenditure. The Amsterdam Treaty failed to eliminate the compulsory/non-compulsory distinction but it did strengthen the role of the European Parliament in the fight against fraud and its role in expenditure under the second and third pillars.

As the European Parliament grows in stature, so its importance to the business community increases. There are a number of points at which enterprises can realistically and legitimately attempt to press their case. As in national parliaments, business can lobby their own member. Membership of European pressure groups and more informal networks can help ensure that MEPs from a number of member states are contacted. This can be important in two ways: first, by influencing the reports and deliberations of the Parliament and, second, by opening another avenue by which to pressure national governments and, therefore, affect the deliberations of the Council of Ministers. This latter strategy can be particularly useful if the MEP is from the same political party as the ruling national party. In addition, membership of a standing committee indicates that an individual MEP takes a particular interest or has a certain expertise in a particular subject. Expert witnesses, including senior executives from major European companies, are also frequently invited to give evidence in front of parliamentary committees.

The European Court of Justice

Often relatively neglected in discussions regarding EU institutions, the European Court of Justice (ECJ) has nevertheless played a major role in the development of the European Union (see Box 2.7) and its interpretation of EU regulations and directives has frequently had a significant impact on the business environment. The Court itself is based in Luxembourg and comprises fifteen judges and nine advocates-general who deliver opinions on cases brought before the Court to assist the judges in their deliberations.

Since 1989, the overburdened ECJ has been assisted in its tasks by the Court of First Instance (CFI). Initially, the jurisdiction of the CFI was limited to disputes between the Community and its employees; to actions brought against the Commission under the ECSC Treaty and on certain complaints or disputes arising from competition policy. The Maastricht Treaty extended the role of the CFI but it does not have the authority to give preliminary rulings under Article 177, that is, to interpret the Treaty or Community legislation. This core role remains the sole responsibility of the ECJ itself.

The fundamental role of the ECJ is to ensure that the Treaties and Community legislation are respected. More specifically, the Court has jurisdiction in the following areas:

- *Failure to fulfil an obligation*: these actions enable the ECJ to determine whether a member state has fulfilled its obligations under Community law. Such cases are usually brought by the Commission but they can also be brought by another member state. The Commission has, for example, taken member states to the Court for failure to comply with environmental regulations, especially, but not only, in relation to water quality standards.
- *Proceedings for annulment*: member states, the Commission, the Council and, in certain circumstances, the European Parliament, may apply to the ECJ for annulment of all or part of an item of Community legislation or decision. Individuals and companies may also seek annulment of a measure which is of direct concern to them. In other words, the Court reviews the legality of the acts of Community institutions and can declare them void. In June 1998, for example, seven airlines won their case against a Commission decision to approve Ffr 20 billion of state aid to Air France when the ECJ

ruled that the Commission had failed to provide sufficient justification for its decision which should be annulled. The final outcome of this case is not yet known as, at the time of writing, the period in which the Commission, the government of France and/or Air France can appeal has not elapsed. Nevertheless, this is a notable decision, representing the first time the Court has seriously questioned state aid practices in the airline sector.

- *Proceedings for failure to act*: the Court may review the legality of a failure to act by a Community institution. Such cases are unusual. The most renowned example was the 1985 decision which upheld the action brought by the European Parliament against the Council of Ministers for failure to fulfil its obligations within the Treaty of Rome to develop the Common Transport Policy.
- *Actions for damages*: the ECJ rules on the liability of the Community for damage caused by its institutions or employees in the performance of their duties.
- *Appeals*: the Court hears appeals on points of law against judgements given by the CFI.
- *Preliminary rulings*: national courts, when doubtful of the validity or interpretation of an item of Community law may, and in some cases must, request a preliminary ruling on the interpretation from the ECJ. In addition, individuals may seek clarification of Community law which affects them. Preliminary rulings, which must be accepted and applied by the national court which made the original request for a ruling, form a major part of the work of the ECJ and promote consistency of application and interpretation of Community law across member states. The 1995 *Kalanke v. Freie Hansestadt Bremen* preliminary ruling has potentially far-reaching implications for affirmative measures to encourage the employment of women. In matters of appointments and promotions, the law in Bremen allows employers to give priority to women who have the same qualifications as men applying for the same post in sectors where they are under-represented. This law was invoked by the Parks Department regarding the promotion of a female landscape gardener. The unsuccessful male candidate took his case through various appeal procedures until he reached the German national court. This court was unclear whether Bremen's positive discrimination law violated Community law and sought a preliminary ruling from the ECJ which ruled that such acts are a form of sexual discrimination in themselves. This decision could result in the end of affirmative action programmes throughout the Community. Indeed, the *Kalanke* decision was a determining factor in abandonment of the British Labour Party's attempts to increase the number of female MPs by insisting on all female short-lists of candidates. However, the *Kalanke* decision is open to interpretation itself and there is a view that more flexible affirmative action laws than the one enacted in Bremen are still permissible.

Over the years the Court has made a number of landmark decisions which have clarified the governance structure of the Community, especially on the relative balance of power between Community institutions and member states, or have had a profound impact on policy within the Community (see Box 2.7). Consequently, the ECJ has not always been popular with member states. Indeed, the British government was openly hostile to the Court during the 1996–7 intergovernmental conference and pushed for reforms to rein back its powers, a stance which came to nothing.

From the business point of view, ECJ decisions have had major ramifications for operational matters in many areas. This is the case in issues of competition policy, pension law, employment law, etc. The same decision often pleases one group of enterprises and dismays another. Following a case brought by an Austrian spectacle frame manufacturer, the June 1998 ECJ decision that trademark owners have the right to block imports into the European Union of goods they sold originally outside the Union (so-called 'grey goods') pleased manufacturers of branded goods but was unwelcome to many retailers and their customers. The ECJ can thus be an avenue for firms to try to achieve key business objectives. The Swedish ferry company, Stena Line, for example, pressed Swedish tax authorities to seek a preliminary ruling from the ECJ on whether the proposed 1999 abolition of duty-free sales (on which Stena relied for about 30 per cent of its revenue) contravened Treaty provisions by effectively extending the EU's tax jurisdiction to international waters. The campaign to retain duty-free has been fiercely fought (and ultimately unsuccessful): an ECJ challenge would have represented an attempt to find a legal loophole when lobbying of national governments to reverse the decision originally taken in the Council of Ministers has failed.

BOX 2.7 LANDMARK ECJ DECISIONS

The cases discussed below established important principles which have had a fundamental effect on the way in which the Community operates:

1 The supremacy of Community law (Costa v. ENEL)

In this landmark 1962 judgement, the Court ruled that by virtue of joining the Community, member states had voluntarily 'limited their sovereign rights, albeit within limited fields [that is, those allowed within the framework of the treaties]' and effected a permanent transfer of power to Community institutions. In other words, where there was a clash between Treaty obligations or legislation derived from the treaties and national laws, Community law was supreme. This principle has been confirmed by subsequent decisions, notably the Simmenthal judgement of 1978. In fact, the supremacy of Community law is essential to make the Community workable as, without it, member states would be able to pick and choose which pieces of Community legislation they applied, thereby rendering achievement of Treaty objectives unattainable.

2 The principle of direct effect (van Gend en Loos)

The 1964 *van Gend en Loos* case established the principle that certain provisions of the Treaty have direct legal effect, enabling individuals and companies to claim Treaty-based rights in national courts when there was conflict with national rules. This ruling has been of great practical importance as Treaty-based rights prevail over national law even if there is no Community legislation to operationalise these rights, thereby removing the need to wait for Commission action under Article 169 of the Treaty of Rome to address the situation. The Court has ruled subsequently on direct effect in relation to many Treaty articles including Article 30 (free movement of goods), Article 48 (free movement of workers), Article 52 (right of establishment) and Articles 59–60 (free movement of services).

Indeed, in one of the most famous ECJ rulings of recent years, professional footballer, Jean-Marc Bosman, challenged the system of demanding transfer fees for players even after the expiry of their contract which he claimed breached his right of freedom of movement as a worker within the European Union. He won his case and the 1995 *Bosman* ruling has transformed business practices within Europe's multi-million Euro football industry.

The treaties have enabled the Court to attack discrimination on the grounds of gender in the workplace. Article 119 establishes the principle of 'equal pay for equal work'. In the *Defrenne v. Sabena* case, the ECJ ruled that 'the elimination of discrimination based on sex' is a fundamental right based on general principles of Community law which the Court had a duty to uphold. The

Court therefore determined that Article 119 was in part directly effective, enabling women to claim their right to equal pay in any national court and that equal pay provisions were applicable to both public and private sector employees.

3 The principle of mutual recognition (Cassis de Dijon)

In this 1979 case, the ECJ ruled that national standards could not be used to prevent the free circulation of goods (in this case, blackcurrant liqueur) except on grounds of public health, fiscal supervision and consumer protection. The judgement firmly established the principle of mutual recognition which stated that if a product was lawfully sold and marketed in one member state, it must be allowed free circulation throughout the Community. This ruling greatly simplified the building of the single market by reducing the need to harmonise technical standards and was utilised not only in the case of goods, but also in service sectors and to secure free movement of workers through the mutual recognition of qualifications.

4 State liability for damage arising from failure to meet obligations under Community law (Francovich)

This 1991 judgement made member states liable to pay damages for failure to observe its Treaty obligations. The decision arose when Italian workers were unable to claim back pay from a guarantee fund for bankrupt enterprises because the Italian government had failed to establish such a fund in line with a Community directive.

Following rejection by the Court of Appeal in London in April 1998 of the British government's appeal against a ruling that it must compensate Spanish fishermen for illegally preventing them from operating under the British flag (thus excluding them from the British quota under the Common Fisheries Policy) Spanish fishermen look set to receive compensation approaching £100 million for losses incurred during the period they were excluded from the British quota. The British liability stems from an ECJ decision that actions introduced in the 1988 Merchant Shipping Act to prevent 'quota hopping' (by only allowing fishing boats which were 75 per cent owned and managed by UK citizens to operate under the British flag and share in the British fish quota) infringed Treaty of Rome provisions regarding non-discrimination on the grounds of nationality.

CHALLENGES FOR THE NEXT CENTURY

The ability of the European Union to reform its institutions and policies tends to lag behind economic and market realities. The Amsterdam Treaty, for example, only partially fulfilled the original tasks set for it, leaving a difficult agenda for the next IGC which must take place before the next round of enlargement. Agenda 2000, which was published in July 1997 shortly after the draft Treaty was agreed, set out the following items which need to be tackled beforehand, notably:

- enlargement: both the who and how of completing this process successfully (see Chapter 15);
- reform of internal policies, particularly the broad principles of measures needed to reform the Structural Funds and the Common Agricultural Policy;
- the development of a new financial framework for the period 2000 to 2006, both in support of reform of the above policies and of the enlargement process.

Enlargement negotiations have subsequently opened with six aspiring members and eleven member states have embarked upon EMU. These major developments will keep alive and even escalate the debate about the nature of the EU. In the longer term, the intergovernmental aspects of the EU will come increasingly under attack with greater pressure to develop along federal lines: that is, as a body with distinct separation of powers in which the responsibilities of different levels of governance are defined according to the principles of subsidiarity and allocated in the constitution of the Union (i.e. the treaties). This is at odds with the usual British understanding of the term 'federal' which is popularly viewed as implying a centralising super-state. In fact, the federal model as traditionally understood in the rest of Europe can imply a large degree of decentralisation and power for lower levels of governance. However, the eventual shape and influence of the EU and through it, its member states, will be determined to a large extent by the outturn of the internationalisation tendencies discussed in Chapter 1.

↘ KEY POINTS

- **The momentum of European integration waxes and wanes in line with political and economic cycles.**

- **An understanding of the evolution of the EU and of its institutions helps business understand the context of individual policies and how they can influence the decision making process.**

- **Businesses can attempt to influence the formation of EU policy at both national and European levels, directly or through national and European trade associations.**

- **The European Court of Justice has had a major, and under-rated, role in forging the European business environment.**

- **Reform of the EU and its institutions is reactive and lags behind economic and market realities.**

SUGGESTED FURTHER READING

Archer, C., and Butler, F. (1996) *The European Union: Structure and Process*, Pinter.

Dinan, D. (1994) *Ever Closer Union? An Introduction to the European Community*, Macmillan.

George, S. (1996) *Politics and Policy in the European Union*, (third edition), Oxford University Press.

Maizey, S., and Richardson, J. (1993) *Lobbying in the European Community*, Oxford University Press.

Middlemas, K. (1995) *Orchestrating Europe: the Informal Politics of the European Union 1973–1995*, Fontana.

Nugent, N. (1999) *The Government and Politics of the European Union*, (fourth edition), Macmillan.

Tsoukalis, L. (1997) *The New European Economy Revisited*, Chapters 1–4, Oxford University Press.

Urwin, D.W. (1991) *The Community of Europe: a History of European Integration since 1945*, Longman.

Van Kersbergen, K., and Verbeek, B. (1994) 'The Politics of Subsidiarity in the European Union', *Journal of Common Market Studies*, Vol. 32, No. 2, 215–36.

3

THE SINGLE EUROPEAN MARKET: ASSESSING AND EXTENDING ITS IMPACT

The initial Single European Market (SEM) programme, covering the years 1985–92, was limited, if not minimalist, in the efforts it made towards the realisation of its stated objective. Much of the programme was about catching up with lapsed priorities that were espoused within the founding Treaties of the European Communities. Indeed the Commission always marketed its single market initiative as merely the first phase of moves towards the establishment of an SEM. A true SEM will only exist when all goods and services that can be traded are freely tradable and when potentially mobile factors of production have no barriers inhibiting their right to do so. This means that the moves towards an SEM extend beyond the priorities outlined within the initial programme and will need to be adjusted as internationalisation creeps into more and more product, service and factor markets.

The initial section of this chapter explains the importance of and opportunities afforded to European business from the development of the SEM. After exploring the aims and intentions of the initial programme, an assessment of its impact (in the light of the predicted gains within the initial Cecchini Report) is offered. Thereafter how the SEM has and is being extended to other sectors as well as how the initial action plan is being complemented by further strategies to counter delays, deferrals and omissions in the realisation of the SEM is discussed. Before conclusions are reached, an examination of the external dimension of the programme is explored.

EUROPEAN BUSINESS AND THE SINGLE MARKET

At its heart, the SEM is about improving the performance of European enterprises as a precursor to broader industrial success within international markets. Such success is pivotal in securing the greater levels of employment and investment which are increasingly the core focus of policy makers. Surveys prior to the initial SEM programme suggested that, across a number of sectors, the fragmentation of the European market was inhibiting indigenous business success on the global stage. For a market of a similar size, the US had considerably more efficient and rationalised market structures with fewer firms within core internationally traded sectors (for example, white goods and motor vehicles).

The opportunities from the SEM for business come from a number of areas, not least from the possibilities of the re-organisation of production offered by producing a single product for a single market instead of the multitude of products previously required by different national laws and regulations. Most analysts believe the advantages to European business from the SEM are derived from:

- wider availability of economies of scale in the production process;
- the effects of more intense competition;
- lower barriers to entry.

In theory, the wider opportunities afforded by the availability of economies of scale will offer lower costs of production and, in combination with more intense competition, lower prices. This will have a knock-on effect as lower prices and costs mean that these enterprises are more competitive in both international and indigenous markets. Over time, this enhanced position is likely to lead to greater levels of employment and investment. These benefits should be accentuated by higher levels of product innovation and a greater attention to non-price factors in the production process (for example, through enhanced product quality and design).

Many of the cost effects of the SEM are derived from alterations in the mode and manner in which firms alter their logistical chain. For many enterprises, this means re-establishing a new network of suppliers and distributors across the continent both as a means of entering new markets and as a more direct cost reduction measure. Benefits to the enterprise's logistical chain are derived from:

- *suppliers*: sourcing from new suppliers that offer lower prices and/or better quality inputs to the enterprise;
- *production systems*: developing new locations in order to enter new markets and lower the cost of market entry;
- *distribution systems*: competition in services to the firm (in areas such as transport, warehousing and retailing systems) can further increase efficiencies.

These cost reduction measures will be complemented by new or renewed marketing efforts and promotional systems at the final end of the logistical chain (that is, the consumer).

Naturally, how such efficiencies are realised comes down to the individual enterprise, its requirements and strategy. The response of many enterprises has been to seek the development of more pronounced trans-national networks as a means of rationalising the production process and of providing an entry point into other markets. Porter (1990) disputes this as the most effective mechanism for realising the competitive gains from the SEM. He believes that if enterprises respond to competition by seeking to limit the intensity of rivalry, then they could limit the competitive benefits of the SEM to both enterprises and the economy as a whole. However, given the need for rationalisation of production, some consolidation is necessary. The issue is one of whether this emerges via a process of 'natural selection' (as Porter suggests) or through agreement/co-operation. One of the features of the SEM was the rise in the number of mergers and acquisitions across the EU within services and manufacturing as firms consolidated as part of their strategy to meet the requirements of entering and being competitive within this integrating market (see Figure 3.1). This trend did tend to fall off with the recession of the early 1990s, though mergers and acquisitions per annum settled at a much higher level.

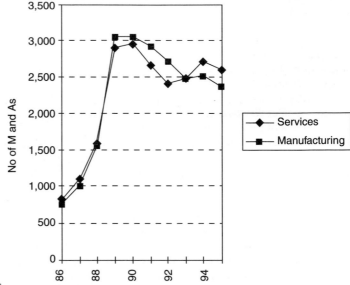

Figure 3.1 **Mergers and acquisitions in the EU (by sector)**
Source: European Commission

THE INITIAL SEM PROGRAMME: INTENTIONS AND OBJECTIVES

The promotion of the SEM was the Community's response to the problems that were evident throughout the European economy in the late 1970s and early 1980s (that is, rising unemployment and slow growth: so-called 'Eurosclerosis'). The 1985 White Paper *Completing the Internal Market* proposed nearly 300 measures to push the development of the SEM. The programme was formalised in the Single European Act (SEA) which was ratified in 1987. Importantly, the SEA set a deadline for the implementation of the initial measures – the end of 1992. It also reformed the decision making procedure to speed up the implementation of SEM-related legislation. The central theme of these measures was to remove the remaining non-tariff barriers which fragmented the EU market (see Box 3.1).

BOX 3.1 THE BARRIERS TO BE REMOVED

The White Paper *Completing the Internal Market* argued that the fragmentation of the European market was sustained by a number of barriers which inhibited factor movements and trade as well as directly imposing costs upon business. Broadly these barriers, which vary in importance on a sector-by-sector or even on a firm-by-firm basis, can be categorised as follows:

- *Physical barriers*: these include border stoppages, customs barriers and other time delaying and cost increasing measures involved in mobility between states;
- *Technical barriers*: these include the absence of common standards across the EU which means developing different versions of the same product for each market; also included are public procurement practices, technical regulations and differing business laws and practices (such as a culture of state support);
- *Fiscal barriers*: these include differentials in the levels of VAT and excise duties among the states.

The prioritising of the SEM by the EU has implications for other core complementary or 'flanking' policies notably:

- the requirement for the EU's competition policy to ensure a level playing field for the business community;
- a more effective regional policy to counter any regional imbalances that result from the advent of the SEM;
- the development of an appropriate social dimension to prevent any erosion of social rights that may arise from the development of the SEM.

In addition, it is important to recognise that the SEM will not be realised by Community legislation alone. It was evident that some form of alignment will need to take place within national legal structures and administrations, attitudes and behaviour of market participants and (as suggested above) the adjustment of complementary policies at both Community and member state levels.

At its most basic, the SEM programme was an exercise in de-regulation from which all members were expected to gain. The gains from the development of the SEM were predicted within the 1988 Cecchini Report which estimated substantial gains both within individual sectors and the economy as a whole. In terms of the sectoral effects (derived from the removal of barriers to trade, economies of scale, competition and other barriers limiting production), Cecchini estimated that the SEM would add 4.3–6.8 per cent to the Community's GDP. In terms of the broader economic picture, it was estimated that the SEM would create nearly two million extra jobs and have overall positive effects on fiscal and external balances as well as on inflation.

THE COMMERCIAL EFFECTS OF THE INITIAL SEM PROGRAMME

Inevitably, the impact of the SEM is directly related to the extent to which the legislation has actually been implemented (see Table 3.3). However, over the period 1985–94, the Commission concluded that the following effects were evident.

Enhanced integration and factor allocation: in terms of trade, the SEM programme led to increasing intra-EU imports for both manufacturing and services, with the rise in the latter being twice the rise in the former. There have also been increases in trade creation relative to trade diversion; indeed there is little evidence that the latter has taken place. These effects differ to the extent in which the sector concerned was sensitive to internal EU trade. This internal liberalisation was coupled with external liberalisation with resulting flows in FDI. The impact of this FDI, the Commission claims, is too soon to tell but it does argue that the SEM has had a more positive impact upon FDI than broader trade liberalisation. Evidence of this growing intra-EU FDI has been typified by the rise in the proportion of EU mergers and acquisitions that are cross-border in nature (see Table 3.1). This is within a generic environment where mergers and acquisitions have increased markedly (see Figure 3.1).

Changes in the nature and pattern of trade: there has been a significant change in the balance between inter- and intra-industry trade, with a marked shift towards the latter. This implies a move away from inter-state specialisation towards more harmonious industrial structures. This reduces the likelihood of asymmetric shocks – an important pre-requisite for the move towards economic and monetary union. In intra-industry trade, adjustment takes place within industries, leaving the EU less exposed to sector-specific shocks. These changes have been enhanced by the nature and effects of FDI. Finally, there is little evidence to suggest that the core of the EU has attracted investment away

Table 3.1 Total mergers and acquisitions in the EU (% by nationality of partners)

Source/type of merger	1986–9	1990–5
National	70.1	70.8
Community	15.5	18.7
International	14.4	10.5

Source: European Commission

from peripheral areas therefore overcoming the fear that the SEM would widen regional disparities. However the absence of any such evidence may be due to the fact that such mobility may only be realised over the medium to long term.

Efficiency and competition effects: efficiency and competitive effects have generally been realised through substantial restructuring of European industries, although this rationalisation has not been as great as suggested by the forecasts within the Cecchini Report. Few of the efficiency gains have been realised through technical improvements. More often, any efficiencies were directly related to economies of scale, notably in terms of fixed investments in marketing, brand evolution, R&D expenditure and the development of new production processes. Competition has undoubtedly increased in intensity with cost efficiencies generally being passed on to consumers but there is limited evidence for the convergence of prices across the EU. This is more evident within consumer and equipment goods industries than it is for other sectors such as energy where agreement on even limited opening of markets occurred a long time behind schedule. Generally, the more goods and services are traded, the greater the evidence of price convergence. As the liberalisation process expands so convergence is likely to become more widespread.

Employment, income and convergence: the Commission has calculated that the SEM has added 1.1 per cent to the growth rate of the EU and also created around 300,000 jobs during the period 1985–94. However, this figure should be treated with some suspicion given the tremendous difficulties in estimating and isolating the effects of the SEM. There has been some degree of economic convergence with the four cohesion states (Ireland, Spain, Portugal and Greece) exhibiting faster growth rates than the rest of the EU as a result of the SEM. In part, this is driven by the fact that these states had a lot of catching up to do, so their growth rate might naturally be higher. Once again, these figures are inconclusive as aggregate figures are skewed by the impressive performance of Ireland and, to a lesser extent, Portugal and thus tend to overstate the levels of actual convergence of the cohesion states.

THE IMPACT UPON MANUFACTURING

In manufacturing, the abolition of customs and fiscal formalities and the gradual elimination of technical barriers have been the two great contributions to the development of a SEM. In terms of customs and fiscal formalities, the simplification of procedures has reduced by about two-thirds the supplementary cost of cross-border shipments. Such savings have added 0.7 per cent to the value of intra-EU trade (around ECU 5 billion). The benefits from technical standardisation have been slower in their realisation with unharmonised standards still affecting some 25 per cent of EC output. Even where agreements have been reached, some operators have found it difficult to get these standards into common acceptance.

The effects of the SEM have not been uniform across manufacturing sectors. The European Commission has identified a number of sectors where the SEM has had the greatest effects, notably textiles, chemicals and motor vehicles where the SEM has accounted for 80 per cent of the changes in market share of intra-EU imports. Across manufacturing, there have been gradual increases in intra-industry trade (notably motor vehicles and chemicals). In those sectors where there has been strong predominance of inter-industry trade (such as food and textiles) evidence of increased intra-industry trade is emerging.

In the manufacturing sector, intra-EU FDI has differed between northern and southern Europe. The majority of FDI in the north has been based on technology intensive sectors (such as engineering, transport equipment and machinery). In the south, cross-border FDI has been based upon more technologically basic products such as textiles, clothing, timber and wooden furniture. In total, 31 per cent of intra-EU FDI was within the manufacturing sector. This (relatively) low figure reflects the greater tradability of manufacturing goods, therefore negating the necessity for FDI.

Largely in anticipation of the advent of the SEM, the EU manufacturing sector underwent a substantial amount of mergers and acquisitions (see Figure 3.1). The vast majority (nearly two-thirds) were domestic in nature. Such trends have led to an increase in the concentration within manufacturing. Right across the manufacturing sector, the concentration ratio (the market share of the top four firms) increased from 20.5 to 22.8 per cent between 1987 and 1993 (see Table 3.2). However, France, the UK and Belgium saw domestic concentration decrease; Germany tended to buck this trend. Many sectors have seen industry concentration rise by more than 5 per cent, notably in those related to public procurement (for example, telecommunications), food sectors sensitive to the SEM (such as pasta, starch, oils and fats) and in others such as electrical machinery. Generally this trend has been strongest in those industries that are more technologically intensive and therefore more susceptible to the SEM and the rationalisation it is expected to stimulate. Those industries where non-price competitive factors such as branding, marketing and advertising are important (such as motor vehicles and consumer chemicals) showed more moderate changes in concentration which was largely due to changes within domestic markets. This may be due to the nationalistic preferences which continue to segment the EU market.

Between 1985 and 1992, there was an increase in firm size within manufacturing in all large EU states except the UK. However, firm size does not appear to have been greatly influenced by the SEM as growth was greatest in those sectors least exposed to the changes. This reflected the fact that the intensity of competition rather than the SEM itself was the factor driving changes in average firm size. There is no evidence to suggest that enterprises have re-organised production and increased the size and scale of their operations as a result of the SEM. Efficiency gains from the SEM were, not surprisingly, more evident in larger manufacturing firms.

The SEM has increased markedly the intensity of competition within manufacturing. Evidence suggested that, across all industries, the advent of the SEM imposed significant constraints upon price–cost margins of the magnitude of a 1 per cent reduction per annum since 1986. Thus, the Commission concludes, had there been no SEM, price–cost margins would have grown faster. The effects have been greatest in those sectors especially sensitive to changes driven by the SEM such as those involving high technology (for example, office equipment) and those which had moderate non-tariff barriers before the SEM (for example, consumer electronics). These effects have extended beyond the most SEM sensitive sectors through networking and strategic reactions. For example, the Commission notes how the impact of the SEM on the glass sector has driven change upstream within the soda ash industry. This underlines the spillover effects initiated by the SEM. Finally, the process of price convergence has also been evident in the

Table 3.2 Changes in concentration in EU manufacturing

Industry type	CR4[1] in 1987 (%)	CR4 in 1993 (%)	Change in CR4
Average for total manufacturing	20.5	22.8	2.3
Conventional industries	13.2	14.4	1.2
Advertising intensive industries[2]	22.3	23.6	1.3
Technology intensive industries[3]	32.9	38.9	6.0
Industries with both high advertising and R&D expenses[4]	30.1	32.4	2.3

Source: European Commission

Notes

[1] CR4 is the share of output represented by the four largest enterprises.

[2] These are largely food related industries

[3] These include telecommunications equipment, chemicals, etc.

[4] This includes sectors such as pharmaceuticals, soaps, detergents, etc.

manufacturing sector especially within those industries that are highly tradable within the EU and beyond. Between 1985 and 1993 prices were estimated to have converged by 3 per cent across all sectors.

A survey conducted by the European Commission in 1996 indicated that manufacturing was generally positive about the impact of the SEM, although over 60 per cent felt that the SEM had failed to remove all obstacles to trade within their sector. A third of manufacturing enterprises surveyed felt that the SEM had been a success for them. This relatively high figure may be due to the scale of the firms within these sectors. There is a largely negative opinion that the SEM has had a tangible impact upon domestic performance and has only really had an impact in European markets. In addition, on average over 70 per cent of firms reckoned that the SEM had had little or no effect upon enterprise strategy with 60 per cent estimating that the SEM had no impact on sales to other EU states. This indifference is compounded by the fact that around 50 per cent perceive that the SEM is of little importance to enterprise strategy. Overall this must make depressing reading for the Commission. Whether the limited impact is understated by the research, is limited by the incomplete nature of the SEM itself or indeed because firms had already undertaken a European strategy prior to the SEM is a matter of conjecture. However, it is perhaps an indicator that the SEM is more important as a background measure or facilitator than as a direct stimulant to business progress.

THE IMPACT UPON SERVICES

The SEM was successful in establishing a legal framework for services. However because such measures have only come into force since 1993, it is too soon to assess their full effect. This problem is not assisted by the uneven implementation of legislation. Since the introduction of the Single European Act, intra-EU trade in services has increased on average by 3.1 per cent per annum. The emerging importance of services within the SEM has been cemented by the fact that the bulk (almost two-thirds) of FDI within the EU has been within this sector. These features reflect the following characteristics:

- the high rate of growth of service sectors within the EU relative to other parts of the economy;
- the high level of protection of services in the period before the SEM, thus FDI expansion was an inevitable consequence of barrier removal (most notably within financial services);
- the lower tradability of services relative to manufactured goods (thus necessitating FDI for market entry);
- firm specific assets;
- the importance of proximity to consumers within these sectors.

Since 1993, services have tended to form the majority of mergers and acquisitions within the EU, a feature which is driven by the delayed introduction of market opening measures within this sector. Continued resistance by national bodies to full implementation of the SEM measures for services is likely to further deny commercial gain from trans-national rationalisation (see for example, the banking and transportation sectors). The effect of the SEM upon services varies from sector to sector. Those that were heavily exposed to the SEM (such as road freight transport – see Chapter 10) have undergone dramatic restructuring resulting in increased concentration at both the EU and national level. This restructuring has had generally positive effects both upstream (final consumers) and downstream (manufacturing) enabling large cost reductions in service consumption. Some more protected industries (such as telecommunications, airlines or retail banking) have shown only slight changes in concentration.

Evidence of efficiency gains within the service sector is difficult to establish due to the nature and problems of measuring service activities. Generally, there has been evidence (albeit limited) of efficiency gains in those sectors that have been most exposed to the SEM process – for example, the distribution sector has undergone sharp cost declines. In the more protected sectors, efficiency gains have been less obvious and where they have occurred it is unlikely that they are related solely to the SEM (for example the wider use of technology in banking). In telecommunication services, the SEM can be credited with stimulating technological change and delivering other efficiencies although the full effects are still to be realised. Across the EU in airlines and banking, no significant changes in efficiency were observed.

Across all service sector industries, there have been increases in the intensity of competition, even in protected sectors or where the implementation SEM measures has only been partial. Despite this, the overall trend was not as strong as in the manufacturing sector due again to the incomplete nature of service de-regulation. Thus increases in the intensity of competition are driven more by domestic rivalry than by any developments at the EU level. At the EU level, new competition has been aided by both new entry in certain market segments (airlines, telecommunications) and the ending of conduct regulations which restricted marketing strategies (airlines, banking). In road freight transport, there has been a sharp decline in prices with corresponding efficiency gains in the distribution sector. These have led to an alteration in the sourcing patterns of retailing and manufacturing firms. In addition, competition within the service industry has been hindered by the persistence of a number of competitive distortions such as state aid.

Like manufacturing firms, service sector enterprises seem to be less affected by the development of the SEM than originally supposed. Just over a fifth of service companies in a recent survey believed that the SEM had been successful in removing barriers within this sector with only 16 per cent believing that the programme had been a success for their firm. In addition, nearly three-quarters believed the SEM had had an indifferent impact upon the sector and two-thirds saw little corresponding success for the SEM within their

CASE STUDY 3.1 THE IMPACT OF THE SEM ON MANUFACTURING: THE CASE OF CHEMICALS

The chemical industry represents a sector for which intra-EU and international trade has always been a core concern of enterprise strategy. The SEM contained no legislation that was specifically directed at the chemical sector but offered a series of amendments to existing legislation for the development of common standards across a broad range of topics from the classifying of substances through to marketing of preparations. This is complemented by SEM legislation which made trade easier for operators within the sector.

For the chemical industry, the SEM programme has reduced obstacles to trade within Europe and increased the intensity of competition. This should imply lower prices and reduced costs. However, a survey conducted for the European Commission indicated the SEM and other initiatives would lead to short term increases in production costs within the sector. These effects vary according to the nature of the legislation though measures related to the environment (such as eco-labelling, packaging and classifying and registering chemical substances) have tended to have the greatest impact upon costs. The effect of such measures upon the international competitiveness of enterprises within this sector has been minimal as these environmental costs are a small percentage of total costs. In any case, the industry sees the SEM as low down the list of salient factors affecting industry performance. Factors such as the economic cycle, generic market trends and technology tend to be more significant. The impact of the SEM has been negated by delays in areas such as energy liberalisation and by the uneven implementation of agreed standards and procedures.

Despite this, most chemical companies feel that the SEM has been generally positive in terms of market performance. Since 1987, intra-EU exports have increased relative to total exports. This rise can be partially attributed to a declining global market share for EU chemical companies. The SEM has increased competition within the sector notably in southern Europe which has been translated into lower real prices. There has been a narrowing of prices across the EU due to this increased competition but this process has been limited by local market conditions, different specifications and variable costs of distribution. Concentration has increased but its detrimental effects may be offset by more intense competition.

The cost effects of the SEM upon industry are difficult to discern. All that can be concluded is that the SEM has played a role in the process, partly by aiding mergers and acquisitions and joint ventures. Whilst the SEM has facilitated more efficient sourcing, it has not had any discernible impact as this was already a regular industry feature. Liberalisation elsewhere within the SEM programme has had a positive aspect on the cost function of enterprises notably with regard to trade facilitation and transport de-regulation.

Overall, the SEM has impacted upon the industry with a resulting response in strategy. The increased competition has led to more mergers but there has been little in the way of upstream or downstream integration. Beyond this the SEM has had little extra effect upon the strategic decisions of enterprises. Further progress is still required by the industry notably with regard to the application of standards, harmonisation of VAT rates, the creation of a single currency, the formation of a single energy policy and the persistence of state aids in a number of member states.

country as a whole. Many firms (between 60 and 89 per cent of those surveyed) had witnessed no discernible increase in domestic competition over the period. However, the level of price competition in domestic markets had shown greater levels of intensity. Around three-quarters of those service sector firms surveyed noted that the SEM had no impact upon enterprise strategy. The only area where the SEM has had a modicum of impact was in product development.

CASE STUDY 3.2 THE IMPACT OF THE SEM UPON SERVICES: THE CASE OF INSURANCE

It is generally felt that the insurance sector has yet to reap the full benefits of the SEM. The sector is worth over ECU 500 billion in premium payments and companies have long complained about the absence of a Single Insurance Market (SIM). Signs exist of a more competitive market but much remains to be done before a full SIM is realised. Over the period 1989–95, there were three major actions towards the SIM: the 1988 Second Non-life Directive, the 1990 Motor Services Directive and the 1992 Third Life and Non-Life Directive. In total, these sought to operate a harmonised SIM from July 1994 through a single system for authorisation and supervision of insurers by host states (the so-called European Passport). Overall, the freedom to provide services was only practised by a few undertakings. Operators were still hesitant to take advantage of the changes due to a number of regulatory obstacles, notably:

- the legal principle of the 'general good', which is incorporated into EU legislation, has presented a legal minefield as it is constantly undergoing revision;
- a lack of harmonised practices in carrying out insurance operations in the EU;
- the incorrect implementation of legislation.

There has been increased upstream and downstream co-operation as the larger enterprises respond to the challenges of more intense competition. To stay ahead of rivals, these companies are implementing new technology to improve distribution channels for products (away from agents, etc.). However the impact of the SEM upon competition is only felt in limited segments of the insurance market. EU insurers believe their success in developing an SIM will be related to overcoming the major regulatory obstacles to the cross-border implementation of insurance products and services.

A consequence of the limited changes towards a SIM is that most investment plans are still focused upon the national market with less than 20 per cent of undertakings investing beyond national borders. Thus there has been no real change in strategy since the advent of the SEM. In addition, the anticipated convergence of market structures (also leading to more intense competition) has simply not happened. In fact, such lack of convergence has merely led to a consolidation of undertakings within national markets which has weakened the smaller players. If leading players do move into new European markets, it is more often through merger and acquisitions than through FDI.

There has also been little concern with the harmonisation of prices or policy conditions for similar products offered by operators between member states. Despite this, since 1989, there have been efforts by insurance enterprises to develop 'Euro' products based upon offering identical insurance products across a range of countries. This is one area where the development of the SIM has had a tangible impact. However real and total uniformity is lacking, thereby

---

continued

preventing customers from comparing products and prices across states. These problems of transparency will be overcome by the introduction of the Euro which will further intensify competition and force the pace towards an SIM.

There has been a clear trend towards cost reduction by insurers. For most, the reason for this is internal and there is little or no credit given to the SIM for these phenomena. Despite this, the SIM is having a limited impact as insurance undertakings integrate one or more functions at the European level. Thus information sharing and unifying promotional efforts offer economies of scale based upon a recognition that enterprises see a SIM emerging. In practice, yet again the majority of these economies are only realised at the European level after they have been fully implemented at the national level.

Over the period examined (1989–95), enterprises have developed strategy around the need to meet competitive concerns and make investments to sustain or enhance position. These developments should be credited to domestic competition rather than to the SIM which has played a largely incidental role in the strategy formation process. In the short term, when a European market does emerge, it will be in selling cover to commercial undertakings operating in this dimension. How and when this feeds through into the personal market is difficult to predict. Differences between states over the desirability of the SIM are still marked. Disputes persist as to whether mutual recognition or harmonisation is the best way forward. Pressure upon the sector is growing as insurance becomes more closely intertwined with other sectors such as banking. This is demonstrated by a number of high profile mergers such as the merger of the Belgo-Dutch banking/insurance group Fortis with Belgium's Generale Bank and the takeover of Royal Belge by the French insurance giant AXA–UAP.

DEVELOPING THE SEM

The initial programme highlighted above was, as suggested, merely the first stage in an ongoing process. The priorities for the second phase of SEM development focus upon:

- delays in the initial SEM programme, such as uneven implementation of legislation;
- deferrals in the initial SEM programme, including issues, such as taxation, that were politically and economically difficult to achieve and were therefore shelved in order to promote work in those areas where agreement was possible;
- omissions from the original programme: that is, to extend SEM opportunities to more actors (such as SMEs) and to more sectors (such as energy) as well as establishing a series of facilitatory measures (such as the development of a series of corresponding infrastructures: see Chapter 9).

Officially the second phase of the SEM started on 1 January 1993. The Commission's priorities for this phase were highlighted within the 1993 Strategic Programme 'Making the Most of the Internal Market'. In many senses, this proposes a scrutiny role for legislators ensuring that EC law is implemented into national law, that the law is enforced fairly, that no new barriers emerge and that a constant re-evaluation of SEM legislation occurs to ensure and sustain its relevance to operators.

In the light of the assessment of the impact and effectiveness of the SEM programme, the Commission has proposed an Action Plan for the SEM. The Action Plan forms the basis for a new political commitment to the SEM. The plan seeks to use the movement towards economic and monetary union (EMU) to secure completion of the SEM, highlighting how its completion is integral to the attainment of EMU. Consequently, the Commission sought to ensure the adoption and implementation of measures to coincide with the introduction of EMU on 1 January 1999.

The Action Plan is based upon comments made to the Commission by member states and very much reflects the themes within the aforementioned strategic programme. Consequently, in setting priorities and objectives, four strategic targets (of equal importance) have been prescribed.

1 *Making the rules more effective*: to restore credibility in the SEM, rules need to have the confidence of business and of member states. This requires the proper enforcement and simplification of EU and national laws related to the SEM.

2 *Dealing with key market distortions*: notably those related to tax distortions and the continued presence of anti-competitive actions within the European business environment.

3 *Removing sectoral obstacles to market integration*: there needs to be an examination of laws to pinpoint remaining barriers and to prevent the emergence of new impediments. This may require changes in the attitudes of national administrations.

4 *Delivering a single market for the benefit of all citizens*: the aim is to secure an SEM that works not merely for businesses but also for employees by sustaining and enhancing levels of employment and offering increased levels of social protection. In addition, the aim is to secure measures that increase personal freedom and offer benefits to consumers.

As a means of realising this, the Commission proposed a three-phase approach which was endorsed by the Amsterdam Council in 1997.

Phase one will be based upon short term measures that do not require additional EU legislation. Success within this phase relies upon a number of practical steps taken at the EU and at national level to give effect to previous commitments notably with regard to meeting the first strategic objective noted above. This phase will typically need to include elimination of all delays in transposing SEM directives into national law (see Table 3.3), effective implementation of telecommunication and energy measures and the closer involvement of citizens in the SEM development and review process.

Phase two includes measures that have been proposed but need to be fully adopted as far as possible before 1 January 1999. This phase includes the proposals for the European Company Statute, the transparency mechanism for information society services and the directive on the liberalisation of gas supply.

Phase three involves areas where progress is relatively immature due to the novelty of the action or where advancement is likely to be, or is proving, difficult. In these areas, when the Commission comes up with proposals, other institutional bodies in the decision making process should give a 'fast track' approach to their implementation. The stage of development for phase three measures is by no means uniform. Typical amongst the actions either proposed or needed include the modernisation and more coherent application of VAT, cross-border mergers, phasing out of restrictions upon investment funds and the abolition of frontier controls.

Overall, the development of the Action Plan is designed to give the process of the creation of the SEM (which is essential to the development of economic and monetary union) an extra political and commercial impetus. This requires all states to renew their commitment to the SEM. The strategy does not require a new White Paper but a series of practical non-legislative measures. The issue of effective enforcement is key. It was evident soon into the initial programme that there would be uneven implementation of legislation by the end of 1992. Indeed, seven years on, the legislation included in the initial action programme was still not fully implemented.

Table 3.3 Non-implementation of SEM rules,
2 February 1999 (%)

All directives	
Belgium	5.0
Denmark	1.1
Germany	2.5
Spain	1.8
Greece	4.8
France	4.4
Eire	4.6
Italy	5.1
Luxembourg	4.9
Netherlands	1.9
Austria	1.9
Portugal	5.5
Finland	0.7
Sweden	1.3
UK	2.7

Source: European Commission

The European Commission has very little power in practice to achieve compliance from states. Its most effective weapon is perhaps to name and shame those states who are not meeting their commitments as well as they might. This underlines the importance of the commitment offered by states to the realisation of the SEM. Member states are now committed to honouring a timetable for implementing outstanding legislation. This required that the majority of all remaining SEM legislation should have been implemented by mid-1998 – a goal which was not actually achieved. To ensure compliance, there are 'problem-solving' mechanisms for dispute resolution involving both formal (infringement procedures) and informal (co-operative agreements) arrangements for overcoming disputes. These operate on both a bilateral and multilateral basis. Within the Action Plan, member states have to provide contact points to allow their own citizens to monitor and question SEM enforcement within their own state.

The European Commission has made a determined effort to simplify EU legislation under the Simpler Legislation for the Internal Market (SLIM) programme. The aim is to develop a simpler legislative environment within which the SEM can be realised. This applies to national as much as to EU legislation. The simplification of legislation was also driven by a desire for effective legislation that did not impose added costs upon business. This was of special importance for enabling SMEs to realise the benefits of the SEM. To date, it has had some success in achieving the stated objective as teams of experts examine legislation to ensure its simplicity and easy comprehension.

The entire process of legislation for the development of the SEM requires close co-ordination between national and supranational administrations. These administrations essentially have a market surveillance role to determine the effectiveness of SEM measures at the sectoral level. This can ensure that measures are monitored and reviewed and therefore respond adequately to the concerns of business and consumers. This is especially important given that SEM legislation is implemented at the national level. This requires national bodies to oversee the implementation of legislation and report back to national and supranational administrations. The issue of surveillance is especially important in the area of technical standards where the failure to implement product conformity sustains discrepancies and limits market development. In these cases, it is up to national bodies on the ground to inform and pressurise for these standards to be met. If this is to be effective, businesses and consumers need to be aware of how to complain. For many states, such bodies are only embryonic. These are enhanced by the Commission's Citizens First programme to inform consumers of their rights in the evolving SEM.

THE EXTERNAL DIMENSION OF THE SEM

The logic behind the development of the SEM was that ultimately increases in the intensity of intra-EU competition would improve the competitive positioning of EU enterprises in the global marketplace. However the intensity of competition is not solely an indigenous phenomenon (see Chapter 17) as competition from foreign based enterprises would stimulate the process of adjustment and increase levels of competition within the European marketplace. It was an oft-mentioned concern that the development of the SEM would lead to a more inward looking EU that would seek to exclude non-EU enterprises from access to its markets. This so-called 'Fortress Europe' scenario was a real and genuine concern for non-EU states. In practice, such fears were to prove unfounded even though Europe remains, at best, a flawed trading partner.

The fact that the Uruguay Round of multilateral trade talks existed alongside the establishment of the SEM means that the moves to liberalise Europe internally were being matched by less vigorous action to liberalise its trade with non-members. Indeed the acceptance of the global move towards liberalisation may have in part been fuelled by the success that Europe was having in the process of internal liberalisation. To European firms, the re-organisation stimulated by the SEM could now be exploited to gain market share within broader international markets.

The impact of the SEM upon non-EU enterprises is derived not only from its impact upon external access but also from its effects upon FDI flows. Both of these have been integral to the European Commission's examination of the impact of the SEM.

External access to the European market

External access to the EU market was helped by the fact that the SEM removed a plethora of national restrictions which impeded non-EU access to the European market. In general these were replaced with a common EU-wide approach to external competition. The clothing and textiles sector was especially prone to this method of national control. These barriers were a problem when there were differences between states in the danger posed to domestic producers from particular types or sources of imports (such as textiles and clothing from China). Thus some states would let the goods in; others would seek to impair their access. It is felt that if the SEM has had an adverse impact upon trade, it is in the area of technical harmonisation especially where EU-wide agreements may have raised the height of some barriers. This reflects the fact that technical barriers are the most important barrier for third party products. In other areas, improvements to the business environment stimulated by the development of the SEM (in areas such as service provision, business law and taxation) have had as great and as positive an impact upon foreign firms as they have had upon EU enterprises. However given the diverse product ranges it is not easy to assess the full impact of these changes.

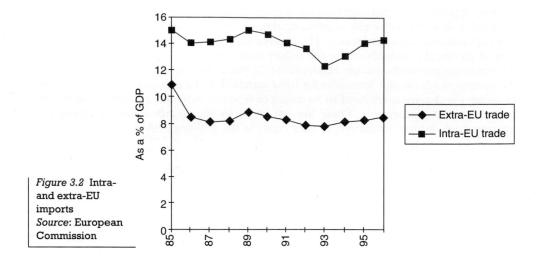

Figure 3.2 Intra- and extra-EU imports
Source: European Commission

The evidence provided in Figure 3.2 suggests that the SEM has tended to have little impact upon extra-EU imports. This is a pattern that is broadly reflected in intra-EU imports. Overall trends in intra- and extra-EU imports tend to correlate closely with the state of the trade cycle.

Foreign direct investment

Most of the FDI stimulated by the advent of the SEM were flows between EU states. However there was a tangible impact upon extra-EU FDI. Inward investment by the Japanese and the US has been primarily market seeking. In the former case, FDI has normally been based around greenfield development; whereas the US has tended more towards merger and acquisition activity. FDI (especially from Japan) tended to be stimulated more by factors such as market growth and the rise of the Yen in the mid-to-late 1980s than by the SEM. Most of this Japan–EU FDI tended to flow into the EU rather than out of it. EU–US FDI exhibited more equal bilateral flows. Some states have been traditionally hostile to FDI, fearing foreign ownership of core strategic resources or that indigenous operators would be undermined by such flows. However, as the EU economy slowed, so EU states became more hospitable and even began to compete for these flows.

The trends for FDI over the period are reflected within Figure 3.3. These show the steady growth of FDI within the European economy and how, as economies internationalise, the interdependence between them grows. In the post-1993 period, these flows have increased further, though the recent Asia crisis could retard these flows over the medium term.

CONCLUSION

In total, the true and complete effect of the development of the SEM will only be felt in the medium to longer term. In part this is driven by the fact that the SEM (even in its original form) is still incomplete. In addition, the impact of the SEM has also to be felt more fully before firms start to re-organise processes to maximise its opportunities. The importance of the SEM cannot be overstated. The development of the SEM has

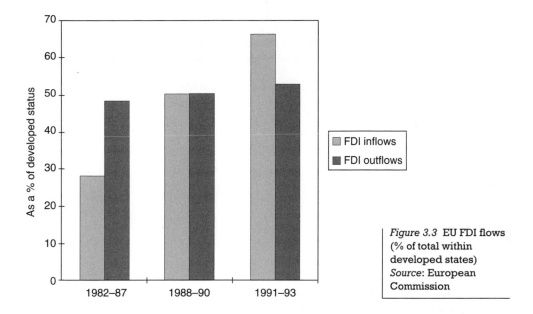

Figure 3.3 EU FDI flows (% of total within developed states) *Source*: European Commission

tended to become less of an issue as progress towards EMU has risen up the agenda. It is important, however, to underline that the realisation of the SEM is integral to the process of achieving EMU. It is unlikely that a full SEM will be realised in the near future but if the EU is serious about the EMU process then states need to renew their commitment to the SEM programme.

➤ KEY POINTS

- **The Single European Market Programme seeks to unify the fragmented national markets into an integrated whole.**

- **The initial programme only had limited success in achieving its stated aims.**

- **The EU has moved into the next phase of SEM development notably by extending its relevance and ensuring the full implementation of legislation.**

- **Generally, the SEM has been coupled with greater openness to the global marketplace, both in terms of trade and FDI.**

SUGGESTED FURTHER READING

Buchan, D. (1996) *The Single Market and Tomorrow's Europe*, Kogan Page.
Cecchini, P. (1988) *1992: The European Challenge*, Gower.
Emerson, M., Aujean, M., Catinat, M., Goybet, P. and Jacquemin, A. (1988) *The Economics of 1992*, Oxford University Press.

European Commission/ DG II (Industry) (1996) 'Economic Evaluation of the Internal Market', *European Economy*, 4.

European Commission (1997) 'Action Plan for the Single Market', *CSE*, (97)1.

Helm, D. (ed.) (1993) 'The European Internal Market', *Oxford Review of Economic Policy*, Vol. 9, No. 1.

Porter, M. (1990) *The Competitive Advantage of Nations*, Collier Macmillan.

4

TAXATION AND THE EUROPEAN BUSINESS ENVIRONMENT: THEMES AND ISSUES

Of all the areas of policy that will impact upon the development of the European business environment, there is perhaps no more controversial topic than taxation. The means and method of taxation go to the very heart of national sovereignty, helping to explain why agreement on removal of this source of EU market and trade distortion has proved so difficult to achieve. Yet the twin forces of regional integration and globalisation imply development of a more harmonious tax system that removes commercial distortions. Initially, this chapter seeks to examine the economic importance of taxation as a determinant of economic performance. Thereafter the issue of harmonisation is explored, highlighting policy efforts within the context of the SEM directed at the process, rationale and impediments to greater approximation. The chapter also addresses the issue of harmonisation on a global level and the factors that will drive and feasibly influence future tax trends and their impact upon the European business environment. Finally, broader aspects of taxation are explored, notably within the context of the moves towards EMU and of the need to build a fiscal system that aids the development of a competitive economy.

THE ECONOMIC IMPORTANCE OF TAXATION

Traditionally, the economic importance of tax was understood solely from the macro-economic perspective, that is, the extent to which governments, by altering the levels, rates and scope of taxation can affect economic performance and development. More recently, the emphasis has changed and tax policy is examined increasingly from a micro-economic perspective, that is, how variations in the tax level have a direct influence over personal and corporate incentives. Whilst taxation is undeniably important as a macro-economic determinant of economic performance, its ability to be fully influential and effective (within integrating economies) is dubious and is undermined as the likelihood of leakages between economies increases. Integration can also render high tax policies prohibitive if the mobility both of factors of production and of commodities facilitates (as seen later in this chapter) the likelihood of overseas purchases where the tax burden is lighter. This economic interdependence undermines, in theory at least, the principle of tax sovereignty.

It is popular to link higher tax rates with the lower rates of economic growth experienced by many developed economies since the 1970s. This linkage is justified to the extent that taxation interferes with the following economic phenomena.

- *Saving and investment*: increases in tax are likely to lower net rates of return, lead to more consumption (as opposed to saving) and thereby diminish available funds for investment. This issue is compounded by taxes that fall directly upon company profits. Both effects will lower investment within the economy. This can be overcome if lower domestic savings are matched by incoming foreign savings. This is difficult within a global economy that is still relatively closed to such exchanges. Tax can also affect the location of foreign capital as multi-national companies seek to organise production to minimise their tax burden.
- *Tax and labour*: the rise in labour taxes has been a notable feature of developed economies since the 1960s. These taxes drive a wedge between what an employer pays and what an employee receives. In areas with inflexible labour markets, this burden tends to fall upon employers, whilst the reverse is true in flexible labour markets. In many EU states (aside from the UK), the former is the case with the consequence that labour is replaced by capital with a resultant rise in unemployment. If inflexible labour markets prevent such substitution or limit changes in the relative prices of labour and capital, the result is a loss in the productive capacity of the economy.
- *Tax and human capital formation*: higher labour taxes can affect the quality of human capital. Under a progressive tax system, the benefits from undergoing training and education are lowered. A similar effect is felt if the result of higher labour taxes is a lower labour supply as workers are prepared to remain idle or wait for higher paid jobs rather than accept those that offer a gross reward that is below their expectations. A balancing act also needs to be performed in terms of labour and physical capital: the more preferential treatment of one implies the relatively unfavourable treatment of the other.

These effects underline the difficulties in developing a tax policy that can best complement the economic growth and performance of an economy. Most governments have settled on trying to balance the need for investment in both capital and labour as a means of securing the desired levels of growth. In this context, most states take a pragmatic view, cutting taxes where it is felt such action would maximise the benefits for economic performance.

The theme of taxation within the European Union and its concerns for business extend beyond the desire to urge tax reform to stimulate the economic performance of the EU. The key focus of supranational taxation strategy is based upon identifying the distortions represented by national tax systems within the context of the integration of economies. The moves towards the Single European Market (SEM), and more recently economic and monetary union (EMU), have highlighted challenges for taxation systems both in terms of ensuring fair trade and of meeting, and sustaining, the fiscal criteria associated with moves towards the single currency (see Chapter 16).

THE HARMONISATION ISSUE: THE THEME FOR INTEGRATION

At the heart of tax harmonisation lies the removal of disparities in national tax structures to the point where they no longer affect the operation of free markets and therefore the allocation of resources between states. This process requires merely an approximation of tax structures not uniformity. Tax structures can differ between states in a number of ways:

- in the definition of what is taxable;
- the levels of tax;
- the form of tax applied (whether, for example, it is applied in an direct or indirect manner);
- the underlying social, economic and political rationale behind the form and nature of the tax system;
- the manner and effectiveness of enforcement.

The perceived requirement for tax harmonisation arises from the nature of trade between European states. Much of the trade is of an intra-industry nature. Therefore differing tax rates can distort competition within the European marketplace. Tax harmonisation seeks not only to remove distortions but also to ensure that the tax system is compatible with the objectives of the EU.

There are two alternative approaches to the process of harmonisation:

- the equalisation approach: this involves standardised tax rates and bases;
- the differentials approach: which implies the tax system should meet the same broad economic objectives across the EU and which involves co-ordination between states to minimise cross-border spillovers.

In practice, moves towards tax harmonisation are a hybrid of both approaches.

BOX 4.1 THE TREATIES AND TAX HARMONISATION

The desire for tax harmonisation was recognised within the Treaties of the European Community/Union via the following articles:

- Article 95 which states that taxes imposed upon imported goods should not exceed the tax imposed upon the domestically produced equivalent;
- Article 99 which authorises the European Commission to submit proposals for the harmonisation of indirect taxation to eliminate distortions;
- Article 105 which defines harmonisation as not more than an 'approximation of the laws of member states';
- Article 220 which requires member states to eliminate double taxation by agreement between them;
- Article 100 which implies that tax harmonisation can only occur via unanimity;
- Article 73D (of the Maastricht Treaty) which requires member states to distinguish between residents and non-residents for tax purposes.

Within integrating economies, differences in relative tax levels directly affect the comparative prices of goods and are therefore likely to have a direct impact upon the terms of trade both within and between economies, leading to changes in the pattern and volume of trade. This has further implications in terms of:

- the distribution of income between citizens;
- the distribution of income between member states;
- trade relations with states outside the economic union.

Thus, the effects of taxes and tax changes are similar to those derived from changes in tariff structures and will affect many aspects of the commercial environment such as income distribution, economic growth, allocation of resources, balance of payments and, obviously, government revenue.

An increasingly internationalised environment and mobile resource base offer direct incentives to authorities to use the tax system as a trade weapon. Tax, of course, is not one of the major factors determining a firm's location decision but it can be influential. Consequently, authorities can develop a tax strategy which offers the highest returns to the increasingly mobile factors of production as part of their economic development strategy. Thus authorities can use taxes as a means to boost the economy in the following ways (Owens 1993):

- *tax competition for foreign investment*: FDI is proving ever more central to employment generation in the EU;
- *tax competition for financial and commercial activities*: incentives can be offered to relocate head offices, distribution centres and so on within a particular state;
- *tax competition for skilled labour*: the quality of human resources is an increasingly important factor in determining competitiveness.

There can also be rivalry between states for the tax base (that is, who and what is taxed) as a means of increasing the revenue accruing to state coffers. This generally occurs in two notable areas:

- *tax competition and interest bearing deposits*: a state can attract funds through the way in which it treats these deposits. Investors inevitably look towards those areas which minimise their tax obligations and therefore offer the highest net returns.
- *the rise of multi-national enterprises and the division of their tax base*: given that these enterprises operate in many states, there is a premium in deciding how to allocate the income and expenses of such companies among the countries in which they operate as a means of minimising tax commitments.

Consequently, an absence of harmonisation can lead to distortionary tax competition between states as they seek to attract inward investment at the expense of employment in partner states. Such developments may be counter-productive to the economic efficiency within the EU in a number of ways:

- tax competition may result in under-taxation as a consequence of beggar-thy-neighbour policies;
- tax differentials may result in location distortions resulting in misallocation of resources and operational inefficiencies for the economy concerned;
- distribution problems from an absence of common rules may occur as a result of firms operating in more than one state.

Consequently, competitive taxation policies to attract inward investment amount to little more than a restatement of the beggar-thy-neighbour policies prohibited by Treaty commitments. Thus tax co-ordination over tax competition is required to ensure a fair trading environment.

The ongoing process of integration is creating a series of interdependencies between national tax systems. Harmonisation is one manifestation of this trend and the pressure for alignment of tax structures will grow as the integration process deepens. The European Commission is increasing the importance given to harmonisation as a means of overcoming the harmful effects of tax competition and is developing a tax strategy that seeks to balance the various political and economic interests of member states via:

- a code of conduct for business taxation: this requests member states to refrain from those activities sourced from the tax system which are harmful to the process of competition within the EU;
- a European solution in the area of taxation of income from savings: this requests that member states agree on the core elements needed for a directive on a minimum withholding tax;
- measures to eliminate withholding taxes on cross-border interest and royalty payments between companies.

Despite this agenda, the Commission's efforts have to date had minimal impact. The Commission is shying away from concerted action, fearing a backlash from member states who are using these devices to generate employment. This is especially potent as they scramble for foreign investment via tax incentives. Importantly, tax competition is no longer solely an issue between EU states but is increasingly a bone of contention within states. Indeed even states who complained vociferously about tax competition to use it as a tool in their economic development strategy.

Gaining agreement on tax harmonisation is problematic due to:

- the unanimity rule that applies in fiscal matters;
- the piecemeal fashion in which taxation is usually dealt.

Consequently, some commentators have suggested a looser approach to the process of tax harmonisation derived from tax diversity. This system based upon tax co-ordination seeks to maintain diversities that are inherent within the system in terms of preferences for form or manner of taxation. Differences within the tax system will persist to the extent that they do not represent impediments to the development of the SEM, balancing integration within a framework of national sovereignty.

INDIRECT TAX HARMONISATION: THE CHALLENGE OF THE SEM

Indirect taxes are incorporated into the final prices of the goods upon which they are imposed. Thus where the cost of production is identical (or at least approximate), differences in tax rates or principles of application will lead to differing price levels. The potential impact of this upon cross-border trade has facilitated a three stage approach to the harmonisation of indirect taxes (see Figure 4.1). Generally, if an indirect tax is applied at the point of origin of the good (that is, where it is produced), it is more likely to have a trade distorting effect; due to their generally greater effects upon relative costs/prices. This distortion is reduced when goods are taxed where they are consumed – the destination principle.

Value Added Tax

Much of the concern over indirect tax harmonisation relates to Value Added Tax (VAT) which was devised in 1967 to overcome the lack of neutrality in domestic tax systems. The tax system is based, at the insistence of member states, on the destination principle, where the tax is levied at the consumption stage and the tax revenue accrues to the state where the good is consumed. The fact that the tax is based upon 'value added' at each stage of manufacture avoids double taxation.

Despite the theory, it is increasingly felt that the destination principle is not enough to ensure trade neutrality and a closer approximation of tax rates is also needed as it is

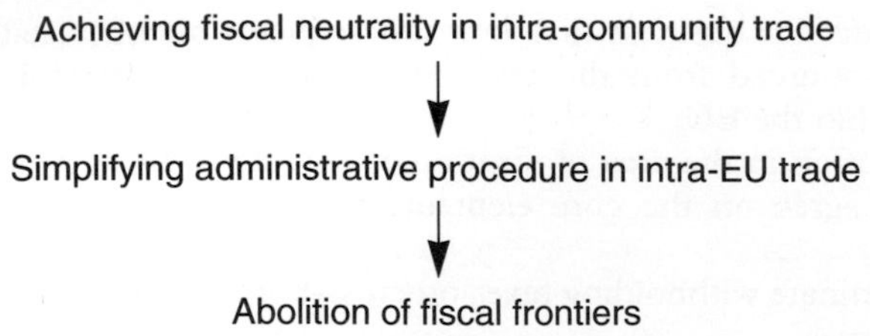

Achieving fiscal neutrality in intra-community trade

↓

Simplifying administrative procedure in intra-EU trade

Figure 4.1 **The strategy
for indirect tax
harmonisation**

↓

Abolition of fiscal frontiers

difficult to police a system where controls on tax rates were absent. This relates to ongoing disputes between states on:

- whether the tax should be levied upon the production or consumption of the commodity;
- the inequality of treatment of commodities between states;
- what goods should be exempt;
- jurisdictional issues over who collects, determines and obtains revenue from the tax.

With the development of the SEM, the destination principle as the central organising idea behind VAT has been challenged by the fact that:

- freer mobility of goods and services makes it more difficult to determine that the place of purchase is the place where the commodity will be consumed;
- with the removal of frontiers, a method was needed to implement the border tax adjustments required under the destination principle. A zero rating for exports is generally used though the Commission wishes to see a clearing house established where tax authorities from the importing states reimburse the authorities of the exporter.

Little agreement between states has been possible. Thus despite the establishment of the above principles, taxation differentials remain an evident barrier to the integration process: over the period 1972–98, the differential between the highest and lowest rates of VAT in the EU has fallen by only 2 per cent. This was underlined by the Cockfield Report (the 1985 Single Market White Paper) which pinpointed fiscal barriers as one of the three primary impediments to the completion of the SEM. Subsequently, the Commission proposed balancing the desire for harmonisation with a degree of flexibility to limit the impact upon national budgets and sovereignty. Inevitably such proposals drew fierce criticism from a number of states. As a result, these proposals were gradually watered down with merely a degree of approximation required between states. Whether this matters or not is debatable. The experience of the US indicates that the persistence of inter-state tax differentials renders harmonisation unnecessary. Despite this apparent evidence, the EU is pursuing some form of approximation of tax rates even if, in fact, it may not be required. Existing tax rates across the EU are indicated in Table 4.1 with the standard rate being subject to a minimum rate of 15 per cent.

However, the implementation of the 'transitional' regime between 1993 and 1997 has been successful although it has merely delayed the problem of finding the appropriate regime that encompasses the assorted concerns inherent within the tax harmonisation process. Until 1997, the EU had a hybrid system in which personal imports were taxed at the rate prevalent in the country of origin and imports by registered traders were taxed at the destination. Thus the development of a VAT system that is not fully trade neutral remains elusive. Businesses are still operating in a trading area where the tax system and its administration not only distorts trade but also adds not unsubstantially to the costs of

Table 4.1 VAT rates in EU member states, 1 January 1998

Member states	Super-reduced rate	Reduced rate	Standard rate
Belgium	1	6	21
Denmark	—	—	25
Germany	—	7	15
Greece	4	8	18
Spain	4	7	16
France	2.1	5.5	20.6
Ireland	3.3	12.5	21
Italy	4	10	20
Luxembourg	3	6	15
Netherlands	—	6	17.5
Austria	—	10/12	20
Portugal	—	5/12	17
Finland	—	8/17	22
Sweden	—	6/12	25
UK	—	5	17.5

Source: European Commission

cross-border commerce. Many of these problems are derived from the transitional nature of the regime and are compounded by disagreements as to whether the destination or origin principle should be the mode of the EU's tax system. The latter is still strongly opposed as:

- states with a narrow export base and a high propensity to import will lose out;
- states with low tax will enjoy an artificial competitive advantage;
- it is seen to interfere with the sovereignty of states.

The EU is currently shifting towards the development of a definitive VAT regime based entirely upon origin. This principle has been chosen due to the fact that it favours producing over consuming countries and offers advantages in terms of:

- simpler administration;
- alleviating the problem of cross-border shopping;
- overcoming the problem of tax competition;
- offering greater security over tax revenues.

Despite this, efforts to overcome the complexity of the system are likely to be thwarted. Member states are still protective on this issue. The Commission has set out to avoid multiple VAT registrations and has achieved a success with the entry into force of the EU Transfer Pricing Arbitration Convention, which is based upon the OECD definition of arm's length pricing and an arbitration mechanism where disputes emerge. There has, in practice, been little progress in meeting the apparently inconsistent aims of achieving a tax system that aids the SEM whilst preserving the maximum degree of sovereignty for states.

Moves towards a definitive system have stalled and the transitional hybrid system has been prolonged beyond the deadline (1997) originally envisaged. Intermediate action has focused upon closer administrative co-operation; a feature that is becoming integral to national taxation strategies. One legacy of this improved co-operation is the improvement in statistical information upon taxation available to authorities. This does not, however, cover the inadequacies of the transitional regime. By pursuing a more realistic agenda the Commission has adopted an incremental path to the development of a definitive system. To this end, the prolonged transitional phase will be modified by a new system based upon three pillars:

- the uniform application of VAT throughout the Community;
- the 'overdue' modernisation of VAT;
- a shift towards an origin based system.

The objective of these actions is to move towards a situation where each tax payer has a single place of taxation for all supplies within the EU. The implication of this desire is a greater move towards harmonisation in tax rates and overcoming the legal uncertainty which is potentially damaging to business. Such pressures are likely to strengthen as the EU continues to move towards EMU. To attain this objective, a co-operative framework has been established under the Fiscalis programme as a precursor to the proposed moves noted above. Fiscalis should also improve the current functioning of VAT systems to prevent fraud.

Excise taxes

Excise taxes are levies upon certain products that account for a large proportion of disposable income and the demand for which is sensitive to changes in price. In addition to the usual revenue raising reasons, these taxes are also levied to influence the consumption of commodities (such as carbon based products, tobacco and alcohol) that are detrimental to public health. Like VAT, states vary markedly in the implementation of these taxes and such differentials can have a detrimental effect upon competition and trade within the SEM. Rates vary widely across the EU due to differences in the socio-economic priorities of states and to the different patterns of consumption between states.

Excise taxes can be applied in one of two ways:

- *a specific tax*: where the tax is based upon a specific amount of the product;
- *an ad valorem tax*: where the tax is levied as a proportion of the selling price.

In some cases, a combination of the two is used. Generally the former tends to be favoured by the northern states and the latter by the southern states. Problems are further compounded by the myriad of ways that the tax can actually be applied and collected.

In pushing for harmonisation, the key concern is not to undermine excise duties as a source of revenue: though this has to be balanced by the desire to remove distortions to competition. Over the years, a number of proposals have been forthcoming which have tended to focus upon the harmonisation of tax structures rather than rates. The lack of success in making any real progress stems from the familiar conflict between the removal of distortions and the maintenance of maximum state sovereignty. Once again this has proved difficult to achieve and has been further hindered by inter-state differences in consumer tastes, cultural attitudes and social policies.

Efforts towards the harmonisation of rates have gained a new emphasis with the push to the realisation of the SEM. Given the political unreality of achieving a single rate, the aim became the attainment of a minimum rate for each product. Over the longer term, market forces may align the rates – a process aided by the consequences of increased cross-border shopping. To date, minimum rates for alcohol, alcoholic beverages, cigarettes, mineral oils and tobacco have been introduced – something achieved on the proviso that these minimum rates are re-examined every two years.

Efforts have also been made to harmonise energy taxes based upon a perception that fuel excise duties need to bear some relation to the cost and maintenance of roads, as well as to the environment and to trade distortions. In practice, very little progress has been made but minimum rates for duties upon most motor fuels and heating oils have been established. The desire is to extend this action to cover all energy products to remove distortions in inter-fuel competition. Despite such intentions, divergences in duties are still evident.

CASE STUDY 4.1 CHALLENGING TAX DIFFERENTIALS: THE RESPONSE OF UK RETAILERS

When, in 1993, the European Union abolished limits upon alcohol imports for personal consumption from other European states, major UK alcohol traders feared the worse in terms of lost revenue and employment. Indeed by October 1993, it was estimated that such trade was costing British retailers somewhere in the region of £500 million per annum. Tesco, a major UK supermarket, expected its revenue from alcohol sales would fall by 6.5 per cent. This, Tesco and other major alcohol retailers believed, would only get worse as the Channel Tunnel opened, not only bringing the continent closer in temporal terms but also lower cross-channel fares as the ferry companies responded to this new competition.

The initial strategy of these companies was to appeal to the Treasury to lower UK excise duties to allow UK companies to compete on a more even playing field. Given that the UK Treasury was also a loser as a result of this trade, they felt they had a good case. However when successive budgets merely increased the duty differential between the UK and France, alternative strategies had to be formulated to protect market share of off-sales alcohol. Thus over 1994–5, the major UK alcohol retailers in the UK opened up subsidiaries in the Channel ports that became the focus for this cross-border shopping. Essentially, the purpose was to attract British customers to familiar high-street names by selling them alcohol they could buy at home at a discount of around 40 per cent below prices in the UK. The irony of British enterprises having to go to France to sell cheap beer to Britons is not lost on many.

The first to make the move was Sainsbury's who opened an off-licence in Calais. The shop is specifically targeted at British consumers and sells the brands that are the most popular in its UK stores. Within nine months, such was its success that the shop was extended. Tesco followed suit in 1995, also establishing a Calais-based operation to tap into this corner of the UK alcohol market. The aim is to use the Tesco brand to attract UK customers instead of using its existing local (since sold-off) chain – Catteau. Indeed, in a mere three months after it opened, the store Tesco Vin de Plus was the company's biggest wine and spirits operation with 90 per cent of its customers being British. This success was despite entry into a market that was already highly competitive with several large hypermarkets and independent British alcohol warehouses (such as Beers R'Us) competing for the same cross-channel trade. These large UK supermarkets have been followed by a number of specialist UK off licences, notably Victoria Wine, Unwins and Thresher.

THE RISE OF DIRECT TAX HARMONISATION

The increased attention given to direct tax harmonisation arises from the consequences of the increased mobility of labour and capital across the EU. Over the longer term, such effects could have a profound impact upon the capacity of states to levy taxes. They may also have detrimental consequences for the objective of regional development and feasibly create the need for compensatory mechanisms between states as their tax base erodes.

Direct taxes are even more fundamental sources of revenue for member states. They have not been so prominent in the debate about the role of tax harmonisation but as interdependence deepens, their impact upon the European business environment will become more pronounced. Again there are differences between states about the base and rates of direct tax. Harmonisation is an evolutionary process that has initially focused upon corporate tax structures. Personal income tax has largely been ignored. The reasons for this, over the short term, are derived from the greater mobility of capital, compared to labour, across the EU.

Corporate tax

The process of economic integration requires neutrality with regard to international flows of finance as well as to the individual investment decisions of enterprises. The harmonisation of corporate tax is not only required to overcome these problems but also to ensure the integration of capital markets – a pre-requisite for the efficient allocation of capital. The harmonisation of corporate tax is proposed because:

- the distribution of corporate tax revenues between states is seen as inequitable;
- tax differentials cause administrative difficulties for both business and governments;
- tax differentials distort competition within the Community.

Corporation tax affects the incentive to invest, the risks attached to such investments and overall levels of business saving. Differences in the level of corporation tax between states will, therefore, create opportunities for states to attract investment by offering lower tax rates and therefore potentially higher post-tax profits for enterprises. The effect is not only important in terms of new investment location decisions but may also offer direct incentives for enterprises to relocate between states. These effects could not only be detrimental for the overall efficiency of the European economy but could also undermine tax revenues in some states. The issue is further complicated by the large number of multi-national companies that have subsidiaries within several EU states and by the principle of non-discrimination against foreign owned enterprises. In a survey of 8,000 multinational enterprises undertaken for the Commission in 1992, 48 per cent of respondents said that taxation was an important issue in deciding where to locate a production plant. This figure varied between sectors and was as high as 78 per cent for financial services.

Differences in corporate tax rates can be problematic in the process of integration in the following areas:

- on withholding taxes on interest rates, royalties and dividends which result in double taxation;
- on the treatment of losses: the periods over which taxes can be carried forward or backward varies between countries;
- on the unevenness of bilateral tax treaties that fail to eliminate double taxation.

The result is that enterprises seeking to reorganise their European operations face considerable tax barriers, a feature which is exacerbated by the fragmented and compartmentalised tax system. In order to iron out discrepancies, action has been taken (in directive form) on:

- *inter-company payments*: to eliminate the double taxation of profits distributed by subsidiaries to the parent company (still to be agreed);
- *mergers and acquisitions*: this seeks to facilitate re-organisation by allowing tax payments of capital gains to be deferred (this has yet to be implemented);
- *consolidation of losses*: this allows companies to offset losses within branches or subsidiaries against those made by the parent company;
- *transfer pricing*: there has been agreement to provide for arbitration to ensure that companies are not taxed twice.

Like other forms of taxation, agreement on corporate taxation has proved elusive. The process has been aided by a recognition (from the EU) that the active pursuit of harmonisation was fruitless. In the immediate aftermath of the initial SEM programme (1985–92), efforts were made to remove the inconsistencies within the tax system that could hurt the development of the SEM, notably the removal of double taxation of cross-border income flows.

The corporate tax breaks given need only be considered as contravening EU law to the extent that they are discriminatory. Thus a state should not simply be punished just because it has lower taxes. The Irish have been particularly vulnerable to accusations that they have engaged in unfair tax competition. The resulting pressure has led to the Irish dropping their special low corporate tax rate of 10 per cent upon manufacturing (as well as their normal rate of 32 per cent) by 2003. In its place they will have a single rate of 12.5 per cent. This has drawn criticism from high tax states (see Figure 4.2). The fear that this could lead to a rush to Ireland by enterprises has to be overstated due to the imperfect mobility of both capital and labour across the EU. Thus the conclusion is that tax competition only really exists at the margin and can be beneficial only to the extent that such rivalry keeps the overall level of taxes suppressed. Despite this, concerted efforts are still in train to overcome the corporate tax barriers to the realisation of the SEM. The Ruding Committee recommended the following series of actions:

- the abolition of withholding tax (which is levied on interest and dividends) on cross-border flows;
- the elimination of double taxation within the Community;
- the improvement of the tax environment for SMEs: these enterprises face particular tax hurdles when seeking to expand activities in international markets (see Chapter 8).

Attempts have been made to harmonise the role of withholding taxes in cross-border portfolio investment but, despite recognition of the problem, progress has been slow. Tax differences remain and it has been difficult to reach agreement in key areas (notably the elimination of cross-border taxation). The Commission has persistently tried to implement these recommendations but has, once again, found its efforts resisted by member states.

Failure to achieve harmonisation has led to a change of tack by the Commission which has recently issued recommendations on the taxation of cross-border workers and SMEs. Recommendations have no legal force and highlight how little real power the Commission

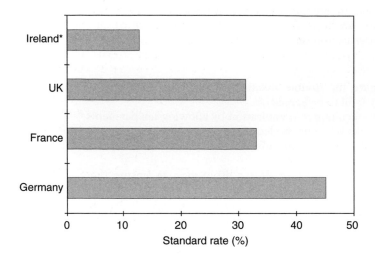

Figure 4.2 Corporation tax
differentials in the EU
Source: European Commission
Note * Tax rate applies from 2003

has in the process of tax harmonisation. With regard to saving, harmonisation is still being pursued, though again this is still being resisted by some states.

The need for harmonisation has been highlighted by issues related to fiscal dumping and tax competition. In an era of slow growth, there is a view that some states have used favourable corporate tax rates to attract business at the expense of employment elsewhere within the EU – a trend heightened by the moves towards EMU which could exacerbate the problem of predatory tax competition and differentials between states. The Commission is trying to develop a code of practice to counter the distorting effects of such action. Any code would though only be voluntary and involves no obligations from states to comply with its recommendations.

FISCAL FEDERALISM: A NECESSARY RESPONSE TO EMU?

It is becoming apparent that tax harmonisation will need to be included in any agreement for fiscal co-ordination within EMU. In 1998, ministers started to recognise that tax policy is an issue of common concern within EMU. This is a consequence of the EMU Stability and Growth Pact (see Chapter 16) which seeks, for reasons of 'mutual benefit', to constrain budget deficits after the start of EMU in 1999. States are keen to avoid tax competition within EMU and it has been proposed that states co-ordinate their budgets, thereby limiting the opportunities for states to utilise taxation systems to replace the exchange rate as a weapon to give their national economy an artificial competitive fillip.

A solution to these problems could be provided by a move to a more distinct form of fiscal federalism. This implies that, so long as the effect of tax differentials is neutral upon trade and factor mobility, decisions about its levels can be devolved to member states or even lower. The issue of fiscal federalism revolves around where tax powers should lie. Not all taxes affect trade and therefore there is little case for the harmonisation of all taxes (see aforementioned issue of tax diversity). Basically, the fiscal federalist literature implies that:

- progressive taxes, due to their impact upon the mobility of workers and capital, are best assigned to higher levels of government;
- company taxes, that are likely to create strong spillovers especially in terms of mobility of tax bases, are also best assigned to higher levels of government;

- lower levels of government are best used for those occasions where the tax base is immobile and where distortions are therefore minimised;
- tax bases that are distributed unequally across an area are best centralised to avoid inequalities both in terms of inequities and allocative distortions.

The need to delegate to a higher body will, of course, not be needed if there is sufficient co-ordination between the separate independent actors to alleviate spillover. However such a solution is unlikely given:

- the unwillingness of tax authorities to consider international implications of tax policies;
- the amount of information actually exchanged is below that needed to negate spillovers;
- the costs of undertaking such co-ordination are high.

It is for these reasons that a case for the transfer of power towards some supranational body can be argued. Power for the supranational level is further justified if:

- the tax base is supranational in nature;
- centralised taxes are a necessary response to cross-border tax externalities.

However, the relative immaturity of the EU as a federation and its generic heterogeneity tends to undermine the case for such a transfer of power. The extent to which this will change as EMU progresses is a matter for conjecture. There is little to be learnt from existing federations: each one is unique in terms of how it taxes and organises its distribution mechanisms. In most federations, the trend has been towards harmonisation of tax bases as opposed to tax rates. Tax rate harmonisation is felt to be unnecessary if there are significant inter-regional transfers.

THE EVOLVING CONCERNS OF EUROPE'S TAXATION STRATEGY

In 1996, a group was convened by the Commission to identify areas of tax policy relevant to the supranational level of government and to determine a sea change in the development of the EU's tax policy. The aim of the Commission is to take a holistic view of tax strategy to ensure it meets broader EU aims, notably the challenges posed by:

- the desire to stabilise tax revenues: an evident need as tax bases become more mobile;
- the aim of achieving economic growth which respects the environment;
- the objective of promoting employment: given the apparent strong correlation between the level of Europe's labour taxes and unemployment rates.

These themes should come as little surprise. Their continued rise up the agenda of the EU has highlighted the persistent importance of overcoming fiscal impediments to the SEM. Of greater note is the desire to utilise the tax system to meet the employment and competitiveness challenges prevalent within the European business environment.

As budget deficits are reduced, so efforts to promote employment require more innovative fiscal policy solutions. If taxes are to be lowered, without making budget deficits stray from the EMU targets, then the shortfall in revenue has to be compensated by alternative sources of revenue or by reduction in government expenditure. Options being explored are a raising of indirect taxation (VAT and customs duties), the establishment or raising of eco-taxes or the taxing of movable or fixed assets. An early proposal was the extension of excise duties to all energy forms (see Chapter 14). This has been resisted by business. Further revenue may be raised by the determination of a definitive VAT system. The Commission is flexible as to how member states finance reductions in labour taxes though those tax advantages that help SMEs are proving popular with all bodies at both national and supranational levels.

Increasingly the Commission is taking a pragmatic view on taxation strategy and has placed an initial emphasis upon closer co-ordination of tax policies. This suggests a move from centrally administered harmonisation towards approximation based upon decisions which respect national sovereignty. Concrete action by the Commission is increasingly likely to be based upon loosely defined guidelines and frameworks.

On the whole, the EU seems to favour an agenda which lowers taxes to improve the performance of business and which therefore drives wealth creation. This has been part of a concerted response to European business which believes that the EU's relatively high taxes penalise indigenous entrepreneurship and deter foreign direct investment. Greater indigenous EU competition has lowered tax rates within states whilst expanding the tax base. The consequence is a more complex tax system and an increased administrative burden for enterprises. A particular problem has been the rising cost of compliance with VAT regulations.

The challenges of developing more employment have not been aided by broader tax proposals in areas such as energy and carbon dioxide. As a unilateral action by the EU these are likely to increase the relative costs of European business thus hindering the ability of the tax system to support employment creation (see Chapter 14). (Although the impact of such taxes could be offset by the efficiencies gained from the full fruition of the SEM.) In closed economies, these tax issues are largely irrelevant but in a global economy, such cost increasing measures will be to the detriment of European business. Such taxes, it appears, are best implemented by multilateral (possibly global) agreement.

Of note has been the proposal to extend excise duties to all energy products, including gas and electricity, to compensate for reductions in taxation upon labour. It has been claimed that such moves would create nearly 150,000 jobs by the formative years of the new millennium. The proposal, which sets minimum excise duties, has met with a lot of resistance from the EU's Mediterranean states who would experience the most significant rise in duties whereas the more environmentally conscious northern European states have generally been more positive about the proposal. Industry itself has been extremely hostile, arguing that the proposal does more to undermine the possibility of sustained employment than actively create it. The fear is that the increases in tax will be translated into either lower profits (therefore lower investment) or higher prices (therefore lower market share in global markets).

There has been agreement between states to introduce some experimental cuts in VAT in labour intensive sectors. It is proposed that the standard VAT rate of 17.5 per cent be cut to around 6 per cent for targeted sectors such as cobblers, cleaners, hairdressers, painters and repairers. Initial studies have indicated that a 10 per cent cut in the costs of these services would amount to around a 1 per cent increase in employment within the targeted sectors. The ability of such a scheme to meet these objectives can only be achieved when the fear of a neighbour's tax regime destroying jobs in another part of the Union is removed.

TAXATION AND THE GLOBALISATION PROCESS

Whatever taxation regime the EU decides to adopt for internal trade, it will in turn be influenced by the fact that European business is conducting an increasing proportion of its trade with third countries. Thus its taxation proposals and decisions must be viewed from the perspective of the reaction of competing economies. Indeed this global perspective has proved influential in many aspects of the EU's tax strategy and is reflected in the conclusions of the second Monti report which stresses the employment generating aspects of the taxation system.

Decisions to co-ordinate tax policies within the EU offer opportunities to advance the competitive positioning of European business but these advances can be undone if the broader environment is not considered. Of particular concern, from the processes of globalisation, is the emergence of an ever more salient form of tax competition. This problem is compounded by the fact that there is no global body (such as the WTO in the case of tariffs and subsidies) to monitor and challenge tax-induced competitive distortions. In the short term, globalisation will affect tax authorities by:

- making the tax base more mobile, thereby stimulating tax competition;
- making it increasingly difficult to collect and determine taxes that fall outside their jurisdiction;
- changing the functioning of tax authorities.

Many of the problems that tax competition poses on an EU scale (as noted above) directly parallel the problems faced on a global scale. Clearly global harmonisation would solve such problems but given the problems of harmonisation evident in the EU, such an ambition in a global setting sounds fanciful. Any scheme has to address the issues of:

- minimising revenue loss;
- sustaining fiscal sovereignty;
- limiting new options for tax evasion;
- complementing the competitive position of an economy;
- minimising transitional costs.

It is these criteria rather than any economic efficiency arguments that will determine the acceptability of any proposals. Given that harmonisation is impractical and tax competition is self-defeating, the only realistic option is for explicit co-ordination between states. This implies that guidelines for the global tax system and a system of multi-lateral agreements need to be established. This, in turn, requires mechanisms to ensure compulsory arbitration where disputes occur.

There has been action within the OECD to overcome possible problems arising from differing taxation policies. Many of these initiatives are influenced by, and are instrumental upon, the actions of the EU. To stimulate the alleviation of market distortions, the OECD has established a Model Tax Convention designed to overcome impediments to cross-border investment derived from double taxation. This convention, if adhered to, should help alleviate the aforementioned distortions. The convention has no legal force but merely acts as a guide to national policy makers and relies upon their goodwill to ensure its effectiveness. The convention works by allocating taxing rights between the resident and source country, requiring the former to eliminate double taxation where there are competing taxing rights. By 1996, there were 225 treaties between OECD states and over 1,400 world-wide based upon the OECD's convention, underlining its influence upon bilateral tax treaties within the OECD and beyond.

The OECD is growing more prominent in these areas as it acquires power to discuss and address tax issues related to the process of globalisation, notably:

- *avoidance and evasion*: OECD states have agreed to co-operate closely on tax evasion and have developed a number of legal tools such as the multi-lateral convention upon administrative assistance in the tax area;

- *tax competition*: in 1996 the OECD was charged by ministers to develop measures to counteract this problem;
- *taxation of foreign income*: this project seeks to overcome disturbances within portfolio investment derived from this system;
- *tax treaty override*: this seeks to highlight and hopefully remove inconsistencies between national and international tax treaties.

The expanding role of the OECD in this area highlights how states are seeking global solutions to common problems derived from the tax arena. Many states see the OECD as a useful forum in which to air multi-lateral problems and to achieve common solutions. Over time, it is expected new tax problems will emerge with the acceleration of electronic commerce, via the Internet, and as environmental taxes move up the international agenda.

The impact of globalisation is likely to be formalised eventually. The US, EU and Japan are putting pressure upon all states to accept the OECD's code on tax competition and are looking to the EU to take the lead on this issue. Tax is also an issue that is moving up the agenda of the G8 states who are starting to address issues of tax competition in their discussions. This is progressing with the explicit commitment of all G8 states.

CONCLUSION

Tax harmonisation has proved difficult. However, the environment could change as the move to EMU takes hold and it starts to have a more profound impact upon reducing the barriers to companies moving funds across borders. This would add further incentives to the desire of firms to exploit capital movements for commercial advantage. This issue is compounded by technological change, which has added to the freedom of companies to shift funds where and when they want. Most large states support some form of co-ordination. Smaller states who have directly benefited from tax competition are proving to be more resistant.

KEY POINTS

- **Tax harmonisation is regarded by the Commission as necessary to ensure the objectives of the SEM.**

- **Tax competition is becoming a more prevalent feature both within the European and the global business environment.**

- **Tax harmonisation has proved difficult due to issues related to national sovereignty.**

- **Pressure to change tax systems and frameworks is growing due to EMU and**

SUGGESTED FURTHER READING

Cnossen, S. (1996) 'Company Taxes in the European Union: Criteria and Options for Reform', Fiscal Studies, Vol. 17, No. 4, 67–97.

Commission of the European Communities (1996) *Taxation in the European Union: Report on the Development of Taxation Systems*, COM (96) 546.

Kanavos, P. (1997) 'Tax Harmonisation: the Single Market Challenge', in Stavridis, S., Mossialos, M., Morgan, R. and Machin, H., *New Challenges to the European Union*, pp. 269–96, Dartmouth.

Keen, M. (1993) 'The Welfare Economics of Tax Co-ordination in the European Community', *Fiscal Studies*, Vol. 14, No. 2, 15–36.

Leibfritz, W., Thornton, J. and Bibbee, A. (1997) *Taxation and Economic Performance*, OECD Working Paper, (97)107.

Lockwood, B., De Meza, D. and Myles, G. (1995) 'On the European Union VAT Proposals: the Superiority of Origin over Destination Principle', *Fiscal Studies*, Vol. 16, No. 1, 1–16.

Owens, J. (1993) 'Globalisation: The Implications for Tax Policies', *Fiscal Studies*, Vol. 14, No. 3, 21–44.

Radelli, C. (1996) 'Fiscal Federalism as a Catalyst Policy Development: in Search of a Framework for European Direct Tax Harmonisation', *Journal of European Public Policy*, Vol. 3, No. 3, 402–20.

Swann, D. (ed.) (1992) *The Single European Market and Beyond*, Routledge.

5

EUROPEAN INDUSTRIAL POLICY: MEETING THE CHALLENGES OF INTERNATIONAL COMPETITIVENESS

Industrial policy has a pivotal influence over the development of the European business environment by setting the framework within which other policies will seek to influence the performance of enterprise. The internationalisation of economies means that this framework is increasingly market orientated and is shifting the policy emphasis away from direct state involvement in the economy towards one of passivity. Initially this chapter seeks to examine the role of industrial policy within integrating and internationalising economies in terms of achieving the core policy goal of international competitiveness. Thereafter, the impact of European integration upon national industrial policies and how globalisation is increasing the prominence of supranational policy are explored. Finally, the policy measures intended to promote the international positioning of European-based enterprises are examined.

THE NATURE OF INDUSTRIAL POLICY AND INTERNATIONAL COMPETITIVENESS

A commonly used perspective on the role of industrial policy is offered by Krugman and Obstfeld (as quoted in Nicolaides 1993): 'industrial policy is an attempt by a government to shift the allocation of resources to promote economic growth'. This implies two key characteristics of policy:

- that government pursues policy to manage the rise of growing and emerging industries;
- that government pursues policy to manage the performance of declining and/or poorly performing strategic industries.

Thus policy is increasingly about shifting resources from declining towards growing sectors. Such resource re-allocation needs to be carried out in a manner to minimise any negative socio-economic impact. Increasingly, therefore, at the hub of industrial policy is an attempt to manage the consequences of structural change within the business environment and to ensure that such changes have an overall positive impact upon the economy. This implies that the changes occur with no large transitional costs in terms of output or employment. Thus ideally, as resources are no longer required in declining sectors, they can readily be absorbed into growing or emerging areas of the economy.

Broadly there are two major types of industrial policy:

- *generic policy*: these policies apply equally to all sectors and include measures such as education, healthcare and others that improve the general economic environment at both a micro- and macro-economic level;
- *selective policy*: these policies apply to particular sectors.

The latter tend to be more activist than the former but, in practice, industrial policy tends to exist as a hybrid of both sets of policies.

Across most industrialised states, there has been a sea change in industrial policy as it is actively seeking to promote structural change rather than limit it. Thus instead of working in spite of or even against markets, policy is increasingly complementing the changes associated with these forces. Despite this shift, policy continues to focus upon aspects of market failure. Within this context, Curzon-Price (1981) differentiates between *negative* and *positive* industrial policies. The former seeks to slow down the process of change (by, for example, protecting declining sectors from international competition); the latter seeks to accelerate transition within a framework of pre-established socio-economic priorities. In a global economy, that the latter is coming to dominate the former should come as little surprise.

Overall, an industrial policy comprises the combination of all measures that have improvement in the competitive positioning of industry as an explicit aim. There can be little debate that this is the desired outcome of all forms of policy for this is the basis of growth and sustainable employment; though there can be considerable debate about how to achieve it. However the traditional stance of industrial policy as a device to maximise the interests of nationally owned corporations is out of date, a concept which has disappeared as a result of the global economy and the increased interactions between states. In this context, the nature of industrial policy has to change. International competitiveness is no longer simply an issue for indigenous firms but for all enterprises located within an economy. An economy's success within international markets is dependent upon the competitiveness of all enterprises that source or locate themselves within it.

There is an increased recognition that policy to stimulate the EU's international competitiveness has to be based upon the following guidelines:

- intangible factors (such as education) are more powerful drivers of medium term competitiveness than tangible factors (such as state subsidies);
- innovation and intellectual property are the strongest drivers of the competitive environment;
- relative costs and productivity affect growth and profits – though 'capital deepening' (that is, high levels of capital intensity within enterprise operations) tends to be counter-productive in terms of both profits and employment.

Traditionally, a strong manufacturing sector has been the basis of the EU's international competitiveness. Under pressure from increased international competition, many 'mature industrialised economies' are seeing this traditional strength replaced by growing commercial advantage in the service sector. Economists are divided over the impact of this trend. Many doubt if services can be as tradable and productive as manufacturing products. This shifting competitive advantage of EU states is derived from the pervasive impact of technology and freer trade and their combined impact on the global business environment. Thus accepting these processes means that the richer states will have to rely upon the service sector and knowledge-based or capital intensive industries to sustain and enhance their position within the global economy. This implies that the quality of an economy's factor base is going to become an increasingly important determinant of competitiveness. This is especially pertinent for labour which is the only factor of production that cannot be easily or quickly duplicated across the global economy (see Chapter 13).

Despite the above, what is actually meant by 'competitiveness' is still somewhat opaque. Factors such as costs of production, technological development or exchange rates are all used as indicators of competitiveness. In practice, competitiveness is a hybrid of all these phenomena as each will determine, to varying degrees, businesses' abilities to successfully sustain a presence within their respective markets. Over the medium to long term, sustenance within markets requires a constant appraisal and renewal of labour skills and capital. In other words, it is enterprises not states that compete and it is within this context, that the role of national policy needs to be re-assessed.

THE ROLE OF NATIONAL INDUSTRIAL POLICIES IN AN INTEGRATING EUROPEAN ECONOMY

As with many policies featured within this text, industrial policies are formed at both a national and supranational level. Increasingly within an integrating European economy, inconsistencies between national industrial policies need to be removed as part of the commitment of member states to meeting their Treaty obligations. Community policy has traditionally differentiated between national and Community interests. This implies that there is a neat segmentation between these two domains. As the integration process proceeds and as previously distinct national economic and industrial structures coalesce, such a differentiation becomes increasingly difficult to sustain. This integration extends markets and increases the potential for the division of labour beyond the national borders.

Many of the perceived benefits derived from the integration process can be directly undermined by inconsistent national policies. States by their actions may limit the intensity of competition, re-nationalise parts of the common market or disrupt the process of structural change. In a period of slow growth (and rising unemployment), these problems may be particularly acute. The response may be a desire by the supranational institutions to develop an agenda to which all states can agree: thereby reducing the incentive for member states to indulge in 'beggar-thy-neighbour' policies *vis-à-vis* other EU states.

This issue is compounded by the rise of globalisation which looks likely to undermine further the ability of nation states to maintain independent policies with substantial discretion. Part of this is driven by the fact that national oligopolies, which were frequently perceived as national champions, are being replaced by international equivalents. Despite this trend, these businesses are still likely to reflect the traditions of enterprise and innovation derived from their national base. Overall, the consequences of globalisation for national industrial policy, according to Sharp in Hughes (1993), limits the role for the state to:

• provide support for science and technology infrastructure and an efficient system for the diffusion of technology;

- provide support for the process of competition and fair play;
- the alleviation of institutional failures especially in terms of an education system that impedes the quality of labour;
- provide support for those technologies which are strategic and in which a state lags behind competitors;
- the negotiation of common rules for trade on a global basis.

The outcome of these conclusions is that the role for the state within internationalising/integrating economies will ultimately be passive and limited to sustaining value added to the economy concerned. The inaccuracies of direct assistance, the leakages of support from the national to the international economy and the increased mobility of factors of production all limit the ability of states to develop national policies that will have the desired effects. Increasingly, therefore, the purpose of policy is not to maximise the value of assets under national ownership but to maximise the value of the productive activities of local people. As Reich (quoted in Boltho, 1996) notes:

> What is the role of the nation within the emerging global economy in which borders are ceasing to exist? Rather than increase the profitability of corporations flying the flag, or enlarge the world-wide holdings of its citizens, a nation's economic role is to improve its citizens' standards of living by enhancing the value of what they contribute to the world economy.

This implies that developing national industry is not the core issue. The key issue is about developing a location where industry – irrespective of the nationality of ownership – can flourish. This has been an ever-increasing theme within national economic development where foreign direct investment is becoming an important determinant of national wealth.

The effectiveness of national policy is further undermined by the gradual gains in legislative power made by supranational bodies. National – and indeed EU – policy may also be undermined by a 'user-led' process where economic actors, desiring consistency of treatment across the states where they have operations, shift production accordingly. The international marketplace will give firms increased freedom from state influence. They can use this power in combination with the desire of states to attract investment to determine the form of industrial policy that most suits them. This represents a potentially very influential constraint upon the form and nature of industrial policy whether it be at national or supranational level.

Community interest (see below), as a justification for strengthening the EU role in industrial policy, tends to be defined in an uncontentious manner, partially as a result of the desire of European states to ensure industrial policy is compatible with the principle of subsidiarity. Consequently, the Community interest is identified by common concerns and issues such as the legacy of industrial change. Importantly, it should not be taken as proof of a convergence between states in the substance of policy; it may simply reflect areas of mutual concern. Where there is a convergence of policies, there is debate as to whether this is driven by the EU or is a natural consequence of the process of business interaction across-borders.

Geroski (see Cowling and Tomann, 1989) argues that the case for a European industrial policy has to be based upon:

- the fact that there is a prima facie case for supranational industrial policy;
- the undermining of the viability of national policies by spillover.

This implies that there is no natural reason to accept a European policy as an inevitable consequence of increased intra-EU business interaction. There is little point in shifting the jurisdiction of policy beyond the domains of the activity it is designed to affect if the degree of market internationalisation is not that apparent. Accordingly, Geroski argues policy needs to be conducted at as local a level as possible due to a belief that:

- policy requires highly detailed information if it is to be properly defined, which gives local bodies a greater advantage;
- policy increases in complexity as more parties become involved;
- policies applied at a local level can be tailored to suit local preferences.

This is likely to be undermined by viability issues related to the ability of policies to meet nationally defined objectives where strong externalities between states are evident. Policy, if it is to be effective, needs to cover the entire market within which particular enterprises are operating. If it does not, it is likely to fail in terms of meeting its objectives. If the situation is characterised by several national markets within which the firm operates, there is still no clear rationale for dispensing with national policy. National policy is only dispensable when the economic market exceeds national boundaries. Thus national policy is undermined where:

- national and economic markets are not synonymous and as a consequence trade barriers emerge due to segmentation based upon national boundaries;
- externalities undermine the effectiveness of national targeting or support mechanisms by enabling other states to benefit from domestic centred actions.

Consequently, there must be realism in terms of national policy and how it responds to the integration process. European policy is a complement to not a replacement of national policies. It is at best a co-ordination device to enable national states to achieve as many of their goals as possible.

For these and other reasons, the influence of the member states over the development of EU industrial policy is prevalent and is still an area where unanimity is required. Even in those cases where the Commission does have a greater degree of discretion, it is still constrained by changing political interests and divergent concerns of the member states. This lack of consistency is not helped by disputes within the Commission over the relative domains/interest of competition and industrial policies. There is obvious scope for disputes between DG III (the industry directorate) and its desire to develop 'European Champions' with the pro-market agenda of the competition directorate (DG IV). These disputes are, however, becoming less common with both the traditionally more activist industrial policy states (notably France and Germany) moving towards passivism in policy form. These positions have arisen from a realisation that interventionism is not particularly effective in the modern global economy.

THE EVOLVING SUPRANATIONAL POLICY: THEMES AND ISSUES

Despite the evidence presented above, many feel that there is a case for the establishment of a more high profile European policy to supplant a national industrial policy due to the need to:

- eliminate inefficiencies derived from competing policies;
- reduce unfairness derived from the unequal allocation of resources between EU states;
- reduce the potential and incentives for a 'beggar-thy-neighbour' scenario;
- account for policy spillover;

- have the correct analysis and information with regard to common problems;
- develop a consensus between states;
- implement policy in a coherent and transparent manner.

Currently, it is difficult to imagine that industrial policy at the supranational level will ever replace national initiatives in terms of importance. However the integration of markets is breeding a degree of convergence between national policies which is broadly in line with measures being established at the supranational level. The power of European industrial policy is a direct derivative of the powers granted to the Commission by the member states. To date, this has in practice meant two things:

- the Commission sanctions as compatible with EU law national/inter-governmental industrial policy actions;
- the Commission establishes broad generic frameworks for promoting the industrial competitiveness of European-based business.

Such actions reflect the lack of formal power that the EU has in the development of industrial policy (see below). As suggested above, industrial policy covers many areas that can both implicitly and explicitly influence the competitiveness of business. There are three distinct, Treaty-based areas in which the Commission has direct influence:

- trade policy;
- competition policy;
- technology policy.

It is feasible to argue that the EU's competencies in industrial policy could be extended to other policies such as regional and transport policy in so far as they affect the performance of European enterprises in international markets.

The nature of the EU's evolving industrial policy was reflected within the Maastricht Treaty's provision on industry (see Box 5.1). This puts the EU's industrial policy firmly within the liberal camp reflecting as it does the position that structural change is not an issue for the state but for the agents of change themselves, that is, enterprises. Policy actions are perceived to be the mere catalyst of competitiveness by stimulating change via developing clear and predictable conditions for enterprises. This is a policy position which is increasingly reflected within national measures.

The establishment of a Community policy is based upon the aforementioned aspects of the concept of Community interest. Jacquemin and Marchipont (1993) believe this can be defined according to the following criteria:

- the avoidance of the emergence of industrial or technological dominance which would lead to a deterioration in the Community's economic position;
- establishing a firm grip for European enterprises in major foreign markets;
- closing the gap or developing generic technologies;
- developing sources of community production that maximise value added;
- limiting 'losses' from national or Community policies.

The challenges the EU economy faces are derived from changes in the global economy such as lost ground in growing markets, slow pace of innovation and relatively high costs of production. These challenges are derived from, and accentuated by, the growing liberalisation of the global trading economy.

BOX 5.1 TITLE XIII: INDUSTRY

This article of the Treaty upon European Union provides the first clear Community competence for the development of European industrial policy. The purpose of policy is, within a framework of open and competitive markets, to:

- accelerate the adjustment of structural change;
- stimulate the development of initiatives to support business development;
- promote co-operation between enterprises;
- ensure the results of the research and development policies and other innovation initiatives are dispersed throughout the economic body.

The trends within European industrial policy reflect the pressures upon its economy resulting from the process of globalisation. Globalisation requires new solutions for international competitiveness. The targeting of specific industries and other active policy measures become increasingly difficult to establish with any great effect within such an environment. Policy reflects a belief that the European economy needs to exploit world markets to prosper. The ability to export depends upon developing the portfolio of goods and services that are demanded in the global marketplace. This implies that change must not be deterred and that new and emerging sectors must be stimulated.

There is a desire to develop a range of policies that overcome the inadequacies of past experience and meet the needs of European-based enterprises to be successful on the global stage. European enterprises and economies now need to compete and adopt new technologies to push their global success. As a consequence policy needs to:

- enable EU based firms to stay ahead of rivals;
- recognise that investment in capital stock and the labour force will be increasingly paramount;
- aid the diffusion of new technology and best practice;
- enable labour to adapt to changes within economy.

These concerns were expressed more fully within the White Paper *Growth, Competitiveness and Employment*. Industrial policy's entire basis is moving increasingly towards the free market as a job creation mechanism. The challenge is that new solutions are required. There can be no protectionism, no massive government expenditure, no direct competition in terms of labour costs or any decline in the treatment of labour. This issue reflects a key concern of how Europe is to compete in a global economy where there are vast differentials in wage rates (see Chapter 13).

As suggested, policy that seeks to promote national or European champions is missing an important facet of the global economy. In a world of multi-national companies, the development of 'champions' is increasingly irrelevant. Thus policy needs to complement the strategies of all firms that invest in the European economy, irrespective of ultimate ownership. Consequently, establishing the pre-requisites under which these firms can be successful is essential and this has become the pivotal theme in European industrial policy and which largely mirrors events going on elsewhere in the global economy, notably the US.

EUROPEAN SOLUTIONS TO GROWING INTERNATIONAL COMPETITION

Jacquemin and Marchipont (1993) highlight that any industrial strategy for Europe needs to recognise that:

- the promotion of human capital is vital to economic success;
- sectoral initiatives need to be based on adequate market and qualitative information;
- there needs to be close interlinkages between international competitiveness policy and technology strategy;
- the globalisation of business needs to be taken into account;
- there needs to be understanding of generic technologies.

Towards the achievement of these concerns, the EU has developed a generally hybrid industrial policy where both generic and sectoral initiatives are followed.

Generic strategies

The largely passive nature of European industrial policy mirrors the relative lack of power of central supranational institutions in industrial policy development. As a reflection of this stance, the following broad principles tend to guide policy:

- the promotion of permanent adaptation to industrial change within the context of open and competitive markets;
- coherence with all other policies;
- a series of horizontal measures (that is, non-discriminatory actions affecting all sectors) to address industrial problems at both the sectoral and regional level.

As a consequence, and as suggested by Table 5.1, these measures are based upon the improved functioning of both European and global markets. It is these factors, the Commission increasingly believes, that will provide the basis for stimulating private sector investment and thereafter an improved commercial performance. EU industrial policy seeks to provide a generic environment that is both predictable and transparent to commercial actors.

Table 5.1 underlines that the active promotion of competition (from both internal and external sources) act as a catalyst in stimulating international competitiveness. These catalysts are not enough on their own for they need to be complemented and supported to ensure that when firms do make decisions, it is the European economy that receives the benefits. Thus pre-requisites such as education, training and infrastructure networks need

Table 5.1 Promoting structural adjustment

Pre-requisites	Catalysts	Accelerators
• Competition	• Internal market	• Research, development, technology, innovation
• Economic context	• Commercial policy	• Training
• Educational level		• SMEs
• Economic and social		• Business services
• Cohesion		
• Environmental protection		

to accompany such a strategy. Furthermore, to ensure that the catalysts are to have an on-going impact, they need to be accompanied by a series of accelerators that will spread and enhance the positive effects of competition and extend the benefits of liberalisation to SMEs, for example.

These concerns were reflected in a deliberate step by the Commission to develop a clearer industrial competitiveness strategy for the EU. To push the competitiveness of European industry, a number of broad measures were suggested:

- the promotion of intangible investments such as training;
- the development of co-operation, notably in pre-competitive actions such as research and development;
- fair (though, noticeably, not free) competition;
- the modernisation of the role of public authorities.

The common theme is the identification of the strengths and weaknesses of the European economy as a basis for policy direction. It is these strengths that are perceived as necessary for securing the success of the European economy on a global stage. All businesses located within the EU, irrespective of the nationality of ownership, are to be the focus of policy measures. Consequently these factors are needed to ensure not only that indigenous industry has the basis for global success but also that the European economy is attractive for foreign direct investment. Increasingly, the EU believes that the development of indigenous industry requires the development of more fulsome alliances (often with non-EU companies) to assist in the rationalisation of production amongst European enterprises as well as to promote the dispersal of 'know-how' throughout the entire economy.

This theme was very much central to the White Paper *Growth, Competitiveness and Employment*. That is, the economic success of the area depends upon the international competitiveness of all enterprises located within the EU. In the era of global capital mobility, the notion of European champions is dead as a concept. Industrial policy needs to be formed solely within such a global context. Such policies form an initial starting point upon which mutual agreement on a global basis can be formed. Global inter-dependence often dictates a form of interaction between global bodies which reflects and complements growing integration between states and regional economic groupings.

Themes within the European industrial policy are heading further towards a liberal position. The aforementioned White Paper was the first to really consider such issues on an EU level. Policy needs to address the cost-based issues which are increasingly central to industry's concerns. There is no intention by the EU of copying the Japanese model of targeting which it perceives as being out-dated. In this context, many feel that the EU policy needs to evolve further and become even more liberal. This is especially true with its stance towards labour market issues. Consequently, it is increasingly advocating that the key areas of policy should be:

- greater flexibility both in terms of real wages and working time;
- a topping up of low wage incomes;
- a fundamentally revised attitude towards entrepreneurship;
- markedly enhanced education and training;
- better educated markets to avoid destabilising capital flows and less investment.

This stems ultimately from the inability of the EU to create the desired level of jobs. These measures are not the exclusive preserve of the EU and need to find a translation in national economies. Some states are reluctant to accept anything which may mean the creation of jobs at the price of moving to US-style uncertainty. Over time, the EU may have little choice to accept some hybrid of EU/US models. Such a model may have to be accepted as the information society and more intense international competition starts to become a reality for more and more enterprises.

BOX 5.2 BENCHMARKING THE COMPETITIVENESS OF EU INDUSTRY

The purpose of benchmarking is to analyse the relative position of European enterprises on an on-going basis and to assess them against continuously improving best practice world-wide. It is a tool for promoting the convergence of best practice on a global basis and therefore a device for improving European competitiveness. The idea is to adopt the practices of other, often non-EU, enterprises to achieve the set objective. The result is a work programme that seeks to operate on a number of levels.

- *Enterprises*: a programme to identify manufacturing and managerial processes which a company needs to improve. These practices will essentially be based upon the experience of other enterprises both within and external to the EU.
- *Sectors*: to sustain its competitiveness, EU industry needs to consider key benchmark areas such as price and quality of service.
- *Framework conditions*: advocates the broad factors of industry that need to be benchmarked such as productivity of labour and capital, growth, job creation and employment.

The key areas for improvements, based upon the perceived weakness of European industry are:

- costs scenarios;
- key inputs for competitiveness such as price and quality;
- infrastructure;
- skills;
- innovation;
- environmental efficiency.

Much of this co-operation will need to be developed in collaboration within and between member states. Towards the attainment of benchmarking, the EU has established a high level group, developed a series of pilot projects and sought to establish a network of expertise on the issue.

Sectoral strategies

Table 5.2 presents some indicative evidence of the sectoral support given or sanctioned by the EU. For simplicity's sake, the sectors involved are divided into three distinct groups; though there will inevitably be some overlap between them. The sectors are differentiated as follows:

- declining sectors: these tend to involve primary production;
- restructuring sectors: these tend to be manufacturing based and frequently suffer from excess capacity;
- Emerging sectors: these seek to utilise Europe's perceived economic strengths for the purposes of employment creation.

The forms of assistance given will vary on a sector by sector or even on a firm by firm basis. Generally, the EU will use, either singly or in combination, competition, trade or technology policies to offer the required level of support. There may also be opportunities for further funding from, for example, the Structural Funds.

Table 5.2 Sectoral support from the EU

Declining sectors	Restructuring sectors	Emerging sectors

• Shipbuilding
• Coal
• Steel
• Textiles and clothing
	• Motor vehicle
	• Aviation
	• Aerospace
	• Synthetic fibres
	• Transport
		• Electronics
		• Audio-visual
		• Biotechnology
		• Pharmaceuticals
		• Information and
		  communication
		  technologies

Many of the declining sectors are given support on the basis that it is needed to overcome the consequences of decline in terms of employment or regional imbalance. Such a decline is often derived from rising costs of production and/or the inability to face the consequences of more competition within global markets. Many European shipbuilders and steel producers have faced declining market shares, and coal has been hit by a decline in economically viable resources. Many of these enterprises would not survive without the support given or sanctioned by the EU. States differ on the validity of such support. Northern European states such as the Netherlands and the UK are hostile whereas France and Spain are more amenable to these methods of support. In many of these sectors, attempts have been made to co-ordinate the removal of over-capacity in the EU. In practice, this has proved very difficult. The steel sector is an evident case where such agreements have proved difficult, largely because the consequences in terms of employment have been equally unpalatable for many states. The EU has made attempts to limit the forms of anti-competitive aid though states have proved themselves fairly adept at circumventing such attempted controls.

The 'restructuring sectors' tend to have substantial over-capacity but their political and economic importance often hinders the rationalisation process. The problems are generally similar to those experienced within the steel sector. The Commission seeks co-operative solutions to these rationalisation problems. In the aviation sector, this has been typified by the development of Airbus Industry (see Case Study 5.2). Action in this area is justified by the fact that the market under concern is global not European and that co-operation stimulates a more efficient allocation of resources and eliminates destabilising competition. The transport sector has also been an area where methods to distort competition have been evident. There are numerous cases where the EU has sought to curtail the subsidies given to airlines: an area where there is evident surplus capacity (see Case Study 6.1). The car industry is also protected but growing international competition has made the companies face up to the challenges posed by this. The voluntary export restraint (VER) is due to be reviewed by the turn of the millennium and car operators are unlikely to get as much protection as before. In any case, given the globalisation of car production, such protection seems increasingly anachronistic. Overall, more intense competition may benefit the EU car industry in terms of global competitiveness, but many of its players seem reluctant to forfeit the support given.

The 'emerging sectors' represent the progressive elements of structural change within the European economy. Successive research and development initiatives have sought to stimulate the technological development of the EU as a precursor to its economic success (see Case Study 5.1). The sectors prioritised reflect the perceived advantage that the EU has in knowledge-based, value-added and increasingly technological activities. These activities are based upon the strong competitive advantage that the EU has derived from its education and science systems. The priorities reflect how policy makers see the EU as successful in the emerging global economy. Many of these activities proposed by the EU are remote from the market. As a consequence, the EU favours a co-ordinated and co-operative approach to technological development. A major theme is the development of the information society supplied by a strong indigenous information and communication technology (ICT) sector. Once this market reaches a critical mass, it will form the basis of successful audio-visual and electronic sectors. The purpose of these actions is to narrow the technological gap between the EU and its major competitors. Where possible the EU seeks to stimulate research to give European industry a head start in future technologies. In this area, it has limited success and notable failures such as the high definition television (HDTV) technologies. In sum, the focus is upon basic research not upon companies.

CASE STUDY 5.1 THE FIFTH FRAMEWORK PROGRAMME

This is the latest of the EU's joint initiatives upon research and development. Carrying on from the Fourth Framework (1994–8), the new programme, covering the period 1998–2002, seeks to ensure that European research efforts can show direct relevance to the general public and therefore directly complement the core priorities of stimulating growth, competitiveness and employment within the EU. The Fourth Framework resulted in just under 3,000 projects involving 10,000 participants. The results from these projects demonstrated the need for better targeting, greater involvement by SMEs and the pinpointing of resources more accurately to avoid spreading efforts too thinly. In response to the process of globalisation, the EU seeks to target resources at those sectors that exploit Europe's competitive advantage where substantial market growth is expected (for example, biotechnology). Effective targeting is pivotal for EU resources are a mere 4 per cent of the total available. This underpins the need for enhanced co-ordination between EU, national and international research efforts.

The core priorities for the Fifth Framework programme reflect the concerns of focusing efforts to address societal problems. These priorities are:

1 unlocking the resources of the living world and the ecosystem;
2 creating a user friendly information society;
3 promoting competitive and sustainable growth;
4 enhancing human potential;
5 innovation and involvement of SMEs;
6 confirming the international role of European research.

The effectiveness in meeting these priorities will be enhanced by efforts to improve co-ordination, enhance flexibility and improve response capability and effective management. These provide the focus of the six major programmes. The first three are 'thematic' programmes on general topics; the latter three are more 'horizontal' themes that are, as suggested, not sector specific. Across all aspects, the EU will seek to involve non-EU players in the process to ensure Europe benefits from 'know-how' elsewhere in the global economy. To enhance the relevance of the framework to 'everyday life', a number of key actions in subjects such as health and food, multimedia contents, sustainable mobility and the 'city of tomorrow' are anticipated.

continued

Overall, the themed research and development areas reflect a growing proximity between these efforts and market processes. This is a response to a concern that the impact of these technologies will be felt greatest upon the performance of the EU economy when the research responds to user and market needs. The European Commission wants to replace unanimity in voting upon R&D with qualified majority voting. It feels that the unanimity rule results in a concentration upon national and sectional interests instead of an overall focused strategy. This change to the R&D process was facilitated by the relevant title within the Amsterdam Treaty. The EU also wants a reserve fund to meet emergency research issues such as those stimulated by the BSE crisis.

The European Commission proposed an expansion in the level of funding in the Fifth Framework by 3 per cent. This is a token amount but it sought to draw attention to the inadequacy of EU research funding which compares poorly with the US and Japan. The Commission wanted ECU 16.3 billion but eventually had to settle for ECU 14 billion. The allocation of funding within the thematic (first activity) within the Framework is reflected within the accompanying table.

Themes within the Fifth Framework

Thematic activity	Typical projects	Funding
Improving the quality of life and management of human resources	• Food, nutrition and health • Control of infectious diseases • The 'cell factory' • Environment and health • Sustainable agriculture, fisheries and forestry (including integrated development of rural areas) • The ageing population	ECU 2,239 million
Creating user friendly information society	• Systems and services for the citizen • New methods of work and electronic commerce • Multimedia content and tools • Essential technologies and infrastructures	ECU 3,363 million
Promoting competitive and sustainable growth	• Innovative products, processes and organisations • Sustainable mobility and intermodality • Land transport and marine technologies • New perspectives in aeronautics	ECU 2,389 million

Thematic activity	Typical projects	Funding
Energy, environment and sustainable development	• Sustainable management and quality of water • Global change, climate and biodiversity • Sustainable marine ecosystems • The city of tomorrow and cultural heritage • Cleaner energy systems • Economic and efficient energy systems	ECU 2,088 million

The funding for the other areas are:

• Second activity (international aspects of research): ECU 458 million;
• Third activity (SME participation): ECU 350 million;
• Fourth activity (human potential): ECU 1,205 million.

In addition to these funds, finance is available from the Euratom Framework programme to stimulate nuclear research and development.

THE IMPORTANCE OF MANAGEMENT PRACTICES

As mentioned above, the core drivers of competitiveness lie within the actions of the enterprise itself not of policy makers. Inevitably the success of an enterprise in achieving such advantage depends upon management practices within it. Such management practices need to ensure:

• the stimulation of innovation within the production process;
• the maximisation of operating efficiency;
• the realisation of structural adjustments.

The implementation of these objectives depends upon a number of critical success factors such as effective leadership, investment in modern equipment, a focus upon core competencies and the introduction of new practices. Many studies have indicated the link between modern management practices and enhanced business performance, notably with regard to organisational innovation and the management of people.

As globalisation begins to spread, so the need for a more speedy adaptation of these practices emerges. This is especially true as competition between enterprises shifts away from 'hard' factors such as economies of scale towards 'soft' factors such as core competencies, speed to market, reputation and service. Thus firms are increasingly competing in areas of product/service differentiation based upon value-added and flexibility. The realisation of these factors has been based upon major investments, a focus upon core business, the development of networks and organisational innovation.

The above implies that policy needs to add velocity to the processes that lead to change and eliminate those that delay it. This requires increasing the exposure of enterprises to competition, helping enterprises (especially SMEs) acquire the management skills required to promote change, lowering the institutional impediments to change and establishing fora within which enterprises can co-operate to overcome the challenges created by the need to alter to enhance competitiveness.

INTERNATIONAL COLLABORATION IN INDUSTRIAL POLICY

In areas of pre-competitive or remote market activities, there is substantial collaboration between economies that would otherwise be competitors. A notable example has been those actions taken within the forum of the Group of Eight (G8) states for the development of the information society and the agreement between the EU, Japan and the US over the subsidies given to the shipbuilding sector within the framework of the OECD.

In addition, there are specific measures to promote EU–Japan collaboration. This has been a result of programmes such as Vulcanus which seeks to enable EU companies to develop closer links with Japan via the exchange of students and, in some cases, know-how. Perhaps a classic case of growing interdependence between industrial policy systems was the EU's decision to offer support to the Airbus Industrie as a challenge to the dominance of the US (via Boeing) of the global market (see Case Study 6.2). However this spillover has been more evident within competition policy (see Chapter 6). This interdependence need not always be confrontational as is suggested by the experience of trade and competition policies. For not only are there moves to get common agreement in these areas, but in areas such as technology the EU will actively seek the involvement of non-EU (frequently US and Japanese) enterprises as an expression of the development of market distant technologies.

CASE STUDY 5.2 DEVELOPING EUROPEAN CHAMPIONS: A STRATEGY FOR THE EU AEROSPACE INDUSTRY

The aerospace market is growing and one in which the EU wants its enterprises to gain an increasing share. To the European Commission, the market for civil and military aviation is global therefore it believes that a fragmented European response to this challenge will undermine the effectiveness of its strategy. For this reason, the EU has actively promoted co-operation between independent EU operators to enable them to take on the large US companies (notably Boeing) who have tended to control and dominate this market. Airbus and the European Fighter Aircraft are two open expressions of this co-operation. Each of these reflect the fact that it is the four largest EU states (France, Germany, the UK and Italy) that dominate European production in the aerospace sector. Importantly, the defence industry is one area where the European Commission can do little to create a common market.

Airbus has been no doubt the most visible and controversial aspect of the European aerospace's strategy to gain market share. A result of co-operation between British Aerospace (UK), Aerospatiale (France), Daimler–Benz (Germany) and DASA (Spain), the Airbus consortia now competes in intense rivalry with Boeing over market share within the civil aviation market. This issue has led to continual friction between the EU and the US (see Case Study 6.2) and to loose bi-lateral agreements, that seem to amount to very little, to constrain state support for their respective enterprises. The EU has always justified the sanctioning of support to Airbus because not only does it believe it is consistent with its market economy investor principle (see Chapter

6) but also because it believes Boeing receives indirect subsidies via the NASA space programme. Whether its techniques are fair or not, there can be little doubt that Airbus has been a success: it now possesses over 35 per cent of the market. But given that the vast majority of the market is held by Boeing (something that can only be enhanced by the McDonnell–Douglas merger), Airbus is still very much a poor second to the US company.

To overcome this, the European Commission is pushing for further rationalisation of the sector, notably by overcoming political problems between constituent partners over the development of Airbus. Despite its success, Airbus still tends to produce too expensively with production split across a network of sites within the four partner states. The enterprise itself argues that its network is designed to exploit the specialised skills of the partner concerned. In practice, however, the network tends to be based more on political pride than on efficiency.

The 1997 Commission document *The European Aerospace Industry* concluded that, despite agreements for co-operation, the EU industry was still too fragmented and that any restructuring was proceeding far too slowly. In comparing the EU industry to the US, the document noted that as a result of restructuring in the latter there are only three suppliers across the entire market (both civil and defence) compared to the EU which has six civil aircraft producers, six fighter aircraft producers, three helicopter producers, twelve missile producers, six defence electronic producers and five satellite prime contractors. This US advantage is reinforced by the fact its industry has only to deal with one government.

The Commission is evidently in a position only to prescribe, the response to such challenges is up to the firms themselves. The Commission recommends the development of European clusters within each of, and indeed across, the market segments. Complete consolidation, as in the US, is politically impractical for the time being. Any rationalisation needs to be accompanied by:

- pinpointing aerospace research for support under the EU's research and development programmes;
- the extension of public procurement rules to defence products;
- facilitating the integration with the development of a European company statute;
- developing a truly uniform certification process and therefore lower costs;
- intensifying standardisation activities in this area.

Progress towards this objective was facilitated in early 1998 when Airbus announced its intention to restructure its operations to allow it to become a limited liability company by 1999. Its development into a single corporate entity is an important step in the consolidation of the aerospace industry in Europe. Assets will be transferred from partners to the enterprise according to the importance of the function. The flotation of Airbus is essential to enable it to compete directly with Boeing and to approach the private sector for funding for project development, notably its planned 'Super-Jumbo'. The extension of this trend to other sectors very much depends upon member states and their commitment to loosening the grip of national champions for the purpose of developing much broader consolidated, largely market led 'European champions' through a rationalisation of the number of firms within the sector. There is likely to be resistance from management within indigenous firms who may see their power undermined by the creation of such enterprises. In practice, their hands may be forced as a third power in aerospace industry emerges from South East Asia and as national aerospace budgets are continually cut. Most national governments are keen for their enterprises to become involved in alliance formation though this need not always be for rationalisation reasons but merely to protect their position.

CONCLUSION

At the heart of the EU's industrial policy is the pursuit of the international competitiveness that can secure much needed growth and higher levels of employment. The actions of the EU itself tend to be passive with the states taking the primary role in the policy process. The measures that the EU undertakes amount to very little more than establishing a generic framework within which national policies can be developed. Where the EU does have Treaty-based power, it often finds itself under challenge from the member states. The policy itself is very liberal, believing that more intense competition is the only route for Europe if it wants to achieves its stated objective. Whilst many states agree with this stance, their support is tempered by a desire to offer certain companies and sectors specific support despite the fact that they go against the grain of what commercial investors would do. Thus overall the EU finds itself with a hybrid policy; that is despite its desire for more liberal competition, the hostility of certain states mean that it cannot make consistent efforts in this direction.

⭷ KEY POINTS

- **Industrial policy seeks to manage the decline of old and the emergence of new industries.**

- **There is a shift away from active (interventionist) towards passive industrial policies throughout Europe.**

- **Supranational policy has a dual focus of offering both generic and sectorally specific support to European industry.**

SUGGESTED FURTHER READING

Audrtesch, D. (1989) *The Market and the State*, Harvester Wheatsheaf.

Boltho, A. (ed.) (1996) 'International Competitiveness', *Oxford Review of Economic Policy*, Vol. 12, No. 3.

Bangemann, M. (1992) *Meeting the Global Challenge: Establishing a Successful European Industrial Policy*, Kogan Page.

Commission of the European Communities (1995) *Panorama of EU Industry*, Brussels.

Cowling, K. and Tomann, H. (1989) *Industrial Policy After 1992*, The Anglo-German Foundation.

Curzon-Price, V. (1981) *European Industrial Policy*, Oxford University Press.

Hughes, K. (ed.) (1993) *UK Competitiveness and Industrial Policy*, PSI.

Jacquemin, A. and Marchipont, J.-F. (1993) 'New Challenges facing the Community's Industrial Policy', *Annales des Mines*, December, 20–4.

Kassim, H. and Menon, A. (eds) (1996) *The European Union and National Industrial Policy*, Routledge.

Lawton, T. (ed.) (1999) *European Industrial Policy and Competitiveness: Concepts and Instruments*, Macmillan.

Nicolaides, P. (ed.) (1993) *Industrial Policy in the European Community: A Necessary Response to European Integration*, Martinus Nijhoff.

Stavridis, S., Mossialos, E., Morgan, R., Machin, H. (1997) *New Challenges to the European Union: Policies and Policy Making*, Dartmouth.

6

EU COMPETITION POLICY: COMPLEMENTING THE INTERNATIONALISATION OF BUSINESS

Central to many of the EU's actions within the European business environment is the belief that nothing is better for competitiveness than competition itself. This underlines a belief that intense competition within both indigenous and global markets is a pre-requisite for the successful performance of European business. In this context, the role of competition policy is to seek to preserve the desired intensity of competition within the EU by setting a series of rules and regulations which limit the ability of enterprises to operate in a manner which is contrary to this objective. This policy stance represents an important sea change, for in many EU states the traditional thinking was that economic success could be influenced by limiting the intensity of competition faced by indigenous firms. Frequently such strategies failed and look increasingly outdated within internation-alising economies. The growing interdependence between states (especially within the context of the EU) implies that there is little to be gained from policy makers offering favours to indigenous over foreign enterprises.

The initial focus of this chapter is to examine the perceived benefits of competition and therefore why it is actively pursued by policy makers. Thereafter the themes and form of competition policy within the EU are explored. Subsequently, the key issue is to examine the processes of change that are affecting competition policy development within the EU, notably the trends towards European and global integration.

THE BASIS AND FORM OF EU COMPETITION POLICY

Economic theory perceives competition to be a social good as its maintenance is regarded as pivotal in ensuring efficiency gains both within enterprises and the economy as a whole. This improved efficiency is expressed in many ways: first, in terms of the prices charged to consumers which are expected to fall as competition intensifies; second, from the pressure for greater cost efficiency within enterprises; and third, from the greater choice of goods and services which arise as more firms enter a particular market. These efficiency gains will be stimulated by the presence of the following four factors which intensify the pressure of competition (Porter, 1990):

- advanced and specialised human resources, technical infrastructure and other factors of production;
- sophisticated and demanding home consumers;
- home based suppliers;
- capable, committed and competing local rivals.

Whilst policy may seek to increase the intensity of rivalry between enterprises, it also recognises that too much competition may be detrimental to the performance of European business. The uncertainty induced by excessive competition may limit investment, increase commercial risks and consequently result in retarded economic development. This is especially true of actions that are deemed pre-competitive (for example, research and development). In addition, too much competition may run counter to the objectives of economic and social cohesion. Policy makers may also decide to limit the extent to which certain sectors face competition for social or political reasons. This may be the case where excessive exposure to competitive forces over the short term may result in detrimental employment consequences – this is a common fear within many of the staple industries (for example, coal, steel etc.).

Competition policy has been traditionally based upon the notion that the larger the number of firms in a market, the greater the benefits to the economy concerned. This stance was inevitably corrupted as the state started to play an increasingly prominent role within the economy. This traditional view point is based upon the perspective that, aside from state control, monopolies are always and everywhere bad. Thus where monopolies are deemed to be 'natural', as was the case for many of the network sectors, there was a strong case for state ownership. This position has been increasingly challenged as policy makers have started to realise that monopolies need not necessarily be detrimental if they are not accompanied or supported by insurmountable (often state determined) barriers to entry. This is important, for it implies potential competition has as big a role to play within market structures as actual competition. Knowing that other firms have the right and ability to enter the market should act as a constraint upon the actions of incumbents even if they hold a monopoly position. This challenge to the traditional policy stance has been supported by the gradual erosion of the notion of 'natural' monopoly (see Chapter 11). Competition is increasingly possible and prevalent within sectors previously regarded as naturally monopolistic, whether it is through bidding for a franchise (as in the case of the UK rail sector) or where services are provided in a competitive manner over a commonly owned infrastructure (as witnessed in many of the network sectors).

Broadly, there are two types of competition policy:

- *form-based*: the analysis of competition is based on an examination of objective, often quantitative, criteria such as market share or structure;
- *effects-based*: where the examination of competition is based upon the effects of the actions of enterprises within the sector concerned.

In terms of competition, the former stresses that the performance of an industry depends upon the structure of the sector concerned which then determines the conduct and eventually the performance of the enterprises. Effects-based competition policy is more concerned with the conduct of the participants within the sector than market structure per se – that is, a monopoly is only bad when it abuses its position. This is the broad logic of much of the EU's competition policy.

THE CORE FEATURES OF EU COMPETITION POLICY

The measures within the EU's competition policy reflect the integration process, especially within the context of achieving the objectives of the SEM. They seek to ensure that the actions of all operators, whether the state, publicly owned/controlled enterprises or private business, are compatible with the objectives of the free and fair competition encapsulated within the SEM programme. Thus policy (as identified in Box 6.1) has within its scope the ability to liberalise protected markets, remove competitive distortions sourced from the state and curtail the activities of enterprises that abuse dominance or seek, via collaboration, to limit the intensity of competition.

BOX 6.1 EU COMPETITION POLICY INSTRUMENTS

Apart from the Merger Control Regulation, EU policy instruments are based upon Articles in the Treaty of Rome.

Article 85 prohibits any collusion between undertakings which may restrict competition to the extent that such collusion has an effect upon trade between states and therefore inhibits the development of a single market. Activities that would typically be declared illegal under this Article include price fixing, quantitative restrictions on production, investment on R&D, market sharing and tying of supplementary conditions to sales. Such agreements may be allowed if they are able to fulfil the following conditions simultaneously:

* the agreement contributes to improving production, distribution or promoting technical or 'economic progress';
* there are significant benefits to consumers;
* restrictions are avoided that are not indispensable to the attainment of conditions above;
* the agreement does not preclude competition in a substantial part of the market for the product in question.

Article 86 prohibits undertakings that hold a dominant position from abusing this advantage to the extent that their actions preclude competition within the single market or at least a significant part of it. Measures that would be considered 'abusive' include predatory pricing, unfair trading conditions and discrimination between consumers or suppliers. There is no exemption clause so any conflict between scale efficiencies and competition is deemed not to exist due to the ease of market access.

Article 90 applies the conditions of Articles 85 and 86 to state-owned enterprises or firms that have been given special or exclusive rights. Thus despite being neutral on property rights, the Treaty maintains that state ownership does not imply a right to distort competition. Member states are allowed to grant special or exclusive rights for certain 'legitimate national objectives' but they should not contravene the rules of competition. If application of competition rules threatens to undermine essential public service elements of these enterprises then these special or exclusive rights are exempt.

Article 92 specifies that any assistance given by the state which distorts or threatens to distort competition by favouring certain undertakings or the production of certain goods, in so far as such action distorts trade, is incompatible with the common market. As mentioned below (see Case Study 6.1), aid is assessed according to the 'market economy investor principle' which means aid is compatible with the SEM if the parties can prove a commercial investor would have behaved in a similar manner. If aid promotes technological or economic development, provides advantages to consumers, enables the relief of natural disasters or of a serious disturbance within the economy of a member state then it is permissible under EU law.

The Merger Control Regulation: this seeks to prevent undertakings from creating or strengthening a dominant position on the market by acquiring control of another enterprise. Only mergers with a clear Community dimension are caught by the regulation leaving member states considerable scope for discretion in this area of policy. Policy is based upon three criteria:

- *size*: mergers with a worldwide turnover of over ECU 5 billion and an EU wide turnover of over ECU 250 million (assuming this revenue is earned across more than one state) would come under the regulation (though as noted, this has been extended to include mergers below this size that have a discernible Community Dimension);
- *impact*: assessing the effects of the merger on the SEM;
- *competence*: determining whether the assessment of the merger should take place at the EU or the national level.

These in combination determine the extent to which a merger has a community dimension.

Within the context of the Treaty of Rome, EU competition policy is an instrument to achieve the specified objectives of balanced development, free trade and harmonious growth. The Treaty on European Union has broadened these objectives to include social and environmental concerns as well as the emerging industrial policy. In terms of meeting these objectives, competition policy will seek consistency with other policy areas. If there is a clash in policies (as there has been between competition and industrial policies), it is more often due to the nature of the policies followed by the member state(s). Clashes between EU industrial and competition policies are gradually being alleviated as the former starts to stress open and competitive markets. As a complement to the broad pro-market themes stressed by industrial policy, competition policy has emphasised the following themes.

- *State aid*: direct support is designed to push the managed, market led decline of the staple industries (such as steel) and to lower their use in those sectors where market forces are gradually being extended. Direct support is put forward in other sectors to meet the concerns of technological and regional development (for example, to attract FDI).
- *Liberalisation*: this intends to extend the benefits of the SEM to consumers by lowering the prices in key, previously protected, services such as telecommunications and energy. The process also seeks to extend and enhance infrastructure quality and capacity as a means of delivering an improvement in the quality of services.
- *Co-operation*: the policy allows for inter-firm co-operation in pre-competitive actions such as research and development or in areas where the market is global in nature.

These are in addition to the themes of protecting competition engendered within Articles 85 and 86. The desire is to draw a distinction between the activities of firms that seek to progress and restructure European industry and those activities that partition markets (thereby denying the realisation of the SEM) and delay the onset of structural adjustment. Thus competition policy, in line with the objectives of industrial policy, seeks to establish the conditions under which enterprises can be successful on a global basis.

COMPETITION POLICY AND THE PROCESS OF INTEGRATION

Competition policy in the EU takes effect at both national and supranational levels. EU policy is only effective to the extent to which the actions of economic actors impede/ distort trade between significant parts of the EU. As the SEM has led to increased interaction across-borders so the pertinence of EU competition policy has increased (as generally reflected in Figure 6.1). As more firms seek to move into other markets so the activities of incumbent operators (and of states) start to have a greater negative impact upon the functioning of the European marketplace. Clearly EU measures have little relevance in highly local/regional or niche markets where national competition policy will come to the fore.

The need for common rules is based upon a desire to maintain the level playing field which is at the heart of the SEM. The intention is that all firms face the same sets of rules and conditions with a simultaneous limit upon the discretion available to the member states in so far as their actions could undermine this objective. The administration of rules by a single body is also likely to lead to greater consistency and predictability in the outcome of policy. The issue is therefore that integration and the increased interaction of firms across-borders have implications for the development of national policy and the way it is administered. Firms crave consistency and efficiency in the market in which they operate. Frequently this requires policy implementation by a single body. To have many different decisions from a multitude of different bodies or the same one from all is both time-consuming and a waste of resources.

As firms start to internationalise, so there will be a desire on the part of enterprises for a single set of uniform rules to oversee their activities. Competition works to service the market within which the action of enterprises has effect. As firms internationalise, and as the network economy becomes more evident, so there is an inevitable blurring of the

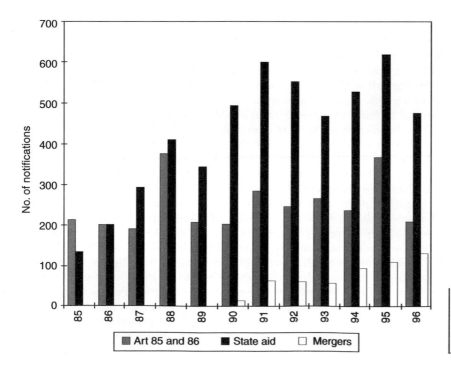

Figure 6.1 **The evolving case load of EU competition policy** *Source*: European Commission

boundaries between national and international markets. The relevant market for the application of EU law can now be defined on a national or regional level. Thus the national/regional market is deemed to represent a substantial part of the overall EU market and restriction of competition within this area could be detrimental to competition within the EU as a whole. In short, in line with the process outlined in Chapter 1, there is a growing interdependence between economies driven by the actions of enterprises. In this context, there can be no neat division of labour in terms of the administration of competition policy between states.

The process of integration has notably led to a convergence in national competition policies as states reform domestic policy to achieve greater consistency with the EU's competition policy. However this trend tends to apply more to the antitrust provisions than it does to mergers. In most cases, a realignment of policy has taken place. This measure is perceptibly better than straightforward co-ordination which may come unstuck due to asymmetric information between states and incentives for cheating. Where rules are harmonised, such problems are, at least partially, overcome. Thus harmonisation is a market led process driven by the integration of states. Such uniformity may work to create an environment where commercial players can act with a higher degree of certainty.

The end point of such processes is feasibly the establishment of a single competition authority for a single market. If the process of convergence of policy continues, it would seem that the harmonious implementation of policy needs to be re-thought and re-designed. This trend will largely be dictated by the larger EU states who in many cases have differing agendas. However, this should not downplay the fact that national competition policies will become increasingly obsolete as the examination of markets (even on a regional or local basis) takes on an increasingly international feel. This will be complemented by the fact that national policy will start to transmit its effects across-borders, thereby undermining the uniformity and consistency of the SEM. These co-ordination problems and spillover effects are likely to provide a further rationale for the development of a stronger supranational presence in the development of policy.

The growing evidence of this trend within the EU has increased the pressure for reform. Germany, at the 1996–7 intergovernmental conference (IGC), proposed the development of a politically independent European Cartel Authority. Under this proposal, the cartel authority would have control over the implementation of Articles 85 and 86 as well as the Merger Control Regulation. The European Commission would be left with residual powers to deal with public monopolies, state aid and the general conduct of competition policy. The idea was to make the process inherently more predictable and apolitical. Not surprisingly this has been criticised by the Commission who feel that moves to split policy will lead to inconsistency, confusion, uncertainty and will undermine the need to consider other policies. In short, such a development would do little for the integration process and may indeed hamper it by diluting the synergetic effects and interlinkages between different policies that drive the process. If there is a case for an independent policy body, it is due to the nature of policy making in the European Commission and the ability of politicians to influence this. Business will inevitably be unsettled by such events but this may require reform of existing processes rather than an entirely new institution.

The European Commission also wishes to extend its merger powers. Clearly not all mergers with a 'Community dimension' are caught by the existing legislation. Consequently, the Commission has sought to reduce the threshold at which its powers become relevant. In 1998, the Commission was given limited extra power in this area when it was given scope to vet mergers with a significant cross-border impact that would have previously fallen below established thresholds. In addition, it has gained extra power over multiple filings: where a merger requires submissions before competition authorities in a number of EU states.

The process of increasing power for the Commission within competition policy as a legacy of the integration process is by no means inevitable. There has been considerable effort by the member states to limit the scope and range of its existing powers. A notable case is the example the French government has presented in terms of state aid. The French government has consistently challenged Commission decisions. Indeed in some cases, typically the Air France example (see Case Study 6.1), it has persistently tested the Commission and arguably undermined its authority and credibility as a regulator of competition. This position has also been compounded by the level of subsidies given by Germany to the former East Germany. Many small states feel undermined by the power of the larger states to inject finance into their industry in apparent contravention of EU law.

The moves by Germany to establish an independent cartel agency and the desire of France to weaken the ability of the Commission to dismantle state monopolies both represent attempts to curtail the powers of the Commission. Compound this with the reluctance of other states to sanction any further increases in the power of the Commission in terms of competition policy and there is a powerful coalition resisting the seemingly logical consequences of the integration process. Yet between states, opinions about the role of EU competition policy differ. Some states wish to pursue liberalisation, others do not. Some wish to extend merger regulation, others do not. Some wish to see a closer control over state aids, others do not. Reaching agreement on how competition policy should respond to the on-going process of integration is proving difficult. Reconciliation of differing national preferences regarding the role and influence of the state over the market has made limited progress. Many states accept the SEM but seem unable to accept what it means in terms of internal competition and enterprise restructuring.

At the end of the IGC, there was evidence to argue that there were serious and successful attempts to limit the power of the Commission in competition policy. There are limits imposed upon the Commission's ability to scrutinise unfair practices of banks and on the applicability of the competition laws to public television stations. In addition, the French were successful in getting an article upon public services included within the Treaty. This measure could curtail the ability of the Commission to push through liberalisation measures.

CASE STUDY 6.1 UNDERMINING COMPETITION POLICY: STATE AID TO EUROPE'S AIRLINES

Successful policy implementation relies upon the even, consistent and credible enforcement of the set of principles contained within the policies. Nowhere has this been challenged more forcefully than in relation to the state aid given to Europe's airlines. It has been a long held objective of the European Commission to achieve full liberalisation of air services across the EU. Within this context, assistance given to (usually state-owned) airlines has the capability of undermining the principle of fairness and consistency which is at the heart of EU policy.

The EU has assessed the validity of such aid in line with the market economy investor principle (MEIP). Thus the subsidy or other forms of aid are only deemed to be compatible with the SEM if the Commission believes that a commercial investor would have behaved in a similar manner. Within this context, the aid offered by governments is generally given to cover the huge losses made by certain European carriers, notably Air France, Sabena (Belgium), Iberia (Spain), Air Portugal, Aer Lingus (Eire) and Olympic Airways (Greece). Generally, the EU likes to see aid as a one-off affair linked to the restructuring of the carrier (the so-called 'one time/last time' principle). Part of the problem is that such assistance is frequently not one-off. Air France, for example, has (to date) been given such assistance three times.

Despite its apparent inconsistency with the development of the single market in aviation, the European Commission has persistently approved such assistance. In practice, its hands have been tied by the highly political nature of the sector concerned. Indeed certain aspects of the EU's policy on state aid have been openly contravened. Notably the one time/last time rule has been broken more than once and states and airlines have engaged in strategies (such as uneconomic pricing and aggressive expansion) that would not have been approved under the MEIP. Two companies (Iberia and Air France) who engaged in this successfully argued that such actions were indeed commercial and therefore compatible with the MEIP. Thus the Commission may in some cases have to act retrospectively to ensure its recommendations are adhered to.

Furthermore many industry analysts have questioned the usefulness of the MEIP for state aid decisions. Certain airlines (notably Iberia and Air France) have found ways around this. Indeed one large transfer to Iberia could not, according to the MEIP, be classified as state aid. This coupled with the lack of transparency over the MEIP offers an opportunity for lobbying to get round the provisions of the policy (as Iberia and Air France successfully did) thus undermining its effectiveness. These airlines (and, more recently, Alitalia) have claimed that such interventions were not in fact state aid but a 'normal investment from a major shareholder' and therefore compatible with the MEIP. If these cases set precedents (as the Alitalia case seems to), then the state aid policy is an empty threat as the lack of clarity of the MEIP offers airlines excessive flexibility and freedom of action. This can be noted by the sporadic nature with which these airlines have met the terms and conditions (set by the European Commission) under which the aid was granted.

The problem for airlines is that the overall level of state aid in this sector is increasing in an environment where levels of support across all industry are declining. This is coupled with an evident resentment from those carriers (such as KLM, BA and Lufthansa) who have undergone years of painful restructuring to put themselves on to a commercial footing to compete globally, only to see the rationale for this strategy undermined by the actions of the Commission (a concerned shared by the US). The Commission in these aid cases is having its credibility undermined by the lobbying of member states who have raised the political stakes surrounding the provision of aid. The political nature of the decisions has been such that the conditions attached to the granting of the aid have had negligible impact upon carriers.

The EU claims that the aid granted to the airlines is now under control. Indeed by mid-1997, the airlines that had gone cap in hand to the Commission appear to have turned the corner towards profitability. However it is unlikely to stop further efforts to aid airlines should times once again be unfavourable to them. In addition, the ability of the Commission to grant aid to Air France was successfully challenged by a number of carriers (such as BA, SAS and KLM) in the European Court of Justice which ruled that the Commission was wrong to approve the aid due to insufficient justification; though it did not demand repayment and eventually had little impact upon the Commission's original decision. Thus the Commission, despite optimistic soundings when the original decision was given, has decided to evade the judgement rather than come into conflict with France. Indeed since then it has approved further state aid notably to Olympic Airways. Unless the Commission is prepared to confront the granting of state aids, then it will find itself facing a huge credibility gap in this aspect of its competition policy.

THE INTERNATIONAL DIMENSION OF EU COMPETITION POLICY

As economies globalise, so competition and policy to ensure its maintenance become ever more important. The rules of competition, though not uniform in both form and structure, are pivotal in determining mutual access to markets and need to be applied consistently and fairly to support the globalisation process by ensuring the equal treatment of indigenous and foreign companies. The certainty and fairness of competition policy is also seen as important in determining the necessary prerequisite for foreign direct investment as protection for local operators is certainly likely to deter such flows.

With the development of international competition, problems will inevitably emerge in trying to police geographically dispersed markets. Such problems may be overcome by:

- the application of national competition laws by a large player on an extra-territorial basis: this raises concerns over legitimacy and equity though it may in practice be the only viable solution;
- the establishment of multilateral fora to address actions by states (or regional groupings) that may distort global trade;
- more complete bilateral agreements between trading partners: this has been an increasingly common development within the EU and has been applied with Central and Eastern Europe as well as the US and Japan (see below).

Ultimately the establishment of co-operation is driven not solely by the globalisation process itself but by a desire for enterprises to have greater certainty and for competition authorities to be better informed about each others' policies and how they will affect enterprise operations. These benefits are compounded by speedier proceedings and more legal certainty when dealing with different competition authorities. The end process of such trends, many would suggest, is a broader competition policy agenda based on international co-operation. Bhagwati (1991, as noted in Hay, 1993) dismisses any rush towards formal co-ordination arguing that four principles should determine the extent to which international agreements are needed and where they are not, notably:

- *proportionality*: small effects should be ignored;
- *intention*: policies not designed to favour indigenous enterprise should be excluded;
- *selectivity*: policies that are not specific to a particular sector should be allowed;
- *proximity*: policies for sectors that are only indirectly integrated into the international economy should be excluded from negotiations at this level.

There is a danger that excessive interference in the policies of other states could lead to dissension and conflict and therefore undermine the potential benefits from globalisation. The progress towards harmonised policy should be driven by the extent to which there are evident spillovers between the respective domains of the competition policy bodies. Thus internationalisation of policy is justified where a government's action increases both national and international welfare due to the existence of policy spillovers.

The international dimension of EU competition policy has been shaped by a number of events:

- ratification of the European Economic Area (EEA) agreement;
- co-operation between the EU and Central and Eastern Europe (CEE) upon competition policy;
- completion of the Uruguay Round of multilateral negotiations which led to the development of the World Trade Organisation (WTO).

The EU was the first to practise a policy to deal with the implications of antitrust and mergers for trade. This has been extended to trade with the EU's trading partners in Europe and beyond including both CEE and the Mediterranean states. In this sense, competition policy has been utilised in a pro-active manner to stimulate international trade. Inevitably, the key theme of these actions is to open export markets for EU companies. This practice has not always been reciprocated by the EU's trading partners. These issues can only be overcome within multi-lateral forums such as the WTO. The last GATT round tended to be very passive upon this issue. The extent to which the WTO will deal with this issue is as yet uncertain.

The international dimension: Central and Eastern Europe

As a natural consequence of the enlargement process, the EU is seeking to extend the principles underlining its competition policy towards the potential new members from CEE. The EU negotiates on a bilateral basis with each state, though a common framework tends to apply. The Europe Agreements provide for the implementation of competition rules within three years of these agreements entering into force. To a large extent, these new rules should be based upon EU competition policy. In other cases, the agreements contain a provision to promote the harmonisation of rules where appropriate. This means that the Commission assesses the restrictions on competition between CEEs and the EU upon the criteria laid out within its competition law. There is room for flexibility within the process of approximation as only the basics need to be copied and special situations (for example, for reasons of investment in infrastructure) where the harmonisation can be tempered. To ensure this process is successful, there is technical assistance available for the creation of competition authorities as a means of promoting a more mature 'competition culture' within these states.

In practice, there has only been uneven progress in the implementation of competition policy in these states (notably with regard to state aid policy). The reasons for this situation are derived from:

- incomplete understanding of competition policy;
- the staffing of competition bodies by members of the former Communist regimes who see their job as limiting the excesses of competition rather than actively promoting it.

Such problems require (again, especially with relevance to the problems of state aid) agreement between states upon balancing the desire for flexibility within a common framework and developing an effective monitoring system to ensure compliance with any agreed framework.

A global dimension to EU competition policy

World trade is increasing rapidly yet competition policy is ill equipped to deal with the problems caused by such changes. Europe is interested in developing rules that are seen to be as pro-competitive as those associated with the development of the SEM. As European firms internationalise, so the prosperity of these companies is based upon the rules governing the operation of competition within the state they are entering or within which they have formed a strategic alliance or other form of network relationship.

Globalisation will affect EU competition policy in a number of ways:

- the global strategies of EU enterprises alter the definition of the relevant market;

- competition from imports increases internal competition (a fact reflected within the EU merger regulation);
- EU competition is affected by external factors.

The results of such problems are jurisdictional complexities and trans-national spillovers in terms of respective policy domains. Both of these suggest there has to be some sort of multilateral deal to increase the efficiency of the functioning of global markets. Such actions will inevitably improve the credibility of the functioning of the global trading system.

Europe is increasingly collaborating with the other major players within the global economy (notably Japan and the US) to cement a set of rules for mutual advantage. The EU does have a limited co-operation agreement notably with the US. This co-operation includes the following:

- exchange of information on general issues related to the implementation of competition rules;
- co-operation and co-ordination of the actions of both parties' competition authorities;
- a 'traditional comity' procedure by which each party takes into account the interests of the other party;
- a 'positive comity procedure' (see below).

Within the context of the agreement, the number of mutual notifications between the two regimes has grown markedly throughout the 1990s (see Table 6.1). Table 6.1 highlights that the majority of notifications are based upon inter-state merger activity.

Importantly no part of the agreement can be applied in a manner that is incompatible with legislation in either the EU or the US. The agreement was subject to a challenge from the European Court of Justice who deemed the proper domain for this action was the Council of Ministers. However the agreement has gone through in its original form and was extended in 1998 when positive comity was strengthened. There have been a number of attempts to conclude a similar deal with Japan but this has met with apparent apathy from Tokyo.

Such co-operation between states is born of the oft-mentioned forces of globalisation. The aim is to establish a pluralistic agreement between industrialised states with similar competition rules/cultures. In short, these agreements would consist of a common set of rules and mechanisms for dispute settlement. The European Commission is pushing for an international body within the framework of the WTO to act as a forum for such action. Both UNCTAD and the OECD have made efforts to develop closer co-operation

Table 6.1   EU/US competition policy notifications

	EC notifications to the US	US notifications to the EC	Merger notifications
1991	5	12	3 (EC)+ 9 (US)
1992	26	40	11 (EC)+ 31 (US)
1993	44	40	20 (EC)+ 20 (US)
1994	29	35	18 (EC)+ 20 (US)
1995	42	35	31 (EC)+ 18 (US)
1996	48	38	35 (EC)+ 27 (US)

Source: European Commission

between states. The 1986 OECD recommendation has been used as a reference point for the negotiation of several bilateral agreements but these are fairly weak with no legal basis.

The European Commission report *Competition Policy and New World Trade Order* argued that these flirtations with co-operation between leading industrialised states need to be strengthened due to:

- the conclusion of the Uruguay Round which has resulted in a progressive reduction in the role of state-imposed trade barriers. These could be replaced by other obstacles which could re-impose the division between world markets (see below);
- the increased contradiction between international markets and the scope of competition policy.

Until this report, there has been little co-operation between states because:

- states have not always agreed upon the objectives of competition policy;
- the nature of competition policy has frequently precluded co-operation.

The existing bilateral agreements between states seek to iron out inconsistencies which have established mechanisms for the exchange of information as well as consultation on issues of common concern. The Quadrilateral Group (see below) argues for the extension of these agreements but ultimately perceives that they will be unsatisfactory as multilateral fora need to emerge. To develop a multilateral framework, the following four key elements should be in place:

- the exchange of information between competition agencies;
- a 'positive comity instrument', where one competition body can ask another to investigate and act, if necessary, against certain practices that are against its interests yet outside its jurisdiction;
- a set of substantive rules that seek to counteract actions that have anti-competitive effects;
- a dispute settlement system containing safeguards to ensure strict compliance.

In response to this report the European Commission has called for a stronger international framework for competition policy. The vision is for the WTO to adopt common proposals around which all states involved in trade negotiations would establish their own rules. In addition, there would be a forum for information exchange to avoid legal overlap on cross-border problems. If a state fails to establish the necessary competition rules, WTO rules could be used where there is a dispute between states. Many European firms encountered such difficulties in penetrating emerging economies, notably in Asia. This is also a problem experienced within some more developed states such as Switzerland. Many Asian states are resisting attempts to introduce harmonisation in terms of competition policy due in no small part to the immaturity of their industrial systems.

Giving the WTO a more active role in the development of a multilateral agreement on rules to govern global competition has proved controversial. Not only is it unlikely that, on a multilateral basis, states would be able to agree on much but this is compounded by the fact nearly half the WTO's members have no competition policy to speak of. In addition, some states (notably the US and some EU countries) feel that the WTO has a general lack of expertise and resources to deal effectively with the issues concerned. Thus over the short term, the WTO is likely to play a minimal role with the international aspects of competition being covered by a web of bilateral deals (see below).

The EU has more recently co-ordinated its ambitions for a reform of competition policy on a global basis by supporting, with Japan, Canada and the US, the development of a study group upon this issue. This 'Quadrilateral Group' has attempted to put the issue of reform upon the agenda though this is likely to be frustrated for the foreseeable future. In many cases, as the following section highlights, the issue is one of consistency between trade and competition policies.

In the absence of a global agreement, the EU has gone about developing a series of bilateral agreements in a number of areas of common interest, notably with the US in the area of aerospace subsidies (see Chapter 5). The bilateral relationship with the US extends to developing a warning system whereby each partner informs each other when it is dealing with cases that may affect the others' interests, co-operation and co-ordination in enforcement activities and provision on comity (see Table 6.1). The need for such co-operation has been reinforced by the experience of the Boeing/McDonnell–Douglas case (see Case Study 6.2). The co-operation between the authorities is growing as the number of transatlantic mergers (either actual or proposed) across a number of industries such as telecommunications and pharmaceuticals grows.

CASE STUDY 6.2 THE INTERNATIONALISATION OF EU COMPETITION POLICY: THE BOEING/MCDONNELL–DOUGLAS CASE

The Boeing/McDonnell–Douglas case provides a notable example of the growing problem of consistency between different competition policy regimes. It also underlines for many the inadequacies of existing co-operation agreements for managing interdependencies between different areas where the market under examination is essentially global in nature. In early 1997, Boeing proposed a $14 billion merger with its US-based rival in the Aerospace industry, McDonnell–Douglas to create the world's biggest aerospace enterprise. The merger would give it over 65 per cent of the market for commercial jet aircraft compared to the 32 per cent of its leading EU-based rival, Airbus. The US competition authorities quickly cleared the merger believing that rationalisation was required in the global aerospace market and that McDonnell–Douglas was no longer a viable concern in this context.

To the EU took a different position arguing that the concentration would be potentially harmful. This is especially with reference to protecting the market share and positioning of Airbus. The EU's concerns were focused upon the power of the new company over the civil aviation market, notably with regard to the exclusive deals the enterprise has with leading US carriers (such as American Airlines and Delta) to supply all their aircraft in the future (this contract was, however, awarded after an open competition in which Airbus was also a bidder). A further fear was that the linkage between civil and defence interests could further undermine the position of Airbus in the global market as well as the possibility that the subsidies given to its defence sector could overspill into its commercial activities. These would give the new enterprise, so the Commission argued, excessive power and leverage over the global market for these commercial activities. If Boeing went ahead with its merger without the approval of the Commission, then the new enterprise would have faced a fine of more than $4 billion.

To the US administration, these concerns smacked more of European protectionism than of legitimate concerns for maintaining competition within this market. With the prospect that the EU could reject the merger, the US considered retaliation including tariffs upon EU imports, limiting flights between the US and the EU and registering an official protest with the WTO. The threat of such measures brought the two to the brink of a trade war. Such brinkmanship was eventually overcome by late concessions from Boeing who terminated its twenty year sales contracts with the US airlines. The deal thus eventually received approval despite continuing French unease; though the EU does leave open the possibility of action if the commitments made by Boeing are not realised.

The actions of the EU in extending its jurisdiction to include a merger between two US companies highlights the extension of jurisdictions and how an era of mega-mergers as a response to globalisation may necessitate an emergence of rules to meet mergers with a global effect. In these circumstances, differences in policy may lead to trade wars and result in inefficiencies within the international business environment as businesses are required to meet differing rules from different regimes. This leads to complexity and time consumption in the process of regulatory clearance. This again implies a fuller role for the WTO to establish such rules and to replace the friction implied by bilateral negotiations. The Boeing/McDonnell–Douglas deal highlighted the dangers and problems of a set of inconsistent rules where each merger that is international in nature may be subject to both differences in commercial and political priorities and to the criteria upon which their actions will be assessed. Indeed the merger has led the EU to question and re-assess the bilateral aviation deal that it has with the US which sets limits on government aid to their respective manufacturers. The deal is based upon an assumption of a diversified market and not upon single national champions as the Boeing deal suggests.

THE LINKS BETWEEN TRADE AND COMPETITION POLICIES

Implicit within this chapter has been the perspective that common competition rules are a necessary co-requisite to trade liberalisation within Europe. As mentioned, the WTO does not have any competition laws although the promotion of market access is its fundamental objective. The WTO permits certain actions that inhibit fair trade. However, this definition of unfair trade differs from that followed by domestic competition laws due to its wider meaning permitting importing states to use trade policy instruments to protect local firms without the need to consider their effects upon competition on a local or international level. Such an example is the use of anti-dumping duties. Dumping is a form of competitive behaviour though it is deemed unfair on the basis that it can lead to monopolistic positions emerging. This situation is problematic for it gives no account of the market power of the dumping firm. This points out an obvious issue for domestic competition, for this is being altered by actions other than competition policy. Trade policy bases its decision upon the state of the competitors rather than the state of competition within the market which is the case for competition policy. In addition, VERs have implications for competition policy since within oligopoly settings, domestic producers are able to form agreements with exporters to lower sales in particular markets. The consequence of such activity is higher prices and less competition within these markets. These arrangements are frequently agreed to by governments. Thus there appears to be inconsistency between competition policy and its desire to increase competition as a social and economic good and the actions of trade policy that seek to limit rivalry within the same markets. Frequently there is a choice of instruments in use that, the Commission claims, it is hard to justify and have a detrimental effect upon trade. Subsidies have been a notable case with the dispute between Airbus and Boeing an evident example.

The Commission which is in charge of both of these policies is accused of being uncertain of the links between these two (Montagnon, 1990). Operating the above paradox is attractive for industry in that it aids industrial development to the extent that it is able to compete on foreign markets. Despite the honest intentions of this stance, such protection is rarely temporary. It can frequently delay the necessary adjustment of industry: a declared objective of the EU's industrial strategy (see Chapter 5). Whilst there is no intention of building a 'Fortress Europe', these effects could emerge almost incidentally for they limit external competition and lead to the development of cartels within the EU.

The solution to such problems is that the two policies, trade and competition, need to be more closely co-ordinated. Montagnon (1990) argues there needs to be more effective ways of co-ordinating these diverse aspects of policy. One solution is to develop a commission that assesses this overlap and offers recommendations to policy measures based upon its results. There is no formal means via which DG IV, the Competition Directorate, can get its opinions known within the formation of trade policy. There is an evident need to sustain competition and it is suggested that the EU splits issues on trade policy to represent the interests of competition within Europe.

On an international level, the conclusions of the Uruguay Round noted three major problems in developing a framework of multilateral rules for the removal of the inconsistency between trade and competition policies.

- Anti-competitive private practice can impede effective market access as well as the competitive process: a locally dominant firm by abusing its position and working to exclude competitors limits the supply of goods into the market and may eventually result in a series of international cartels which divide up the world market.
- Trade measures can impede the competitive process as well as block effective market access.
- Various regulations can frustrate both market access and the competitive process (for example, standards).

The OECD has come to recognise the mutually reinforcing nature of trade and competition policies. These problems are only slowly being removed at the international level. Successive rounds of trade liberalisation have limited the scope for governmental measures to distort international competition. There is a fear that governments may be replaced by private sector restrictions on market entry. Competition policy is a possible remedy to this problem and OECD states have undertaken to:

- improve co-operation between national competition authorities;
- increase the convergence of competition laws and policies;
- extend scope and coverage of competition laws;
- assess actual enforcement of competition laws;
- examine cases from both a competition and trade policy perspective.

Despite such progress, uniformity to alleviate these problems cannot easily be overcome and substantial progress is still required. What may happen is that the emergence of trading blocs elsewhere in the global economy may be a powerful factor in resolving these issues as the process may become simpler. The development of regional trading blocs could become a powerful force to reduce the uncertainty of global competition.

CONCLUSION

Competition policy is integral to the internationalisation of the European economy. It defines the rules of entry and play within the game of competition. Clearly competition policy is both reactive and proactive to the integration process but as internationalisation proceeds, the former is becoming more evident. As the internationalisation process continues, there is an evolving process to reorientate national rules initially based on a European norm. Over time, pressure for a further reorientation at the international level is developing. To offer a prognosis regarding the end point of the process is an exercise in conjecture. Over the short term, a likely, indeed necessary, measure, is to offer greater powers to multilateral bodies to remove inconsistencies within the world trading system. Such measures do not seem imminent on a multilateral basis but are becoming ever more common on a bilateral level.

◣ KEY POINTS

- **Competition policy seeks to maintain the intensity of competition in order to sustain the objectives of the EU.**

- **Competition policy has extensive powers to regulate the activities of enterprises to the extent that these activities contravene Treaty objectives.**

- **Policy is reacting to the process of integration via a gradual extension of policy scope and of new powers.**

- **Globalisation also requires a re-examination of the EU's competition policy.**

SUGGESTED FURTHER READING

Commission of the European Communities (1993) *XXIIIrd Report on Competition Policy 1993*, Brussels, 1994.

Fishwick, F. (1993) *Making Sense of Competition Policy*, The Cranfield Management Series, Kogan Page.

Hay, D. (1993) 'Competition Policy: the Assessment', *Oxford Review of Economic Policy*, Vol. 9, No. 2, 1–27.

Kuhn, K., Seabright, P. and Smith, A. (1992) *Competition Policy Research: Where Do We Stand?*, CEPR Occasional Paper.

Montagnon, P. (ed.) (1990) *European Competition Policy*, Pinter.

Nicolaides, P. and van der Klught, A. (1994) *The Competition Policy of the European Community*, European Institute of Public Administration.

Porter, M. (1990) *The Competitive Advantage of Nations*, Free Press.

Riley, A. (1997) 'The European Cartel Office: a Guardian without Weapons', *European Competition Law Review*, Vol. 17, No. 1, 3–16.

7

REGIONAL POLICY: PROMOTING EVEN DEVELOPMENT FOR EUROPEAN BUSINESS

The goal of social and economic cohesion, European Union jargon for ensuring that wide disparities in income do not impede the process of European integration, has become an increasingly important driver behind many aspects of EU policy as integration deepens and changes the geography of Europe. EU regional policy, as in other areas, is designed to improve the environment in which businesses in problematic regions operate. Business location decisions arise from a complex mixture of factors, including market potential, the general macro-economic context, the local labour market (particularly the availability of appropriate skills) proximity to suppliers and to the market, the quantity and quality of infrastructure, the type of activity involved and a miscellany of social, cultural and quality of life factors.

Many of the policies outlined in other chapters have, often inadvertently, had an impact on the above factors. This chapter discusses explicit EU initiatives intended to redress regional imbalances within Europe and to create a platform for more even development throughout Europe. Accordingly, the first section examines the nature and extent of the EU's regional problem. It is then followed by a discussion of the rationale behind Europe's regional policy. The chapter then traces the evolution of the EU's regional policy, including the current debate of the reform needed to accommodate enlargement to the east. Social and economic cohesion is not the sole preserve of regional policy and the Structural Funds: other EU policies also have an impact on regional development and the concerns of business. The chapter therefore concludes with consideration of two examples of potentially positive regional benefits for enterprise from two related policies – TENs and enterprise policy.

THE NATURE OF EUROPE'S REGIONAL PROBLEM

The nature and extent of the EU's regional problem is manifold, covering a variety of types of region, which face the following problems:

- Border regions encounter problems because infrastructure and general development plans tend to take place within the framework of national boundaries and neglect the economic synergies which would occur in the absence of borders. In addition to general regional development policy, the abolition of internal border checks as a result of the SEM and the development of trans-European networks (TENs) should help overcome some of the problems besetting these regions.
- Declining industrial regions have previously experienced prosperity based on heavy industries such as steel and coal mining but have subsequently declined. Such regions exist in many member states, including Belgium, Spain, France, Italy and the United Kingdom and are the subject of EU action under Objective 2 of the Structural Funds (see Box 7.2).
- Rural problem regions experience low incomes and are frequently subject to depopulation as the unemployed and low paid move to cities and regions with better economic prospects. Objectives 5a and 5b are designed to assist such regions (see Box 7.2).
- Island regions encounter particular problems because of their geography, a factor which, at the prompting of Greece, was recognised in the Amsterdam Treaty.
- Lagging regions have always tended to be below the level of development of other regions and exist in Greece, Spain, Portugal and, increasingly to a lesser extent, in Ireland. Such regions experience a number of problems, especially relating to rural development, border problems and peripherality. Objective 1 of the Structural Funds covers lagging regions (see Box 7.2).
- Peripheral regions are located at the edge of an economic area and are the casualties of the core-periphery model of development which appears to predominate within the European Union, both at a national and a supra-national level. Many of the more prosperous regions within countries lie in the centre or around the capital city. At EU level, the prosperous core sweeps from south eastern England through Benelux, France and Germany into northern Italy with the most disadvantaged regions away from the core, particularly, but not only, in the Mediterranean region.

The extent of regional problems is usually measured in terms of GDP per head and levels of unemployment. Table 7.1 sets out GDP per capita for the EU (12). The accession of Sweden, Austria and Finland did not add to the EU's regional problems in any significant way. The figures indicate some reductions in disparities between member states, especially as a result of substantial improvements in the relative position of Ireland, which has seen annual average growth rates of almost 5 per cent during the 1990s compared to an average of less than 2 per cent in other member states. This strong growth has resulted in a growth in average Irish GDP per capita from 61 per cent of the EU average in 1986 to 97 per cent in 1996. Significant relative improvements have also occurred in Portugal but not to the same extent as in Ireland.

Aggregate figures however underestimate the disparities within member states as shown by Table 7.2 and Figure 7.1. In five member states, GDP per capita in the richest region is over twice that in the poorest region. For example, as a result of reunification, Hamburg, the richest region, is 3.5 times better off in terms of GDP per capita than Germany's poorest region. In total, forty-six (almost one-quarter) of EU regions register GDP per capita below the EU average. These regions are located in eight member states, including all thirteen regions in Greece, eight in Spain, seven in Germany, six out of seven of Portugal's regions, five in Italy, the four overseas French departments, two in the United Kingdom and one in Austria. Nine regions are 1.5 times or more the EU average or above and four of these are located in Germany. Only four regions, two in Greece, the French overseas departments and the Azores, are half the EU average or below. Neither Portugal nor Greece have a region at the level of the EU average but in recent years, the Balearics in Spain have moved up to the EU average.

Table 7.1 GDP per capita (EU (15) = 100), at current prices and in PPS

	1960[1]	1973[1]	1986	1996
Belgium	98.0	104.1	102.8	112.1
Denmark	116.5	111.5	112.1	119.3
Germany[2]	123.2	115.8	116.1	108.3
Greece	34.9	51.4	59.2	67.5
Spain	59.0	76.7	69.8	78.7
France	106.2	111.6	109.8	103.9
Ireland	59.9	58.1	60.8	96.5
Italy	86.9	93.7	100.4	102.7
Luxembourg	153.3	139.4	137.3	168.5
Netherlands	115.5	110.2	101.8	106.8
Portugal	37.9	54.6	55.1	70.5
UK	123.8	104.7	98.6	99.8
Austria	n.a.[3]	n.a.	103.2	112.3
Finland	n.a.	n.a.	99.7	96.9
Sweden	n.a.	n.a.	111.5	101.2
US		154.2	146.3	148.2
Japan	54.5	93.6	105.8	120.7

Source: Eurostat and European Commission, *Sixth Periodic Report on the Regions*

Notes:
[1] 1960 and 1973 relate to EU(12) = 100; [2] in 1996, Germany excluding the new länder = 118.5; [3] n.a. = not available

Table 7.2 GDP per capita by region (EU (15) = 100) (highs and lows within member states)

	Low	High
Belgium	80.7	173.1
Denmark	119.3	119.3
Germany	55.1	192.5
Greece	43.8	76.8
Spain	54.6	100.6
France	78.3	159.9
Ireland	96.5	96.5
Italy	59.2	132.5
Luxembourg	168.5	168.5
Netherlands	74.9	134
Austria	71.5	166.6
Portugal	50.0	88.5
Finland	74.1	128.9
Sweden	92.4	123.1
United Kingdom	73.1	140.4

Source: European Commission, *Sixth Periodic Report on the Regions*

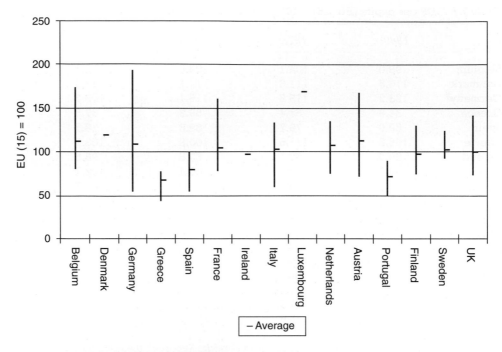

Figure 7.1 GDP per capita by region (highs and lows within member states)
Source: European Commission, Sixth Periodic Report on the Regions

Similar patterns are also apparent from unemployment figures (see Table 13.1). In 1998, unemployment ranged from 2.2 per cent of the labour force in Luxembourg to 19.5 per cent in Spain. However, Spanish unemployment is concentrated and exceeds 30 per cent in Andalusia and Extremadura and also disproportionately affects the young. Indeed in Asturias and Cantabria and in parts of southern Italy, unemployment for those aged below twenty-five is over 50 per cent. Within Germany, unemployment rates in the new länder are up to three to five times higher than in other German regions.

THE RATIONALE FOR REGIONAL POLICY

Regional policy attempts, among other things, to encourage business to locate and develop in regions which they would not otherwise contemplate as potential locations. At least, this is the theory: regional policy is frequently criticised for aiding companies to invest in a particular region when they were intending to do so in any case. Nevertheless, the question still remains why the European Commission and member states consider it appropriate to engage in apparently interventionist policies when the direction of most of their policies is towards making the market work more efficiently? Indeed, a purist view of market forces sees non-intervention leading eventually to a reduction of regional disparities. A large, barrier-free market with full factor mobility enables economic operators to specialise, leaving everyone better off. Alternatively, over time, the prosperous core areas become congested and expensive, losing some of their attractiveness to the benefit of less prosperous regions. There could even be positive spillover effects from rapidly growing areas in less dynamic neighbouring regions.

In practice, EU regional policy, although perhaps not that of member states, is not concerned with granting direct incentives for companies to invest in particular locations. Indeed, it would be inappropriate for the Community to discriminate in favour of or against individual regions. Rather, as Box 7.1 shows, the specific actions of EU regional policy are concerned with improving the business environment by enhancing the skills of the labour force, improving infrastructure and helping small and medium enterprises (SMEs). In other words, EU regional policy is, to a large extent, consistent with other aspects of EU policy: it is intended to help the market work more effectively.

Nevertheless, an explanation is still needed as to why regional policy is considered important. Indeed, as regional policy appears to have become less central to economic policies in a number of member states, regional and structural polices have taken on an enhanced role within the European Union to the extent that implementation of proposed reforms will involve the allocation of over one-third of the EU's budget to structural spending in contrast to the late 1970s when the equivalent figure was 5 per cent.

There are a number of reasons for efforts to reduce regional disparities, regardless of whether the implementing authority is a member state or the EU itself, including concerns of equity and fairness. The exclusion of significant groups or regions from economic prosperity is regarded as inequitable and can lead to alienation from the economic and political process with potentially damaging consequences. Regional disequilibria also signal an under-utilisation, even a waste of economic resources. Problems also accrue to disadvantaged regions: in the United Kingdom, for example, overheating in the south east of England has often caused the authorities to dampen down economic activity to control inflation. Although this may have been an appropriate policy for the more buoyant regions, it can be singularly damaging for the less prosperous regions of the country which have much less pronounced economic cycles or frequently lag behind core regions: that is, although the economy is overheating in the south east, other regions may only just be emerging from the previous economic downturn. If it is thus appropriate to try and attain more balanced growth within member states, so must it be similarly appropriate, and even more difficult, to do so within the European Union as a whole as it approaches economic and monetary union (EMU).

In addition to the above, fairly persuasive arguments for regional policy in general, there are a number of reasons which are specific to the European Union for conclusion of European-wide regional policy. First, regional policy is seen as a support to integration generally. The Treaty of Rome speaks of 'harmonious development'. There has long been a view held within the Community that excessive disparities and regional polarisation could contribute to a loss of support for the European Union if these effects are associated with the integration process. The importance of cohesion has increased with successive enlargements and with policies such as the Single European Market (SEM) and EMU, which could, without countervailing regional measures, increase regional disparities. This argument was used successfully by some of the relatively disadvantaged member states to justify major increases in Structural Fund spending in both 1988 and 1992.

Second, many EU policies affect Europe's geography and regional policy is regarded as a way of offsetting any negative effects on regions. The SEM stimulates industrial and service sector restructuring (see Chapter 3) with impacts on the geographical pattern of business location. SEM-inspired restructuring is difficult to disentangle from restructuring caused by other events and the full effect of such restructuring is only likely to be felt over a much longer time period than has elapsed already. Therefore, any precise matching of regional policy with regional disadvantage caused by the SEM is impossible. Other policies also have regional implications. For example, the Common Agricultural Policy (CAP) with its bias for historical reasons on products grown in northern Europe, can be said to favour northern farmers relative to poorer farmers in southern Europe.

Third, regional policy at EU level can help the co-ordination of member states' policies. This can help reduce wasteful competitive bidding between member states trying to attract inward investment. It can also provide a forum in which to tackle regional problems which cross borders – a role which has been taken on by Community Initiatives (CIs) in particular (see Box 7.3). This co-ordinating role can also extend to assessment of the links of social and economic cohesion with other EU policies.

Fourth, without large-scale redistribution from central EU funds, member states with the biggest regional problems are also those with the least ability to afford these measures. EU funding allows for a degree of Community solidarity, providing assistance for member states exhibiting large regional disparities, both within their own territory and from the Community norm. The reverse side of this argument is that, given these circumstances, leaving regional spending to these poorer member states will result in a relatively ineffective attack on regional disparities.

Fifth, member states can export their regional problems or benefits to other member states, a factor which will become more prominent as the European market becomes more integrated. The effects of strong growth in one region will spill over into neighbouring regions in other member states: regional policy can help more disadvantaged regions benefit from this effect by improving labour market skills, for example, so that when the opportunity for growth occurs, the region can take advantage of it. EU policy in non-structural areas can also bring about positive spillover effects: growth in one region benefiting from the SEM, for example, can spill over into neighbouring regions.

EVOLUTION OF EU REGIONAL POLICY

Apart from the Mezzogiorno in southern Italy, regional disparities did not constitute a major problem among the original members of the European Community which was reasonably homogeneous in terms of its economic structure and level of development. Nevertheless, the Treaty of Rome did contain the seeds of a regional and structural policy. The preamble committed the signatories to move towards 'ever closer union' and expressed the anxiety of the original Six 'to strengthen the unity of their economies and to ensure their harmonious development by reducing the differences existing between the various regions and the backwardness of the less favoured regions'. The Treaty also set up the European Social Fund (ESF) and the European Agricultural Guidance and Guarantee Fund (EAGGF) which were two out of the three funds making up the Structural Funds at the 1988 reform.

Circumstances began to change in the 1970s. Economic growth (hit by high real oil prices and international recession) and the 1973 enlargement (which brought the United Kingdom with its declining industrial areas into the Community) gave regional issues a much higher profile. Indeed, it was the entry of the United Kingdom which led directly to the establishment of the European Regional Development Fund (ERDF) in 1975. At this stage, the ERDF was relatively small, comprising only 4.8 per cent of the EU budget, and was allocated according to national quotas rather than to any objective European criteria relating to regional divergence.

BOX 7.1 MILESTONES IN EU REGIONAL POLICY

1958   Original structural instruments, the ESF and the EAGGF, come into existence to support the implementation of Community policies

1975   ERDF set up following the first enlargement to foster redistribution from richer to poorer regions

1986	Integrated Mediterranean Programme (IMP) set up to help the Mediterranean regions of France, Italy and Greece cope with competition from two new members – Spain and Portugal
1987	Single European Act contains economic and social cohesion as a Community priority for the first time
1988	ESF, ERDF and Guidance section of EAGGF given clear objectives and brought within the framework of the Structural Funds to improve co-ordination. Structural spending doubled
1992	Edinburgh Summit adopts second package of structural measures leading to a further doubling of Structural Funds
1993	Financial Instrument for Fishing Guidance (FIFG) added to Structural Funds
1993	Maastricht Treaty establishes Committee of Regions and the Cohesion Fund
1997	Agenda 2000 sets out the basic principles for Structural Fund reform within the context of further enlargement
1998	Detailed proposals brought forward for Structural Fund reform – beginning of struggle between net contributors and net beneficiaries

The 1981 (Greece) and 1986 (Spain and Portugal) enlargements continued the 'tradition' of introducing new members with living standards significantly below the Community average. The southern enlargements enhanced the scale of regional problems and were sufficient in themselves to justify a big expansion of regional spending. The 1986 enlargement also gave Greece, France and Italy the opportunity to use their bargaining power at the Council table to negotiate the 1985 Integrated Mediterranean Programme (IMP). Among other things, the IMP was intended to compensate existing Community regions which could lose out as a result of the accession of Spain and Portugal. This was not the first, or the last, time that member states extracted regional policy concessions in exchange for agreement in other policy areas. The IMP was more important however than as a quid pro quo for enlargement: it presaged coming reforms of regional policy itself through its rejection of a piecemeal project approach in favour of medium term programming and the co-ordinated use of instruments, which were key features of the 1988 Structural Fund reforms.

The Iberian enlargement also coincided with a big push towards further integration in the form of the Single European Market (SEM). Although expected to bring large gains in aggregate terms, the SEM would not necessarily benefit all and it was feared that weaker regions, particularly those on the periphery, might be harmed by it. Increases in regional spending were regarded as necessary to offset potential negative impacts of the SEM. The Single European Act (SEA), which was introduced to facilitate the introduction of the SEM, strengthened the Community's legal base for policies with a strong regional dimension by the inclusion of Title V (Articles 130a–130e) on social and economic cohesion. Although not explicitly defined, measures to achieve social and economic cohesion are intended to ensure EU progress is not threatened by economic and social tensions caused by unacceptable disparities of wealth. Indeed, Article 130a explicitly states that 'in particular the Community shall aim at reducing disparities between the various regions and the backwardness of the least-favoured regions'. Article 130c gave the ERDF the explicit treaty base, which it had previously been lacking, and Article 130d required the Commission to submit proposals within one year for reform and rationalisation of existing Community financial instruments so they could contribute more effectively to the objectives of social and economic cohesion.

Accordingly in 1988, the most radical reform of regional policy to date took place. In addition to a doubling of the funds available for structural reform to ECU 60 billion, the three Community funding mechanisms with an impact on social and economic cohesion – the ERDF, the ESF and the Guidance Section of the EAGGF – were brought together under the umbrella of what became known as the 'Structural Funds' in an attempt to co-ordinate their activities in relation to explicit Community objectives. A fourth instrument, the Financial Instrument for Fisheries Guidance (FIFG), has been incorporated into the Structural Funds since 1993. The reforms themselves were organised around the following four principles which remain relevant:

- *Concentration*: Structural Fund activities were required to contribute to the attainment of a set of key objectives (see Table 7.2). The objectives were subsequently amended to take account of changing conditions. Objective 6 (development of regions with extremely low population densities), for example, was added as a result of the 1995 enlargement. The original Objectives 3 and 4 on youth and long term unemployment were amalgamated to make a new Objective 3 in 1992 when a new Objective 4 on helping workers adjust to industrial change and new production techniques and organisation was introduced. The introduction of priority objectives enabled Structural Fund spending to be determined according to goals set at Community level rather than by member states, each following their own different priorities.
- *Programming*: the Structural Fund objectives are used to develop a programmatic approach to regional spending in which the Commission and member states together draw up plans for a period of three or six years. This allows for longer term planning (spending was previously committed annually) and for greater coherence among projects. In addition, the Commission has developed a number of Community Initiatives (CIs) which are designed to deal with common problems which have a Community dimension (see Box 7.3).
- *Partnership*: this involves close co-operation between the Commission and authorities within member states at national, regional and local level through the planning to the implementation stage.
- *Additionality*: Community assistance is intended to complement the activities of member states rather than replace them.

BOX 7.2 1994–99 STRUCTURAL FUND OBJECTIVES AND THEIR ROLE IN BUSINESS DEVELOPMENT

Objective 1: economic adjustment of regions lagging behind

As Figure 7.2 shows, Objective 1 funding accounted for the lion's share of Structural Fund spending during 1994–9 and was directed predominantly towards Spain, Portugal, Ireland, Greece, eastern Germany and the Mezzogiorno region of Italy. About 25 per cent of the EU population lived in areas eligible for Objective 1 spending (that is, areas in which GDP per capita is less than 75 per cent of the EU average). Objective 1 funding was spent on:

- direct investment to create jobs;
- development of infrastructure (including trans-European networks) and for environmental protection;
- services to small firms (advice, networking, etc.) to maximise local and regional development potential;

- investment in health and education infrastructure;
- vocational training;
- rural development measures (for example, tourism, adaptation of rural structures, rural heritage).

Objective 2: conversion of declining industrial areas

Objective 2 spending has been directed towards the United Kingdom, France, Germany and Spain and has accounted for slightly over 10 per cent of Structural Fund spending and affects about 16 per cent of the EU's population. Objective 2 spending includes:

- investment in new productive activities;
- investment in infrastructure, especially for the restoration of industrial sites and environmental protection;
- services for small firms – vocational training, research and development, employment aids.

Objective 3: combating long term employment and the integration of young people and those threatened with exclusion into the labour market

- temporary employment aids for the young and long term unemployed;
- improved training and employment structures;
- vocational training and guidance;
- equality of opportunities for men and women in the workplace.

Objective 4: the adaptation of workers to changes in industry and systems of production through measures to prevent unemployment

The development of new skills via:

- anticipating new labour market trends and the related skills requirements;
- vocational training and retraining, including assistance for adaptation of training systems.

Objective 5a: adapting agricultural and fishery sectors in line with CAP reform

- support for agricultural incomes;
- investment to reduce production costs, improve living and working conditions and promote economic diversification.

Objective 5b: economic diversification of rural areas

The promotion of alternative activities in rural areas by:

- investment in infrastructure to create jobs outside agriculture (for example, in tourism and small firms) and to protect the environment;
- providing services for small firms.

Objective 6: development of regions with extremely low population density (about 0.4 per cent of the EU population)

To encourage people to stay in remote areas by:

- development of new activities likely to broaden employment opportunities;
- aid to help these areas adapt to changes in agriculture, mostly forestry;
- development of human resources through training.

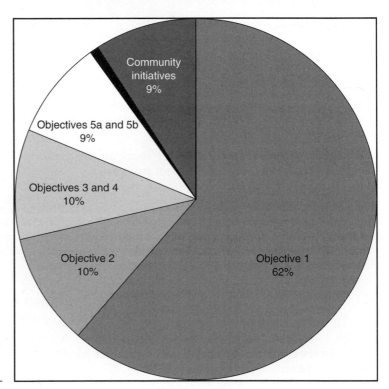

Figure 7.2 1994–99 Structural Fund spending by objective
Note: Objective 6 was less than 1%

The process of reform has continued. The 1992 Edinburgh Summit agreed to a further substantial increase in Structural Fund resources to ECU 141.5 billion (at 1992 prices) for the period 1994–9, more than doubling existing funding. Other changes agreed at Edinburgh refined the 1988 reforms, such as fine tuning of the priority objectives, rather than representing a radical new departure.

The Maastricht Treaty, which was agreed in 1991 and came into force in 1993, underlined the importance of social and economic cohesion. The goal of economic and social cohesion was introduced into Article 2 and the strengthening of social and economic cohesion was introduced into Article 3 for the first time as a key element of Community activity. The main concrete developments within the Maastricht Treaty affecting the regions were the creation of the following forms of assistance:

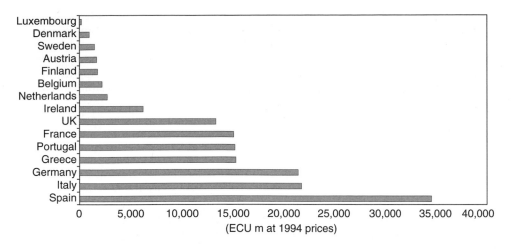

Figure 7.3 1994–99 Structural Fund spending by member state (ECUm at 1994 prices)

BOX 7.3 1994–99 COMMUNITY INITIATIVES

The following 13 Community Initiatives were approved for 1994–9

Name of initiative	Amount (ECU million)	Objective
Interreg II	3,447.6	Cross-border co-operation; development of energy networks; international co-operation on water management, etc.
Leader II	1,722.6	Local development in rural areas
Regis II	600.0	Support for the most remote regions
Employment	1,784.0	Vocational integration of women, young people, the disabled and the excluded
Adapt and Adapt-BIS	1,623	Updating for the labour force
Rechar II	448.8	Conversion of coal mining areas
Resider II	564.2	Conversion of steel areas
Retex	562.8	Diversification within areas dependent on the textile industry
Konver	744.3	Diversification of areas dependent on military activities
SMEs	1,054	Improved international competitiveness of SMEs
Urban	800.1	Restoration of crisis-hit urban areas
Pesca	290.3	Restructuring of the fisheries industry
Peace	300.0	Support for peace and reconciliation in Northern Ireland and the border counties of the Irish Republic

Source: European Commission

- *The Committee of the Regions (CoR)*: the CoR is an advisory body made up of representatives of regional and local bodies which is consulted by the Commission and the Council on issues relating to education and youth, culture, public health, TENs, economic and social cohesion and in other cases where it is considered appropriate. The creation of the CoR was generally welcomed as representing an opportunity for greater participation in the decision making processes of sub-national entities. However, its role as yet is relatively limited.
- *The Cohesion Fund*: the Cohesion Fund was set up in part as the price for achieving ratification of the Maastricht Treaty by the cohesion countries, namely Spain, Portugal, Greece and Ireland. The Cohesion Fund was established to ease the preparations of the Union's poorer countries to meet the EMU convergence criteria and set aside ECU 15.5 billion for spending on transport infrastructure and the environment during 1994–9 for countries with GDP of less than 90 per cent of the EU average.

The Amsterdam Treaty had relatively little to say about social and economic cohesion, apart from the introduction of a declaration on the specific problems of island regions which opens the possibility of the introduction of integrated programmes for these regions. However, major reforms to the Structural Funds are on the agenda, necessitated by the conclusion of new budgetary arrangements for the Union for 2000 to 2006 and the prospect of the accession of a number of Central and Eastern European countries during this period.

REGIONAL POLICY AND THE STRUCTURAL FUNDS AFTER 1999

Following the publication of Agenda 2000 in July 1997 which, among other things, set out the general principles of Structural Fund reform for the period 2000 to 2006, the European Commission published further details of the proposed reform in March 1998. In addition to the usual aim of improving operational efficiency and effectiveness, a number of other factors are driving this reform. The Amsterdam Treaty introduced an employment chapter into the treaties for the first time: Structural Fund activities and the focus of the ESF in particular are being directed towards meeting the objectives of this chapter. EMU was launched on 1 January 1999, bringing with it potentially de-stabilising economic changes for some regions. Increasing internationalisation has the potential to damage some regions. Most dramatic of all, the enlargement of the European Union to incorporate several Central and Eastern European (CEE) states will make the current Structural Funds unworkable without significant changes to the ways in which they operate. None of the applicant countries has a GDP per capita greater than any current EU member. Indeed, the average GDP per head in the applicant countries is less than half that of Portugal and Greece at 32 per cent of the EU average. As such, the extension of existing policies to potential new members would require the transfer of the equivalent of over 10 per cent of CEE GDP to them (the equivalent for Greece has been 3 per cent). Not only is this beyond the willingness and capacity of existing member states, it exceeds the capability of the CEE countries to absorb such funding.

Proposed reform retains and, in some cases, builds upon the 1988 principles of concentration, programming, additionality and partnership and adds new elements of simplification and monitoring. The key features of the proposed reform are as follows:

- *Greater concentration*: concentration is sought at the following levels:
  - concentration on three policy objectives and three Community initiatives (see Box 7.4);

- concentration on areas of priority assistance directed towards an integrated approach to development aimed at regional, national and Community priorities;
- geographical concentration so that 35 to 40 per cent of the Community's population will be eligible for assistance in 2006 rather than 51 per cent as in 1998.

● *Partnership, decentralisation and simplification*: the draft reform proposals announce the Commission's intentions to broaden and deepen its partnership with interested parties throughout the policy process, from preparation of the original programme through to its implementation, monitoring and evaluation. At present, genuine partnership relates to limited stages of the process. In addition, although there has been significant progress in involving regional authorities, the participation of local authorities, environmental bodies and bodies at local level engaged in Structural Fund activities such as the social partners, local voluntary organisations and non-governmental bodies remains patchy. The Commission therefore intends to bring forward proposals for these organisations to be involved in implementation of the Structural Funds at all levels and make explicit the role which various groups should play at different stages. In order not to slow down the process, the operation of partnership will be adjusted, where appropriate, in line with the extent of financial involvement of the partners. In broad terms, however, it is envisaged that the Commission's role will be essentially strategic, concentrating on the overall goals and priorities of each programme whereas member states will take on the roles of monitoring, management, evaluation and control. This clearer division of responsibilities should make for more effective management and also serves the goals of subsidiarity. One of the criticisms frequently levelled at EU regional policy is that it is too removed from the member states and regions themselves who know better than anyone else the nature of their problems.

● *Monitoring and transparency*: greater clarification of roles and the decentralisation of policy make it both easier and more essential to improve monitoring of Structural Fund programmes and their transparency. A Monitoring Committee will continue to oversee implementation of programmes but in a more involved manner. In addition, greater detail in implementation reports and closer involvement of the Commission with the Monitoring Committee will enable the Commission to execute its responsibility for budget transparency. This will also facilitate the development of more efficient procedures for the disbursement of funding.

● *More developed financial engineering*: Structural Fund spending has traditionally taken the form of direct grants. In order to achieve greater leverage from structural assistance and in response to criticism from the Court of Auditors, greater use of financial instruments apart from grants is anticipated by the Commission. This could take the form of reimbursable aid, preferential interest rates, loan guarantees or equity stakes. Such an initiative will allow closer co-operation with the work of the European Investment Bank and the European Investment Fund, both of which are heavily involved in projects with a strong regional dimension. In addition, such financing will focus greater attention on the returns from regional projects and help the promotion of public private partnerships (see Chapter 9) for the implementation of major infrastructure projects.

BOX 7.4 PROPOSED NEW STRUCTURAL FUND OBJECTIVES

Proposals emanating from Agenda 2000 aim to replace the present six Structural Fund objectives with three new objectives. Two of the three new objectives are to be based on regions and the third upon human resources.

Objective 1: regions whose development is lagging behind

Objective 1 remains the same but will also include those remote regions of the Community which are covered by the current Objective 6. Eligible regions must comply with the 75 per cent rule (see below). Lagging regions continue to suffer from lack of economic potential, inadequate infrastructure, low employment and skills shortages. About two-thirds of total Structural Fund spending will be directed towards these issues.

Eligibility of regions for Objective 1 funding will be determined by strict applicability of the criterion that GDP per capita should be 75 per cent or less of the EU average. In addition, only regions qualifying for Objective 1 funding will, in future, be eligible for state aid under Article 92 (3) of the Treaty of Rome ('that is, aid to promote the economic development of areas where the standard of living is abnormally low or where there is serious underemployment'). Assistance to current Objective 1 regions no longer qualifying for funds will be gradually phased out with the result that the regions eligible for Objective 1 funding will qualify for no more than 20 per cent of the EU population compared to 25 per cent at present.

Objective 2: areas undergoing economic and social conversion

Objective 2 funding will apply in industrial, rural, urban and fisheries dependent regions which face major restructuring needs, including the restructuring of services. Eligibility for funding will depend on close collaboration between the Commission and member states. The Commission proposes that eligible regions should account for no more than 18 per cent of the EU's population and that compared to present population eligibility under Objectives 2 and 5b, no member state should see a reduction of more than one-third in its population eligible for funding.

Objective 3: development of human resources

Objective 3 will support the adaptation and modernisation of policies relating to education, training and employment in regions not covered by Objectives 1 and 2. The starting point will be the Employment Chapter introduced into the Amsterdam Treaty and the new procedures for drawing up national employment action plans (see Chapter 13).

Community initiatives

The present thirteen Community Initiatives (CIs) are to be reduced to three to cover trans-national, cross-border and inter-regional co-operation in regional, economic and rural development – that is, measures with a clear Community interest. Each CI will be financed by only one of the three Structural Funds: the ERDF for cross-border, transnational and interregional co-operation; the Guidance section of the ERDF for rural development and the ESF for combating social exclusion. In total, the CIs will be allocated 5 per cent of Structural Fund resources.

Unlike previous reforms, however, the proposals for 2000 to 2006 do not suggest major increases in spending. The Commission has stated that spending will remain at 1999 levels in relative terms throughout the period, that is, 0.46 per cent of GDP or ECU 275 billion at constant 1997 prices. Of this total ECU 210 billion is to be allocated to current member states to fund the above proposals. Of the remaining ECU 65 billion, ECU 20 billion will be allocated to the Cohesion Fund and ECU 45 billion to new members, which includes pre-accession aid.

By the summer of 1998, discussions over the proposals for Structural Fund reform had only reached a preliminary stage. However, it is clear that, even if the broad principles of the reforms are accepted by member states, there is likely to be extensive debate around the details of the proposals, especially the allocation of funding. Concentration of funding means that regions which are currently eligible and in receipt of EU Structural Funding will cease to be so. It is unlikely that member states will give up such funding without a struggle. Indeed it is possible, that present beneficiaries of Structural Fund spending will try to make their support for enlargement conditional on continuation of such support. Similar tactics have been used in the past as the cost for agreement to other key policies such as the SEM and ratification of the Maastricht Treaty. The position this time is complicated by the fact that net contributors to the EU's Budget, particularly but not only Germany, wish to restrain EU spending and certainly do not wish to see it increase without a fairer degree of burden sharing among member states. This is compounded by the disciplines of EMU which places extra pressure on spending restraints.

LINKS BETWEEN SOCIAL AND ECONOMIC COHESION AND OTHER EU POLICIES

Although Structural Fund spending is central to the EU's attempts to reduce regional disparities and to promote the goal of social and economic cohesion and, as discussed above, some policies may not have a positive effect in this respect, other policies complement and support the Structural Funds in their goals. The following two sections use the examples of enterprise policy and TENs to demonstrate the direct link between these policies and the Structural Funds (that is, the use of Structural Funds themselves to fund SME initiatives and TENs projects) and how the objectives of the two policies coincide.

Regions and small and medium-sized enterprises

Encouraging the development of SMEs is pivotal to the EU's strategy for renewing growth, competitiveness and employment as well as to regional development. Chapter 8 highlights many of the generic problems that SMEs face in realising their potential. SMEs in many of the 'less favoured regions' are finding that these generic problems are compounded by the weak economic position and strong presence of agricultural activities (and correspondingly lower incomes) within their indigenous region. In some areas, (such as Denmark and Ireland) the major problems faced are national in nature, due largely to the relatively large percentage of national output derived from agrarian activities, rather than from the simple fact that they are located in a 'less favoured region'.

In general, SMEs in 'less favoured regions' find that their performance is retarded by the following characteristics.

- *Inadequate infrastructure*: most regions find that their remoteness from major markets was compounded by a lack of supporting communication and energy infrastructure (see Chapter 9).
- *Poor access to external information*: SMEs, especially within southern Europe are finding that an inability to obtain advice on funding, a lack of contact with R&D institutions/ service firms and relatively poor access to EU-wide SME support initiatives was also impeding success. These problems are inevitably not assisted by remoteness from major urban centres or by a poor quality local workforce.
- *Restricted local industrial environment*: within 'less favoured regions', there tends to be an absence of both a culture of entrepreneurship and a well ingrained work ethic.

- *Absence of qualified workers*: 'less favoured regions' tend to be unable to attract skilled workers, a problem compounded by comparatively lower education and training levels.

Despite the presence of these specific disadvantages in 'less favoured regions', SMEs may be able to benefit from a number of advantages such as low workforce turnover rates, lower payroll and premises costs, more space for expansion and a more attractive living environment for staff.

Policies to encourage SME development in less favoured regions evidently need to address the weaknesses already identified. Consequently much effort is focused upon overcoming 'environmental' impediments such as inadequate infrastructure and the problems derived from the characteristics of the local industrial climate. These broad measures are complemented by more specific SME focused measures (see below) which offer financial assistance and thereby increase the level of 'soft investments' (that is, not direct assistance but finance for training, networking etc). This strategy very much reflects a 'localisation' approach to regional development; seeking endogenous solutions to regional problems.

Support from the EU for SMEs in 'less favoured regions' come from a number of sources. The ERDF devotes on average 10 per cent of its resources to measures to stimulate the economic environment of SMEs. ERDF assistance is aimed at encouraging the demand for and supply of services to support SME activity. Generally such services encourage SME exports/internationalisation, advice and information and assistance for raising finance. This is supported by the efforts of the ESF which offers assistance to SMEs in education and training. Over the period 1994–9, the ESF devoted some 14 per cent of its funds towards this objective. This was complemented by the ADAPT initiative which offers funding to enable SMEs to respond to the changing requirements of the labour market. Finally, the SME initiative targets SMEs in Objective 1 regions enabling them to adapt to the single market and generally improving their competitiveness at an international level through assistance in changing production and organisation systems, the more rational use of energy, stimulating co-operation and improving access to finance and credit.

Infrastructure, the regions and the business environment

Social and economic cohesion is one of the fundamental objectives behind the TENs programme (see Chapter 9). Article 129b of the Treaty on European Union specifically urges the Community to 'take account in particular of the need to link island, landlocked and peripheral regions with the central regions of the Community'. The Maastricht Treaty also provided for the establishment of a Cohesion Fund which had the specific role of providing Community finance to trans-European transport networks and the environment in member states which have a GNP of less than 90 per cent of the Community average as part of their EMU convergence programme.

Underpinning the link between TENs and social and economic cohesion is the assumption that the inadequate quality and quantity of infrastructure are closely connected with low levels of economic development and that the existence or otherwise of adequate physical infrastructure can be a key determinant in decisions about business location and enterprise competitiveness. Indeed, the fact that the EU's lagging regions are also those with the poorest infrastructure endowment in terms of number of telephone lines, the number of faults per line, road and rail provision, etc. would appear to give some credence to this view.

The reality can be more complex. In addition to inadequate infrastructure, there can be many other explanations for relatively poor performance such as distance from the market and shortages of skilled labour. Infrastructure improvements also act as facilitators which improve the possibility for further economic development – they do not provide the improvement in themselves. Apart from the creation of jobs during the construction phase and the much smaller number of additional jobs required for the operation of the infrastructure, improved infrastructure is a necessary but not sufficient condition for enhancing the economic performance of lagging regions. Enterprises themselves need to grasp the opportunities provided by the improvements to the business environment.

Nevertheless, EU policy makers anticipate a range of potential benefits accruing to disadvantaged regions as a result of improvements to each of the major infrastructure networks, explaining why infrastructure played a major part in ERDF spending long before the modern TENs programme was born at the end of the 1980s and why transport infrastructure, along with environmental protection, was chosen as the destination for Cohesion Fund spending. Indeed during the period 1975–88, infrastructure accounted for almost 80 per cent of all ERDF commitments, ranging from 37 per cent of all ERDF spending in Germany to over 85 per cent in Spain, Portugal, Greece, Luxembourg and Italy.

In theory, transport TENs hold out the prospect of creating better spatial balance within the European Union by linking more regions to major networks and by reducing the negative business impact of long distances through speedier access, thereby reducing the imperative to locate in central areas and increasing the attractiveness of more peripheral regions. Transport infrastructure improvements, therefore, help to neutralise the disadvantages of the distance of peripheral regions from more economically prosperous regions. Improved services, greater intermodalism and the connection of missing links increases the speed of journeys, thereby saving time and reducing costs. The development of trans-European transport networks should therefore improve inter-regional and international access to the peripheral regions of the Union through the reduction of travelling time and enhance their attractiveness as business locations. Achievement of this goal relies not only on the construction of the major networks but also on ensuring the secondary networks are effectively connected to the major networks.

The impact of telecommunications on social and economic cohesion is complex. At its most integrative, telecommunications infrastructure can facilitate spatial harmonisation within the European Union by removing physical and geographical obstacles to integration (that is, 'reduce distances') without the more adverse environmental effects of transport harmonisation. High quality telecommunications networks, which today involve fax and data transmission as well as efficient telephone systems, are an essential pre-condition for modern business. Border regions in particular may benefit from greater telecommunications liberalisation and greater integration of networks: as with other networks, telecommunications systems were developed from a national perspective resulting in the charging of short distance cross-border calls at high international rates.

BOX 7.5 EXAMPLES OF TENS-RELATED STRUCTURAL FUND SPENDING

ERDF funding has been extended to many infrastructure projects over the years. The examples given below are only a small selection of more recent projects. Several of the projects below have also received funds from the European Investment Bank

Transport
- main roads in Ireland, Northern Ireland and Italy;

- Athens–Thessaloniki rail link;
- Via Egnatia and Pathe motorways in Greece;
- Cork–Dublin–Belfast rail link

Energy

- construction of the Algeria–Morocco–Spain gas pipeline;
- introduction of more natural gas to more Spanish towns and cities;
- introduction of natural gas to Portugal and interconnection of the Spanish and Portuguese gas networks;
- the main pipeline in the project to introduce natural gas to Greece and funding of the work to build the high pressure gas supply network
- the gas connector between eastern Germany and western Poland and work on other sections in Germany and Poland as part of the Russia–Belarus–Poland–European Union gas pipeline
- electricity connector between Spain and Portugal

Telecommunications

- development of advanced telecommunications networks (ISDN) in Greece

Advanced telecommunications networks can both increase and reduce the amount of decentralisation within the European Union. Efficient communications enable organisations to maintain good links with subsidiaries and customers in more peripheral areas or outside their region. They also allow firms to maximise their gains from lower costs in peripheral regions whilst simultaneously building up effective links with more central regions. Good telecommunications can also act as a substitute for travel through the use of video-conferencing facilities.

Telecommunications advances also make possible and complement more profound changes in work and organisational patterns. Teleworking, which the Commission forecasts in its Europe 2000+ study will involve ten million EU workers by 2000, is expected to yield the greatest benefits for isolated regions. Improved telecommunications grant access to greater quantities of information and help companies in outlying regions utilise opportunities offered by the SEM. The skills base of the labour force in disadvantaged regions can be improved by access to open and distance learning.

Telecommunications advances also herald cost savings to small and medium-sized enterprises, which can have a key role to play in regional development, and change the factors influencing business location and employment patterns. Such technological advances reduce the need for physical mobility in terms of meetings etc. and reduce the requirement for employees to live within daily travelling distance to the workplace.

In the energy area, the TENs programme aims to improve cohesion by linking unconnected regions to the Community's gas and electricity networks. The extension of such networks will increase the choice of energy sources within the peripheral areas which will, in turn, through increased competition and reduced costs, improve the overall competitiveness of these regions. Connection to the Union's major supply networks will also improve the security of supply of these regions, which tend to be the most dependent on non-Union suppliers and have the most limited variety of energy sources.

CONCLUSION

Structural Fund spending has steadily increased in importance since the mid-1970s when the ERDF was established to the point where it is anticipated to account for one-third of EU spending early in the twenty-first century. Reform is under discussion. Previous reforms have resulted in massive increases in spending, but this will not happen this time given the numerous constraints on EU funding. Rather, the emphasis is on increasing the effectiveness of the Structural Funds by concentrating their efforts on fewer more focused objectives, both geographically and thematically.

From the perspective of business, Structural Fund spending is intended to reduce some of the locational disadvantages experienced by less economically buoyant regions. In this respect, through its efforts to create a more favourable environment for business (for example, through measures to improve labour market skills and infrastructure quality), the activities of the Structural Funds are entirely consistent with other EU policies such as TENs and enterprise policy. Box 7.5 gives examples of TENs projects which are part-funded by the ERDF as a result of their contribution to social and economic cohesion. In the future, if the Commission is successful in pushing through its reforms, there will be opportunities for business, as one of the social partners, to become more involved in the formulation of Structural Fund programmes and projects.

KEY POINTS

- **Regional disparities remain wide within the EU but there have been some improvements in the relative positions of Ireland, Portugal and Spain. Inclusion of the countries of Central and Eastern Europe in the Union will widen the disparities further.**
- **The intent of Structural Fund spending is to improve the business environment within targeted regions, particularly by enhancing skills, improving the quality of infrastructure and facilitating the growth of small and medium enterprises.**
- **Structural Fund spending is mutually supportive of a number of other EU policies such as TENs, enterprise policy and labour market policy and is used to offset the unintended negative regional impact of other policies.**
- **Structural Fund reform has become essential as a result of EMU and, particularly, eastern enlargement, but proposed reforms are likely to encounter strong resistance from regions and member states which will cease to be eligible for funding.**
- **Greater concentration, partnership, decentralisation, transparency and more developed financial engineering will be the guiding principles of reform.**

SUGGESTED FURTHER READING

Amin, A., and Tomaney, J. (eds) (1995) *Behind the Myth of the European Union: Prospects for Cohesion*, Routledge.

Artobolevskiy, S. (1997) *Regional Policy in Europe*, Jessica Kingsley.

Bachtler, J. and Turok, I. (1996) *The Coherence of EU Policy: Contrasting Perspective on the Structural Funds*, Jessica Kingsley.

European Commission (1994) *Europe 2000+: Co-operation for European Territorial Development.*

European Commission (1997) *Agenda 2000: For a Stronger and Wider Union.*

European Commission (1998) *Reform of the Structural Funds: Explanatory Memorandum.*

Williams, R. (1996) *European Union Spatial Policy and Planning*, Paul Chapman.

8

EUROPEAN ENTERPRISE POLICY: REALISING THE POTENTIAL OF SMALL AND MEDIUM-SIZED ENTERPRISES

The focus of enterprise policy is upon facilitating the success of small and medium sized enterprises (SMEs) in an increasingly challenging business environment. The needs and requirements of larger enterprises are more adequately reflected in a range of other policies such as those related to trade, competition and industry. In addition, SMEs face unique problems that require specific policy solutions. The need for such policies within the European business environment is underlined by the fact that over 99.8 per cent of all enterprises within the EU are classified as SMEs (see Table 8.1). Despite this, SMEs have often been neglected within the policy process.

Traditionally, policy makers have treated SMEs as young, marginal firms needing protection in the face of open competition. This attitude is changing as many policy makers increasingly recognise that SMEs are among the most dynamic enterprises in Europe and are central in sustaining the EU's competitive position. Importantly SMEs are becoming ever more significant in job generation within the European economy accounting for 66 per cent of all employment (Table 8.1). An increasingly central goal for policy makers is to push the success of European SMEs by encouraging them to exploit the trend towards the internationalisation of markets. This represents an important sea change in strategy as SMEs have traditionally focused upon local/regional markets. Such a narrow market base is inadequate if SMEs are to aid the competitiveness of the European economy.

Initially this chapter explores the core policy challenges and initial reactions from policy makers to stimulate the development of SMEs within the EU. Within this framework, the chapter will seek to analyse these policies and their success especially with regard to the ability of policy measures to encourage SMEs to exploit the internationalisation of markets. This latter concern will explore particular solutions to support this objective especially with regard to networking and the broader adoption of information and communication technologies (ICTs) within SMEs. Before conclusions are reached, an assessment of policy measures will be given.

Table 8.1 Main indicators of SMEs and LSEs

	SMEs	LSE
Number of enterprises (1,000)[1]	18,555	35
Employment (1,000)[1]	73,810	38,220
Average enterprise size (persons employed)[1]	4	1,035
Turnover per enterprise (ECU million)[1]	0.5	175
Value added per occupied person (ECU 1,000)[1]	35	55
Share of labour costs in value added (%)[1]	52	53
Labour productivity[2]	2.1	2.8
Unit labour costs[3]	2.5	1.7
Profitability[4]	0.4	0.4

Source: ENSR

Notes

[1] 1996 figures

[2] Real value added per occupied person (averge annual change in %: 1988–98)

[3] Labour costs per employee, adjusted for labour productivity (average annual change in %).

[4] Difference between value added and labour costs, adjusted for imputed wage of self-employed, as % of value added (average annual % change: 1988–98)

THE EVOLUTION OF EUROPE'S ENTERPRISE POLICY

The rising importance of SMEs within the European economy is derived from a number of factors, notably that these enterprises:

- are largely responsible for employment growth;
- predominate within the increasingly important services sector;
- tend to undertake activities that are less prone to international competition;
- employ more young people and women than larger enterprises;
- employ more part-time workers and consequently offer opportunities for job sharing and other flexible employment practices;
- are major beneficiaries of the process of downsizing in large enterprises through their involvement in outsourcing and sub-contracting activities.

SMEs have a perceived 'flexibility', especially in terms of demand, structure and volume of production, which allows them to keep ahead and abreast of rapid changes within the European economy and which has been a vital factor in promoting their growth. Larger enterprises have tended to encounter problems dealing with rapid changes within their operating environment. Additionally, it is perceived that SMEs have a number of other advantages over large scale enterprises (LSEs) namely less internal bureaucracy, a consensual management style, a generally more highly motivated workforce and better labour relations.

Whilst SMEs may offer tremendous potential, they do face specific problems. The European Commission's own figures suggest that over half of SMEs fail within five years of start up. The Commission identifies five factors to explain this relative weakness:

- the increasingly intricate legal, fiscal and administrative environment which is particularly burdensome for SMEs;
- an inability to access research programmes and exploit their results;
- relatively inadequate management and training capabilities;
- additional borrowing costs arising from the higher risk attached to lending to SMEs;
- scale impediments in accessing new markets.

These problems are compounded by more generic problems related to their relatively poor productivity (when compared to larger enterprises) as well as lower returns to scale and poorer labour/working conditions (see Table 8.1 for further comparative performance statistics).

BOX 8.1 DEFINITION OF SMALL AND MEDIUM-SIZED ENTERPRISES

Member states have traditionally employed differing definitions of what constitutes a SME. However, in order to operate a common policy for SMEs and to provide an appropriate focus for policy, a single definition of SMEs was required. The Commission has, therefore, adopted a definition (see below) which is applied to all Community programmes for better targeting of policy initiatives.

Criteria for SMEs

	Medium sized	Small	Micro-enterprise
Maximum number of employees	< 250	< 50	< 10
Maximum turnover (m ECU)	40	7	—
Maximum balance sheet (m ECU)	27	5	—

Source: European Commission

To be classified as an SME, and therefore to benefit from EU Enterprise Policy, a firm has to satisfy the employees measure and one of the financial criteria. In addition, the firm must be independent: in other words less than 25 per cent of the enterprise is owned by another enterprise or group of firms.

There were no specific policies for SMEs at the EU level until the mid-1980s, although many more generic EU policies affect the development of these enterprises to varying degrees. As integration progressed, the lack of an EU policy framework for SMEs became an increasingly glaring omission. This changed in 1989 when a separate Directorate General for SMEs (DG XXIII) was created. The role of DG XXIII was to administer a series of SME-focused measures (which formed the embryo of the EU's enterprise policy) which sought to:

- safeguard and improve the environment for business during the completion of the internal market and beyond;
- develop policies that enable SMEs to exploit the opportunities created by the internal market;
- ensure consistency between enterprise policy and other EU policies.

Traditionally, the EU as a policy making body has been regarded as potentially damaging to SMEs. In particular, the plethora of regulations emanating from Brussels are frequently criticised for imposing unnecessary extra costs upon SMEs. There is, therefore, a need for the EU to balance the promotion of free trade (which is generally good for SMEs) alongside the need for regulation which is potentially costly for these enterprises.

Enterprise policy is a wide ranging domain covering diverse areas and policy actions. The initial measures for a Community Enterprise Policy were reflected in the year for Small and Medium Sized Enterprises in 1983 and were established on the basis of Article 235. There were two initial stages in the development: first, the setting up of a SME task force in 1986; and, second, the decision to provide enterprise policy with increased resources in the wake of the Single European Act. This facilitated the creation of the aforementioned DG XXIII to provide, as suggested above, a primary focus for SME development. In order to achieve its objectives, EU policy focuses upon regenerating the institutional framework, stimulating information diffusion and reinforcing human capabilities.

The increasing importance of SMEs (and of associated policy measures) to the European economy was reflected within Title XIII of the Treaty Upon European Union which highlighted the importance, within the context of improving competitiveness, of initiatives to develop these enterprises. Article 130 provides a new and more specific legal base for Enterprise Policy and was later complemented by the 1993 White Paper *Growth, Competitiveness and Employment*. The White Paper forms the basis of many of the current efforts to support the development and commercial success of SMEs through increasing the awareness of these enterprises of the consequences of internationalisation and helping SMEs to exploit them within Europe and beyond.

Despite such objectives, SMEs are, and will remain, over the short to medium term at least, strongly affected by local factors such as the education and training systems. These are areas of the institutional framework of SMEs that are still very much determined at the national level. Consequently, a great deal of EU action is focused upon convergence of these conditions where appropriate, as a precursor for pan-European SME growth. To this end, policy has to date concentrated upon overcoming conventional impediments to internationalisation such as poor information, lack of experience, inadequate resources and restrictive government regulations.

THE EMERGING CHALLENGES FOR EUROPE'S SMES: THE INTERNATIONALISATION OF MARKETS

The exploitation of international markets is not a concern for all SMEs. On a global level, the OECD estimates that internationalised SMEs account for 25 to 35 per cent of world manufactured exports with, it is estimated, only 1 per cent of manufacturing SMEs being truly global. Another 5 to 10 per cent show an extensive degree of internationalisation whilst a further 10 to 20 per cent draw between 10 to 40 per cent of their turnover from international activity. Thus only a third of European enterprises (assuming a straight extrapolation of the figures) are likely to be affected to any great extent by the internationalisation process.

Despite this, evidence from the OECD suggests that those EU SMEs with the highest degree of internationalisation represent some of Europe's fastest growing enterprises – showing growth as much as two to three times above the average enterprise growth rate. These SMEs tend to operate in narrow niche markets which enable them to exploit their specialist skills and market positioning more effectively.

As the network economy becomes more prominent, so more firms will become exposed to global competition even though they have not formulated their own international strategy. This 'indirect' impact is felt not only through increased competition within internal markets from foreign enterprises but also as a result of their position as suppliers to enterprises with international strategies. In addition, SMEs are also affected by internationalisation as potential takeover targets for foreign enterprises who wish to establish a subsidiary in another market. These trends are underlined by the five possible strategic paths which SMEs can feasibly follow in the internationalisation process (Cafferata and Mensi, 1995):

- *indirect internationalisation*: where the SME is a sub-contractor of a larger firm which is more actively engaged in the process;
- *occasional export*: where the SME offers the same terms to foreign competitors but where exports are a low proportion of its overall turnover;
- *deliberate export orientation*: where the SME purposefully looks for markets abroad;
- *export led business development*: where the enterprise is in perpetual search of new export markets;
- *research to find competitive advantage abroad*: where those firms that are already selling abroad seek opportunities for new markets by having access to better commercial knowledge.

Evidence suggests that European SMEs are not seriously concerned with the competitive threat from the Pacific Rim or indeed the US: although the latter is feared more than the former (see Table 8.2). This reflects the core issue that, for the majority of European SMEs, internationalisation means Europe, more particularly developing a strategy in response to increasing levels of intra-EU competition.

Trends indicate that the SMEs' share of international trade is growing faster than that of larger enterprises. As suggested above, SMEs tend to export more to neighbouring countries than to the broader global trading environment, a situation which is aided by similarities in commercial culture and common trade regulations with members of the same trading group. Their ability to exploit the potential of the network economy, to develop new customer–supplier linkages and to enter new markets is dependent upon the quantity and quality of available information and the manner in which the enterprise utilises it. This is especially important given that many SMEs are based in single locations and thus face considerable spatial barriers in developing an international strategy and in establishing cross-border networking. This increases the prominence of ICTs within this group of enterprises as much as it does for larger firms (see below).

Table 8.2 Impact of internationalisation upon mean SME turnover growth and employment

Dimension of globalisation	Impact upon turnover growth	Impact upon employment growth
Exports within the EU	+*	+
Exports outside the EU	+	+
International co-operation	+*	+
International sub-contracting	+	+
International marketing efforts	+	+
Subsidiaries in other EU states	+	+

Source: ENSR Enterprise Survey

Note: * Not significant

THE IMPACT OF THE SINGLE EUROPEAN MARKET

Over the short to medium term, internationalisation is most likely to effect SMEs in the sense that their markets are becoming increasingly European in nature. Indeed, as mentioned later, this has become a primary focus of the policy debate. Successive surveys have indicated the progressive influence of the Single European Market (SEM) upon SMEs: nearly three-quarters of such enterprises have been challenged or threatened by more intense competition generated by the SEM. On the other hand, SMEs have benefited from higher levels of demand generated by relaxed market access. This under-lines that, although larger enterprises have been affected to a greater extent by market integration, SMEs have also become involved in cross-border contacts and international competition.

Encouraging SMEs to exploit the opportunities of the SEM is an important EU policy priority, as it:

- will allow new efficient operators to enter the market thus breaking the repressive hold of incumbent operators;
- increases the number and variety of active participants in the market;
- increases the range of specialisation in the market;
- increases the exposure of local firms to prevailing best practice and the latest innovations.

European Network for SME Research (ENSR) sub-divides SMEs into a number of different groupings according to the extent that they are affected by the advent of the SEM and include:

- *Sheltered local players*: these are micro-enterprises who are reluctant to venture beyond their home market which is frequently regional as opposed to national in nature. The SEM has little relevance to this grouping.
- *Indifferent local players*: similar to the above but with higher levels of employment. They have experienced no increase in the level of competition recently and observe little opportunity or threat from the evolving SEM.
- *Skilled Europeans*: medium sized enterprises who are experienced in the export of goods and services to the EU. They are strongly challenged by the SEM especially in terms of changed VAT procedures, the simplification of customs procedures and harmonisation of products/production processes.
- *Challenged product harmonisers*: these are manufacturing SMEs which have benefited from the increased trading opportunities from the SEM, a process which has been facilitated by the need to harmonise production processes and products to EU norms.
- *Challenged international players*: these are experienced exporters who regard the SEM as an opportunity. They are frequently medium sized enterprises who have directly benefited from the trade liberalisation measures such as easier customs procedures and reduced borders delays.

Overall, the development of the SEM has generally benefited SMEs. Aside from the demand side factors noted above, the removal of technical, fiscal and physical barriers has had a positive impact upon export growth, turnover and employment (see Table 8.1). In addition, higher levels of foreign direct investment, cross-border co-operation and competition have had positive impacts not only on exports but also on employment and turnover growth. One of the key aspects of SME policy is to spread such benefits further throughout the EU's SMEs. Consequently, the EU has prioritised the development of information packages to inform SMEs of legislative changes brought in by the SEM programme. Issues of concern relate in particular to standards, testing and CE conformity marking, innovation and intellectual property, trade practices and competition law.

A network of Euro-information centres has been established to make SMEs aware of the legislation that affects their operations and to provide them with assistance, information and advice relating to areas of the EU's competence. In addition, it also hoped to entice SMEs to become involved in new markets from which they were previously excluded (such as public procurement) and in other markets where they have traditionally been outperformed by larger enterprises. Again, structures such as the Euro-information centres are designed to identify those areas of the evolving SEM which are of particular relevance to SMEs.

TOWARDS AN INTEGRATED POLICY FOR SMES

Given these trends, policy towards SMEs is based upon a recognition that internationalisation is an irreversible process. Consequently, actions need to be based upon strengthening the position of SMEs to respond to these challenges. The development of an integrated policy for SMEs is based upon the perceived need to co-ordinate the array of policies and events that will influence the performance of SMEs within such an environment. Co-ordinated action is regarded as essential if policies are to achieve the objective of maximising the impact of SMEs upon the European economy. Thus an integrated policy has been designed to increase the effectiveness of all policy measures (at local, regional, national and supranational levels) that are likely to affect the development and performance of SMEs. In this context, the aim of the integrated policy is to achieve:

- a simplified and improved administrative environment;
- an improvement in the financial and fiscal environment;
- a greater degree of internationalisation;
- a strengthening of competitiveness by improved access to research and development, innovation, information and training;
- a greater level of entrepreneurship.

Broadly, these objectives are to be met via three sources: concerted actions within states, assistance within the framework of enterprise policy and guidance within the context of other Community policies.

In terms of these objectives, it is important to identify those policy measures designed to assist the performance of SMEs within the framework of internationalising markets. In this context, policy is likely to be both reactive and proactive in the sense that it seeks to respond to, as well as encourage, the internationalisation of SMEs. The integrated programme was in direct response to the White Paper *Growth, Competitiveness, Employment* which identified SMEs as a vital link between growth and employment; a link dependent upon SMEs exploiting the opportunities within international (notably European) markets.

At the Madrid Summit in 1995, policy towards SMEs became more ambitious, highlighting the desire to offer cost effective targeted help for these enterprises. This was very much driven by the need for Europe to create employment within a difficult macro-economic climate. The Madrid SME policy paper recommended:

- the reduction of the burden of red tape upon SMEs;
- improvement of SME access to the decision making process;
- the direction of assistance towards SMEs that create jobs;
- the reduction of market distortions and inefficiencies;

- improved integration of SMEs into the EU's research and development programmes;
- enhancement of the competitiveness and internationalisation of SMEs.

This Madrid paper shifted the emphasis of SME policy away from simply offering opportunities in international markets towards aiding the development of these enterprises wherever possible to maximise the number of jobs created. Directing SMEs solely towards international markets risked undermining their full employment creating effects. This is not to downplay internationalisation: the earlier measures remained important in complementing the broad changes that were happening in the EU. However, policy also began to recognise that, in periods of slow growth, it was SMEs which tended to suffer the most.

The nature of the integrated programme reflects the generally passive nature of EU policy towards industry, recognising that the impact of SMEs upon the European economy and their success within global markets is ultimately an issue for the entrepreneur alone. Consequently, the best course of action for policy makers is to facilitate the success of these enterprises by seeking to address the unique problems that SMEs are likely to encounter in rapidly changing markets. To aid such actions, there is limited direct funding for the development of SMEs within the EU budget under the following programmes/initiatives.

- The multi-annual programme for SMEs: this established a series of Euro-Information centres to provide assistance to SMEs in terms of network formation, legal issues and information about new markets.
- Regional funding: the European Investment Bank, European Investment Fund and the Structural Funds all offer funding opportunities for SMEs in the peripheral or lagging regions of the EU.
- The SME initiative: this programme focuses upon stimulating indigenous enterprise growth within Objective 1 regions of the EU (see Chapter 7).
- Research and Development: this seeks to tap the innovative potential of SMEs by offering support for innovation.

Not surprisingly, both implicit and explicit policy measures are likely to have the greatest impact upon cost functions. Measures that lighten administrative and regulatory costs, contribute to lower financial risks and enable SMEs to fully exploit the benefits of their size (as well as overcoming its handicaps) will have the greatest effect. Such action will inevitably be assisted by the rapid dissemination of best practice throughout the economy. There are in truth a whole raft of measures that can be utilised within the framework of an integrated programme. The crux though, is to minimise the negative and maximise the positive features of these enterprises.

Table 8.3 indicates the three types of measures used to promote SME development. The first two actions are set in the context of the development of the third. The co-ordination between states is based upon using the supranational organisation as a means of disseminating information with regards to best practice relevant to SMEs. Within the above framework, the integrated programme supports a number of initiatives to promote the success of SMEs in ensuring the maximisation of their impact in terms of international markets and employment (see Table 8.4). As mentioned above, policy measures focus upon removing unnecessary impediments derived from the financial and regulatory measures. The rationale of these policy measures is based upon encouraging these enterprises to use their domestic markets as a base for the internationalisation of their activities. Consequently, all measures are designed to aid success, initially at least, within domestic markets. Table 8.5 highlights the core policy actions undertaken in Europe at both national and supranational levels to support the globalisation of SMEs.

Table 8.3 The framework for the integrated SME programme

Concerted actions within member states	Contributions from the EU
1 Measures to promote mutual consultation between member states and joint co-ordination, as appropriate, concerning actions in favour of SMEs.	2 Measures for SME development under other relevant Community policies (e.g. Structural Funds, R&D, EIB and EIF); 3 Measures for SMEs developed within the framework of the communities' specific SME policy (i.e. multi-annual SME programme)

Table 8.4 Key aspects of the integrated programme

Broad framework	Specific measures
Concerted actions	• access of SMEs to the information society • forum on entrepreneurship • forum in craft and small enterprises • forum on commerce
Actions under other Community policies	• simplifying SEM legislation • loan guarantees for employment • EIF equity for SMEs • introduction of the Euro • instrument for trans-national investment in Europe • support for international co-operation • innovation in SMEs • market orientated technological development
Specific SME policy actions	• third multi-annual programme for SMEs

Source: European Commission

To overcome the traditional impediments to the integration of SMEs into international markets, the EU has acted in a number of ways. Though constrained by its limited budget, the EU has set up (as mentioned above) a number of specialist information centres to overcome deficiencies with regard to knowledge and financing in foreign markets. It has also sought to develop measures within multilateral fora to:

• aid network development to share best practice;
• assist foreign investment;
• establish inter-firm co-operation agreements for the purposes of market entry;
• offer training for improvements in the quality of management within firms;
• support enterprises which exhibit the highest growth potential;
• improve access to SME supporting services;
• alleviate trade barriers with third countries.

Table 8.5 Typical policy initiatives to support the internationalisation of SMEs

Nature of assistance	*Type of programme*
Finance	• *Export insurance and loan guarantees*: most states offer support to enable SMEs to cushion the risk involved in foreign trade. Most European schemes cover losses in connection with sales and investments abroad. • *Development finance and venture finance* to grant these potentially high risk enterprises access to the capital needed for expansion. • *Direct grants or subsidies for export promotion*: these can vary from market intelligence or trade fairs (UK) to loans for exports (Netherlands).
Business environment	• *Network development and joint ventures*: most states have support programmes to foster collaboration via information provision and to aid partnership formation. • *R&D*: assorted support from direct subsidies (France) through to limited grants for micro-enterprises (UK) to support innovation. • *Industrial parks/free trade zones*: ready-made sites or support for financing of developmental locations (Greece). • *Subcontracting*: incentives or encouragement for MNCs to use SMEs as suppliers (UK and Eire). • *Arbitration*: support to settle international disputes. • *Integrated assistance*: state networks of support offices to provide a 'one-stop-shop' for SME assistance (UK, Finland, Portugal).
Capability	• *Consultancy and advice*: a network of support offices (above) to offer advice on export strategies (Netherlands, UK). • *Research and technology transfer*: direct grants (Netherlands) and secondment schemes (UK) to encourage managers to adopt best practice. • *Information technology and logistics*: grants (Netherlands) or advice (Portugal) on new technologies.
Access	• *Information and advice about foreign markets and related matters*: provision of export intelligence or aid in the establishment of contacts in foreign markets. • *Inward access*: stimulation of investment in the indigenous economy by foreign SMEs

Source: OECD

Pragmatism is essential in this environment in enabling SMEs to exploit the opportunities afforded by the SEM as well as in meeting the challenges posed by the emerging internationalisation of markets on a broader scale.

The integrated policy will be directly complemented by the Third Multi-annual Programme (1997–2000) for SMEs. This gives a specific budgetary basis for measures to support SMEs by focusing upon overcoming impediments to SME success in increasingly international markets as well as to maximising their employment impact within the context of the EU-wide Employment Pact. The EU asked the member states for ECU 180 million to support the Multi-annual Programme but for many states this was simply too much. The animosity arose from the conviction of member states who feel that they can do a better job (typical national policy actions are summarised in Table 8.5). This has brought a negative response from the small business lobby who feel that many of the EU's industrial policy initiatives are designed to support the development of larger business and that they also require specific policies at the supranational level.

CO-OPERATION BETWEEN SMES

The encouragement of co-operation between SMEs is central to the EU's strategy for their development. Co-operative agreements are seen as a means by which they can exploit the internationalisation of markets and engage in research and development initiatives: an area within which the Commission is keen to promote SME involvement. Co-operative agreements between SMEs are also important in allowing these enterprises to overcome the problems associated with small scale production. In other cases, these agreements can provide a feasible method of allowing SMEs to compete with large business without a corresponding loss of independence. Central to this theme is the development of the enterprise within the context and framework of the network economy. Such networks can work in many ways to strengthen the positioning of SMEs. In some cases, SMEs can overcome financing problems via joint ventures and strategic alliances. Despite the benefits of engaging in such activities, such action remains the exception rather than the rule. This is due to the absence of an obvious need to undertake this strategy due to factors such as localised markets and the cost of co-operation. This is expected to change as SMEs confront the challenges and implications of internationalisation. Co-operative agreements are liable to make it easier for SMEs to do business in other states and are integral to strategies that seek to overcome impediments to market access.

SMEs start to feel the pressures of more intense competition, if they may start to actively engage in co-operation. Inevitably such events will vary on a firm by firm basis. Sectoral co-operation may occur as a direct result of public sector led initiatives to offer commercial guidance to a group of enterprises who may have been vulnerable had they been left in isolation. This highlights the key point, that co-operation between SMEs is frequently a result of policy stimuli – as is the case within the EU's research and development initiatives. These, in turn, need to be complemented by a commercial culture that more readily accepts the notion of co-operation over individualism – a feature that would inevitably be reflected in the regulatory structure of the state concerned.

To date, many SMEs do not believe cross-border co-operation to be that important for commercial success. This is likely to change as many more SMEs start to see their markets internationalise. In other words, the desire for co-operation lags behind the commercial need for SMEs to engage in it. Thus market structures may fail to adjust to new competitive threats that could undermine SME strategies. The effort required to develop co-operative networks of SMEs often precludes their formation. Many SMEs do not regard co-operation as necessary. However within certain sectors (such as those with active pre-competitive research and development), the rationale and policy support for such co-operation is more apparent. Generally the major obstacles to cross-border co-operation (aside from those noted above) are:

- the immaturity of the levels of communication and of the development of networks to enable successful access to other markets;

- the wide variations in business culture between states: this applies especially to consumer habits, market structures and regulations.

Indeed to speed up SME networking as a means of aiding their international success, there may be a case for the public sector to act as a clearing house for the establishment of such co-operative agreements. To this end, fora such as the Business Co-operation Network, the Europartnertariat (developing co-operation between SMEs in areas supported by the Structural Funds) and Euromanagement (promoting managerial skills to meet the needs of the SEM) all seek to assist the networking capabilities of enterprises.

The active encouragement of co-operation between SMEs by the EU is seen as a means of developing specialisation, complementarity and of allowing for the development of common externalities which realise competitive advantage within open markets. Such a stance has been heavily influenced by the experiences of, amongst others, France and Germany. The focus is not upon assisting individual firms but networks of firms. These networks of SMEs can be primary agents in the convergence of institutional structures needed for their successful integration into international markets. This has been complemented by the Europartenariat where the public sector seeks to stimulate linkages between SMEs to stimulate international trading opportunities. Such networking is likely to increase over the coming decades. Scepticism has been frequently voiced about networking as it can be difficult to identify the benefits from a large number of SMEs coming together. This is especially true if these interlinkages are unplanned or poorly structured.

THE INCREASING IMPORTANCE OF ICTS FOR SMES

An increasingly important factor within the integrated strategy for SMEs is to increase the penetration of ICTs. ICTs are of growing importance for SMEs in enabling them to exploit the internationalisation of markets and in enhancing their flexibility in the light of changing markets (see Figure 12.1). These technologies enable SMEs to exploit foreign markets without the need to physically locate within the target markets. The result has been a number of successive policies to enable these enterprises to exploit the potentialities of electronic commerce. Indeed one of the key themes of the Bangemann Report was to ensure that 40 per cent of Europe's SMEs were utilising this technology by the end of the millennium. As highlighted in Chapter 12, this has resulted in a policy response from both the member states and supranational bodies to stimulate an awareness of these technologies by SMEs. This has been complemented by the Group of Eight (G8) initiative upon the development of a global marketplace for SMEs (see Case Study 8.1).

It is inevitable that information becomes of increased salience within the gradual internationalisation of SMEs. ICTs have essentially a supporting role. This varies on a firm by firm basis as individual SMEs adjust strategies in response to their changing environments. As the process of internationalisation becomes increasingly important for these enterprises, so the need for good quality information grows to enable them to respond quickly to the changing requirements of customers within ever more geographically dispersed markets.

Uncertainty relating to the technological environment and competition frequently impedes the ability of SMEs to implement new technology. This is compounded by a general uncertainty about how to use this technology for competitive advantage. If technology is imposed upon these enterprises by large customers or suppliers then this could further increase their vulnerability. In addition, the relatively poor resource position of these enterprises also impedes the successful implementation of ICT systems. Indeed, because SMEs tend to react to, rather than promote, change, they operate according to a short-term time horizon which may preclude the wider use of ICTs. This is compounded by a lack of training in ICTs within SMEs.

CASE STUDY 8.1 INTERNATIONALISING SMES: 'A GLOBAL MARKETPLACE FOR SMES'

In order for SMEs to access international markets, the EU has, within the framework of the G8 (though non-G8 states are also involved in the project) initiated a programme entitled 'Global Marketplace for SMEs'. This programme is a series of initiatives to stimulate the adoption of ICTs within SMEs and to demonstrate to these enterprises how the information society can be used for internationalisation strategies. Projects are targeted to the extent that they facilitate competitiveness and increase participation in global trade by SMEs. Towards this objective the initiatives seek to:

- aid the development of an electronic environment for the open and non-discriminatory exchange of information (in areas such as data products, technologies and human resources) as a means of overcoming obstacles of distance, time and borders for the benefit of SMEs;
- expand global electronic commerce to encourage SMEs to sell within markets where they do not have a direct physical presence (see Table 12.3).

The initiative encompasses three themes: a global information network for SMEs (providing a means of access to ICTs); establishing SME requirements (identifying what SMEs require to use these technologies with confidence); and the provision of international testbeds for electronic commerce (to stimulate awareness and spread usage of this technology). Much of the effort within the programme involves sharing the results of projects to integrate SMEs (via the information society) into the international business environment. In turn, much of the effort at the European level is the result of co-ordination of national and supranational initiatives. Most European states have introduced national initiatives directing electronic commerce at SMEs. At the trans-national level, a number of networks have been established as a means of providing on-line information for SMEs to enable them to access the information necessary to enter European and international markets (such as BC-NET: a network of consultants etc. which helps SMEs find partners to stimulate their internationalisation). These are complemented by around thirty pilot projects across specific industry groupings such as TradeNet (a virtual research and development enterprise and electronic marketplace involving a number of companies including Rover), Shopping 2000 (a French project to connect all actors in the purchasing chain from the supplier through to the final consumer via on-line catalogues etc. within sectors such as DIY and Furniture) and Agroweb (a project designed to support the exchange of agricultural produce in southern Europe and Mediterranean areas).

POLICY ISSUES FOR SMES: LIMITS AND IMPEDIMENTS TO POLICY SUCCESS

As mentioned above, great weight is placed upon SMEs as a means of restoring growth within the EU. A key part of achieving this rests upon SME exploitation of what are increasingly integrating markets. Whilst integration may benefit the EU, the process does not always meet with universal approval from SMEs. Some policies proposed in the name of integration could have counter-productive effects. Experience has highlighted that SMEs were deeply concerned about the threat to profitability from increased competition and more especially from the added social costs implied by the Treaty upon European Union. Surveys have indicated that nearly two-thirds of SMEs believed that these increased costs would have a negative impact upon their performance. The position differs between states with German SMEs most concerned while the British (initially due to its opt out) less so. Though, in practice, the full anticipated effect of the Social Chapter has not been felt as many states tend towards more flexible social models (see Chapter 13).

EU policy directly targeted towards SMEs has also been criticised. The UK's Confederation of British Industry (CBI) has criticised DG XXIII arguing that it is too weak, has minimal impact and should be abolished. The CBI claims the EU can only find a role in so far as it supplements national policy. DG XXIII is not sufficiently influential to achieve this due to insufficient resources and a generally low profile within the Commission. This they claim undermines the ability of the Commission to achieve anything substantial. The CBI also underlines the need for better targeting of resources as a requirement of a more effective policy. For while SMEs create jobs, only 4 per cent of SMEs have created 50 per cent of these new jobs while the craft sector, an important focus of DG XXIII, has little desire to expand. Thus, argues the CBI, support to the craft sector should be phased out with greater focus placed upon the 4 per cent that are the major employment creators and the further removal of unnecessary rules. This, the CBI argues, is best achieved by merging parts of DG XXIII into DG III (Industry) and DG XV (Single Market). As a consequence, it believes there is a need for a major shift in EU SME policy to increase its effectiveness. This viewpoint is not shared by all: many SME representatives believe that handing power to DG III would be inappropriate as it is more concerned with large, rather than small business.

SME lobby groups believe that SME policy should be an integral element of general economic policy. There is coverage for SMEs within Article 130 but they feel more depth needs to be added in terms of:

- measures to simplify administration and decision making procedures;
- a more effective best practice policy with regards to SMEs;
- the targeting of support at efficiency alongside transparency and coherence with regards to EU law.

Typically, the concerns of SMEs within the EU (and its economic and institutional structures) are broadly similar to those of larger business. There is a general opposition to a multi-speed Europe, a desire for speedier and more transparent decision making and a conviction that the process of economic integration should be centred around the concerns of competitiveness and open markets. In short, wealth creation is the major priority and this needs to be reflected within EU policy and practice.

Better access by SMEs to the process of policy development is also regarded as essential if their requirements and concerns are to be considered. Within this context, SMEs point out that policy needs to:

- be simply and effectively administered with greater co-ordination between environmental and support measures to aid the development of SMEs;
- ensure micro-SMEs are made more aware of support measures;
- ensure better co-ordination between local, regional and national authorities.

Reducing the often mentioned regulatory and administrative burdens is made problematic by the fact that no universal position is obtainable on this issue. Some SME burdens are someone else's benefits. For example, social protection works to the benefit of workers but potentially against the interest of SMEs. Clearly a balance needs to be struck. Addressing these issues requires a more credible and inclusive policy process. To complement this issue, there needs to be a central forum for the resolution of regulatory and administrative burdens that limit the internationalisation of SMEs. In short, the issue has to be responded to in a pragmatic manner.

Deloitte Touche (1995) has also looked at the appropriateness of EU SME-based policies. It noted that many SMEs have benefited from the SEM yet its lack of completion was hindering their further success. Once again, the single biggest factors were cost related. The regulatory costs of the SEM were perceived as too high and needing to be reduced further. Most states have tended to give this short shrift. Despite this, it was keen to point out that most of the barriers faced by SMEs emanate from national as opposed to supranational authorities. There are also a number of requirements that have still not yet been fully met, most notably the provision of greater quantities of market information and linguistic training for managers. Most favour EMU as this would be a great cost reduction measure (especially for SMEs with large export sales) and EU measures to provide low cost finance are regarded positively. Overall, most EU initiatives were felt to be of use to SMEs but more could be done by the EU to help the search for business partners and market information. In part, these concerns are overcome by the development of assorted business information schemes such as those offered by the network of business information networks. The biggest threat to SMEs, the impact of regulatory cost derived from national authorities, is beyond the remit of the EU.

Evidence presented by Clay, Creigh-Tyte and Storey (1996) concluded that policy has tended to focus upon the wrong areas. In the case of the UK, policy has done little to reverse long term relative economic decline, has tended to increase regional divergence, dissipated productivity improvements and has done little to lower unemployment and provide quality jobs. They also note that public money has been wasted on trying to develop SMEs as many individuals would have turned to self-employment in any case (due to the long term restructuring of industry that has occurred since the late 1970s) and policy support has been ineffective in achieving its stated aim of SME development.

The employment consequences of SMEs were further explored by the OECD (1996). Again, their evidence suggests a reluctance to be optimistic about the ability of SMEs to create the desired levels of employment. Looking at selected OECD states, it notes that rates of job creation and job losses tend to be higher in SMEs than in larger enterprises: reflecting the more volatile nature and dynamics of SMEs. Indeed many studies found a negative relationship between job creation and size of enterprise. However this finding was not uniform.

A survey by the European Foundation for Entrepreneurship (Roure, 1996) highlighted a number of key factors or 'myths' about SMEs that need to be considered by policy makers:

- only certain types of SME are job creators (see above);
- new companies are not the only source of employment creation therefore attention also needs to focus upon the problems of existing enterprises;
- dynamic, employment creating enterprises do not belong solely to new and high growth sectors;
- entrepreneurs do not belong only to the young educated classes but cross all ages and educational achievements;

- growing companies tend to be built by teams, not by a single entrepreneur;
- dynamic firms target niche markets where they can be leaders or strong challengers and do not focus upon large, growing markets;
- dynamic companies have to target export markets;
- growing companies compete using high quality products and superior services and are not low cost producers;
- successful companies rely upon investment in human capital and not upon some unique technology;
- dynamic enterprises tend to be self-financed with assistance from bank loans and are therefore not party to sophisticated forms of finance.

Many of these factors are already integral to the policy strategy undertaken by the EU and member states. Overall, policy needs to be user-led, reflecting the experience of those enterprises which are contributing to net employment creation in the EU. Measures that follow the concerns of policy makers and not the experience of these dynamic entrepreneurs would logically be expected to fail.

The development of a wide range of intermediaries in policy implementation has, in many cases, not really helped the performance of SMEs but has led to a waste of resources and a lack of planning. This has also led to poor co-ordination and risks of overlap between different authorities. Despite the increased consideration given to SMEs within policy, there are still some gaps in information and communication between these enterprises and policy makers. This is especially true of those enterprises within peripheral areas and of micro enterprises. There has also been great difficulty in developing standard models and schemes for SMEs within different parts of the EU. A legacy is that each region, in terms of the requirements of its indigenous SMEs, needs to be examined on an ad hoc basis; though exchanges of information and best practice between enterprises of all sizes have proved useful.

An inevitable conclusion is that policy needs to be more focused upon the more dynamic enterprises and not upon all SMEs. The latter route has tended to spread resources too thinly. The reports above indicate that the experiences of 'dynamic firms' can be readily transferred to policies being followed elsewhere in the EU that can impact upon SMEs. Indeed they tend to support the conclusion that existing firms are as, if not more, important in terms of job creation than new firms. In addition, there is little evidence that SMEs can pull the EU economy out of a period of slow growth. Larger enterprises tend to be much more cyclical. Despite evidence that SMEs can create jobs, the results of the above surveys should lead one to conclude that policy is correct in the nature of its support for SMEs. If firm size is significant in determining employment creation, it is also important to first note why a firm is small. Economic theory suggests that structural change, cyclical effects, technological change, alterations in market environment and changes in tastes will all determine the size of an enterprise and its ability to create the levels of employment desired.

CONCLUSION

Problems in developing SMEs persist. The hurdles these enterprises encounter differ on a spatial, sectoral and even on a firm by firm basis and there is no standard model or scheme that can be applied to these enterprises. The processes of integration and internationalisation are having a generally progressive impact upon SMEs. Over the short term, the impact of internationalisation is derived more from developments associated with the opening of European markets and has less to do with progressive globalisation. SMEs face problems in exploiting these markets. If policy is to enable these enterprises to exploit them, then it needs to pinpoint those SMEs for whom the process exhibits greatest relevance. Policy studies indicate that targeted policies are likely to be the most effective but policy must still be hands off as the success of a SME depends upon the skills and strategies within the enterprise itself and not upon those of policy makers, however laudable their intentions.

✎ KEY POINTS

- **SMEs form the vast majority of enterprises within the EU.**

- **A core policy initiative is to seek to expand SMEs into international markets.**

- **Internationalisation is however only relevant to a select group of SMEs.**

- **Much other policy effort is centred upon developing a regulatory and administrative environment that is cost-minimal to SMEs.**

SUGGESTED FURTHER READING

Blili, S. and Raymond, J. (1993) 'IT: Threats and Opportunities for SMEs', *International Journal of Information Management*, Vol. 13, No. 6, 439–48.

Cafferata, R. and Mensi, R. (1995) 'The Role of Information in the Internationalisation of SMEs', *International Small Business Journal*, Vol. 13, No. 3, 35–47.

Clay, N., Creigh-Tyte, S. and Storey, D. (1996) 'Public Policy towards Small Firms: Spreading the Jam too Thinly?', *Journal of European Public Policy*, Vol. 3, No. 2, 253–71.

Commission of the European Communities/DG III (1994) 'SMEs and Internationalisation', *Panorama of EU Industry*, pp. 139–46, Brussels.

Commission of the European Communities (1996) *Integrated Programme for SMEs*, COM (96) 329, Brussels.

Confederation of British Industry (1995) *Adding Value: the Role of EC SME Policy*, Policy Statement, London.

Deloitte Touche (1995) *EU Initiatives for SMEs: Are the Policies Appropriate?*, London.

European Network for SME Research (1996) *Fourth Annual Report of the European Observatory*, Brussels.

European Voice (1996) *UK bosses call for end to SMEs directorate*, 4 January, p. 22.

OECD (1995) *Best Practice Policies for SMEs*, Paris.

OECD (1996) *Small Business, Job Creation and Growth*, Paris.

OECD (1997) 'Globalisation and: Ten Small and Medium Sized Enterprises' (Vols 1 and 2), Paris.

Roure, J. (1996) 'Mastering Enterprise Myths about Entrepreneurs', *Financial Times*, 23 December, p. 12.

Schreyer, P. (1996) *SMEs and Employment Creation: Overview of Selected Quantitative Studies in OECD Member States*, OECD/STI Working Paper, 1996, No. 4.

9

TRANS-EUROPEAN NETWORKS: BUSINESS AND THE EMERGING NETWORK ECONOMY

The emergence of trans-European networks (TENs) on the agenda of the EU has been driven by the changing strategic requirements of European business. The gradual liberalisation of European markets has increased the commercial salience of mobility and accessibility within modern economies underlining the role of TENs as the physical support for the increasingly international actions of enterprises and consequently as a powerful factor in the integration of European economies. The development of TENs is split across three broad sectors:

- transport;
- telecommunications;
- energy.

BOX 9.1 FEATURES OF THE NETWORKS

There are three distinct aspects to the development of networks upon which TENs concentrate:

- *nodes*: that is geographically fixed points such as airports, seaports, telecommunication terminals or liquefied natural gas (LNG) terminals;
- *links*: that is links between nodes such as roads, rail track, pipelines and telecommunication cabling;
- *services*: that is the deliverables over the links including transport services, electricity flows and advanced telecommunication services such as e-mail.

As will be noted, the focus of the TENs programme has been on the links except in aspects of telecommunications where efforts have concentrated on deliverables.

Overall, this chapter is designed to complement the respective chapters on the network sectors involved in the TENs programme. Within this context, the initial theme of this chapter is the importance of these infrastructures for the development of business within the European economic space. Thereafter, the rise of TENs as a policy issue is briefly accounted for. An examination of the key network sectors follows with the emphasis upon common (as well as sector specific) themes and problems inherent in the development of these infrastructures. Finally, the push to develop an external element to these networks is addressed.

THE COMMERCIAL IMPORTANCE OF NETWORK INFRASTRUCTURE

Infrastructure evolution has been pivotal in defining the form and nature of the commercial development of the European economy. As the European economy has evolved, so the supporting infrastructure has had to adapt to its changing requirements in terms of mobility and accessibility (see Box 9.2). The link between economic development and infrastructure is well understood by policy makers and provides the rationale for infrastructure policy.

BOX 9.2 THE HISTORIC ROLE OF INFRASTRUCTURE IN EUROPEAN ECONOMIC DEVELOPMENT

Historically infrastructure has played a pivotal role in the economic transition of Europe. Different stages of economic development placed unique demands upon the supporting infrastructure. Four broad periods can be identified.

- *The Hanseatic period* (from the thirteenth to the sixteenth century) based upon inland and coastal waterways connecting cities along rivers and coastal areas in northern and western Europe.
- *The golden age period*: (from the sixteenth to the eighteenth century) based upon big improvements in maritime transport systems.
- *The Industrial Revolution*: (from the middle of the nineteenth century to the First World War) in which the invention of the steam engine revolutionised transport systems.
- *The information revolution*: (from the 1970s onwards) in which the development of advanced telecommunications infrastructure is promoting new industries and growth.

The core benefits from infrastructure come from the quality and quantity of the service provided over it. The key function of infrastructure is to provide network services between physically separate locations. Consequently the rationale for policy makers to stimulate increased investment in the provision of infrastructure lies in the more efficient delivery of the network services through spatially dispersed markets. The better the quality of infrastructure, the better the quality of the services that are delivered over it. Network services such as transport, energy and telecommunications are all core to the operation of business: the cheaper these services are available to enterprises, the more the opportunities for efficiency and the competitiveness of European business are enhanced.

The realisation of these cost benefits from the development of TENs is closely related to the progressive liberalisation of service provision within these sectors. Thus infrastructure provision alone is insufficient to deliver the benefits expected of its development. Within the EU, the development of infrastructure supports the consequences of freer trade and integration (especially in the light of the SEM), notably in terms of:

- *the volume effect*: the need for infrastructure to support the anticipated increases in trade associated with liberalisation;
- *the interoperability requirement*: the need for physical and technical network compatibility of networks to ensure interoperability;
- *the dimension effect*: the recognition, within national planning systems, that the development of infrastructure has effects beyond the borders of the nation state concerned;
- *the quality requirement*: TENs are needed to ensure the quality of network services to sustain the competitive position of European business;
- *the cohesion effect*: the provision of infrastructure has a pronounced impact upon the attempts to promote more even business development across Europe's economic space (see Chapter 7).

Furthermore, the development of infrastructure within the EU enables enterprises to take advantage of the opportunities for efficient trans-national production and to exploit the international division of labour as well as facilitating the use of just-in-time production techniques. This is, of course, in addition to the fact that these networks are a representation of the physical mobility and accessibility required by the legal changes offered by the advent of the SEM.

The potential benefits from the development of TENs in terms of the performance of enterprises explain why the issue has risen up the agenda of the EU. These networks will be powerful factors in promoting the cost-space and time-space convergence associated with the development of a more capacious, efficient and evenly developed series of infrastructure networks. The issue of even development is important given that the services delivered by these infrastructures are of generic interest across the socio-economic spectrum: communication, mobility and access to energy are necessities for modern day living. These public interest concerns can and have operated as a constraint upon the liberalisation of network services and have the potential to undermine the competitive benefit to enterprises derived from the development of these advanced infrastructures.

THE EMERGENCE OF TRANS-EUROPEAN NETWORKS

As stated above, the emergence of TENs was a derivative of the moves within Europe towards construction of the SEM. Indeed the initial TENs documents were set very much within this context. Thus meeting the concerns of enterprises to exploit the opportunities of the internationalising markets was initially very much the dominant theme of the EU's infrastructure strategy. Explicit powers to develop these networks were formally given within title XII of the Treaty upon European Union (see Box 9.3).

BOX 9.3: TITLE XII: TRANS-EUROPEAN NETWORKS

Article 129b, paragraph 2

This title outlines not only the role of the Commission in the development of TENs but also the priorities of such networks, namely that:

- their development should be market led and financed;
- these networks should be physically integrated;
- the networks should, even where not interconnected, be compatible with each other to facilitate future integration;
- access to these networks should be as broad as possible to ensure the aims of economic and social cohesion.

Over time, the emphasis of TENs has extended beyond meeting the requirements of the SEM to become a more all-embracing policy that directly complements and involves other themes of integration such as economic and social cohesion (see Chapter 7) and the shift towards the information society (see Chapter 12). More importantly, TENs became a key feature of the EU's strategy for competitiveness insofar as they provide the means of enabling firms to derive greater value added from infrastructure.

The development of TENs is born of the osmotic process of interaction between national infrastructures which is based upon the chain of events in Figure 9.1. This highlights the market driven context of their development. Increased user demand (largely driven by increased freedom of movement) for national and trans-national infrastructure creates a situation in which commercial interest in the condition of a state's infrastructure is not solely the concern of indigenous enterprises. Such spillovers highlight the need for movement towards a set of integrated infrastructures that aid mobility and accessibility in a broader context than previously defined: that is, national infrastructures become mere sub-groups of a broader international network of networks.

Currently, Europe is at the stage where the interdependencies between national infrastructures have been recognised and concerted efforts are underway to remove obstacles to their integration. The implication, over the short term, is that national planners need to take a broader perspective in the development of domestic infrastructures (see below). The lack of a trans-national dimension is reflected in a number of deficiencies across networks.

- *Nodes (such as airports)*: these have been developed to meet national needs and access to them is often impeded by national laws and regulations. This is compounded by the inability of certain nodes to deal with the rising interactions across space.
- *Links (such as pipelines and roads)*: many of the links needed to meet the requirements of the SEM either do not exist or are inadequate to meet the demands placed upon them. Within many states, networks tend to be based upon a national core-periphery model radiating from capital cities and declining in quality and intensity as frontiers approach. This is clearly inadequate as cross-border interaction increases.
- *Services (such as passenger and freight movements)*: a lack of compatibility between networks hinders the functionality and value added derived from the network. The value to businesses from network services will be complemented by the liberalisation of service provision.

It was the White Paper *Growth, Competitiveness, Employment* which pushed the development of TENs towards the top of the EU's agenda. Within the framework of markets established by the Treaty upon European Union, the Commission outlined a range of priority projects to alleviate bottlenecks in core regions and to bring peripheral areas more closely into the hub of the European economy. The White Paper also highlights potential

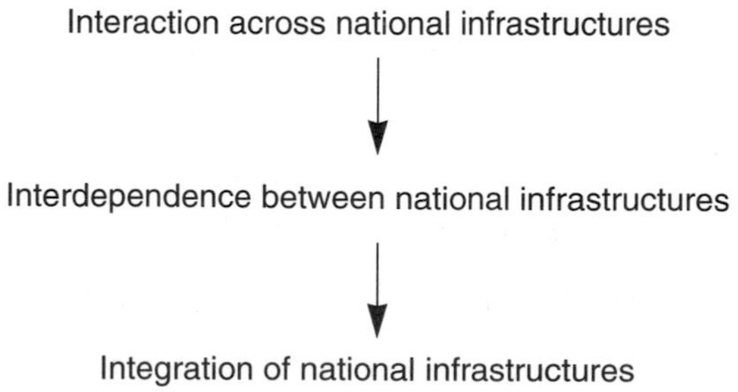

Interaction across national infrastructures

Interdependence between national infrastructures

Integration of national infrastructures

Figure 9.1 The integration of national infrastructures

options for the support which the European Commission could offer projects to aid their realisation (see below).

THE NETWORK SECTORS: GENERIC THEMES AND POLICIES

Unlike most industrial companies, utility enterprises have, to date, tended to remain nationally focused with the emphasis upon meeting domestic demand. This approach has been compounded by regulatory structures which have governed network management and reinforced the national focus of the business. However, this national focus is changing as liberalisation across these sectors becomes more prevalent. As enterprises start to operate internationally and as utilities begin to exercise rights of entry in other markets so the interdependencies between national networks (see Figure 9.1) become more evident.

Most of the priorities within the TENs programme have focused upon strengthening links as opposed to upgrading nodes. This is due to:

- the spatial fixation of TENs;
- the greater ability of nodes to attract commercial funding;
- concerns that EU intervention may distort inter-nodal competition.

Across the network sectors involved in the development of TENs, a number of themes and generic concerns were apparent within the priorities established by the European Commission.

Transport

The needs of transport infrastructure cut across diverse modes to contribute to the goal of sustainable mobility (see Chapter 10), implying that each of the transport networks (road, rail, inland waterways, coastal shipping, airlines and integrated transport) complement each other. Indeed to help transport flows, these networks were aided by developments in other sectors, most notably by efforts to apply telecommunications technology to traffic management, thereby underlining the growing linkages between the network sectors.

Priority projects within the transport sector reflect a political compromise between the member states (who are keen to get hold of Commission funding to develop domestic infrastructure). The priorities established also need to be compatible with the objectives of a more environmentally friendly transport system: this is reflected in the relative priority given to rail over road infrastructure in terms of Commission funding. The TENs initiative is not an attempt to dictate which transport modes to develop but to respond to user requirements. The priority is to reduce the dependence on roads for the bulk of freight and passenger traffic: a dominance which has been accentuated by the increased provision of better roads within the core regions of the EU.

In the light of the White Paper, the Christophersen Group identified fourteen priority projects. These projects are of relative maturity and are distributed across the sector as follows:

- *rail* (both high speed and conventional) covers five projects including efforts to develop an embryonic trans-European high speed rail network in various parts of the EU;
- *combined road/rail links* account for a further five projects. These are distributed fairly evenly across the EU and reflect the aforementioned desire for complementarity between different modes of transport;
- *road networks* comprise a further three projects. In this case the Commission is keen to

pursue road as a tool of cohesion and not simply to promote a mode of transport across the EU which may deliver environmental problems;
- *air transport*: priority is given to one airport (Milan).

Generally the priority projects fall into two broad categories:

- those designed to relieve congestion in the core of the EU such as the Paris–Brussels–Cologne–Amsterdam–London high speed rail network;
- those intended to lessen the isolation of peripheral regions.

Transport TENs projects incorporate much more than the fourteen priority projects. The Christophersen Group also identified twenty-one projects of 'further importance' and within the transport infrastructure guidelines, a much broader range of projects of 'common interest' have been identified for development.

Energy

The central theme of energy networks within the TENs programme is to ensure the security of supply at reasonable costs for European business (see Chapter 11). The desire is to broaden the supply of energy in some member states (for example in extending gas to Portugal and Greece) and ensure that all areas have access to a diverse array of energy sources. The development of gas and electricity networks is closely linked with the liberalisation of the energy sector and is necessary to ensure the rights of access and transit which are integral to the liberalisation process.

The development of TENs in the energy sector is related to the interconnection of gas and electricity networks. Generally, the core themes are to integrate national infrastructure and to extend networks to ensure a diverse and secure energy supply throughout the EU. The specific themes within each sector are outlined below.

- *Electricity*: the concern here is interconnection between areas ensuring that all parts of the area can be supplied from anywhere else within the EU. This underlines the apparent close linkages between liberalisation and the notion of security of supply. Furthermore, the EU wishes to ensure access to energy sources by the more remote areas: an essential pre-requisite for any business wishing to locate in these areas and integration of European electricity networks with external networks.
- *Gas*: a major concern with gas is to account for the growing imports of gas from external sources such as North Africa and Russia. Thus the major concern is to use TENs as a means of ensuring the security of supply of energy for the EU. The other major concern within priority projects is to provide access to gas to those peripheral areas that are without it. Furthermore, there is a desire to interconnect isolated networks into the main European network.

Telecommunications

Priorities for the development of the telecommunications networks are closely linked to the development of the information society within the European Union (see Chapter 12). Information infrastructures are becoming an increasingly important factor in determining the competitiveness of the economy and will have an all pervasive effect on the quality of factors of production and markedly alter the cost, time and spatial aspects associated with the emerging global marketplace.

Initial actions within the TENs programme were, as with the other networks, designed to meet the information requirements of administrations in attempting to manage the effect of the SEM in terms of factor and commodity flows. This theme was later subsumed within the concerns of the White Paper *Growth, Competitiveness, Employment* which sought to use these networks as tools to promote the broader technological development of the European socio-economic body. The White Paper took a stronger technological approach by also identifying the necessary network technologies to support the requirements of business.

The market-led strategy for the development of networks was based upon achieving a critical mass for these technologies by utilising a core of commercial and semi-commercial applications. The success of these applications would lead to the development of services of generic appeal across a broad range of users. Consequently, the following broad areas were identified as priorities:

- *networks for citizens*: this involves networks that have a strong social impact such as education, health care, teleworking and transport;
- *networks for SMEs*: this involved the development of networks for groups of enterprises whose demand for services would otherwise be ignored by the large telecommunications suppliers.

Environment

Environmental networks tend to take a back seat in the TENs programme. These were not included within Title XII of the Treaty on European Union. However, serious consideration has been given to the development of these environmental networks, especially in terms of water resources and waste management. Importantly the Cohesion Fund is allocated between investment in transport and environment infrastructure.

THE FINANCING OF TRANS-EUROPEAN NETWORKS

The financing required for infrastructure in the EU is vast. Indeed the White Paper *Growth, Competitiveness, Employment* estimated that the transport networks required expenditure of ECU 220 billion (of which ECU 82 billion was represented by the priority projects) before 2000 with ECU 13 billion required in energy and ECU 67 billion in telecommunications. These sums, if anything, underestimate the scale of the investment needed in EU infrastructure if it is to meet the requirements of the European economy.

The role of business in the development of TENs is not only as a user of network services but increasingly as a provider of the networks themselves. The desire of the EU to involve the private sector in developing infrastructure, when combined with the scale of the resources required, represents the biggest impediment to the realisation of TENs. This is partly driven by the practicalities of an environment where the public sector is retreating (due to fiscal retrenchment, the requirements of EMU, etc.) and does not possess the funding levels required to develop TENs in the manner envisaged within the EU's plans. The problems of attracting commercial investment is not uniform across the sectors involved in the development of TENs.

- *Telecommunications*: this sector has already received substantial investment in infrastructure derived from the onset of competition within the sector. Any financing problems are derived from the desire of the public sector to meet, over the short term, the broad socio-economic requirements of the information society (see Chapter 12). Investments in infrastructures to meet the needs of business have little trouble attracting funding.

- *Energy*: in the case of energy, problems of meeting TENs objectives arise more from planning and administrative problems than from the inadequacy of financial resources. The private sector has considerable experience of investment in energy TENs within this sector (see Chapter 11).
- *Transport*: this is the sector with the most evident financing problem. Consequently, the rest of this section is concerned with the problems within this sector.

The problem of getting private sector financing into transport infrastructure is compounded by the commercial risks that developers face, namely:

- in the promotion and preparation stage of the project, there is still no guarantee that the project will take place;
- the high risk construction phase due to the likelihood of cost overruns throughout the lifetime of the project;
- the uncertain revenues once a project starts operating and the potential for policy changes to undermine the viability of the project.

This situation is compounded by a commercial culture that is not, for the most part, accustomed to investment in large scale infrastructure projects and does not readily accept the scale of investment required by transport infrastructure. The banking system has already proved reluctant to offer financing on the scale required and especially over the time horizon (frequently twenty years plus) needed for commercial return from infrastructure. This position is compounded by the variations in the ability and experience of banks to finance these projects over the lifespan of the trade cycle. These, and other market failures, have meant that the public sector cannot abrogate responsibility for the development of infrastructure. Consequently, much of the development of transport networks is expected to take place within the context of public private partnerships (PPPs).

Public Private Partnerships

Despite the desire for private sector led development of TENs, it is evident that much of the funding to ensure the development of these networks will still come from the public sector. According to some estimates 25 to 33 per cent of total funding will be derived from this source. Most of this money comes from national public sectors with supranational funding, aside from the actions of the EIB and the EIF, being largely incidental. Public funds are designed to support commercial finance within the context of a PPP. Generally, the role of PPPs is to:

- function as a risk sharing device between public and private sectors to encourage network development;
- ensure that anti-competitive effects of network development are precluded;
- sustain a public service element within network development.

Public sector support is not only important in terms of finance but is also essential in political terms. Regulatory uncertainty can also undermine the feeasibility of a project. The form of the PPP will vary on a case-by-case basis along with the commercial viability of a project. Thus PPPs need to be pragmatic in development and the nature of public involvement in the development of TENs will vary according to:

- the extent to which the developers are state owned;
- the attitude of the state to infrastructure;

- the attitude of the state to commercial investment in infrastructure;
- the opportunity cost of resources devoted to infrastructure;
- the willingness of the private sector to invest in infrastructure;
- the perceived risks of the project;
- the externalities associated with a project.

The PPP is therefore a balancing issue which revolves around injecting sufficient public sector resources into a project to lower risks sufficiently to stimulate the desired levels of private sector investment. If the public sector does not plough in enough resources or fails to offer other ways of lowering commercial risk, then TENs will not be realised in the manner desired. Such a problem has already been evident throughout the TENs initiative.

The role of the EU

The role of the EU in the development of TENs is defined by the terms of the Treaty upon European Union and is very much based upon complementing rather than directly assisting their realisation. Thus in order to achieve the TENs' objectives the EU may, according to the Treaty:

- establish a series of guidelines covering the development of TENs of common interest;
- establish measures to achieve the interoperability of networks;
- support the financing of these projects.

There are a number of supranational funding sources for the development of TENs, namely:

- the Cohesion Fund;
- the TENs budgetary line;
- Structural Funds.

These are complemented by other supranational sources (not directly linked to EU funds) notably:

- the European Investment Fund (EIF);
- the European Investment Bank (EIB).

These sources do not cover the full cost of the development of TENs projects and as such merely seek to supplement existing financing, whether from the private or the national public sector.

Any support is not unconditional. The aid is given upon the precondition that the projects are commercially and technologically feasible. The Cohesion Fund and the Structural Funds are directed towards the attainment of a specific objective, namely the promotion of even development within the EU. The most specific measures are related to the TENs budgetary line. This offers around ECU 2.4 billion across all TENs sectors. The support given has to bear in mind that it needs to work with commercial operators in the development of projects: hence the conditions of commercial and technological viability. This finance is generally used to support and overcome initial uncertainties derived from factors such as an absence of feasibility studies for the prioritised projects.

As noted, this finance is merely incidental to the overall levels of funding required for the development of TENs. In fact it is as little as 0.1 per cent of the total needed. These efforts represent a disappointment for the European Commission which originally envisaged a much greater effort via a series of bonds to lend as much as ECU 7–8 billion per annum to TENs projects. These efforts were squashed by the Council who felt it inappropriate that the Commission should increase its borrowing at a time when all other European public sectors are doing the opposite. Thus the Commission finds its direct efforts to support TENs severely limited.

Instead of a direct Community device to aid the financing of TENs, a compromise emerged with extra money given to the EIB (which saw its lending facilities increased) and the creation of the aforementioned EIF (a joint venture between the EIB, the EU and commercial banks) which could offer an extra billion ECU to these projects. The rationale behind this compromise was the experience that the EIB had in the development of infrastructure projects. Despite these actions, the development of projects will remain a bottom up policy with member states taking the primary role in their development.

The money to develop TENs does exist within the EU economy: the challenge lies in attracting this finance into the development of these infrastructures. Existing methods are unable to achieve this objective. A consequence is that the initial fourteen transport priority projects are exhibiting financing gaps which are as much as 40 per cent of the total required. The reasons for this gap include:

- an economic climate which was inappropriate for the calls for finance from the private sector;
- the inexperience of the private sector in financing long term, high risk infrastructures;
- the inadequacy of current or proposed PPPs, leaving the private sector exposed to a prohibitive degree of risk.

The easy solution to these issues would be to offer more public money. But this is only part of the problem. There still needs to be a clearer regulatory environment for private operators. The insistence of many member states on strong public service commitments within network sectors will inevitably deter commercial involvement. This commitment may need to be diluted if TENs are to be realised. In addition, there needs to be a re-appraisal of the financing methods for these infrastructures, although this problem may be alleviated as the EU gains more experience in the development of these infrastructures. Whatever the problem, the development of these networks requires greater commitment from member states.

The financing issue for the member states is compounded by the fact that they are the paymasters of the EU's budget. This has already brought the Commission into conflict with the member states on a number of occasions, notably in the case of the proposed Union Bonds. Most states are seeking to lower public deficits and are reluctant to grant the Commission more power in this area. This has been typified by the public spats between the Commission and the member states over attempts to expand the level of funding for the TENs budgetary line (see below).

To strengthen efforts towards the development of TENs, the Commission is pushing for a doubling of the funds available from 2000 to 2006. Such pressure is derived from an environment where the requests for funding are three times higher than the amount available. The Transport directorate is pushing to expand the amount available to ECU 5 billion. As a complement to this, the TENs financing regulation is being altered to make available finance on a multi-annual basis as opposed to the current granting of loans on a year-by-year basis. This should, if passed, give greater certainty to the TENs financing environment.

CASE STUDY 9.1   PRIVATE FINANCE IN INFRASTRUCTURE: THE CASE OF EUROTUNNEL

Everywhere people are talking about the Channel Tunnel, and technical folk say it can be done and must be done. The problem is capitalism.

(Lenin, Pravda 1913)

The core of the problem suggested in the above quotation is that there is a real and genuine reluctance to put private investment into projects that require long term funding. As part of the Treaty establishing the development of the Channel Tunnel in the early to mid-1980s, there was an insistence by the UK government that it be developed via private finance alone. This represented the first barrier in the development of the Channel Tunnel as many banks were reluctant to offer long term financing. The repayment period required by the eventual operators was twenty-two years. Japanese banks were comfortable with this; the European banks did not like it but on the whole could live with it but US banks would not even contemplate these conditions. Thus of the 225 banks involved in the funding of the Channel Tunnel, only two were from the US. These problems were compounded as the costs of construction rose to twice their anticipated levels and as revenue flows became increasingly uncertain. Consequently, when the operator, Eurotunnel, took over the Tunnel from the constructors, it found itself shouldered with high levels of debt that would dog the formative years of the Tunnel's life. Part of the problem was that the company had to accept the terms agreed between the construction companies and the financiers; something over which it had apparently little control.

When the Tunnel opened in 1994, the operating company had an £8 billion debt which required interest payments of £2 million a day. Thus soon after it came into operation, Eurotunnel was forced into financial restructuring and suspended these interest payments. These problems were compounded by uncertainties over revenue flows: in 1995, for example, turnover was less than 50 per cent of the predicted flows. Consequently, it was difficult to envisage flows of traffic that would allow interest payments, let alone operational costs, to be met. This problem was not aided by the delay in the Tunnel becoming fully operational and by more intense price competition with the ferries. Given this environment, it is not surprising that less than a year into its operation the enterprise sought to reschedule its debt. To Eurotunnel there was little doubt that it would generate revenue; the issue was whether this would be quick enough to prevent further increases in its debt mountain. The original plan of breaking even in 1998 (and therefore start repaying debt) started to look fanciful. By late 1995, the company was technically bankrupt, only surviving on the goodwill of its banks.

By late 1995, Eurotunnel had revised down revenue figures and its worst case forecasts suggested that the company would not be able to repay its total debt and accrued interest until 2052. As its crisis deepened, so Eurotunnel sought to shift blame, seeking compensation for these losses from other parties, notably the construction companies whom it blamed for much of the delay and consequent increases in debt and the national train operators whose poor performance has also hindered revenue flows. Problems were worsened when shareholders, whose share value took a battering, called for state intervention and for trading in Eurotunnel shares to be suspended.

In retrospect, the basic problem was that the project was not economic. Many banks lent under official pressure; others due to a lack of other funding opportunities. Eurotunnel, if it threatened bankruptcy, had tremendous leverage over the banks who would see little return on their £8 billion outlay. In early 1997, Eurotunnel turned to the French and UK governments to support its efforts. They felt that the governments owed Eurotunnel money due to the regulatory uncertainty induced by issues such as the privatisation of rail. Confidence in the project was further hit when the single largest group of investors in project finance, the Japanese banks, started off-loading debt at a highly discounted rate.

The overriding conclusion is that all or most of the investors who have put money into the project will have to accept they are not going to get their investment back in its entirety. This is inevitable as the company's debt levels rise inexorably towards £9 billion. In practice, Eurotunnel was not able to meet the costs of interest let alone repay the principal debt. The project was re-financed with the banks taking around half of the equity in Eurotunnel in a debt-for-equity swap. This should cut the horrendous interest bill that Eurotunnel faces. By mid-1997, the situation between the banks and Eurotunnel and its shareholders had deteriorated to such an extent that the former were openly considering appointing a new operator. In part, this was driven by shareholders who were unhappy at seeing their shareholdings devalued and were refusing to endorse the restructuring plan with no obvious likelihood of compensation or potential return.

One bright spot in this otherwise troubled birth was the provisional agreement by the French and UK governments to extend Eurotunnel's licence to at least ninety-nine years up to 2086 in exchange for 25 per cent of the company's pre-tax profits. It is hoped by then that the venture will be in profit and the concession can then continue indefinitely. This was core to getting the shareholders to agree to the restructuring plan. This was eventually approved in July 1997 with the debt deal finally agreed to by all creditor banks in November 1997. With this agreement, Eurotunnel's future was finally assured. The consequence of this deal is a cut in its interest bill by 40 per cent.

Events were not helped by the Channel Tunnel fire which stopped full revenue flows for over six months and which reduced turnover by over 25 per cent in the first half of 1997. By the end of 1997, there was evidence to suggest that Eurotunnel had finally turned the corner when it reported its first ever operating profit. However, it does not expect to deliver full year profits until 2004. The financial restructuring has also enabled it to deliver sustained profits into 1998 as it regains the market share lost after the 1996 fire. This was tempered by evidence that the UK and French governments wanted more from their deal with Eurotunnel; notably an increased share of pre-tax profits if Eurotunnel fails to promote more freight traffic. It was finally agreed that the government's would share 59 per cent of pre-tax profits in return for the extension to the licence. This has been aided by a French agreement to create a trans-European freight corridor. Despite making profits of £56.8 million for 1997, the effects of interest payments still put the firm heavily into loss to the tune of £611 million.

On the UK side of the tunnel, the position of Eurotunnel has not been aided by the uncertainty surrounding the Channel Tunnel rail link which ran into financial trouble before a sod of earth was turned. The failure of London and Continental Railways (the consortium established to build the link) to raise the cash has highlighted flaws within the UK's Private Finance Initiative. The experience of the Eurotunnel seems to suggest that greater public sector commitment (as mentioned) is needed to balance public and private sector risks. This is something many governments are reluctant to do.

The lesson suggests that the financing of large infrastructure projects via private sources needs to be reconsidered. Other methods such as government financing for construction accompanied by the privatisation of its operation may need to be considered. The experience of Eurotunnel is a worrying example for the TENs programme. Eurotunnel may have staved off imminent collapse but it is still not out of the woods. Much of its success into the future depends upon its ability to meet the revenue targets. Over the next few years, it has also other challenges to meet, not least of which is the end of duty-free sales. This may lead to a more level playing field in cross-Channel traffic as the revenues from high margin duty free sales are abolished placing upward pressure on ferry fares.

FURTHER ISSUES IN THE DEVELOPMENT OF TENS

Whilst the financing problem is undoubtedly the greatest barrier to the development of TENs, it is by no means the only one. Across all TENs sectors, further problems exist which are related largely to administrative and regulatory hurdles. The nature of these problems is largely idiosyncratic to the particular TENs sector. Within telecommunications, there is a need to balance the progressive liberalisation of the sector with the need to foster co-operation between rival companies as a means of developing infrastructures. Too much competition within the sector is a problem, for excessive levels of rivalry may create a degree of uncertainty that prohibits the levels of infrastructure investment desired. Thus the EU has pursued a policy of managed competition (at least over the short to medium term) where a degree of rivalry is allowed although entry is ultimately limited. Within the energy sector, problems are generally more related to administrative and legal constraints than to finance per se. These constraints stem from a number of causes but the expression of environmental concerns has excited a lot of local interest to resist the development of energy infrastructures, especially in the electricity sector. Such factors make the authorisation procedure long and cumbersome; a feature that increases the overall cost of projects and limits the ability of operators to respond to market conditions.

The problems of each of the network sectors are also compounded by the desire of a number of states to maintain a high public service dimension in the development of networks. This offers an apparent contradiction with the desire of the EU to involve the private sector and other commercial operators in their development. This public service element has held up liberalisation across a number of sectors. In telecommunications, the liberalisation of the sector has gone hand in hand with attempts by operators to define a minimum 'universal service obligation'. This is an uncertain concept that will evolve with technology. Similar efforts are being made elsewhere usually by offering state subsidy to sustain levels of service in otherwise unprofitable activities.

Despite the supranational nature of these projects, there are still many challenges from their development for the member states. These challenges stem from a change in the nature of the culture of infrastructure provision. As economies integrate, so there is likely to be a greater spillover between states in terms of network development. Such integration and externalities could lead to an impasse as some states may benefit from the development of infrastructure for which they do not pay. This is evidently still a problem due to the state maintaining a large role for the state in infrastructure finance. Clearly states may be reluctant to invest in the network when other states may benefit from its provision without having contributed to its development. A way to remove such an impasse is to promote mutual investment in networks.

Getting national planners to recognise the European element in infrastructure development is also proving problematic. Planners within member states traditionally created infrastructure to meet national and local requirements. In this context, the European element of infrastructure planning was an afterthought: in an integrated European business environment this can no longer be the case. This needs to be compounded by speedier decision making within member states based upon a realisation that the national network in an integrated Europe is a mere sub-network of a larger European series of networks and that prolonged administrative procedures have a spillover effect upon other member states and are potentially damaging to indigenous enterprises. Therefore there has to be an appeal to the broader economic interests of the states based upon a recognition that isolation in network development is anachronistic and commercially damaging. Thus integration will be driven by economics not compulsion. Consequently a short term role for the EU is to seek to co-ordinate national infrastructure policies to create a 'virtual single network' via the interconnection and interoperability of national sub-systems.

In some sectors, the consideration of international factors in network development implies a cost upon national operators. For example, in telecommunications and transport adoption of standardised formats for some forms of technology and modes of transport will inevitably prove costly. This has been the case for the development of the European Integrated Services Digital Network and rail networks. Such problems provide a justification why future networks should be interoperable and interconnected from day one.

An interrelated issue is attempts by member states to control the power of the Commission via the application of the principle of subsidiarity to the development of TENs. Thus Title XII of the Treaty upon European Union provides the EU with a more co-ordination role with the member states taking the primary role. Individual network guidelines set the parameters for the application of the principle of subsidiarity to each network. The guidelines conclude that the development of networks falls between member states and the EU. For example, the development of guidelines is a Community role: but the details and timing are a job for the member states. In practice, subsidiarity reflects the political and economic realities of TEN development. The EU has developed for itself a facilitator role in which TENs develop in response to need and via the co-ordination of national policies.

THE EXTERNAL DIMENSION OF TRANS-EUROPEAN NETWORKS

The Treaty upon European Union highlights the desire to develop and extend TENs to third countries, both on the European continent and beyond. The desire for international interoperability of networks reflects:

- the need for networks to reflect the internationalisation of markets;
- the desire to extend TENs to potential new members of the EU;
- the potential for economic success of the EU beyond its own political borders.

The external element is especially strongly motivated by the desire to integrate the EU with Central and Eastern Europe. The break up of the Soviet Union and the collapse of Communism has markedly increased the salience of extending infrastructure into Eastern Europe. This is driven by the factor/resource endowment of this region and by the desire to enter new markets and to provide incentives for these regions to continue with the reform process. This process has been strengthened by the increasing liberalisation of trade between the two sides of Europe. Eastern European infrastructure needs to reflect changing trade patterns and not the old political objectives which frequently motivated the former Communist regimes.

Many of the transport links to Eastern Europe were in a state of chronic disrepair: as economic ties strengthen and trade grows, so these crucial arteries threaten to clog up totally. Several projects are being planned, particularly in the transport sector. In addition, there is the desire to strengthen energy ties given the fact that the EU gets a considerable amount of its energy from the east of Europe. The theme of transport has led to the establishment of a five point plan to build a European-wide transport network via:

- establishing pan-European corridors and areas as a framework for ensuring efficient transport systems within the European continent;
- preparations to extend TENs to other states as a pre-requisite of accession;
- a common approach to transport technology;
- the encouragement of intelligent transport technology;
- closer co-operation in research and technology.

The ability to develop infrastructure in these areas is troubled by financial problems and by the absence of a legal framework to support the involvement of the private sector in the development of these networks. In the latter case, the European Bank for Reconstruction and Development (EBRD) has been pivotal in establishing PPPs for the development of infrastructure in these regions. Such action has been particularly successful in tele-communications and energy. The development of transport has been more problematic. The initial concern has been to upgrade existing corridors before any new networks are developed. Substantial gaps are still evident in the development of these projects. The EBRD has estimated that the CEE states need $40–60 billion for motorways, $30–40 billion for rail and $100 billion for telecommunications.

The EU's PHARE programme has focused upon the alleviation of certain number of transport bottlenecks especially in terms of border crossings. Its actions are most effective when they are co-financed with the EIB, the EBRD and the World Bank. These bodies have a much wider role than purely financial. They are also involved in the development of a wider regulatory structure within these regions, underlining the broad catalytic role these institutions play in the development of pan-European networks.

The energy sector has external connections beyond the European continent. Indeed, the development of networks in these areas extend to North Africa. Again the reason for the development of these networks essentially concern the security of supply. Despite this, there are concerns about the political stability of these states which could endanger the EU's primary concerns in extending networks to these regions.

The development of telecommunication networks has the strongest global element. The globalisation of trade and the emerging information society has bred a desire to ensure that development of Europe's advanced infrastructure is interconnected and inter-operable with global networks. Therefore much of the work to standardise networks in Europe is set within the context of global requirements. The G8 initiative on the develop-ment of the information society reflects the desire for interoperability in many key TEN initiatives as part of developing global information infrastructures. This has been further enhanced by the number of European network operators that have become involved in alliances to develop global enterprise networks to meet the unique communication requirements of multinational enterprises.

PROGRESS TOWARDS TENS

The progress towards the development of TENs varies markedly across the sectors concerned. In transport, the financing problems are living up to the trouble anticipated. With the establishment of a TENs budgetary line, member states put forward bids which inevitably exceeded the funds available. To try and kick start the development of these projects and to overcome funding issues, the EU tried to use savings from the Common Agricultural Policy to put extra funds into these projects. This was resisted by Germany and the UK who felt that extra funding was irrelevant given a lack of confidence by private investors and technical problems. The European Commission believes that construction is being delayed as much by the aforementioned lack of confidence as it is by financing problems. This confidence gap is, according to the Commission, best closed by public equity support. The private sector still feels that the commitment from the public sector is insufficient to stimulate greater involvement by commercial actors and thus a lack of desire to develop PPPs by these bodies remains.

The development of energy TENs is proving more successful and over half the priority projects are on their way to completion. This has happened despite slow progress towards liberalisation within this sector. There have been delays in the development of projects in the electricity sector which have run into local/regional impediments due to environmental and other concerns. Once these are out of the way, the Commission aims to start funding for further projects of common interest for which it has agreed to partially fund feasibility projects.

Preparatory action for the development of the telecommunications networks is underway though initial actions came across resistance from network operators and a lack of funding from commercial actors. The development of networks has been aided by the actions of other bodies. Of note has been the European Telecommunications Standards Institute (ETSI) led 'European Information Infrastructure' initiative. This has focused upon achieving initial interoperability for Europe's emerging advanced broadband infrastructure. Whilst there has been substantial investment in telecommunications infrastructure, much of this funding has been directed towards meeting the requirements of business and not the broader socio-economic objectives of the TENs programme.

The legal framework for TENs has been hindered by disagreements between member states and the European Parliament. Part of this is derived from a continued reluctance of member states to adapt national priorities to build TENs. The administrative procedures are also still ill-suited to the development of commercial provision of infrastructure across-borders. The EU has sought to help by developing a help desk to smooth the process of administration of evolving projects.

A proposal that ebbs and flows on the agenda is the development of a European Infrastructure Agency (EIA). According to the Federal Trust, this would be an independent body which would have the power to evaluate TENs projects from a European dimension. It would draw upon the expertise of the financing bodies and industry in its work. In addition, it could take on board best practice to stimulate successful development of PPPs and provide advice to public bodies on infrastructure development. In the past, such proposals have met with hostility from the member states who were reluctant to cede power to such a body. The body is now envisaged as a co-ordinater but there is still little evidence to suggest that many member states have warmed to the idea.

CONCLUSION

TENs are an important complement to the ability of enterprises to function successfully within the integrating European economy. Despite this, TENs are still very much at an embryonic stage within the EU. This is partially due to the uneven state of liberalisation within the TENs sectors but also due to the fact that, for many priority projects across all the areas, the private sector seems to be unwilling to commit the funds needed to secure their development. The experience of Eurotunnel does not provide an example that would inspire many private operators to become involved in infrastructure development. However there is considerable private sector involvement within both telecommunications and energy sectors (see Chapters 11 and 12). Future private sector involvement in the transport sector seems increasingly to rely upon greater levels of public sector support coming forward to support more fully the strategies of commercial operators. This currently seems unlikely.

✎ KEY POINTS

- **Trans-European networks were born of the desire to complement the mobility and accessibility requirements of the SEM. This objective has been expanded to include the desire to achieve sustained economic growth.**

- **The sectors involved are transport, energy and telecommunications, though much of the policy effort is directed at transport.**

- **The realisation of TENs is to be through public and private sector partnerships though there are few, to date, that have proved successful.**

- **Progress has been varied across the sectors with each facing its own unique problems. Transport TENs, in particular, are facing huge financial difficulties.**

SUGGESTED FURTHER READING

Adonis, A. (Rapporteur) (1995) *Network Europe and the Information Society*, Federal Trust Report.

Cowie, H. (Rapporteur) (1996) *Private Partnerships and Public Networks in Europe*, Federal Trust Report.

Commission of the European Communities (1990) *Towards Trans-European Networks: for a Community Action Programme*, COM (90) 585, Brussels.

Commission of the European Communities (1993) *Growth, Competitiveness, Employment*, COM (93) 700, Brussels.

Commission of the European Communities (1994) *Financing the Trans-European Networks*, SEC (94) 860, Brussels.

European Parliament (1994) *The Financing of Trans-European Transport Networks*, DG (Research), Working Papers W-7, Luxembourg.

European Round Table of Industrialists (1989) *Missing Networks: the European Challenge*, Brussels.

Griffith-Jones, S. (1993) *Loan Guarantees for Large Infrastructure Projects*, EEC, Luxembourg.

Johnson, D. and Turner, C. (1997) *Trans-European Networks: the Political Economy of Integrating Europe's Infrastructure*, Macmillan.

Lawton, T. (ed.) (1999) *European Industrial Policy and Competitiveness: Concepts and Instruments*, Chapter 8, Macmillan.

Nijkamp, P., Vleugal, J., Maggi, R. and Masser, I. (1994) *Missing Transport Networks in Europe*, Avebury.

Stavridis, S., Mossialos, E., Morgan, R. and Machin, H. (1997) *New Challenges to the European Union: Policies and Policy Making*, Dartmouth.

Stoffaes, C. (1993) 'Europe and the Major Networks', *Annales des Mines*, December, 30–6.

10

TRANSPORT POLICY: TOWARDS EFFICIENT AND EFFECTIVE MOBILITY

> Efficient, accessible and competitive transport systems are vital to the society and economy of the Union. They ensure the well-being and quality of life of its citizens as well as the prosperity of its businesses. The links they provide are essential for the internal cohesion of the Union both in regional and social terms. At the same time transport policy must reconcile the need for mobility with the imperatives of ensuring a high level of safety and of protection of the environment.
>
> (*The Common Transport Policy Action Programme, 1995–2000* [COM (95) 302])

The Community's founders signalled the importance of transport in the development of Europe by according it its own title within the Treaty of Rome (Articles 74–84), the only sector apart from agriculture to be treated in this way. Why does transport merit such special treatment? The answers are various and relate to the characteristics of the sector itself, its role in fostering European integration and, increasingly, to the way in which transport has evolved throughout Europe. Efficient transportation systems are essential for the competitiveness of European business and to the process of European integration. The first section explores the contribution of Europe's transport sector to Europe's corporate and economic well-being. The following section traces the evolution of the EU's transport policy, drawing out some of its key features and its interaction with market developments. Given that the challenge of liberalisation posed similar problems across modes, the next two sections concentrate on policy in two sectors – road haulage and civil aviation. Road haulage has been chosen because of its dominance in the carriage of goods around the Community and because the single market has wrought major changes in the way shippers and hauliers conduct their business. Airlines have been chosen as the second mode because remaining barriers demonstrate the difficulties of achieving a genuine single airline market and because of ongoing controversy surrounding strategic alliances and 'open skies' negotiations with third countries. The chapter concludes with analysis of the dominant themes of transport policy as the European Union enters the twenty-first century.

THE IMPORTANCE OF TRANSPORT TO EUROPEAN BUSINESS

Transport is an important sector in its own right. It accounts for approximately 6 per cent of EU GDP, almost 30 per cent of EU energy consumption and about 40 per cent of public investment throughout the EU. In 1994, 5.8 million people worked in the EU's transport sector (4.5 per cent of total employment in the EU (12)), of which 3.6 million were in land transport; 228,000 in water transport; 293,000 in air transport and 1.7 million in support services including travel agencies, tour operators, cargo handling and storage. Regardless of any other considerations, the well-being of such a major sector must be of concern to policy makers.

An efficient transport system supports and promotes all other economic activities. Transport is an important cost factor for most sectors and efforts to control these costs have major spillovers for competitiveness. In particular, transport and related costs form a high share of the costs of high volume, low value-added goods such as construction materials and liquid products and initiatives to control their transportation costs effectively extends the market of such sectors. Table 10.1 demonstrates that logistics costs of 10 ten per cent of total revenue are commonplace in many sectors. Such costs include not only transportation but also warehousing, administration and the carrying of inventories, all of which are affected by the efficiency of the transport system. Efficient transport services also reduce the time taken for supplies and components to reach manufacturers, thereby enhancing the viability of just-in-time management, and the time needed for a product to reach its market – an important factor in time-sensitive sectors, such as the food industry. In short, not only is an efficient and competitive transport sector an important element in cost control and the development of competitiveness but it also provides a general stimulus to growth and brings more firms into direct competition with each other with secondary effects for competitiveness.

Table 10.1 EU logistics costs as a % of revenue by sector

	Transportation	Warehousing	Administration	Inventory carrying	Total
Automotive	2.7	2.3	1.2	2.7	8.9
Chemicals/petroleum	3.8	2.3	1.5	2.6	10.2
Computer/electronics	2.0	2.0	2.5	3.8	10.3
Electrical machinery and appliances	2.5	2.6	2.9	4.6	12.6
Food, beverages, tobacco	3.7	2.2	1.7	2.8	10.4
Machine tools/metal products	2.3	2.2	1.9	2.9	9.3
Paper/paper products	4.7	3.0	2.1	3.6	13.4
Pharmaceuticals	2.2	2.0	2.1	2.5	8.8
Wholesaler	2.9	3.0	2.2	2.9	11.0
Retailer	2.3	3.0	1.6	2.0	8.9

Source: European Commission, *The Single Market Review: Transport Networks*

Transport also plays an important role within the context of European integration. By facilitating and encouraging trade, an efficient transport sector and integrated transport network enables European business to take maximum advantage of the Single European Market (SEM). Indeed, the absence of an efficient European-wide transport system jeopardises the achievement of a genuine single market by limiting the quantity of cross-border trade within Europe. The realisation of these benefits depends both upon the liberalisation of Europe's transport sectors and upon the construction of genuine trans-European transport networks (see Chapter 9).

The condition of transport services has great significance for other policies, particularly the environment, an area in which congestion and vehicle emissions from the inexorable growth of road freight and passenger transport are increasing and seemingly intractable problems. Transport also has implications for public health and safety: increased vehicle usage pollutes the atmosphere with adverse consequences for respiratory disease and almost 50,000 people are killed and 1.2–1.3 million injured each year on the EU's roads. The promotion of social and economic cohesion through regional development is also a primary Community objective in which transport plays a key role. The Maastricht Treaty gives the Community the power to develop trans-European transport networks to satisfy the 'need to link island, landlocked and peripheral regions with the central regions of the Community' – a response to the view that there is a direct correlation between the level of economic development and the quantity and quality of infrastructure. Transport policy also has implications for external commercial policy, not only in relation to efforts to facilitate the accession of potential new member states but also in the negotiation of transit rights and in the Commission's attempts to gain the right to negotiate airline agreements with third parties, particularly the US, to protect the integrity of the SEM.

EVOLUTION OF THE COMMON TRANSPORT POLICY

Although its translation into practical measures was limited for many years, the legal framework of the Common Transport Policy (CTP) has been in existence since 1958 in the form of Articles 74–84 of the Treaty of Rome. The guidance given by the Treaty to the Council of Ministers on the development of the CTP was relatively vague and applied only to rail, road and inland waterways. The inclusion of air and sea transport was only confirmed later following a decision by the European Court of Justice (ECJ). More specifically, Article 75 empowered the Council of Ministers to formulate:

(a) common rules applicable to international transport to or from the territory of a Member State or passing across the territory of one or more Member States;
(b) the conditions under which non-resident carriers may operate transport services within a Member State;
(c) any other appropriate provisions.

Certain derogations are allowed under specified circumstances for the protection of living standards and employment. State aids are also sanctioned 'when they meet the needs of co-ordination of transport or if they represent reimbursement for the discharge of certain obligations inherent in the concept of public service' (Article 77).

In 1961, the European Commission published the Schaus Memorandum, which represented the first attempt to establish comprehensive and specific objectives and principles to enable the Commission to operationalise the CTP. The main thrust of the Memorandum lies in the need to introduce more competition in the Community's transport markets, but it does presage the later TENs initiative by alluding to the need for co-ordination of investments and the integration of transport systems. The Memorandum identified three key principles (see below) for the CTP which are entirely consistent with the subsequent evolution of the CTP and the TENs programme from the 1980s and beyond:

1 The elimination of difficulties in the general implementation of the common market arising from national transport regulations: this principle underpins later attempts to liberalise individual transport sectors as part of the SEM initiative (discussed more fully below in relation to road haulage and airlines).
2 The integration of transport throughout the Community: the originators of the CTP intended to establish common rules for transport between member states and to admit non-resident EU carriers to the markets of fellow member states. In later years, this integration increasingly referred to physical integration of transport systems through the TENs programme as much as to the creation of common rules, the impact of which would be jeopardised without physical integration.
3 The organisation of the transport system: this was initially interpreted to mean the introduction of a more competitive transport system. It also came to imply organisation of transport according to European rather than national requirements, both via regulations and by the development of a trans-European transport network.

BOX 10.1 MILESTONES IN THE COMMON TRANSPORT POLICY

1957	Common Transport Policy accorded its own section within the Treaty of Rome (Articles 74–84)
1961	Schaus Memorandum establishes comprehensive principles and objectives for the CTP
1982	European Parliament takes the Council of Ministers to the ECJ for failure to introduce the CTP in line with its Treaty obligations
1985	ECJ supports the European Parliament and requires the Council to table measures to liberalise transport services
1985	Single Market White Paper contains transport liberalisation measures
1987	Agreement on first airline package
1989	Transition agreement on the lifting of road haulage cabotage restrictions
1990	Agreement on second airline package
1991	Rail directive 91/440
1992	Agreement on third airline package
1993	Removal of most short sea coastal cabotage restrictions
1993	Maastricht Treaty gives the Community the legal base to develop trans-European networks
1994	Essen Council confirms the fourteen priority transport TENs identified by the Christophersen Group
1995	Publication of the 1995–2000 Common Transport Policy Action Programme
1997	All airline cabotage restrictions lifted
1998	Full cabotage liberalisation – road haulage

Despite this early flurry of activity, implementation of these CTP principles was limited for some time. For nearly thirty years, the transport provisions of the Treaty of Rome were interpreted to mean harmonisation of conditions, particularly of technical and social standards but progress was slow. Forging the CTP was made more difficult by the high and varying levels of state intervention and regulation in all transport sectors. In the road haulage sector, for example, cabotage restrictions and bilateral trade quotas were in operation; prices were regulated via compulsory tariffs; entry to the road haulage sector was strictly controlled by licensing systems and the range of taxation systems meant that competition was far from fair. Although the details varied, controls on price, quantity and market entry were also endemic in other transport sectors. State ownership, particularly in the rail and airline sectors also resulted in high levels of state aid. In short, for a variety of reasons, member states had seen fit for many years to protect their transport industries and to isolate them from the forces of competition – a situation which was clearly at odds with the principles of the Schaus Memorandum.

BOX 10.2 KEY TRANSPORT TERMS

Cabotage

The transportation of goods or passengers wholly within the territory of one country by lorries, vessels or aircraft owned by nationals of another country. Restrictions on cabotage were operative in the road haulage, short sea shipping, inland waterway and aviation sectors until the SEM campaign succeeded in lifting of such restrictions. A limited agreement on reducing road haulage cabotage restrictions was reached in 1989 and established the principle of ending cabotage constraints. This agreement paved the way for full cabotage liberalisation, not only in road haulage but also in other sectors – a central factor in the opening of transport markets to competition.

Fifth freedom

The right to carry passengers between two countries by an airline of a third country on a route with an origin/destination in its home country. The EU's three airline liberalisation packages have granted authorised EU airlines full fifth freedom rights.

Further complicating factors in the development of the CTP were the diversity of transport structures, national policies and modal preferences within the member states themselves. France, for example, followed a long term policy of developing the rail sector and maritime transport was not so important for the EC (6) as it was for later entrants such as the UK and Greece. Given the various roles that transport policy can play in the modern economy, member states have also often invested their transport policy with a significant role in regional policy and have imposed tight public service obligations on different transport modes. The need to serve its island communities, for example, made Greece resistant towards the lifting of cabotage restrictions in short sea shipping.

Notwithstanding all these difficulties, pressures for a more positive EU approach towards transport policy emerged from the logic of European integration and from the dynamics of long term transport trends. Table 10.2 shows that since 1970 road freight and passenger transport have consistently grown more rapidly than rail in virtually every member state, resulting in a much increased share for road passenger traffic and a halving of the share of rail transport. The switch to road transport is particularly pronounced in the freight sector where rail freight has, in most member states, either declined or demonstrated growth of less than 1 per cent per annum. Inland waterways are either declining or growing only slowly. These trends are anticipated to continue. Based on increasing average journey lengths, development of logistics, the growing use of the private car for leisure, greater intra-EU trade and higher levels of car ownership, forecasts of a doubling of road traffic within the EU between 1995 and 2015 are not uncommon.

Table 10.2 Average annual growth rates of the main transport modes in EU member states, 1970–94 (% change)

	Passenger[1]		Freight[2]			
	Rail	Road	Rail	Road	Inland waterway	Total Freight[3]
Austria	1.6	n.a.	1.0	4.4[4]	1.5	2.1
Belgium[5]	−0.6	2.0	0.1	4.6	−1.2	2.6
Denmark	1.6	2.5	0.4	0.8	–	1.1
Finland	1.4	2.7	1.9	2.9	−0.8	2.1
France	1.5	3.2	−1.3	2.6	−3.4	0.6
Germany[5]	0.7	3.0	0.0	4.3	1.1	2.2
Greece[6]	−0.6	0.3	−3.1	2.9	–	2.8
Ireland	2.1	n.a.	0.2	n.a.	–	n.a.
Italy	1.7	4.4	1.0	5.0	−5.1	4.0
Netherlands	2.5	3.1	−0.8	3.1	0.3	1.2
Portugal	1.6	6.7	3.6	n.a.	–	n.a.
Spain	0.3	4.5	−0.6	5.1	–	4.6
Sweden	1.2	1.1	0.4	1.6	–	1.1
UK	−0.3	2.5	−2.6	2.1	−1.9	1.6

Notes
[1] Passenger figures based on billion passenger kilometres
[2] Freight figures based on billion tonne kilometres
[3] Total freight figures includes transportation by pipeline
[4] Transport for hire and reward only
[5] German and Italian passenger road growth rates refer to 1970–93; German road freight and total freight figures refer to 1970–93; Belgian road and total freight figures and UK inland waterways refer to 1970–90
[6] Greek road passenger transport excludes private cars
Source: European Council of Ministers of Transport, *Trends in the Transport Sector, 1970–1994*

In the 1990s, over 80 per cent of domestic and 60 per cent of intra-EU freight travels by road and private cars account for three-quarters of medium and long distance passenger journeys. This growing dominance of road transport, whose attraction arises from its door-to-door flexibility, has resulted in a transport crisis in terms of both efficiency and the environment. Efficiency problems arise from bottlenecks, growing congestion and delays. Road transport is also the most environmentally damaging transport mode in relation to emissions and land usage. This helps explain why the CTP White Paper published in 1992 was sub-titled 'Sustainable Mobility' and why TENs emerged in the 1990s as a strong complement to the continuing harmonisation and liberalisation efforts of the EU.

The emergence of a more concerted attempt at developing the CTP received further impetus from the European Parliament which, concerned at the apparent transport policy stagnation, took the Council of Ministers to the ECJ in 1982 for failing to fulfil its Treaty obligations. In May 1985, the Court supported the European Parliament's position and required the Council to bring forward measures to liberalise transport services 'within a reasonable time'.

The ECJ judgement preceded wider developments which were to result in important breakthroughs in European transport policy. The British peer, Lord Bethell, had been lobbying for a number of years for the opening of Europe's airline markets. His campaign was helped by the spread of economic liberalism and supply-side economics which emphasise the benefits of competition, deregulation and liberalisation. The 1985 White Paper *Completing the Internal Market* was essentially about removing non-tariff barriers to trade (barriers which, as shown above, were rife in transport) and is an example of the growing reliance on the market as the guardian of competitiveness.

The SEM was the key to the substantial changes which have taken place in the transport sector since the mid-1980s and which, as shown below, have resulted in significant corporate restructuring, particularly of production and distribution networks. In 1988 the Cecchini Report estimated that failure to liberalise Community transport systems would result in costs to business which were 2 per cent higher than they would otherwise be. The additional trade flows and prosperity which were anticipated from the dynamics of the SEM would lead to higher demands for transport services and could be jeopardised by the fragmentation and inadequacy of Europe's transport systems.

These factors resulted in a two-pronged attack on Europe's transport problems: programmes to liberalise systematically all traffic modes within Europe and a campaign to develop trans-European transport infrastructure (see Chapter 9). As a result, the legal underpinnings of a single market in transport in the form of service liberalisation had, in theory at least, been largely agreed for all modes by the SEM deadline of 31 December 1992.

DEVELOPING THE CTP: THE CASE OF ROAD HAULAGE

The European Union has introduced a wide range of single market measures which directly affect the road haulage industry (see Case Study 10.1). Other non-specific measures will also affect this sector. The TENs initiative, for example, could have a major impact on road transport efficiency and result in modal shifts; third country relations have implications for transit rights and EMU will, as with all other sectors, affect road haulage. This section highlights the changes occurring in the EU's road haulage sector in recent years recognising that, although the pressure behind these changes is not wholly attributable to the EU, the CTP has played its part.

CASE STUDY 10.1 SINGLE MARKET MEASURES IN THE ROAD HAULAGE SECTOR

Liberalisation measures abolish border formalities and controls and extend access to the market and to the profession of road haulier across-borders. They are intended to increase competition throughout the EU market, benefiting productivity as a result. The end of cabotage restrictions, for example, will increase opportunities to pick up cargoes for return journeys, thereby boosting competition and the need for greater efficiency and innovation.

Harmonisation measures are intended to ensure that the increased competition between road hauliers from different member states is fair. The safety and social measures are designed to prevent road hauliers gaining a competitive advantage from compliance with lower national standards – a requirement which could place undesirable downward pressure on safety standards throughout the EU in an open market. The impact of harmonisation on hauliers' costs will vary from state to state.

1 Access to the market and to the profession of road haulier

Admission to the occupation of road haulier and mutual recognition of diplomas are both harmonisation and liberalisation measures and are central to the creation of competitive, efficient transport services. Unlike other road haulage SEM measures outlined below, these will tend to lower costs.

(a) Admission to the occupation of road haulier and mutual recognition of diplomas

Conditions which a road haulier must satisfy to operate throughout the EU include:

- a good reputation: that is, no serious criminal record or convictions for infringement of regulations (for example, driving hours, weight, dimensions, safety);
- appropriate financial standing;
- professional competence as demonstrated by professional qualifications or five years management experience in a transport company.

(b) Carriage of goods between member states

For many years, bilateral quotas limited transport between member states. Latterly, these quotas were complemented by annual Community quotas for the carriage of goods by road between member states. From 1993, quotas on carriage of goods by road between member states were finally removed.

(c) Cabotage

Limited cabotage was introduced in 1990 and cabotage restrictions were completely lifted in July 1998.

2 Tax harmonisation

Tax harmonisation applies directly to road haulage in three areas – vehicle taxes, excise duties on fuel and tolls and user charges for infrastructure. Contrary to liberalisation measures, tax harmonisation tends to increase road haulage costs. In 1993, minimum tax rates were agreed on some road freight vehicles and framework conditions were established for tolls and user charges for certain infrastructure costs. This resulted in the introduction of a common road user charge, known as the 'Euro-vignette', in Germany, Denmark, Belgium, Luxembourg and the Netherlands.

From 1 January 1993, minimum excise duties on mineral oils such as diesel have been in effect. Minimum duties allow a wide range of excise duties to co-exist above the minimum and the cost impact of these measures varies from state to state.

3 Safety and social measures

(a) Driving and resting hours

Directives govern regulations on maximum driving hours, minimum rest periods and the age and professional requirements of truck drivers. Vehicles must be equipped with tachographs for compliance purposes.

(b) Transport of dangerous goods and checks on the transport of dangerous goods

Conditions under which dangerous goods may be transported by road and inspection procedures have been harmonised.

4 Customs controls and formalities

Measures include the abolition of frontier checks and formalities relating to road vehicles, their drivers and the accompanying documentation.

5 Environmental regulation

Since 1970, successive directives have set standards for maximum permissible noise emissions from freight vehicles. Other directives have also set limit values for carbon monoxide, hydrocarbon, nitrogen oxide and particulate emissions from commercial vehicles. Further tightening of these standards is anticipated.

6 Technical harmonisation

Directives regulating the dimensions, weights and technical characteristics of commercial vehicles operating between member states have been in force for many years. Proposals to codify these directives into one umbrella piece of legislation and to extend harmonisation to national transport are under consideration.

Devices to limit the maximum speed of heavy freight and passenger vehicles on the Community's roads have been compulsory since 1 January 1993.

7 Safeguard mechanism

In the event of a crisis in the road haulage sector, the Commission may introduce measures to prevent overcapacity.

Road haulage provides the fastest and most flexible option for door-to-door carriage of goods and contributes more than 2 per cent to EU GDP. The majority of road haulage traffic in the Community is domestic with cross-border trade accounting for approximately 3 per cent of road freight transport in tonnage terms. However, given the greater average distance travelled in international haulage, the share of cross-border business in terms of tonne kilometres is much greater at almost 20 per cent of the total. As Table 10.3 shows, the Netherlands and Belgium have a disproportionately larger share of the EU's international haulage sector than the relative size of their economies would suggest. This reflects their location: the North Sea ports serve large swathes of north-west Europe and their domestic market is relatively confined. In addition, the Netherlands in particular has long had a more liberal road haulage regime than its larger neighbours, a factor which has placed Dutch transport and logistics companies in a strong position to cope with

Table 10.3 **Share of member states in cross-border road haulage, EU (12) (%)**

	Tonnes	Tonnes-kilometres
Belgium	20.0	11.1
Denmark	2.6	3.9
France	17.4	19.2
Germany	17.3	14.9
Greece	0.4	1.6
Ireland	0.6	0.2
Italy	5.7	10.9
Netherlands	26.7	18.8
Portugal	1.3	3.7
Spain	4.6	8.8
UK	3.4	6.6

Source: European Commission, *The Single Market Review: Road Freight Transport*

increased competition. The United Kingdom, although also maintaining one of the more liberal regimes for many years, does not have the same market share, largely because of its relative geographical isolation and lack of transit opportunities.

The road haulage sector includes a variety of company types, each of which have responded to the changing business environment in different ways. Specialist hauliers carry large amounts of cargo over long distances: their specialisation can be based on geography, technology (for example, refrigeration) or types of goods carried (for example, chemicals, cars). This contrasts with more generalist transporters who carry bulk, general cargo often in containers. Recent years have seen the evolution of some larger hauliers into logistics chain managers who take care not only of transport needs (which can also be contracted out) but also of warehousing and distribution functions. Larger, more specialised and logistically oriented companies tend to be based in northern Europe whereas southern European haulage companies tend to be much smaller, often consisting of a few vehicles or even owner-drivers.

The structural and strategic changes which are underway in the road haulage sector are the result of the interaction of a complex mix of changes occurring in the business environment. EU policy is only one of these changes, albeit an important one, and is both an agent of change and a response to changes in the business environment. Transport policy changes have an impact on both the consumers of the transport, in this case the shippers, and on the transport companies themselves. The changing demands of shippers feed into the strategic response of the haulage companies.

Regardless of EU initiatives, the requirements of shippers have been changing rapidly. The emergence of logistics as a distinct business function since the 1970s is both a response to the changes in the external business environment (such as internationalisation and the emergence of integrated trading blocs) and a cause of the changes themselves. The holistic approach of logistics to the management of product movement and broader changes in manufacturing have helped change the nature of transport demand. Just-in-time management techniques and shorter product lifecycles, for example, have increased demand for transport and reduced the average size of individual consignments, thereby increasing the number of journeys and placing a greater premium on reliability. Transport companies which can supply a range of integrated logistical services on a cross-border, or even a world-wide, basis are well placed to serve these shippers.

The SEM has been a major factor in the rationalisation of manufacturing and distribution sites throughout Europe and has encouraged the reconfiguration of commercial activities across boundaries. Companies are increasingly tending towards specialised production sites which serve the whole of the European market or beyond rather than producing several of their products at each site to serve smaller, fragmented markets. Pharmaceuticals company, Roussel–Uclaf, for example, has restructured its activities away from six multi-product plants to three specialised plants in different countries. Electronics multinational, Philips has moved away from fifteen national warehouses throughout Europe to a handful of regional centres. Companies are also tending to concentrate on their core business, leading to greater outsourcing of services and components and, in the transportation field, moving away from 'own account' business to 'hire and reward'. International transport statistics indicate there have been significant increases in tonne-kilometres over recent years which have not been matched by increases in tonnage, implying that freight is being transported over longer distances, as expected in view of the above trends.

Because of these changes, shippers have correspondingly rationalised their carriers and are basing their transport and logistics strategies on Europe as a whole or on significant sub-regions of it rather than on individual national markets. This has made business both harder to come by for carriers and has extended the distance over which goods are transported. The hauliers which benefit from this are the larger hauliers with a strong regional and/or logistics speciality and which have the financial clout to invest in the necessary equipment and information technology (crucial for tracking and tracing shipments) and to develop distribution centres. These companies are also increasingly contracting out the physical transport side of their logistics business to smaller companies – an attractive option, given that it is the sub-contractor who has to bear the cost of compliance with national and EU regulations. The contractor simply has to choose the most competitive bid.

Given the increasing trans-national nature of European industry, European logistics and transport companies are increasingly going trans-national themselves and building up cross-border networks. This is evidenced by the large number of subsidiaries maintained by the biggest transport and logistics companies outside their country of origin in the rest of Europe: Nedlloyd, for example, one of the closest to a comprehensive trans-European transportation and logistics company, has 170 European subsidiaries outside the Netherlands and is strong in most EU regions.

In the longer term, these changes could have a substantial transformational effect in the spatial distribution of economic activity throughout Europe, particularly if the result is a clustering and concentration of major production and distribution sites around key nodes and along main trans-European transport corridors. At one level, the emergence of large pan-European logistics providers, often engaged in strategic alliances with shippers who, as has been seen, are integrating and rationalising their activities across Europe, parallels the physical development of trans-European networks (see Chapter 9). The logistics networks which are being developed, like the physical infrastructure itself, are based on achieving time-space convergence accessibility and optimal network management.

The impact of EU measures on hauliers

The impact of SEM measures on the cost structure of the road haulage sector has pulled in different directions. Table 10.4 summarises the outcome of a simulation of the sources of cost changes carried out as part of a study for the European Commission on the impact of the SEM on road haulage. Whereas the liberalisation measures (cabotage, the

Table 10.4 International cost price changes in international transport journeys over 1,000 km as a result of SEM measures (% change)

	Range of cost changes
Cabotage	−3.3 to −4.1
Elimination of border delays	−1.8 to −2.1
Harmonisation of vehicle taxes	−3.0 to +0.4
Harmonisation of excise duties	+9.7 to +12.0
Speed limiting device	+1.0 to + 2.4
Euro-vignette	+1.2 to +1.6
Weights and dimensions	−0.6 to −0.9
Driving and resting hours	0

Source: European Commission, *The Single Market Review: Road Freight Transport*

Note: Simulation based on Belgium, Germany, Denmark, Spain, France, the UK, Greece, Italy and the Netherlands and based upon calculations in Deutschmarks

elimination of delays at borders, etc.) served to reduce costs through improved productivity, harmonisation measures had the opposite effect tending to place upwards pressure on costs. The introduction of minimum excise duties was responsible for the largest share of this upward pressure. The study estimated that the total effect of EC measures on road haulage resulted in an overall increase in costs ranging from 2.5 per cent in Germany to 7.2 per cent in Spain.

Despite these upward cost pressures, tariffs have not risen correspondingly and profits have declined, implying the existence of intense competition. Even before full liberalisation of road haulage cabotage in 1998, cabotage in terms of million tonnes kilometres increased threefold between 1990–4 with over half of cabotage mileage accounted for by the internationally minded Dutch and Belgian hauliers. This represented a new situation for international road haulage: before the mid-1980s, cross-border transport in most parts of the Community was regulated by bilateral tariff agreements, resulting in the absence of price competition and high profits. Competition subsequently emerged not only from the liberalisation measures of the SEM but also from deregulation introduced by member states in their domestic markets, including those of France and Germany, to accustom their domestic haulage operators to the forces of competition before it became a reality. In effect, the prospect of increased competition in cross-border markets encouraged the liberalisation of domestic markets. EU measures therefore had a much wider impact than on cross-border trades – the legitimate target of EU policy.

The combined impact of changes in the road haulage sector has been to create opportunities for both small and large operators whilst increasing the possibility that medium-sized operators will be squeezed between the two. Larger companies have benefited from liberalisation and harmonisation through possibilities of improved network management whilst passing on the burden of increased costs to small operators through sub-contracting. Larger operators also have the financial resources to make the substantial investments needed to reap scale benefits in terms of exploitation of advanced information technology – a requirement which acts increasingly as an entry barrier to trans-European trade, pushing smaller and medium-sized operators more towards national or regional business.

DEVELOPING THE CTP: THE CASE OF AIRLINES

Following the end of cabotage restrictions (apart from a ten year transition period for the Azores and the Greek islands), a single European civil aviation market came into existence in April 1997. Airlines have gained the freedom to set fares on both scheduled and charter services and all intra-EU routes have been opened up to EU operators. This achievement springs from three airline liberalisation packages which gradually chipped away at the substantial obstacles to competition. The First Package (1987) reformed capacity sharing practices so that member states were no longer able to insist that 50 per cent of traffic on a particular route be reserved for the national airline; granted limited fifth freedom rights; introduced more flexible procedures for fare approval and removed single designation provisions. The Second Package (1990) extended the liberalisation measures in the First Package. The Third Package (1992) completed the process: full fifth freedom and cabotage rights are in existence so that licensed EU operators have access to all international routes and are free to charge the fares they wish with some public service exceptions. Domestic markets were fully open by 1997 and member states are required to grant charter services access on the same basis as scheduled services.

Removal of regulatory barriers is only the first step in creating a world beating European airline industry. In its 1994 Report, *Expanding Horizons*, the Comité des Sages, an independent group of experts set up by the European Commission, concluded that 'European airlines pay a heavy price for the fragmentation of their market in Europe . . . In concrete economic terms, the structure of the European airline industry is still very much oriented towards outdated national boundaries.' The result is significantly poorer productivity, lower profitability and higher operating costs than US airlines. In other words, a number of other obstacles need to be removed before the full benefits of airline deregulation can be felt. The roots of these obstacles lie in politics (state aids) and lack of capacity (congestion, air traffic control, slot allocation, inadequate infrastructure):

- *State aids* have been notoriously widespread in the airline sector for many years. Intense political lobbying by member states regarding the survival of their national flag carriers has long defied the European Commission's attempts to eradicate this assistance. State aids seriously undermine the integrity of the single aviation market, allowing recipient airlines to distort trade and escape commercial pressures, thereby significantly reducing incentives to improve efficiency and putting non-recipient competitors at a serious disadvantage. The Commission has drawn up 'one time, last time' guidelines for state aids but, as Case Study 6.1 shows, their eradication has not yet been achieved.
- *Congestion* results from a variety of sources, including too few landing and take-off slots; shortage of terminal and runway capacity and aircraft stands; inadequate surface access to airports and air traffic management systems which fail to keep pace with the demand. Further congestion is anticipated as a result of current trends in air traffic growth and additional growth resulting from airline liberalisation. Congestion at airports and in the skies will prevent the full exploitation of market opportunities offered by the airline liberalisation packages and acts as a market entry barrier. Solutions to congestion in which the EU has a role include:

  - *Physical infrastructure*: improvement of airport infrastructure falls within the remit of the TENs initiative (see Chapter 9). However, the only airport project included on the list of priority projects is Malpensa Airport in Milan. In short, although there is a growing crisis in the provision of key airport infrastructure, the solution will not, in the short term at least, come from the EU. Although some EU funding will be available for airports in peripheral regions, the biggest boost to airport investment will come from the current wave of airport privatisations throughout Europe;

- *Air traffic control*: European air traffic control costs are frequently ten or more times greater than in the US and provide a good example of the damage caused to European airlines by excessive market fragmentation. European air traffic control is run from over fifty centres, causing complex and unnecessary management problems which add to costs and congestion. However, member states are proving reluctant to create a single air traffic management system in Europe.
- *Slot allocation*: given the infrastructure and capacity problems faced by many European airports, the allocation of take-off and landing slots has become an acute problem. The provision of additional capacity or the improvement of operating conditions is the best way to deal with the problem of slot allocation but this will not occur in the short term. Proposals to reform the slot allocation have been delayed until rulings on key strategic alliances have been made (see below).

Airlines in the global marketplace

Airlines account for by far the biggest share of passenger traffic between the EU and third countries. The indivisibility of the global and European markets has resulted in a fierce battle between the Commission and member states over who should have the responsibility for conducting airline diplomacy with third countries. The European Commission has frequently restated its claim to exercise exclusive competency in the negotiation of airline agreements with third countries, thereby ending the practice of bilateral negotiations between individual member states and third countries. However, although they have granted the Commission a limited negotiating mandate in this area, member states are exceedingly reluctant to relinquish further powers to it.

The case for EU competence in this area is strong. Bilateral agreements conflict with the principles of the single aviation market and threaten to undermine it. The Commission regards the bilateral agreements as discriminatory against EU nationals, therefore representing a fundamental breach of the SEM. For example, a bilateral agreement between Belgium and the United States prevents Lufthansa, or any other non-Belgian EU airline, taking advantage of open skies between Belgium and the United States whereas this possibility is open to US airlines. Transport Commissioner Kinnock claimed:

> By unilaterally granting US carriers traffic rights to, from and within the EU while ensuring exclusively for their own air carriers the right to fly from their territory to the United States, these member states create serious discrimination and distortions of competition, thereby rendering EU rules ineffective.

Anti-competitive practices on non-EU routes may also allow carriers to cross-subsidise unprofitable intra-EU routes. Furthermore, bilateral talks tip the balance of the negotiations in favour of the US. Separate negotiations with individual member states enable the US to create a network of agreements which give US airlines access to flights between member states. A fair return for European airlines would include not only access to the US market but also the freedom to fly from one US city to another – a freedom which is currently greatly limited.

If negotiations were conducted on the basis of two large internal markets, there would be more parity between the negotiating partners and a greater likelihood of opening the US market to European airlines on equal terms. However, a fixed determination to guard national negotiating rights within the European Union puts European airlines at a competitive disadvantage compared to their US counterparts and distorts the internal market. As it is, the bilaterals are one-sided and far from genuine open skies deals. Ownership restrictions on non-US nationals, for example, are much stricter in the US than they are for US carriers in Europe and cabotage is a concept which is not entertained by the US authorities.

CASE STUDY 10.2 STRATEGIC AIRLINE ALLIANCES

By 1998, most European airlines had negotiated or were in the process of negotiating strategic alliances, both within the European market and beyond, particularly with larger US carriers. This was partly a response to European liberalisation as weaker airlines search for survival strategies in the absence of protected national markets and as the more confident airlines seek to gain maximum advantage from the new opportunities. However, this trend is not just a European phenomenon. The US alliances hold out the possibility of protecting and increasing their presence on the profitable transatlantic market. The strategic nature of the alliances extend even further and many are aiming to achieve global coverage, looking to possible links with Asian airlines. Following the Asian economic crisis, many Asian airlines view tie-ups as a way of cutting costs and gaining access to more stable markets throughout the globe. As a British Airways director stated, 'It is all about building a global alliance network to counter the other networks that are developing . . . we believe that the way the industry is going is to build pan-national networks.'

The details of alliances vary but they all enable participants to reap economies of scale by combining frequent flyer programmes; by granting partners access to each other's schedules via code sharing and computer reservation systems (CRS) and by providing tie-ins for feeder systems. In some cases, alliances also include limited exchange of equity. In mid-1998, the following four US–European strategic alliances were awaiting approval from competition authorities:

- *The Star Alliance* which comprises United Airlines of the US, Germany's Lufthansa, Scandinavian Airlines System (SAS), Air Canada, Thai Airlines and Varig of Brazil. Probable new partners include Air New Zealand, Japan's All Nippon Airways and Singapore Airlines with Cathay Pacific reportedly considering membership. For a medium-sized European carrier like SAS, which also has links with Qantas and Iceland Air, strategic alliances give its 150 million passengers access to 535 destinations world-wide. The alliance received approval from the US authorities some time ago but in mid-1998 the European Commission's decision was still pending. The EU's approval may be contingent upon the airlines reducing flights between certain cities or restricting co-operation on frequent flyer programmes or on CRS.
- *The Atlantic Excellence Alliance* is composed of Delta of the US, Swissair, Belgium's Sabena and Austrian Airlines. Swissair, Austrian Airlines, Sabena, TAP of Portugal, Turkish Airlines and AOM of France comprise the Qualifying Group which complements the Atlantic Excellence Group and benefits from almost 300 destinations in 125 countries. This alliance is currently looking for Asian partners. Delta is reportedly looking into the possibility of an alliance with Air France which in turn is also considering a link with Continental which is already tied in with Northwest Airlines, thereby demonstrating how quickly alliances can extend seemingly throughout the whole industry with worrying consequences for competition.
- *Northwest Airlines and KLM* of the Netherlands were the leaders in formulating close operational ties but these could become difficult to sustain as additional partners join. In early 1998, Continental and Northwest announced their partnership. As mentioned, Continental is

continued

keen to push ahead with an alliance with Air France, a development which could cause problems for the Northwest–KLM link given the extensive competition between KLM and Air France in European markets and which could be further complicated if Delta and Air France continue to pursue links. This potential competition problem could be intensified by KLM's alliance with Alitalia: as initially envisaged, Alitalia's predominantly short-haul routes would complement KLM's long-haul portfolio. However, the potential introduction of Air France into this network could upset the balance and attract close scrutiny from EU competition authorities. In 1998, both Continental and Northwest signed an agreement with Air China and the search is on for further Asian partners to make this a truly global network.

- *British Airways (BA) and American Airlines.* The European Commission started to investigate this proposed alliance in 1996 and had not ruled on it by the middle of 1998. Approval is likely to be conditional on the surrender of a number of slots at Heathrow Airport: the Commission initially spoke of up to 350 slots but the final number is likely to be less. British Airways has been tireless in developing links and maintains over thirty of differing intensity with large and small carriers worldwide. In 1998, it concluded an agreement with Finnair which significantly improved its coverage in Scandinavia; it reached an outline agreement with Iberia in 1997; developed links with Air Liberté and TAT in France and has concluded a preliminary deal with Polish carrier Lot involving code sharing and possible equity investment. This strategy aims to create a seamless service across Europe. The American Airlines deal is easily the biggest one to date and significantly extends BA's geographical coverage.

This brief outline of the main trans-Atlantic alliances highlights some of the key questions surrounding strategic alliances. Do they represent a legitimate response to the intensification of competition in airline markets or do they inhibit the emergence of the full benefits of liberalisation? In addition, given the frequently shifting composition of some of the alliances, is it possible for regulatory authorities, and indeed for the alliance members themselves, to keep fully abreast of the competition implications of these alliances? These considerations are particularly pertinent in relation to the Northwest–KLM alliance in view of the proposed Northwest–Continental tie-up which could bring Air France into this particular network. The US authorities tend to take a more relaxed attitude to these issues than the European Commission. The position taken is crucial for the future of the airline industry: although the configuration of alliances could prove fluid, the pressures to form them are on the increase and are likely to be around for some time.

The Commission has been trying hard, with little success, to persuade member states of the case for EU-led negotiations. In 1996, it received a mandate to open talks with the United States which concentrated on the 'soft' aspects of open skies – safety, competition, ground handling rules, CRS access, environmental issues – and excluded the crucial issue of market access. Given the preference of member states for negotiating their own agreements, the only interest in talks with the European Union for the US Department of Transport is to secure access for its carriers to fly on internal services within and beyond the EU. This is not within the Commission's remit and can be achieved by the United States through bilaterals. Consequently talks between the US and the EU came to nothing.

Commissioner Kinnock, however, has not given up and in March 1998 began legal proceedings against member states (Austria, Belgium, Denmark, Finland, Germany, Luxembourg, Sweden and the UK) who have concluded 'open skies' agreements with the

US. The member states in question have two months in which to respond to the 'reasoned opinion' which has been sent to them under Article 169 of the Treaties by the Commission. The opinion sets out the Commission's reasons for believing that the member states concerned are breaking the law. If they fail to comply with the opinion, the Commission can take them to the ECJ. If this occurs, this issue is unlikely to be resolved by 2000 at the earliest. The Commissioner has tried to soften the opposition of member states by giving an undertaking that there will be no deterioration in the situation of any member state if the Commission takes over the negotiations.

The Commission has one potentially powerful card up its sleeve – the growth of strategic alliances (see Case Study 10.2) which are increasingly being brought into the debate. The Commission still has to rule on the admissibility of the four main strategic US–European alliances and, if it finds they conflict with the principles of the SEM (which is quite probable as their negotiation is dependent on the conclusion of bilateral 'open skies' deals) the Commission may only allow the alliances to proceed in line with very stringent conditions. In short, the battle over who has the right to regulate relationships between EU carriers and third countries is coming to a head and will involve some heavy political battles which may only be resolved by the ECJ.

CONCLUSION: THE FUTURE OF THE CTP

The CTP has passed through several distinct phases. Almost three decades of relative inactivity in which attempts were made to harmonise disparate aspects of member states' transport policies were followed by a phase from the mid-1980s in which major strides were made in the liberalisation of major transport modes as part of the SEM programme. Latterly, the development of transport TENs has assumed considerable importance as a way of ensuring, among other things, the efficient functioning of the SEM. EU transport policy in the early years of the twenty-first century will build on these broad trends and in particular on the following themes within the CTP Action Programme for 1995–2000:

- Improved quality via 'integrated and competitive transport systems based on advanced technologies which also contribute to environmental and safety objectives': this definition of quality incorporates a number of policies including the development of intermodalism; transport research and development within the Fifth Framework Programme; infrastructure development, via both the networks themselves and improved traffic management systems; and initiatives to improve public transport, which at EU level means further promotion of the 'Citizens' Network' concept which is intended to improve public transport. Efforts to develop 'sustainable mobility' will continue through improvements to the environmental efficiency of existing transport modes and via policies to ensure that user charges reflect the true cost of transport infrastructure.
- Improved functioning of the single market 'to promote efficiency, choice and a user-friendly provision of transport services while safeguarding social standards': single market transport legislation is extensive but enforcement requires greater attention and policies need further development, especially in the maritime sector, one of the more neglected transport modes.
- A broader external dimension to the CTP 'by improving transport links with third countries and fostering the access of EU operators to other transport markets': the maintenance by member states of bilateral reciprocity-based transport agreements with third countries has been identified by the Commission as an important source of SEM distortion and a factor which weakens the EU's efforts to promote its economic interests. The Commission is likely to be tenacious in its attempts to develop a common EU policy regarding transport relations with third countries.

From the business perspective, further developments in these aspects of transport policy will accentuate existing trends in logistics development and raise questions about the impact on competitiveness of environmental issues, particularly those relating to the internalisation of external costs. One of the big problems which has long dogged the airline sector, the high incidence of state aids which has seriously distorted airline competition, may diminish in importance as more state airlines move into the private sector. However, the real test of whether competition will really reign in the airline sector is how the Commission chooses to deal with strategic alliances, the pressure for which is growing ever stronger. Given the growth of these alliances, their constantly shifting composition and their spreading geographical reach, the airline sector provides a strong illustration of the need for the internationalisation of certain aspects of competition policy (see Chapter 6).

✈ KEY POINTS

- **Efficient and effective transport services underpin all forms of economic activity and enable European business to maximise their benefits from the SEM.**

- **Development of the CTP has been slow but the legal framework is now largely in place.**

- **The SEM has encouraged the reconfiguration of business activity across boundaries, requiring and receiving an appropriate response from the haulage sector.**

- **Despite upward cost pressures on road haulage, tariffs have not risen accordingly, indicating a strong intensification of competition.**

- **Airlines are forming global strategic alliances to cope with new competitive pressures.**

- **EU members are unwilling to follow the logic of the single airline market by continuing to grant state aids and limiting the ability of the Commission to negotiate 'open skies' agreements.**

- **Liberalisation and infrastructure development have been the overriding CTP themes of the 1990s and will continue to guide policy. Other priorities for the twenty-first century include quality, sustainable development and external aspects of transport policy.**

SUGGESTED FURTHER READING

Button, K. (1994) *Transport Policy: Ways into Europe's Future*, Bertelsman.

Comité des Sages (1994) *Expanding Horizons: a Report for Air Transport to the European Commission.*

European Commission (1992) *The Future Development of the Common Transport Policy: a Global Approach to the Construction of a Community Framework for Sustainable Mobility*, White Paper, COM (92) 494.

European Commission (1994) *The Way Forward for Civil Aviation in Europe*, COM (94) 218.

European Commission (1995) *The Common Transport Policy Action Programme, 1995–2000*, COM (95) 302.

European Commission (1995) *Towards Fair and Efficient Pricing in Transport: Policy Options for Internalising the External Costs of Transport in the European Union*, Green Paper, COM (95) 691.

European Commission (1996) *Towards a New Maritime Strategy*, COM (96) 81.

European Commission (1996) *A Strategy for Revitalising the Railways*, White Paper, COM (96) 421.

European Commission (1997) *The Single Market Review: Road Freight Transport*, Vol. II/5.

European Commission (1997) *The Single Market Review: Transport Networks*, Vol. II/11.

European Commission (1997) *The Single Market Review: Air Transport*, Vol. II/2.

Johnson, D., and Turner, C. (1997) *Trans-European Networks: the Political Economy of Integrating Europe's Infrastructure*, Macmillan.

Kiriazidis, T. (1994) *European Transport: Problems and Policies*, Avebury.

11

ENERGY POLICY: DEVELOPING COMPETITIVE, CLEAN AND SECURE ENERGY SUPPLIES FOR BUSINESS

Europe's energy sector encompasses some of Europe's largest corporations and poses a wide range of significant policy challenges which demonstrate several recurring themes in relation to the EU's interactions with business. These themes include liberalisation and deregulation, tax harmonisation, public service obligations, environmental issues, enlargement and the development of constructive sectoral relationships with third countries and regions – a process which takes on an additional dimension for energy in view of the demands of security of supply (that is, ensuring that the EU always has good quality, reliable sources of energy available). Not only are these themes central to the development of strategy in Europe's energy producers but they are also a significant to Europe's commercial and industrial energy consumers for whom energy can be a major cost component.

Although EU energy policy comprises a myriad of individual initiatives, all broadly fall within the framework of the following three main themes, or pillars, of energy policy:

- competition and the integration of markets;
- environmental protection;
- security of energy supply.

These themes have always been present in EU energy policy deliberations but their relative importance has varied in line with changes in global energy markets. For example, following the energy price hikes of 1973 and 1979, security of supply became the dominant energy policy concern. However, by the mid-1980s, the return of real energy prices to below pre-crisis levels, the re-emergence of oil surpluses and the single market campaign combined to reduce the relative importance of security of supply issues and thrust competition back to the forefront of energy policy priorities with the additional complication that environmental protection issues were becoming increasingly prominent. The competition and environmental pillars continued to exercise strong influences over EU energy policy at the end of the 1990s. However, security of supply issues are slowly moving back up the agenda as indigenous energy supplies start to decline. The key challenge for EU energy policy in the early years of the twenty-first century is to balance these three objectives to ensure they work in concert and not in conflict with each other.

The chapter opens with a brief discussion of the energy policy interaction between member states and the European Union. The diversity of energy industry structures, supply situations and attitudes to economic management have made formation of a common energy policy particularly problematic. The chapter then discusses in turn each of the three pillars of energy policy before highlighting how the pillars can both complement and conflict with each other. The chapter concludes by analysing the corporate response to the major policy-induced changes in their operating environment.

THE MEMBER STATE–EU ENERGY POLICY INTERFACE

EU energy policy is the result of a complex process in which the often diverse energy supply and demand situtations and different approaches to energy markets within member states have to be reconciled and in which the prevailing market situation invariably has an influence. Agreement on key electricity market access measures in 1996, for example, which had been the subject of long, often tense debate, only became possible because some member states had themselves tentatively started to open up their own markets and think the previously unthinkable in terms of market access. Similarly, several member states have embarked upon a series of reforms in their own domestic energy sectors in preparation for major EU-induced changes. At the end of the 1980s, the electricity supply industry (ESI) in most member states was organised almost entirely on a state monopoly basis. Box 11.1 indicates the extent to which this situation had changed by 1998.

BOX 11.1 STATUS REPORT ON THE LIBERALISATION OF ELECTRICITY IN MEMBER STATES, 1998

Austria	Mixture of state, regional and municipally owned generation and distribution companies. Partial privatisation of regional utilities planned and pressure to end market fragmentation in preparation for opening of EU markets.
Belgium	Generation mostly private but distribution by 600 municipal distributors. Closer ties proposed between Electrabel (electricity) and Tractabel to create a super-utility to compete in liberalised European market. In June 1998, Electrabel and Tractabel form Scandic Energy as vehicle to enter recently liberalised Swedish and Norwegian markets.
Denmark	Cross-ownership in generation, transmission and distribution has resulted in highly integrated industry. Radical opening of Danish market from April 1998.
Finland	June 1995 law liberalised key aspects of Finnish ESI. Consolidation of Finnish power sector secured following the European Commission's June 1998 approval of merger of state-owned oil company Neste and state electricity concern, IVO. Paves the way for privatisation.
France	Limited market opening proposed to secure minimum compliance with Electricity Directive. Dominance of state monopoly, EdF, to be reduced but access to French market likely to remain difficult.
Germany	April 1998 Energy Law, abolished the exclusive concession contracts and demarcation agreements which have impeded competition and kept prices high, thereby allowing all consumers to choose their suppliers. Despite certain

	caveats, this law goes much further than required by the 1996 Electricity Directive.
Greece	State monopoly but partial privatisation and opening of the state-controlled grid to private producers in the offing.
Ireland	Restructuring of state electricity monopoly, the Electricity Supply Board, and the introduction of independent power production, network access and independent regulation likely.
Italy	Italy lags behind other member states in preparations for the opening of the EU's power markets. Gradual liberalisation planned in which state monopoly, ENEL, retains its single buyer status. Privatisation on the agenda but not immediately. ENEL keen to form joint venture partnerships to position itself within the wider European market.
Luxembourg	Electricity supplied by imports.
Netherlands	Reform ongoing for several years. 1998 law to promote effective competition based on TPA and the use of infrastructure as free trade route. Netherlands has a highly fragmented power industry and many high voltage cross-border transmission links, making it vulnerable to competition from third countries.
Portugal	Restructuring of state monopoly, Electricidade de Portugal, has taken place to facilitate its gradual privatisation and the introduction of TPA.
Spain	Gradual liberalisation has taken place over several years. The 1996 Electricity Protocol (in force in 1998) introduces competition in generation and opening of retail market ahead of the EU Directive. A debate is underway about speeding up the liberalisation process and in July 1998 the Industry Minister approved a law allowing three companies from France, Portugal and Morocco to sell electricity on Spanish territory to large consumers.
Sweden	Participant in regional Scandinavian power market. Recent reforms → TPA at level of local distribution networks as well as access to regional grids.
UK	Privatisation of network agreed in 1996 and introduction of competition completed in 1998 with choice of supplier granted to all consumers.

The emerging central precepts of EU energy policy therefore have to be fitted into the constraints, interests and perspectives of individual member states. Thus while in general all fifteen member states feel able to sign up in principle to the three pillars of EU energy policy, the significance attached to each of these pillars varies from state to state, depending on individual supply and demand situations and diverse ownership and market structures.

Greece, for example, has been reluctant to embrace greater competition in its line-bound energy industries (gas, electricity and district heating). Given its limited resource endowment, its location on the south-eastern extremity of the EU and the conflict in the former Yugoslavia, which separated Greece for a time from the UCPTE network which connects up European power networks, further reinforcing its sense of isolation and vulnerability, Greece places a higher priority on security of supply than on competition. The UK, on the other hand, which has among the highest levels of indigenous energy resources in Europe and which already has experience of deregulated energy markets, has placed the opening of Europe's gas and electricity markets at the top of its energy policy wish list. Northern member states generally tend to be more advanced than their southern counterparts in setting environmental standards and goals to reduce emissions from their energy industries and are lobbying hard for similar measures at European level.

The strategic response of energy companies to market opening and environmental requirements will be strongly influenced by their starting point in terms of size and structure. Ownership, organisation and structure of the energy sector within member states ranges from giant state corporations such as Italy's ENEL and ENI, Gaz de France and Electricité de France and huge multinationals such as Royal Dutch Shell, BP and Elf Aquitaine to large, privately owned national companies such as Germany's RWE and Ruhrgas and National Power in the UK to a multitude of smaller and medium size energy companies, many of which are owned by regional or local authorities. Larger utilities are already seeking opportunities outside their national territories in preparation for greater market access throughout Europe. Smaller utilities are likely to become the target of predators anxious to establish a foothold in new markets or alternatively will seek to meet the challenge of extra competition from within a larger group.

THE COMPETITION PILLAR (THE INTERNAL ENERGY MARKET)

The competition pillar has been a constant, usually dominant, theme in EU energy policy since the 1950s. The emphasis of the first decade of the EEC's existence was on determining the broad principles of energy policy and on trying to co-ordinate a common approach to energy policy among the ECSC, Euratom and the EEC. Specific energy actions were limited but policy statements consistently emphasised the gradual creation of a market with the lowest possible prices and the widest possible consumer choice and the free movement of goods in line with the principles of the Treaty of Rome.

BOX 11.2 MILESTONES IN EU ENERGY POLICY

1951	Treaty of Paris establishes the European Coal and Steel Community (ECSC).
1958	European Atomic Energy Community (Euratom) comes into existence.
1968	Guidelines for Community energy policy give priority to competition and consumer interests.
1973	Yom Kippur War – oil prices quadrupled.
1974	International Energy Agency established to co-ordinate the OECD response to crisis, to assess national policies and to research energy. France declines to join.
1974	EC energy objectives for 1985 include 10 per cent reduction in energy consumption; reduction of dependence on imported energy from 63 per cent in 1973 to 40 per cent in 1985; greater use of natural gas (from 2 per cent in 1973 to 25 per cent in 1985) and 50 per cent of electricity to come from nuclear generation.
1979	Iranian revolution – further oil price hike.
1985	White Paper *Completing the Single Market*.
1988	Commission publishes inventory of energy trade barriers – *The Internal Energy Market*.
1990	Electricity Transit Directive adopted.
1991	Gas Transit Directive adopted.
1991	Gas and Electricity Price Transparency Directives into force.
1994	Green Paper on Energy Policy.
1994	Hydrocarbon Licensing Directive into force.
1995	White Paper on Energy Policy.
1996	Directive establishing 33 per cent opening of EU electricity market by 2003 adopted.
1997	Commission adopts proposals for taxation of energy products.
1998	Formal adoption of directive to open up a minimum of one-third of the EU's gas markets within ten years.

The oil price hikes of 1973 and 1979 displaced competition as the pre-eminent theme of EU energy policy for some years. However, the emergence of oil surpluses resulting from the incentives given by high prices to companies to find new sources of supply (sources which would have been unprofitable in pre-price hike days) resulted in the return of competition to the top of the energy policy agenda by the mid-1980s. The re-emergence of competition was also encouraged by the growing popularity of supply-side policies, both at member state level, led by the United Kingdom, and at Community level following the 1985 White Paper *Completing the Single Market*.

The application of SEM philosophy to the energy markets involves the fundamental transformation of nationally based energy markets with a large degree of administrative price setting and central planning into a European-wide market in which cross-border trade is significant and prices respond primarily to market forces. In other words, the aim is to forge isolated or semi-isolated national markets into a functioning, integrated 'whole' operating on market-based, cost-driven pricing via the provision of a 'level playing field' on which energy companies from one member state can compete equally with those from another.

Intensification of competition should increase the efficiency of energy producers, push down prices and improve the competitiveness of European business. EU enterprises are increasingly affected by the globalisation of the world economy. Not only is competition, therefore, more intense for both energy and non-energy companies from other EU countries but they are also increasingly competing in domestic and third country markets against companies whose competitive base is strengthened by lower energy input costs. In 1996, for example, German industrial electricity prices were more than double those in Australia and Canada and were 80 per cent higher than those in the United States.

At first sight, the introduction of competition into energy markets merely represents the application of the dominant economic liberal philosophy to the energy sector in the same way as it has been applied to all other sectors. However, certain perceived characteristics of the energy sector have made the process more problematic. Energy liberalisation began from a situation in which most gas and electricity utilities were structured as either national monopolies (for example, France, Italy and pre-privatisation UK) or as regional monopolies (for example, Germany). The most common perception of energy was that it was a strategic good and a natural monopoly which made it unsuitable for the type of changes which were being undertaken elsewhere in the single market.

Unsurprisingly, therefore, the 1985 Single Market White Paper contained no explicit references to the creation of an internal energy market. However, the general Treaty provisions and SEM proposals outlined in Box 11.3 applied to energy in the same way as to other sectors.

BOX 11.3 APPLICATION OF TREATY AND SEM PROVISIONS TO EUROPEAN ENERGY MARKETS

Treaty of Rome

- *Articles 30–36*: free movement of goods, exceptions to which are allowed on 'public policy or public security grounds'.
- *Articles 85 and 86*: forbids the use of restrictive practices or the abuse of dominant position.
- *Article 90*: public undertakings and undertakings which have been granted special or exclusive rights by member states are required to conduct themselves in line with EU competition rules

unless there is a clash with public service obligations (PSOs). PSO provisions are contained in the 1996 Electricity Directive and were introduced into the Amsterdam Treaty (Article 7d).

- *Articles 92–94* (Treaty of Rome) and Article 4 (ECSC Treaty). Given the inability of the Community's coal industry to compete against imported coal, state aids to the coal sector have become commonplace: since 1965 over ECU 75 billion of state aid have been extended to the coal industry. The Commission has drawn up a set of rules to govern state aid to the coal industry for the period 1994 to 2002.

Application of SEM provisions to energy

- *Technical standards*: EU standards policies apply to energy products and equipment and are central to public procurement policies and the development of energy efficiency under the SAVE programme.
- *Procurement*: energy, along with other previously excluded sectors (telecommunications, transport and water), has been brought within the scope of the Community's procurement rules.
- *Fiscal harmonisation*: the removal of fiscal trade barriers has been one of the least successful areas of the SEM, largely as a result of the unanimity requirement for fiscal measures and the centrality of taxation to the raison d'être of member states (see Chapter 4). In 1997, as a result of shortcomings of the already agreed excise harmonisation and as an alternative to failed attempts to secure agreement on a carbon energy tax, the Commission proposed to extend the scope of excise duties to cover all energy products (see Chapter 14).

The policy initiatives of Box 11.3, although important to the creation of the internal energy market (IEM), failed to address the many energy specific barriers within Europe. In preparation for removing these considerable obstacles, in May 1988 the European Commission published an inventory of barriers in the form of a Working Paper, *The Internal Energy Market*. This formed the base of subsequent proposals to free up the Community's energy markets – a task which has proven much more problematic than originally contemplated.

Given the international integration of oil markets; the large number of players (multinationals, state companies and smaller independents); oil price transparency and the alternatives to line-bound transportation, the oil sector is considerably more open to competition than other energy industries and has taken a relatively low profile in relation to creation of the IEM. That is not to say that the oil sector has been entirely without trade barriers: the 1988 IEM Working Paper, for example, identified a number of specific obstacles in the relatively new Mediterranean members. These were subsequently removed. More widespread barriers persisted in the upstream activities of exploration and production where most oil producing states reserved some or all exploration and production rights to national companies. This resulted in the Hydrocarbon Licensing Directive which brought these activities into line with single market principles through ensuring non-discriminatory access to exploration and production.

Gas and electricity are another matter, however. Initially, it was anticipated that gas and electricity markets would be fully open by 1996. However by 1996, it had only proved possible to attain agreement that member states would open up one-third of their electricity markets to competition by 2003 (see Box 11.4). Negotiations on the final phase of market opening are due to take place only nine years after the directive has been in force. Negotiations on gas market access proved so difficult that they were suspended until agreement on electricity was achieved. Gas negotiations recommenced following the electricity breakthrough and, benefiting from precedents set by the Electricity Directive, resulted in a political agreement at the end of 1997 and formal adoption of the Gas Directive in May 1998.

The Electricity Directive continued the work of the price transparency and the electricity transit directives which were both adopted in 1990. Prior to this, gas and electricity prices for large industrial consumers were unpublished and subject to negotiation and wide variations. The price transparency directive requires member states to inform the Commission of the prices and terms of sale of gas and electricity to industrial end-users. It contributes to the IEM by increasing the market information available to consumers, thereby enabling them to make more informed choices about the sourcing of energy supplies and will come fully into its own only when the gas and electricity markets are totally open.

The directives on electricity and gas transit mirror each other almost exactly. They require member states to take the necessary measures to facilitate the transit of electricity between high voltage grids and of natural gas between high-pressure transmission grids. The transport must involve the crossing of at least one intra-Community frontier. Each directive contains an annex which lists the grid operators subject to its provisions. In cases of non-agreement on transit conditions, the entities involved may request conciliation via a body set up and chaired by the Commission. If the reasons for non-agreement appear unjustified or insufficient, the Commission may take measures to 'implement the procedures provided for by Community law'. These provisions stirred up concerns among both the gas and electricity sectors that they represented the first step along the road to Community regulation of their industries.

Although an important milestone in the prising open of the Community's gas and electricity markets, the transit directives were merely appetisers to the main course of energy liberalisation – the introduction of third party access (TPA), later modified to a choice between TPA and the French-inspired single buyer model (SBM). Nevertheless progress in this area has been slow because of:

- the reluctance of some member states, particularly those lacking indigenous energy resources, to relinquish control of their energy utilities to market forces;
- the perceived need to control 'naturally monopolistic' enterprises such as gas and electricity utilities via national, regional or municipal government;
- fears of national energy monopolies about the erosion of their market control and level of protection;
- the fear of national energy monopolies that they will be left holding their public service obligations (PSOs) while new market entrants will be able to 'cherry pick' the most lucrative parts of the business, unburdened by PSOs;
- expectations that the introduction of greater competition will spell the end of long term contracts without which major infrastructure investments are regarded as too risky.

The traditional view of Europe's gas and electricity utilities as naturally monopolistic implied that effective competition could not be developed for line-bound utilities, thereby creating potential for abuse of market power in the form of artificially high prices and 'monopoly profits'. Given the central and sensitive economic role of these utilities, they have been controlled by public institutions at central, regional or local government level to ensure social obligations were observed and wide energy planning objectives (for example, priority for the consumption of domestically produced coal) were taken into account. The bundling of social obligations (for example, universal service, uniform pricing, social pricing, etc.) onto monopolistic publicly owned gas and electricity utilities in return for protection from competition is often referred to as the 'regulatory bargain'.

However, several member states have increasingly moved towards liberalisation of their gas and electricity markets, including the partial or complete privatisation of state utilities. Problems raised by the 'regulatory bargain' have been among the most difficult to resolve in this process. As some member states have found, problems of creating a competitive environment only begin with the transfer of a publicly owned monopoly into private ownership. Where 'natural monopolies' are no longer under state-ownership, the appointment of a publicly accountable, yet politically independent regulator has been made to try to provide the same economic signals to the monopolist as those within more competitive markets. This has the purpose of contributing to greater efficiency, lower costs, and greater attractiveness to private investors.

In recent years however, there has been a marked change in the perception of electricity and gas industries as 'natural monopolies' – a change which is the result of the disaggregation of the activities of utilities and of the realisation that they are amenable to the introduction of competition. These activities cover:

- *generation*: that is, the actual production of energy;
- *transmission*: long distance transportation of electricity and gas through high voltage grids and high pressure pipelines respectively;
- *distribution*: the physical transportation of energy from the grid to the end user through low voltage grids and low pressure pipelines;
- *supply*: a trading rather than a physical function which includes sales and metering and invoicing and which has both wholesale and retail elements.

While transportation or grid functions such as transmission and distribution are to some extent still considered as 'naturally monopolistic', other functions such as generation, wholesale and retail sales, metering and billing are increasingly regarded as prime candidates for competition. Furthermore, devices such as open access regimes and TPA have promoted the view that even 'naturally monopolistic' infrastructures such as transmission and distribution systems can be made more open to competition. The result of this more relaxed view towards this sector was the compromise reached on the Electricity Directive in June 1996 which was concerned with the following aspects of competition:

- *Competition in generation*: member states may adopt authorisation or tendering procedures for new generation capacity. The authorisation procedure allows generators to build and operate new plant subject to certain technical criteria (such as safety standards, energy efficiency standards, etc.). This procedure is largely driven by commercial criteria, rather than by centralised energy planning. Under the tendering procedure, planning for new plant capacity is in the hands of a central planning authority. Decisions regarding the type and size of new capacity are made through normal energy planning procedures. The competitive element is introduced at the 'building and operating' stage.
- *Retail competition*: member states must open an increasing share of the market to competition under one of two approaches:
  - *Third party access (TPA – either negotiated or regulated)*: under negotiated TPA, grid owners on the one hand and competitive suppliers or customers on the other negotiate conditions of access to the grid. Grid access charges must be published annually to enhance their transparency. Monitoring of the behaviour of the grid owners is likely to be undertaken by regulatory or cartel authorities, although there is no specific provision for this in the directive. Under regulated TPA, grid access charges must be non-discriminatory and published as tariffs (that is, not negotiated but authorised by special regulatory bodies). The Electricity Directive guarantees

open access only to consumers requiring over 100 GWh/per year. Member states will decide which other consumers will be able to choose their suppliers to ensure that the market opening goals are achieved (that is, 33 per cent by 2003).
- *Single buyer model (SBM)*: under the SBM, the 'single buyer' is appointed by the government and functions as the sole purchaser of electricity. The single buyer is obliged to purchase any electricity procured by eligible customers and at the final price which it would charge to the eligible customer minus a published tariff for grid access. The competitive element of the SBM comes from the differential between the price at which competitive suppliers can buy the original electricity from the generator and the resale price at which they can sell to the single buyer.

In line with the principle of subsidiarity, the Electricity Directive sets the broad parameters and principles of electricity liberalisation but leaves the details of implementation to member states. For example, irrespective of whether a member state chooses TPA or SBM, the Electricity Directive clearly defines the level of market opening required to ensure comparable degrees of competition. The Electricity Directive also does not establish exhaustive technical specifications for operation of the EU's post-liberalisation ESI. Any technical arrangements made must conform to competitive principles and not create discriminatory barriers to market entrants nor 'tilt the level playing field in favour of the home team'.

Given the time that it has taken to reach agreement on the Electricity Directive, it is understandable that the parties to the negotiations felt a sense of relief and achievement in concluding the deal. However, in another sense its achievements seem less remarkable. Only one-third of the total electricity market will be open to competition by *the end of the implementation phase* in 2006 when the Commission will review the Electricity Directive with a view to recommending further market opening. While there may be some justifiable criticism that the directive is rather modest and unambitious compared to the original proposals which urged full liberalisation by 1996, this is due to the diversity within the EU's energy sectors rather than to any lack of will on the part of the Commission. When decisions are made which affect crucially important economic aspects of member states such as the performance of their electricity utilities, agreements will inevitably be reached according to the lowest common denominator. This is especially the case when the energy circumstances of individual members are characterised by a wide diversity of resources, policies and historical development. Against such a background, it can seem remarkable that agreement was reached at all. The directive represents a major shift in policy and, as mentioned above, is responsible for a spate of reforms and changes in member states as they prepare for the impact of power market opening in the EU. It also gives some leeway to member states to adapt to the Directive in line with their existing practices.

BOX 11.4 MAIN FEATURES OF THE ELECTRICITY DIRECTIVE

Intermediate stage in attainment of internal electricity market – final phase to be negotiated nine years after directive comes into force.

- *Scope*: common rules for generation, transmission and distribution of electricity.
- *Objective*: an open competitive market in electricity without discrimination in terms of rights or obligations.
- *Public service obligation (PSO)*: member states may impose PSOs on electricity undertakings relating to environmental protection and security, regularity, quality and price of supply.

PSOs must be transparent, non-discriminatory and verifiable and must be notified to the Commission.

- *Generation*: member states can choose between an authorisation or tendering procedures for new generating capacity. The procedure adopted must be objective, transparent and non-discriminatory and must not exclude autoproducers or independent power producers.
- *Unbundling and transparency of accounts*: integrated electricity companies to keep separate accounts for generation, transmission and distribution activities to avoid possible discrimination, cross-subsidisation and distortion of competition.
- *Co-existence of third party access and the Single Buyer Model*: whichever model is chosen, access must lead to equivalent economic results, and to directly comparable market opening and degree of access to markets across member states.
- *Market opening*: progressive and gradual according to the following indicative timetable:

    19.2.1999 – 22 per cent of national markets opened to final consumers consuming over 40 GWh p. a

    19.2.2000 – 27 per cent of national markets opened to final consumers consuming over 20 GWh p. a

    19.2.2003 – 33 per cent of national markets opened to final consumers consuming over 9 GWh p. a.

- *Transitional regime*: to tackle 'stranded investment' problems, member states may apply for a transitional regime if the directive inhibits prior commitments.
- *Safeguard measures*: member states are allowed to take temporary safeguard measures in the event of a crisis in energy markets or a sudden threat to 'system integrity'. Such measures must be proportionate to the crisis and will be subject to Commission oversight.
- *Derogations*: Greece (two years), Belgium (one year) and Ireland (one year) have longer to apply the Directive.

Source: Directive 96/92/C concerning common rules for the internal market in energy.

THE ENVIRONMENT PILLAR

The link between the environment and energy is a key consideration in the formation of energy policy. This has not always been the case. The prime objectives of EU energy policy during its first twenty-five to thirty years, when environmental awareness was rudimentary, fluctuated between common market and security of supply issues. This only began to change in the 1980s with the emergence of concerns in Scandinavia and Germany about acid rain. By the end of the decade, the issue of global warming had moved into the political mainstream, further strengthening the link between environmental and energy issues. Policy initiatives aimed at tackling the climate change problem were bound to have an impact on the energy sector which, although not the only cause of global warming, is a major contributor to it.

The energy sector is subject to the general tenets and principles of EU environment policy within the framework of the Fifth Environmental Action Programme (EAP) (see Chapter 14) and is one of the sectors identified by the Fifth EAP as requiring a special effort to integrate environmental issues into its policy deliberations. In broad terms, the Fifth EAP defined the environmental challenge for the energy sector in similar terms to the challenge for energy policy generally: that is, the need to reconcile economic growth and efficient and secure energy supplies with a clean environment.

Initiatives relating to the energy-environmental interface stress the following areas:

- Development and application of energy-saving technologies and practices, including renewables and co-generation. Union support for this priority comes from individual programmes such as SAVE II (energy efficiency), Altener (renewables) and Joule–Thermie (general energy research and technological development) and from a general commitment to the encouragement of renewable energy sources as set out in the 1996 Green Paper on Renewable Energy Sources which established a target of a 15 per cent share for renewables in primary EU energy demand by 2010;
- Implementation of demand-side measures, the internalisation of external costs and benefits, via the tax system and in non-fiscal ways, and improved co-ordination of consumer awareness initiatives in Community energy saving programmes;
- Reinforcement of energy efficiency standards for appliances and provisions for energy efficiency labelling;
- Development of strategies and targets to restrict and reduce environmentally damaging emissions. These include the EU's climate change strategy (see Case Study 11.1); its strategy to eradicate acid rain; and the Auto-Oil initiative, a long term programme designed to reduce emissions from road transport involving extensive collaboration by the European Commission with Europe's oil and automobile industries.

CASE STUDY 11.1   THE EU'S CLIMATE CHANGE STRATEGY

The increased concentration of greenhouse gases (carbon dioxide, nitrogen oxides and methane) are commonly held responsible for the gradual increase in the earth's temperature which is allegedly having a destabilising effect on the world's ecological balance. Energy's contribution to the climate change problem is significant, with three-quarters of man-made carbon dioxide emissions originating from the combustion of fossil fuels.

The EU has developed its own strategy to deal with climate change which, given the international interdependence of this particular environmental problem, it is also promoting through international fora such as the summit held in Kyoto in December 1997. The Kyoto Protocol stipulated an average 5.2 per cent reduction by 2010 in six greenhouse gases compared to 1990 levels by the major industrialised countries. The EU was assigned a target of an 8 per cent reduction, the United States 7 per cent and Japan 6 per cent. The principle of emission permits was also agreed. In March 1997, the Environmental Council had agreed an objective and a negotiating position of a 15 per cent reduction in greenhouse gas emissions by 2010. Disappointing though this outcome was in relation to the initial negotiating position, attainment of these goals requires success in a number of initiatives, which will have quite profound implications in some areas for energy companies and which also interact with other energy–environment objectives:

- An action plan to reduce methane, particularly from oil and gas production: the application of best available recovery techniques for coal mines; pipeline inspections and minimum leakage standards or voluntary agreements for gas pipelines.
- Technology and innovation: the promotion of technologies which favour greenhouse gas reduction such as combined cycle gas turbines, fuel cells, clean coal, renewables, vehicle and engine improvements, enhanced efficiency of household appliances, electrotechnical

equipment and electronic energy-control devices in the home. This will be carried out via the Fifth Research and Technological Framework programme which includes Joule–Thermie, the energy research programme.

- Energy saving (SAVE II) and energy efficiency standards, including standards for household appliances, home entertainment equipment, office machinery, lighting products, space heating equipment and air compressors along the lines of those agreed for refrigerators and freezers in 1996.
- Renewable energy programmes: according to the Commission, attainment of a 12.5 per cent share of renewables in energy consumption would lead to a reduction in CO_2 emissions of 386 million tonnes per annum by 2010, equivalent to 12 per cent of such emissions.
- Programmes relating to Combined Heat and Power (CHP), energy efficiency improvements in the transformation sector and fuel switching.
- Programmes relating to energy efficiency improvements in heavy industry and large combustion plants: the May 1997 Energy Council indicated that Long Term Agreements with Industry on Energy Efficiency (LTAs) could be an effective and flexible way of implementing energy efficiency measures. Key elements of LTAs are quantified targets for a fixed period, the development of energy efficiency improvement plans for companies and an independent monitoring process.
- Initiatives relating to improved energy efficiency in buildings – a feature of the current SAVE II programme.
- The progressive reduction and removal of subsidies, tax schemes and regulations which counteract the efficient use of energy: this would include the eventual phasing out of subsidies to the coal industry, for example.
- An increase in minimum tax levels to reduce greenhouse gas (GHG) emissions and to improve energy efficiency.
- Integration with other policies: the Commission is anxious that other policies, especially agriculture and forestry policy, environmental and waste management policy, transport policy, research and development policy, fiscal policy, regional policy, should take into account the need to reduce GHG emissions from energy-related activities. In 1997, the Commission published a communication which integrated all proposed climate change measures in all policy areas. For example, greater use of the Structural and Cohesion Funds to help reduce GHG emissions can be expected and, within the context of Common Agricultural Policy (CAP) reform, an initiative to encourage the use of biomass to produce energy could serve both energy policy and CAP objectives.

THE SECURITY OF SUPPLY PILLAR (THE INTERNATIONAL DIMENSION)

The EU is a major net energy importing region. This import dependence relates not only to oil but also to coal and gas (see Table 11.1), two fuels which will see a dramatic increase in import shares in the first two decades of the twenty-first century. Eastward enlargement will increase the EU's external energy dependency: the addition of 1994 CEE imports to EU figures, for example, would have added a further 67 mtoe to the EU's 634 mtoe of net energy imports.

The growing gap between EU domestic energy production and consumption implies an increasing role for energy imports in coming decades (see Figure 11.1) and the need to

Table 11.1 1997 EU energy import dependency by fuel

	Consumption	Production	Net imports	Net imports as % of consumption
Oil (mt)	624	145	479	77
Gas (bcm)	336	199	137	41
Coal (mt)	215	122	93	43

Source: Derived from *BP Statistical Review of World Energy*, June 1998

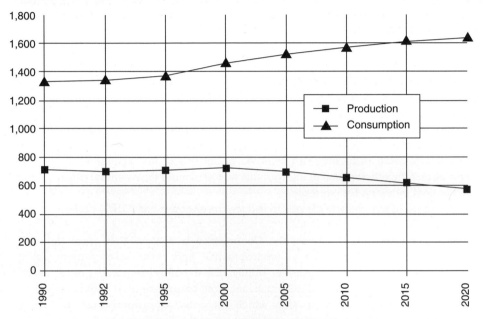

Figure 11.1 EU primary energy supply–demand balance, 1990–2020 (mtoe)
Source: European Commission

pay greater attention to security of supply issues. In the base case scenario of a major forecasting exercise, the European Commission forecast that indigenous energy production will peak at around 720 mtoe by 2000, declining thereafter to 575 mtoe by 2020. In contrast, energy consumption is forecast to rise by a modest 0.7 per cent per annum. This will nevertheless result in an increase in energy demand to around 1,640 mtoe by 2020, of which more than 1,000 mtoe (that is, 65 per cent of total demand) must be met by imports. Failure to secure these supplies will have unacceptable economic and political consequences.

Given the substantial growth anticipated in the EU's dependence on external energy supplies, those countries, groups of countries or geographic regions, possessing substantial hydrocarbon reserves, such as the Middle East, North Africa, and the republics of the former Soviet Union (FSU) will play a crucial role in meeting the energy needs of EU citizens and companies. The European Commission views close energy trade relations as a means not only of securing energy supplies but also as an important tool for promoting economic growth and development (and therefore political stability) among producer nations. Various EU initiatives are intended as long term supply measures by:

- promoting international energy trade and investment to enlarge the number of energy interconnections;
- facilitating inward investment flows to energy producers to develop new oil and gas fields;
- providing transit and investment safeguards which benefit both the energy producer and consumer.

In addition, and particularly in its energy relations with the rapidly growing Far Eastern energy markets, the EU increasingly views energy diplomacy as a means of securing trade and investment opportunities for EU energy producers, equipment suppliers and engineering and construction companies (see Box 11.5).

BOX 11.5 EU ENERGY DIPLOMACY

Central and Eastern Europe (CEE)

PHARE programme established in 1990: PHARE energy projects help prepare the CEE countries for accession by addressing key energy problems, including inadequate energy infrastructure; low energy prices; over-reliance on FSU resources; inefficiency and waste in energy production, distribution and transmission; and poor environmental standards.

Former Soviet Union (FSU)

The Energy Charter Treaty (ECT) aims to provide a legal framework for energy trade, transit and investment. It offers supply security to the EU and inward investment and technology transfer to the FSU.

TACIS (Technical Assistance Commonwealth of Independent States): energy and nuclear safety together account for about 30 per cent of TACIS funding with the objective of introducing a more market-oriented approach to energy supply and greater efficiency in production, transmission, distribution and consumption.

Black Sea

The Black Sea Regional Energy Centre established in Sofia in 1995 under the EU's Synergy programme to promote energy co-operation among countries around the Black Sea, an important energy transit point and central to EU energy security.

Mediterranean

The role of North African and Eastern Mediterranean countries as energy producers and consumers places energy at the heart of the Euro-Mediterranean Partnership (see Chapter 17). The initial work of the European Mediterranean Energy Forum, which met for the first time in May 1997, was aimed at developing a framework for medium term action to cover market opening, energy efficiency, energy investment, infrastructure links and greater co-operation in research, development and technology transfer.

Gulf Co-operation Council (GCC)

Since the early 1980s, driven by the interdependence of their markets, the EU and the GCC (Bahrain, Kuwait, Oman, Qatar, Saudi Arabia and the United Arab Emirates) have sought closer ties. The 1988 EC-GCC Co-operation Agreement covered many economic and cultural issues and contained a commitment to an EC–GCC free trade area. Progress has been limited but the dialogue was relaunched in the mid-1990s.

continued . . .

Asia	The 1995 Energy White Paper urged closer energy co-operation with Asia. In May 1997, the Energy Council adopted a communication on EU energy co-operation with eighteen Asian countries. The EU strategy is driven by the hitherto rapid economic and energy demand growth in Asia, which currently represents 50 per cent of the world energy equipment market, and is aimed at:

- modernisation of Asia's electricity sector, which currently accounts for 80 per cent of annual energy investment in the continent (over ECU 40 bn per annum);
- promotion of natural gas in view of the potential of China, India, Bangladesh, Indonesia and the Philippines in this sector;
- clean coal and CHP technologies: coal accounts for 30 per cent of the region's energy consumption. Its use in power generation continues to grow rapidly with adverse environmental consequences;
- promotion of rational energy use in power generation, industry, transport and urban areas;
- security of supplies in rural areas, especially via the use of renewables;
- development of regional energy resources.

China	The EU–China Energy Working Group was established in 1996 and provides opportunities for EU energy companies in the development of China's under-utilised energy resources. China's rapidly growing fossil fuel demand could destabilise international energy markets and attempts to constrain global CO_2 emissions. China will benefit from technology and know-how transfer and inward investment.
Latin America	The ALURE programme provides limited funding to encourage energy co-operation between the European Union and Latin America.

INTERACTION BETWEEN PILLARS

There is significant inter-linkage between the three energy policy pillars of competition, environmental protection and security of supply. In some cases, the links are complementary and in others, they are conflicting. The promotion of energy efficiency, for example, improves both environmental protection and energy supply security. However, competition measures which lower energy costs to consumers may weaken incentives to enhance energy efficiency and increase demand and therefore could have negative security of supply and environmental effects.

Support for technological research and development is also aimed at making renewable resources more competitive with conventional resources. Promoting Europe as a 'centre of excellence' for energy efficiency technologies will also yield benefits in global terms as countries outside the EU become increasingly committed to improving their own efficiency, environmental protection and supply security levels. Energy efficiency represents a potentially huge export market for European technology and services, a factor which is reflected in energy trade diplomacy.

The energy TENs initiative is a prime example of a policy which incorporates all three pillars (see Chapter 9). There is a strong link between the IEM which removes legal barriers to energy trade, and energy TENs which remove physical barriers to energy trade. Without the physical means to take advantage of the IEM, the benefits of increased competition, greater efficiency, lower costs, greater competitiveness and economies of scale will remain theoretical and elusive. Energy TENs also serve security of supply by improving the efficiency and reliability of existing supplies and by diversifying supply sources and routes. The environmental pillar benefits from increased access to natural gas supplies which emit lower levels of carbon dioxide than other fossil fuels.

CONCLUSION: CORPORATE RESPONSES TO EU ENERGY POLICY

Although the effect of the environmental and security of supply pillars of EU energy policy on European business should not be underestimated, it is the deregulation of markets which will have the most profound long term effect on business practices and strategies and, ultimately, on market organisation in Europe. The ramifications of the reforms will take many years to materialise fully. However, it is already possible at this early stage to speculate about corporate reactions to the opening of the gas and electricity markets by drawing upon the experience of what has already happened and is happening in the US, UK (see Case Study 11.2) and Scandinavian markets which have already experienced liberalisation. This leads to the following conclusions about the possible results of market opening.

Lower energy prices and changes in purchasing practices

Experience in US utility markets, which were open to competition before European markets, provide some guidance over the possible price and purchasing trends. US gas markets have been open for years and electricity market opening is underway, although it has proceeded further in some states than others. Between 1983–94, US well-head gas prices fell by 44 per cent and residential electricity consumers in pilot projects in New Hampshire, one of the fastest states to open its market, have experienced price reductions in excess of 30 per cent. In the United Kingdom, where full competition did not occur until 1998, domestic electricity prices fell by 18 per cent in real terms between 1990 and early 1997 and real power prices for industrial consumers fell by 16 per cent between 1994 and early 1997.

Falling gas and electricity prices will characterise Europe's markets following the introduction of greater competition. This will be particularly significant for energy intensive industries for whom energy prices comprise a significant proportion of costs. In the case of primary metals, building materials and chemicals, energy can account for up to 40 per cent of production costs. Any reduction in such a major cost component will bring significant benefits for competitiveness in such sectors.

Lower prices and the introduction of choice of supplier will also have a major impact on purchasing practices and patterns of major industrial consumers and transfer an element of the commercial risk from the buyer to the seller. The reforms imply a shift from a long term, stable relationship between buyer and seller to a wholesale market for energy similar to that for any other product (the technical arrangements for such markets will vary between member states). The experience so far in the United States and United Kingdom indicates a willingness of consumers, particularly larger industrial consumers, to shift suppliers in search of the lowest cost supplies. One probable development will be the emergence of single buyers for energy for large industrial groups. Previously, enterprises with scattered sites would have purchased their supplies from the monopoly supplier. However, group purchasing of energy, and indeed of other utilities, offers the possibility of obtaining lower prices for bulk purchases. In addition, it enables enterprises to develop expertise in utility purchases, which requires market and technical knowledge, and obviates the need for a number of teams to carry out the same function.

CASE STUDY 11.2 POST-PRIVATISATION RESTRUCTURING IN THE UK ELECTRICITY SUPPLY INDUSTRY (ESI)

The privatisation of the UK ESI took place against the background of massive privatisation of state-owned industries in the United Kingdom and was one of the earliest and most comprehensive attempts at power deregulation in Europe. The process began in 1990 and was completed in 1996 with the sale of Nuclear Electric (renamed British Energy). However, the introduction of competition was phased in over several years and was only completed in 1998 when it became possible for domestic consumers to choose their suppliers.

Upon privatisation, the UK government reorganised the industry in England and Wales into two generation companies (National Power and PowerGen), one nuclear company (Nuclear Electric), twelve regional electricity companies (RECs) and National Grid. Scotland acquired two integrated companies and the Northern Ireland ESI became Northern Ireland Electricity. This structure altered rapidly after privatisation following a series of mergers and acquisitions which resulted in greater vertical integration on the part of the RECs. Foreign utilities, especially from the US, were particularly prominent in this activity. There was also some internal consolidation of utilities as shown by Scottish Power's acquisition of Manweb and the acquisition/merger of local power and water utilities in Wales and north-west England. Southern Electricity bought Southern Water and has obtained a licence to become a distributor of natural gas, giving it the potential to become the country's first regional multi-utility. Many other utilities are following suit in 1998 as a result of the opening of energy markets for gas and electricity consumers.

Examples of post-privatisation mergers and acquisitions in the UK ESI

Regional electricity company	Acquirer/merger partner	Acquisition
East Midlands Electricity		
London Electricity	Electricité de France	
Yorkshire Electricity	Prudential (4.9 per cent US)	
Northern Electric	Failed bid by Trafalgar House	
Eastern Group	Hanson (UK)	
Southern Electric		Southern Water
Midlands Electricity	General Public Utilities and Cinergy (US)	
Manweb	Scottish Power (UK)	
South Western Electricity	Southern Company (US)	
Seeboard	Central and South West (US)	
Norweb	North West Water (UK)	
South Wales Electricity	Welsh Water (UK)	
Generators		
Northern Ireland Power Plant, Kilroot	NIGEN (US/Belgian)	
Northern Ireland Power Plant, Belfast	NIGEN	
Northern Ireland Power Plant	British Gas	

Not all merger and acquisition attempts were successful. The UK government blocked National Power's attempt to take over Southern Electric and a proposed merger with Southern Electric of the US because of concerns about the potential erosion of competition. However, the Hanson Corporation, through its distribution subsidiary Eastern Group, has been allowed to purchase power stations from both PowerGen and National Power, facilitating the creation of an integrated power company.

In addition to mergers and acquisitions there have been a number of investments in independent power producers by both European and US investors. Enron of the US has taken a 50 per cent stake in the world's largest gas-fired power station located in Teesside. Seeboard and AES have a major stake in a development in Medway and Finland's IVO, along with Tomen and ABB, has been active on the south bank of the Humber Estuary.

As competition continues to unfold in the UK, restructuring through mergers and acquisitions and through foreign direct investment will continue, providing a possible template for what might follow in European markets as the Electricity Directive starts to take effect.

Strategic flexibility

Utilities will respond to the new European market situation by assessing their strategic positioning in the market (see Case Study 11.2). One possibility is the development of horizontal integration leading to the emergence of 'super utilities' which bundle together not only gas and electricity sales but perhaps also water and telecommunications. Again this is not unknown in the United States and has taken place to some extent in the United Kingdom. This allows for economies of scale in certain areas (for example, network utilisation, billing and retail activity) and allows one-stop utility shopping for consumers. It also entails the dangers of diversifying out of core areas of business.

Vertical integration throughout the whole of the energy value chain will also become commonplace. Gas producers, for example, will be able to utilise their supplies in electricity generation, thereby reducing some of their commercial risk. Electricity generators have the possibility of becoming increasingly involved in raw material supply. US oil and gas producer, Conoco, and its parent company, Du Pont, a substantial industrial energy consumer, anticipate greater integration of their activities within a liberalised European energy market through the sale of Conoco-produced North Sea gas to electricity and steam generation units on Du Pont industrial sites. Electricity generated in this way can be traded throughout the parent group in Europe. Market liberalisation will also encourage autoproducers to increase their production capabilities to trade beyond their corporate borders.

Geographic flexibility

Closely allied to the concept of strategic flexibility is that of geographical flexibility. That is, with the extension of market boundaries, energy suppliers will enter the utility markets of other member states, either on their own or through the development of joint ventures, strategic alliances or mergers and acquisitions.

In some cases, they will also be driven to develop defensive alliances to protect their domestic markets and will be subject to predatory take-overs. A large degree of cross-ownership and long term contracts can be expected and is happening in the liberalised Scandinavian power market. Norway's Statkraft and PreussenElektra of Germany have become major shareholders in Sweden's Sydkraft. Sydkraft and PreussenElektra have bought shares in Hamburgerische Elektrizitätswerke and PreussenElektra and Statkraft have signed a long term electricity exchange contract and are building a submarine cable between Norway and Germany. All the big European energy utilities are involved to some degree in European markets in addition their own national markets.

The above trends are in their initial stages and can be expected to accelerate as liberalisation proceeds. Indeed, Europe's energy utilities can be expected to undergo their biggest ever changes in the early part of the twenty-first century, largely as a result of the impact of the opening of EU markets.

↖ KEY POINTS

- **Diversity within Europe's energy industry has made consensus on EU energy policy elusive.**

- **The spread of economic liberalism and re-evaluation of the concept of 'natural monopoly' finally made agreement on the key directives in the electricity and gas sectors possible. Member states are embarking upon major reforms in their domestic markets in preparation for the opening of the European market.**

- **Import dependency of the major fuels will grow in the coming decades, increasing the importance of security of supply. An intensification of the European Union's energy diplomacy initiatives can be expected as a partial response to these concerns.**

- **The three pillars of energy policy can and do conflict. The challenge for energy policy is to balance the three objectives.**

- **The corporate response to energy policy changes, particularly market opening, is already resulting in lower prices, group purchasing, restructuring and strategic and geographical re-positioning. This process will accelerate as the implementation of policy proceeds.**

SUGGESTED FURTHER READING

Matalary, J.H. (1997) *Energy Policy in the European Union*, Macmillan.

European Commission documents (unless otherwise stated)

Energy in Europe – regular Commission publication on EU energy policy.
Annual Reviews of EU Energy Policy.
The Internal Energy Market, COM (88) 238.
Electricity and Natural Gas Transmission Infrastructures in the Community, SEC (92) 553.
For a European Union Energy Policy, Green Paper, COM (94) 659.
European Community Gas Supply and Prospects, COM (95) 478.

An Energy Policy for the European Union, White Paper, COM (95) 682.

European Energy to 2020: a Scenario Approach, SEC (95) 2283.

Energy for the Future: Renewable Sources of Energy, White Paper, COM (96) 576.

Common Rules for the Internal Market in Electricity, Directive 96/92/EC, published in the *Official Journal*, OJ L 27, 30.1.97.

Restructuring the Framework for the Taxation of Energy Products, COM (97) 30.

The External Dimension of Trans-European Energy Networks, COM (97) 125.

An Overall View of Energy Policy and Actions, COM (97) 167.

Energy Dimension of Climate Change, COM (97) 196.

12

THE EUROPEAN INFORMATION SOCIETY: STIMULATING THE INFORMATION REVOLUTION FOR BUSINESS

INFORMATION SOCIETY

A society in which the quality of life, as well as prospects for social change and economic development, depend increasingly upon information and its exploitation. In such a society, living standards, patterns of work and leisure, the education system and the marketplace are all influenced markedly by advances in information and knowledge. This is evidenced by an increasing array of information-intensive products and services, communicated through a wide range of media, many of them electronic in nature.

(Martin 1995)

Globalisation, improvements in technology and shifting competitive advantage have all contributed to the pressure on the European economy to make progress towards the creation of an information society. The information society itself has its most potent expression in the increased prominence of information and communication technologies (ICTs) across all forms and size of business. In most corporations, telecommunications and associated technologies now represent the second largest corporate expense, underlining the extent to which these technologies are becoming an increasingly important strategic resource for business (see Figure 12.1). The adoption of these technologies is born not just of the desire to maintain commercial advantage but increasingly out of necessity. The development of the information society will not only influence the environment of European business by offering the potential for improvements in performance but also provides opportunities for the development of new industries to supply the information increasingly demanded by businesses across the evolving global economy. These trends in the use and production of information society related technologies

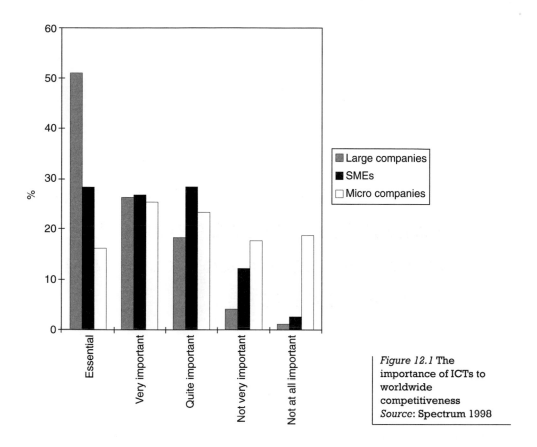

Figure 12.1 The importance of ICTs to worldwide competitiveness
Source: Spectrum 1998

services and applications are perceived by many as pivotal to the continuing commercial success of European business within increasingly internationalised markets (see Table 12.1 for progress on key information society indicators).

Initially, this chapter examines the changes associated with the development of the information society underlining its importance for modern economies. Thereafter, it discusses the policy measures within the EU to stimulate its onset. Finally, the chapter explores the broader issues involved in the onset of the information society which serve to further highlight its importance across Europe's socio-economic spectrum.

THE INFORMATION REVOLUTION AND INTERNATIONAL COMPETITIVENESS

The information revolution is the latest of the logistical and technological revolutions that have characterised the development of the European economy (see Box 9.2). The information revolution has its basis in the preceding industrial society where, since the 1970s, informatics and telecommunications have become the new engines of growth in the global economy driven in no small part by the rising utilisation of these technologies within the increasingly important service sector. This shift towards service sector based economies implies that knowledge will become a key factor determining the quality, utilisation and transformation of resources. The end point of this trend is the substitution of physical goods and processes by their electronic equivalents (that is, the dematerialisation of the

Table 12.1 Basic information society indicators

	Lines per 100 inhabitants[1]	ISDN lines per 100 inhabitants[2]	PCs with modem (% of total PCs)[3]	Internet hosts per 1,000 inhabitants[4]	EDI usage[5]	Teleworkers (% of labour force)[6]
Spain	47.2	0.24	4.6	4.9	3,000 companies	n.a.
Portugal	51.4	1.93	n.a	4.3	0.4 % (750 companies)	n.a.
Belgium	51.8	0.54	6.4	10.4	5–10 %	Negligible
Eire	53.8	0.21	n.a.	10.8	n.a.	9.3 occasional, 1.4 regular
Germany	58.7	3.4	4.0	13.3	7,000 companies	Less than 1
Austria	60.6	1.0	12.1	13.0	1.8 % (5,500 companies)	n.a.
Greece	60.8	0.08	20.0	2.7	300 companies	n.a.
Luxembourg	62.3	0.92	n.a.	11.8	1 %	n.a.
Italy	64.0	0.87	2.6	4.4	Negligible	0.5
Holland	64.9	2.01	34.0	24.7	5 % (30,000 companies)	2.4
France	66.9	3.72	n.a.	5.5	12,000 companies	1
UK	68.4	1.02	30.8	17.0	412,500 companies	20
Denmark	84.3	0.57	25.0	31.4	40% (19,060 companies)	0.4
Finland	84.9	0.57	n.a.	95.2	2 % (3,500 companies)	10
Sweden	107.9	0.73	n.a.	41.0	n.a.	17.5

Source: European Commission

Notes

[1] Conventional, ISDN and mobile at end of 1997
[2] End of 1997
[3] End of 1997
[4] End of 1997
[5] Estimate of penetration rate at end of 1997
[6] Reference date varies from 1994 for France through to December 1997 for Sweden

economy). In addition, increased competitive pressures from the global economy will push companies to combine a range of inputs from an array of sources to develop commercially attractive products and services. This trend underlines the increased importance of the services element within product development.

The central theme behind the development of the information society is accessibility to the information/telecommunications network. By offering universal access, this network will enable the anticipated economic effects to be felt. The basis of the network is a series of information infrastructures which have the physical capability to offer services and applications associated with the information society across the socio-economic spectrum. The ambition is to create a common information area (see Box 12.1), initially on a European level but later on a global level, to support the requirements of an ever growing number of users.

BOX 12.1   THE COMMON INFORMATION AREA

This has its parallel in the SEM. In this case, it is the free mobility of information rather than the traditional factors of production. Increasingly, information needs to be as mobile as any other commercial resource. This implies that the following are interconnected and interoperable and thus can move easily from one economic/social situation to another:

- *information*: this needs to be presented in universally applicable (that is, digital) format and be readily understood;
- *hardware, software and components* (for example PCs etc.) that are readily transferable between economies;
- *physical infrastructure*: developed in line with common standards that facilitate interconnection;
- *telecommunications services*: these need to be usable and accessible whilst possessing uniform functionality and availability across space;
- *applications*: where relevant these should exhibit standard format and functionality and be readily transferable
- *users*: similar levels of awareness and familiarity with technology.

According to Confland (1993), the impact of information upon the competitiveness of an economy is dependent upon four 'permanent' factors namely;

- how ICTs reinforce the enterprise's strategic vision and assist in effective and efficient decision making;
- how the utilisation of ICTs aids the rationalisation and optimisation of production;
- how the application of ICTs promotes the increased reactivity and flexibility of organisations;
- how the use of ICTs stimulates further development of new technology and innovation.

The realisation of such competitive benefits will be driven largely on an enterprise-by-enterprise basis in accordance with the desire to master uncertainty, the substitution of a functional based approach for a product based approach, the development of complementary human resource systems and the aspiration to develop new and better technologies.

Consequently, the information society implies a growing and increasing interlinkage between the productivity and flexibility of an economy and the quality and quantity of the information and communications environment. As mentioned above, this trend is linked into the process of globalisation. In general, ICTs facilitate globalisation as they:

- make skills and know-how portable;
- facilitate a more rapid response to competitive pressures;
- eliminate barriers of distance;
- reduce the communication and transaction costs involved in trade.

As the network economy develops, so these factors are likely to breed a virtuous cycle of integration within both European and global marketplaces, a process fostered by more mature inter- and intra-firm networks.

The application of ICTs within the context of the European business environment is shaped not only by the above commercial concerns but also by the fact that these technologies can have a generally positive impact upon the integration process through:

- *a time–space convergence*: that is, remoteness from markets need not be an impediment to economic success (see Chapter 7);
- *a cost–space convergence*: the form of transportation associated with the information revolution is quicker and cheaper than the physical mobility associated with the industrial society as well as being generally uniform over distance;
- a gradual abolition of geographical and political frontiers for the purposes of communication and business.

Consequently, the use of ICTs directly helps businesses overcome the friction of distance which often precludes entry into, and successful operation within, international markets. Network enterprises more than others have come to realise the importance of ICTs and how differences in information resources can affect the success or otherwise of their business. In other words, the increased space over which management decisions now take effect has altered the parameters of space and time and their functioning in the production process.

The shift to an enterprise sector based upon the increased utilisation and production of ICTs reflects a trend towards Europe's future economic success being firmly based upon its establishment as a knowledge intensive economy. Related policy measures underline the importance of education and training as supports for this process – the commercial benefits from the information society will be driven by 'talented' people. As ICTs become ingrained into both production and education and training systems, so these sectors will become increasingly intertwined. That is, the world of work and learning will converge. This is important, for the competitive advantages of the information society are not derived from the new technologies but from the new skills and learning processes engendered within the associated structural changes. In short, despite the increased commercial salience of ICTs, labour still represents the key component in determining an economy's international competitiveness.

THE EUROPEAN INFORMATION SOCIETY: GENERIC THEMES AND STRATEGY

The European model of the information society is based on a strong ethos of solidarity, in which the key preoccupation is the creation of a socially inclusive information society which avoids cultural and economic isolationism across a broad range of socio-economic groupings. Consequently, the EU's group of experts on the information society emphasised that:

- the information society is about people;
- it is essential to view the information society as a 'learning society' based upon the abilities of people not upon the information within machines;

- ICTs have both negative and positive impacts upon the society in which they are utilised.

Thus, much of the focus within the EU's plans for the information society tends towards the development of new forms of employment and ensuring that social and economic cohesion is sustained. This is based upon a concern that industry not only needs technologies but also requires a supporting infrastructure in terms of education and training systems. Consequently, the EU is increasingly emphasising lifelong learning to ensure that the labour force is adaptable to the dynamics and requirements of the information society. This emphasis applies equally to both education and internal enterprise training systems.

The strategy of the EU for the information society is typified by the following extract from the Bangemann Report (1994, p. 3) which states in its preamble that the information society

> means fostering an entrepreneurial mentality to enable the emergence of new dynamic sectors of the economy . . . means developing a common regulatory approach to bring forth a competitive, Europe-wide, market for information services . . . does not mean more public money, financial assistance, subsidies, dirigisme or protectionism.

Any strategy that emphasises the market as the driver of the information society must also take into account that the transnational environment is the most effective arena in which these changes can be realised as:

- national markets are of insufficient size to realise the needed investment in advanced ICTs;
- many technologies are aimed at niche markets which are too small in any one state;
- the speed and ability of these new services to offer multi-media could allow them to break through linguistic barriers.

Within the context of the transnational marketplace, public authorities throughout the EU are playing a largely market creating function, seeking to push the market for information society services/applications and technologies towards a 'critical mass' and an environment in which:

- telecommunications and other communications technologies should be affordable;
- user demands are adequately expressed;
- there is adequate awareness of ICTs in all parts of the European economy;
- education/training systems readily absorb the implications and dynamics of ICTs;
- new information products emerge that are useful, usable and affordable;
- supply conditions improve to the extent that greater economies are available in the production and supply of ICTs;
- there is a commercial incentive to supply all parts of the European socio-economic body;
- state involvement is largely redundant.

This implies that the information market is currently of insufficient maturity to develop without public sector involvement. Policy actions to overcome this immaturity focus upon the following priorities:

- promotion of the use of ICTs, especially in the delivery of public sector activities;
- stimulation of investment in trans-European services;

- establishment of a complementary regulatory framework;
- development of training and education schemes based upon the utilisation of these new technologies;
- measures to stimulate improvement in the industrial and technological performance of European business.

In practice, the public sector acts as a catalyst, not as a primary driver, in efforts to develop the information society. A lack of financial power means that much public sector action seeks to bring together partners with a mutual interest in developing projects that actively contribute to the development of the information society. The EU also assists in enabling partners to develop an awareness of technologies and guide them in best practice in the use of ICTs. These efforts are supported by financial measures that enable the EU to become directly involved in the onset of the information society (see below). It is important that governments do not encourage firms to force the pace of adoption as staff may be untrained and resist the transformation – changes need to take place in line with the ability of the firm to absorb the impact of these technologies.

DEVELOPING A EUROPEAN INFORMATION INDUSTRY

As has been noted, a key objective of the EU is to ensure that the emerging European necessity for advanced information technologies is supplied by an indigenous information industry (covering the content, telecommunications and IT sectors). Given that these technologies are likely to be accepted globally, this offers the EU opportunities to develop a competitive advantage in the global provision of information society-related technology and services. Inevitably these changes will be supported by a strong indigenous demand for these technologies and from an education and social culture that is generally more open to the information society (Table 12.1 highlights the onset of the information society within Europe).

Despite the objective to develop a competitive niche in the provision of information society-related technologies, the EU has to overcome the relatively poor performance of EU IT companies compared to rivals in the US and Japan. The EU has a large trade deficit in ICTs, something that is unlikely to disappear over the short to medium term. Past failures in terms of targeting ICT enterprises (notably Bull in France and Olivetti in Italy) have spurred the EU into a much more market-led agenda. A core problem restraining growth within the sector is the sheer shortage of trained people, thereby limiting the potential of European business to find a competitive niche in these emerging information industries.

Initial action towards strengthening the European presence in this global market rests upon freer markets and upon facilitating the aforementioned critical mass for information society-related technologies and services. The market for information is being developed within the context of the convergence of the telecommunications, computing and 'content' (for example, the broadcasting and software industries) sectors as the technology used by each becomes broadly similar – as typified by the increased provision of telecommunications by cable TV companies.

Policy makers, if they are to secure a strong indigenous ICT sector, need to ensure that policy works to support all of these sectors and that the enterprises involved in the information society are able to generate the revenue needed to support its development. This not only means more commercial freedom but also greater autonomy from other constraining factors such as state ownership and its implications for resource availability. This, in practice, means that the information society is increasingly tied into the privatisation of the incumbent public telecommunication operators (PTOs) and the liberalisation of previously protected/reserved markets (see below). These PTOs, and their investment strategies within the emerging competitive environment are pivotal to the success of the information society (see Case Study 12.1).

Regulatory and legal framework

Changing the regulatory structure of the telecommunications sector is essential to stimulate the investment required for information society-related products and services. The liberalisation of the European telecommunications sector on a Community-wide basis has been proceeding since 1987. The final phase towards complete open markets began in 1998. This process has not, and will not, occur in a uniform manner as many of the cohesion states have been granted extra time to open markets – often into the early years of the new millennium. Some of the states which were originally given extensions or were reluctant to liberalise (generally out of public service concerns) have, in practice, found that the demands of the emerging information society have created a need to accelerate the process. The initial consequence of such actions will be to breed greater transparency and consistency in national regulations derived from the desire to extend the principles of the SEM to the telecommunications sector. It is anticipated that the application of the SEM to this sector will not only speed up investment in the necessary networks but also stimulate the needed innovation, improve the quality of communications and deliver lower tariffs (and thus stimulate the demand) for these technologies. These processes in combination will have a positive impact upon the ability of EU-based enterprises to minimise the core operating costs associated with the network enterprise: a factor which will aid the ability of these businesses to compete successfully on a global basis.

These measures are complemented by a series of actions to ensure that enterprises have incentives to continue to develop the technology and services associated with the information society. Of particular importance is the protection of intellectual property rights, ensuring that there is no excessive concentration in terms of media ownership and the development of relevant standards to facilitate interconnection and interoperability of respective national and international networks. To achieve this, the EU is looking to the framework established by the SEM in areas such as freedom of establishment and service provision. This is complemented by a directive on the transparency of information services which is designed to prevent a patchwork of national rules with regard to the use of the Internet for electronic commerce springing up across the EU.

The success of the liberalisation is only partially evident. Whilst international call charges are falling rapidly, there is still great uncertainty as to how quickly such changes will be felt in local markets. Already there is limited scope for user pressure to derive greater value-added from information networks and suppliers. For example, major multinational enterprises have combined under the umbrella of the European Virtual Private Network Association to exert pressure upon major suppliers to meet user requirements more effectively. This has been complemented by increasingly competitive market structures as more and more firms enter all aspects of the market for the supply of the services associated with the information society. In addition, many incumbent enterprises have responded to the desire to develop transnational services for business by engaging in alliances with other operators (see Case Study 12.1).

Research and development

This is the research into and development of products and services applications that are of insufficient maturity to be either technologically or commercially feasible and are

CASE STUDY 12.1 EUROPEAN TELECOMMUNICATION ALLIANCES

Public telecommunication operator (PTO) alliances have been prominent in the European telecommunications environment for a prolonged period. The pressures for alliance formation for competitive purposes have grown as European PTOs have started to experience the consequences of the twin forces of liberalisation and globalisation. As the PTO's own revenue bases came under attack and user requirements (especially within the lucrative multinational enterprise market) increasingly stressed global telecommunication solutions, so Europe's largest PTOs embarked upon a round of competitive alliance formation, the most important of which are noted below.

- *Concert*: this is a network of PTOs based around BT's active alliance and joint venture strategy.
- *Global One*: an alliance between France Telecom, Deutsche Telekom and Sprint (a US carrier).
- *Uniworld/WorldPartners*: an alliance between AT&T, KDD (a Japanese carrier), Singapore Telecom and Unisource (an alliance of smaller European PTOs from Switzerland, the Netherlands and Sweden).
- *Cable and Wireless*: less of an alliance, more a 'federation' of a group of geographically disparate telecommunication enterprises concentrated in Europe and South-East Asia.

The major pre-occupation of these alliances has been to offer coverage and uniform service levels across the three major regions within which multinational enterprises operate, namely Europe, the US and Southeast Asia. To strengthen service levels, these alliances have been involved in a round of alliance and joint venture agreements to enhance service levels in these areas and to extend the reach of the respective networks, notably over recent times to Latin America. Across the EU, the pattern of alliance development is reflected in the table below.

European telecommunication alliances

	Concert	Global One	Uniworld	Cable & Wireless
France	JV	Incumbent	O	S
Germany	JV	Incumbent	JV	D
UK	Incumbent	O	S	JV
Italy	JV	O	S	S
Spain	JV	O		S
Denmark	D	O	D	D
Norway	D	O	D	D
Sweden	JV	O	Partner	JV
Netherlands	JV	O	Partner	O
Belgium	O	O	S	S
Switzerland	JV	O	Partner	S
Austria	D	O	D	O
Ireland	O	O	D	S
Portugal	JV	O		S

Source: Ovum

Note: JV – Joint Venture, D – Distribution agreement, S – Subsidiary, O – Own Marketing Office

Thus across Europe, these alliances have developed an extensive network of PTOs and subsidiaries to sell what are frequently branded products. Such an extensive network is important given the large number of users within the EU and the growing level of demand for more advanced services within Europe as a whole. Over more recent times, these alliances have been especially active in attempting to increase the relevance of their service portfolios to SMEs. In turn, the development of these alliances raises issues for competition and other regulatory authorities on both a European and global stage. For example, many alliances were not allowed to proceed unless each of the operators involved had, or committed itself to, liberalised domestic marketplaces: an issue especially relevant for many of the larger operators (such as France Telecom and Deutsche Telekom) and regulators (both in the EU and the US) who were especially keen to secure such commitments before approving these alliances.

The development of these alliances raises obvious issues for the smaller European PTOs. There has been considerable debate about the strategy these enterprises should adopt. This, in some senses, has led to a messy patchwork across the EU. For example, Telefonica (the Spanish PTO) has been shifting between alliances (it moved from being a partner in Unisource into an agreement with Concert which it has since ditched). Such movements indicate that PTO's strategies reflect what is in their best interest and where their greatest opportunities lie. The smaller PTOs will increasingly develop relationships with these alliances in order to secure market positioning as the liberalisation of the European (and global) marketplace continues apace.

complementary to the liberalisation process. The EU seeks a co-ordinated approach in this area for, in terms of research and development (R&D), there is little competition in these products due to their technical and commercial immaturity. This co-ordinated approach to R&D is compounded by a belief that competition in this activity may create a degree of uncertainty that could deter investment and that co-operation allows for synergies in product development. Competition only enters the equation when these products are being marketed to end users.

Support for the development of ICTs has been a recurrent theme within the EU's successive research and development programmes. However, there has been limited success in contributing to the development of the information society given:

- the inadequate resources directed to the R&D effort;
- the relatively poor commitment to R&D when compared to Europe's major competitors;
- the poor co-ordination of R&D at various levels;
- the inability to convert scientific and technological achievements into industrial and commercial successes.

As a response to these issues, there was a concerted attempt within the Fourth Framework programme (1994–8) to make the R&D process more user friendly by taking account of user needs throughout the process. This is needed if R&D is to deliver competitive benefits to enterprises and aid the successful development of the EU ICT industry. In short, research into ICTs has to respond to demand if it is to aid the competitiveness of the EU economy and avoid a culture of engaging in research for its own sake.

Each research programme seeks to build upon the results of the preceding framework programme. The Fourth Framework (1994–8) was concerned with market testing and applying the technology developed under the Third Framework. Many of the schemes within the Fourth Framework programme have been re-nationalised, representing a shift away from a philosophy of totally integrated, uniform solutions towards uniformity via a series of complementary national based actions. Much of the effort within these national based schemes is focused on developing (in combination with other programmes) a series of 'information islands' – large populated areas which, by sharing experiences of technologies, will be a starting point for the onset of the deployment and development of ICTs to support the realisation of the information society.

Proposals for the Fifth Framework Programme (see Case Study 5.1) stress more concretely the theme of the information society as a key issue in future R&D. A core theme within the framework is the emphasis on the user friendly nature of the research undertaken as a pre-requisite to ensuring its marketability and ability to stimulate further innovation. These priorities have been criticised by a number of telecommunications bodies who argue that the needs of industry have not sufficiently been taken into account. In particular, much of the research is too near the commercialisation stage, thereby running the risk of creating distortions within the competitive supply of key information society services. Indeed, since private sector investment is already planned in some areas highlighted under the Fifth Framework, operators are at a loss to explain what value EU support adds to the process. On the other hand, they feel the proposals do little to solve the real problem which is the need for greater effort in pre-competitive research. This is the area in which European telecommunication network operators (ETNO) feel that the EU can best support the market led development of the information society. If the EU's actions seek to promote technologies that are close to commercial maturity, it risks distorting the market for any products or services that consequently emerge.

Deployment

The deployment of the technologies associated with the information society is being stimulated by the trans-European telecommunications network programme (see Chapter 9). The aim is to use Commission funding to encourage the commercial and technological development of a number of networks that are perceived as key to the information society. The priority is to encourage the roll out of those networks that are relevant to SMEs and of those that are of broader socio-economic interest, such as those which support teleworking. The objective is not to develop networks per se but to ensure past research efforts are actually employed within user environments.

The aim of the programme is to use limited Commission funding to overcome initial commercial uncertainty within a number of information society-related services and applications. Thus the EU seeks to cushion the financial risk involved in developing networks that have as yet unproven demand but are likely to be a direct stimulant to the onset of the information society. In practice, much of the development of these networks is occurring as a result of local authorities which are increasingly using the information society as a tool for regional development. This has been identified via the priorities within regional and social funding which have both sought to utilise the information society as a means of achieving their objectives. This has been compounded by the actions of a number of European cities, under the Bangemann Challenge, which are also seeking to utilise technology to enhance regional development, deliver public services and enable local enterprises to have improved access to international markets.

Market creation

The EU has a distinct information market policy. Up to the end of 1994, the IMPACT programme (Information Market Policy Actions) aimed to stimulate the development of a more mature information market. The objective was to strengthen the competitiveness of European information suppliers. The starting point was combining the public sector, as the largest supplier of information, with private information sources so that new 'innovative services' could emerge. The second IMPACT (1994–8) scheme sought to develop 'near market' projects with immediate appeal to various segments of the information market. This action has been complemented more recently by the INFO2000 programme to stimulate the development of a European information content industry to enable it to compete on a global basis as well as meeting the requirements of the European market. The success of this programme is inevitably linked to the existence of sufficient demand for the technology and services involved.

SPREADING THE RELEVANCE OF THE INFORMATION SOCIETY

Integral to the EU's vision of the information society is the inclusion of a diverse range of user groups. Consequently, many of the priorities for the information society supported by the EU are based upon targeting core groups such as:

- SMEs;
- workers in remote areas;
- the unemployed;
- health professionals;
- education and training professionals;
- public administrations;
- economic agents in areas of urban decline.

Policy is focused on overcoming the vicious cycle of low demand that impedes the realisation of the information society within the aforementioned groups. Inevitably, this assistance is complementary to the supply side measures noted above – that is, there is obviously little point in stimulating the supply of something for which there is insufficient demand. Market stimulation derives from the interactions of both sides of the market. Actions such as standardisation and liberalisation are likely to have a positive impact upon the demand for the services and technologies associated with the information society via stimulating a virtuous cycle of take-up driven by lower tariffs and network effects. However, governments need to be careful not to force the pace of ICT adoption where the existing resource base is ill-equipped for it may only have negative effects upon enterprise productivity. This underlines the ultimate policy priority of testing the commercial feasibility of services and technologies that support the EU's vision of the information society.

Aside from increased user involvement within the assorted R&D programmes, other efforts to push demand have focused upon stimulating public awareness of the information society and highlighting how the adoption of these technologies can assist and improve enterprise functioning. SMEs are a particular target for these technology stimulation measures as is apparent in the Information Society Budget Line and the INFO 2000 project.

CHALLENGES FOR THE INFORMATION SOCIETY

Concerns about the consequences of the information society are shaped by whether it will deliver its anticipated benefits in an equitable manner across space and assorted socio-economic groupings. If it does not, then European policy makers will fail in delivering an

CASE STUDY 12.2 STIMULATING ELECTRONIC COMMERCE WITHIN THE EU

Electronic Commerce (EC) is regarded by many within the telecommunications and IT sectors as a core driver behind the shift towards the information economy. A precise definition of EC is illusive, but at its heart is an increased number of commercial transactions or interactions taking place through electronic, rather than through physical, contact. When fully realised, its implications for business development are huge as EC is likely to lead to a full re-examination of business processes and structures. The requirement and expansion of EC has been driven by the process of globalisation which means more dispersed interaction between businesses, administrations and customers. EC should enable any enterprise to organise its operations, target suppliers and pinpoint customers for maximum commercial advantage.

The potential for electronic commerce

Impacts upon business activities	Specific benefits to business	EC-based generic business strategies
• marketing, sales and sales promotion • pre-sales, sub-contracts, supply • financing and insuring • commercial transactions • product service and maintenance • co-operative product development • distributed co-operative working • use of public and private services • business to administration activities (tax, customs, concessions etc.) • transport and logistics • public procurement • automatic trading of digital goods • accounting • dispute resolution	• reduced advertising costs • reduced delivery cost (notably for goods that can be delivered electronically) • reduced design and manufacturing cost • improved market intelligence and strategic planning • more opportunity for niche marketing • equal access to markets (that is, for SMEs vis-à-vis large organisations) • access to new markets • customer involvement in product and service innovation	• electronic marketplace: sales promotion, interactive TV/Internet shopping, • efficient customer response management • electronic trading • supply chain management • vendor managed inventory

It is estimated that EC (for business to business transactions alone) could be worth as much as $75 billion by 2000; with the US established as the strong market leader. In addition, the estimated cost savings are believed to be between 50 to 80 per cent depending upon the sector concerned. Despite this, the use of EC remains very embryonic with most Internet sites being used merely for marketing purposes and very few for EC. Examples of EC exist across a number of sectors such as retailing and distribution. A notable retailing example is the Internet Bookshop which allows for the browsing, selection and payment of books over this medium.

Concern at the slowness with which EU enterprises (especially SMEs) were taking up EC has led to the 'European Initiatives for Electronic Commerce' programme. This initiative is two pronged. First, to secure the uptake by large business by securing the necessary complementary regulatory environment. This requires agreement not only between EU states but also on a global basis upon issues related to network security, privacy, intellectual property rights and clarity over the tax situation regarding transactions over this medium. These are necessary safeguards to ensure that users have confidence in the use of EC. These measures are coupled with a common acceptance of the global agreements upon IT and telecommunications which should secure better access to EC (both in terms of technology and services/applications). The second aspect of the strategy is essentially developmental and centres upon disseminating best practice and reinforcing awareness and confidence in the use of EC. Consequently, a number of EU's schemes contain references to EC developments notably in SME programmes, R&D initiatives (within the Fourth Framework), the G8 Information Society Initiative and the TEN-Telecom programme.

Expanding access to SMEs has been a particular priority. The EU's efforts in this domain are shaped within the context of the G8 Initiative for a Global Marketplace for SMEs (see Case Study 8.1). These efforts have been supported by both the EU's Telematics and TEN-Telecom programmes. The EU seeks to draw upon a wide range of programmes across the EU to develop a system of mutual learning between bodies to strengthen SME access to EC particularly with regard to expanding the capabilities of electronic data interchange. In achieving this objective, limited levels of support and advice will be provided to ensure the traditional hurdles of SME utilisation of EC (such as finance) can be overcome. These actions are insufficient on their own and need to be coupled with a more pro-active public sector, full telecommunication liberalisation and a culture within SMEs that more readily accepts ICTs.

To cement the development, over one hundred SMEs, trade associations and local authorities (under the European Commission's lead) have signed a Memorandum of Understanding (MoU) on Open Access to EC. The MoU stresses co-operative guidelines in EC development for this group, notably common standardised architecture, standards for product marketing and information, the exchange of legally binding documents, payment systems and the rights and responsibilities of users. These are essentially guides to best practice based upon industry agreements covering self-regulation and assorted codes of practice.

information society that is 'socially and economically cohesive'. These challenges for the information society are derived from the nature and consequences of the market led strategy preferred by policy makers. In this case the information society will be dictated by the:

- density of users;
- wealth and income of users;
- differing sensitivities to ICTs;
- quality of human resources.

Spatial and social variation in these criteria will lead to the uneven development of the information society across the EU. The social and spatial consequences of the information society require some form of policy response.

Employment

Given the employment creating rationale behind the promotion of the information society, this concern appears surprising at first sight. The core fear is that the increased application of ICTs to all business functions will cost jobs. History has bred a suspicion of technological change given that every time a new form of technology is adopted by business, lower levels of employment result from changes in the ratio of capital to labour. Concerns about ICTs are particularly salient due to:

- the pervasiveness of ICT across all sectors;
- the speed with which ICTs are being introduced;
- the high level of cross-border mobility brought about by ICTs.

The counter-argument to this fear is that whilst the evolution of the information society may destroy jobs, it is also expected to create new forms and types of employment – a natural consequence of any 'logistical/technological' revolution. The conventional view implies that 'old' jobs that were mundane and low skilled will be replaced with 'new' higher skilled occupations that deliver higher value-added. However, there will be a lag between the destruction of old jobs and the creation of new ones and the emergence of new forms of employment able to absorb the surplus labour. Minimisation of the length of this lag has to be a core policy priority. The application of ICTs will also change work patterns, work organisation and the functioning of labour markets. The adoption of ICTs is symptomatic of broader trends towards more flexible work forces, network enterprises and growing instability for less skilled employment. The requirement of policy is to stimulate flexibility, thereby minimising the disruption within labour markets from the emerging information society.

Increasingly, policy is responding to such challenges by stressing the notion of lifelong learning to ensure that resources are sufficiently flexible to match the changes brought about by the development of the information society. EU social funding has to some extent worked to achieve this and is complemented by a series of actions within local and regional bodies. The EU labour market needs to respond quickly to the challenges posed by the information society if its positive employment effects are to be maximised and its negative aspects minimised. Workers from declining sectors need to be supported via training processes that reflect the skill requirements of the information society. Exploring how the information society can aid sustainable employment is a key objective of policy makers. The success of such strategies requires a more fundamental shift in the mentality of the labour force. Thus it is not simply a case of policy makers taking ICTs to workers but also of workers being willing and able to participate in such changes. But policy can and should only do so much. The employment effects of ICTs will result from decisions taken on a firm-by-firm basis. All policy makers can do is ensure that the transition to the information society takes place with minimal social cost. However, the social challenges of the information society run deep.

Social cohesion

The employment consequences of the information society will obviously have social consequences and its negative effects are likely to be felt most keenly within specific social groupings. In addition, as the information society becomes a greater reality for all groups, effective demand will determine access to information. Lack of effective demand will retard the development of the information society within certain socio-economic groups, especially the low skilled who are likely to be most adversely affected by the changes. The inability to obtain and access information risks creating 'information have and have nots' could reinforce existing social division and economic deprivation. For this reason, the Commission has attempted to define universality of access to certain core services as integral to the development of the information society. This needs to be coupled with the affordability of the necessary technologies.

There is also the concern that the information society could undermine sociability by confining people to an isolated existence both in terms of work and leisure. Consequently, there is a desire that these changes promote new forms of contact with people as well as technology. For these reasons, the Commission intends that the development of the information should be people centred. Thus ICTs are to be utilised in people centred services such as health and education. However, the consequences for social cohesion and ICTs are not totally understood.

A further fear is that the information society will lead to social homogeneity based upon the fact that the majority of the information will be largely US-sourced. Member states have been keen to stem this 'cultural imperialism', in some cases limiting opportunities for US-sourced English language content within the EU's emerging information market. Increasingly, European states are taking counteractive measures to resist potential cultural domination by seeking to ensure that the information society reflects the diversity of Europe.

Regional cohesion

The Commission implicitly recognises that the development of the information society will occur in an uneven manner across the EU (as indicated by Table 12.1). As the information society becomes increasingly important for economic development, such differences could run counter to the EU's objective of economic cohesion (see Chapter 7). Telecommunications liberalisation in the EU has initially led to growing gaps in technological development between businesses located in different areas of the EU. This is inevitable given that investment will naturally focus upon high demand, low cost areas.

There is a concerted attempt by the EU to use its Structural Funds to alleviate such problems at least partially. For some time, the Commission has supported the development of telecommunications in the regions via initiatives funded from the Structural Funds. Indeed, the Commission is keen to promote teleworking as a means of overcoming the economic development problems derived from isolated locations (see Chapter 7). The more mature this becomes, the more opportunities will emerge for these areas to attract investment driven in no small part by time–space and cost–space convergence. These convergence processes should enable the more peripheral regions to benefit from the existence of greater mobility and flexibility in terms of factors of production. Thus much of the EU's challenge for measures to support the information society are focused upon peripheral or under-developed regions as typified by the Regional Information Society Initiative.

The ability to utilise the information society as a tool for regional development is still restricted by the maturity of the local information culture and the provision of supporting infrastructure (both of which are especially lacking in the cohesion states). In practice, much of the development of the information society is occurring on a localised, regional basis and not necessarily in line with the priorities of the Structural Funds. The

Commission has encouraged regional co-operation to overcome vicious cycles of under-development for these regions.

COMPLEMENTARY INITIATIVES: NATIONAL AND GLOBAL ACTIONS

Global actions

The EU is very keen to push the information society as a global phenomenon. The changes noted above are happening on a global level particularly within those states which are considered as the EU's major competitors. A longer term objective of the EU's actions is to ensure that Europe secures its portion of the emerging global market for information society-related technologies and services. Importantly, for many businesses, the development of the European information society is a means to achieve a global presence both within, and external to, the ICT sector. The development of the information society elsewhere in the global economy will be an increasingly important factor in enabling European businesses of all sizes to access international markets.

The global aspect is compounded by the fact that many of the enterprises benefiting from and contributing to the development of the European information society will be neither European based nor owned. This is a natural consequence of the moves towards a globalised economy. These moves will be strengthened by the WTO agreements upon freer trade in information technology and telecommunications services. These will be powerful factors in stimulating the development of the information society within the EU and beyond. A noticeable feature has been the number of mergers and alliances within the sector as a consequence of these global and technological forces.

On a pre-competitive level, the G8 states have agreed to collaborate to stimulate the development of the global information society. On a global level, these states have agreed that the development of the information society is to be based upon:

- dynamic competition;
- private investment;
- a flexible regulatory framework;
- accessibility to technology;
- diverse content;
- global co-operation.

This global co-operation between the G8 states sought to stimulate eleven key projects central to the development of the information society. The theme was one of synergy, mutual interest and information exchange in the key projects which, in turn, should be established within the context of the above principles. This does not preclude the fact that these economies (and the enterprises therein) will still continue to compete within an increasingly globalised market for the technologies associated with the development of the information society.

These actions are being further complemented by a plethora of other bodies such as the ITU, the OECD and the World Bank. In addition, the EU is seeking to extend the scope of its own actions by seeking to integrate its near neighbours (such as Central and Eastern Europe) into the information society as well as seeking to disseminate the technology to less developed states.

To strengthen the twin drivers behind enterprise strategy, globalisation and the information society, the European Commission is calling for an International Charter to co-ordinate the relevant policies on an international basis. This Charter, scheduled to be adopted by the end of 1999, seeks to establish a framework within which co-operation between states in the development of the information society can occur. This will cover areas such as taxation, tariffs on ICTs, intellectual property rights, encryption, authentication, data protection and liability and other rights needed for the development of a global electronic marketplace. These will inevitably be assisted by the WTO agreements on basic telecommunications and information technology as well as by other non-governmental bodies such as the World Intellectual Property Organisation (WIPO).

Currently, global development of the information society is taking place within a plethora of governmental and non-governmental bodies. Such fragmentation risks undermining the realisation of an integrated information society. The Charter would not be a legally binding treaty but merely seeks to develop a unifying framework for all states via three main actions:

- determination of the major issues;
- identification of who should deal with the major issues;
- development of principles to guide organisational decisions.

Industry has broadly welcomed the idea of the Charter with the Global Internet Project which has been established to formulate its response to the Charter. The US government is, however, resisting on the grounds that it is unnecessary and could be a tool for imposing new regulations upon the sector. This position reflects the very pro-market attitude of the US towards the development of the information society.

National initiatives

National action towards the information society is driven not only by the urgency attached to its development but also by the apparent lack of power of supranational bodies. Most national actions broadly fit into line with the socio-economic vision advocated by the EU. The most vigorous actions tend to occur within northern European states, further underlining the uneven pattern of progress towards the information society within the EU.

National actions are, by and large, developed within the context of supranational initiatives. Indeed, joint funding may be available from supranational and national bodies. Actions are frequently regional in nature. This provides a means of testing the technology as a pre-requisite to its wider dissemination throughout the rest of the economy. This is evidenced through initiatives such as the previously mentioned Bangemann Challenge which sets local (frequently city based) initiatives within the broader context of supranational policy.

Policy within states reflects, in some senses, the differing priorities of policy makers. France has tended to take a very proactive line through its programme to develop advanced infrastructure under government guidance. The UK has taken a more passive line: its actions are based upon stimulating an awareness of the technology as a means of demand creation. In other words, some states have identified that the main driver of the information society is business and believe that the social element will follow the maturing market. Other states believe the social and economic elements are of equal importance in the development of the information society.

CONCLUSION

The information society is having an increasing influence over many aspects of European policy (from regional through to industrial policies). Its importance is driven by the need for Europe to re-position its competitive strengths within a global economy in which its traditional employment supporting activities are increasingly being undertaken by third countries. The information society exploits Europe's core competitive strengths such as an educated work force and high rates of product innovation. However, the information society's capacity to yield generic competitive effects depends upon its ability to spread its impact right across Europe's socio-economic spectrum thus ensuring that, in the extreme case, there is no segment of the labour force, region or enterprise that is unaffected by these changes. Maximising the impact of the information society has to be the focus of policy ensuring that both supply and demand work in conjunction with each other to deliver the benefits that are expected from the advent of the information society.

↘ KEY POINTS

- **The development of the information society is central to the future commercial success of the EU.**

- **The information society will have a pervasive influence across socio-economic groupings and businesses.**

- **The information society will be driven by market forces with policy makers reduced to seeking to stimulate commercial forces via a series of largely passive commercially focused measures.**

- **There is a real danger that the information society could reinforce existing socio-economic divisions.**

SUGGESTED FURTHER READING

Bangemann Group (1994) *Europe and the Global Information Society*, Brussels.

Commission of the European Communities/DG III/XIII (1994) 'More Competitive Industry Through Research', *I & T Magazine*, autumn.

Commission of the European Communities (1994) *Europe's Way to the Information Society*, COM(94)347, Brussels.

Confland, D. (1993) 'Information and Competitiveness', *Annales des Annes*, pp. 63–5.

The Economist (1996) 'A Survey of the World Economy', 28 Sept.

European Parliament (1993) *Emerging Technologies: Information Networks and the European Union*, Working Papers (Economic Series), Luxembourg.

Federal Trust (1995) *Network Europe and the Information Society*, Federal Trust Publications.

High Level Expert Group (1996) *Building the European Information Society for Us All*, Jan.

Martin, W. (1995) *The Global Information Society*, Gower.

OECD (1995) *Workshops Proceedings on the Economics of the Information Society*, No. 2, Istanbul, 14–15 December.

OECD (1996) *Workshop on Information Infrastructure and Territorial Development*, Paris.

OECD (1996) *Workshops Proceedings on the Economics of the Information Society*, No. 4, Helsinki, Korea, 6–7 June.

OECD (1996) *Workshops Proceedings on the Economics of the Information Society*, No. 5, Seoul, Korea, 22–3 October.

Public Network Europe (1996) *Dirigisme: Thanks But No Thanks*, February, pp. 39–42.

Public Network Europe (1996) *PNE Yearbook*, The Economist Group.

13

EUROPEAN LABOUR MARKETS: A FLEXIBLE RESPONSE FOR EUROPEAN BUSINESS

> Employers need greater flexibility, in particular more interchangeable skills among their employees and adaptable working patterns, while employees need assurances about their own employability and job prospects. Better organisation of work can offer workers increased security through greater involvement in work organisation, a greater choice of working arrangements, more job satisfaction and the possibility of developing skills and long term employability. In turn, this provides employers with increased flexibility in the form of a more skilled, motivated and versatile labour force, better able to take the initiative, to cope with change and to be more deeply involved in the economic health of the company.
>
> (*Social Action Programme 1998–2000*, COM (98) 259)

The debate about European labour market policy has shifted away from preoccupation with the harmonisation of worker rights and labour market regulations which characterised the 1980s towards the battle against unemployment and the controversy over labour market flexibility. The outcome of this debate is viewed by many as the key to improved competitiveness and ultimately to the creation of more jobs. The labour market flexibility issue is not new. Indeed it was a fundamental element of the former UK Conservative government's opposition to the EU's social dimension. However, it would be too simplistic to claim that the current emphasis on labour market flexibility represents the imminent dismantling of worker rights. Certainly, the 1990s have seen the growth of fears throughout Europe that unemployment is increasingly a structural phenomenon arising from the introduction of advanced technologies and the competitive consequences of globalisation. The 1980s and 1990s have also seen the spread and triumph of neo-liberal economics, resulting in a shift of policy from direct market intervention to enhancing the environment within which enterprises operate. Nevertheless, although there is an emerging consensus that labour market flexibility is about enabling labour markets to operate more efficiently, agreement ends there. Views conflict about what labour market flexibility actually is, and how it can be achieved, and these differences reflect to a large extent previous conflicts about labour market policy and different labour market traditions within the EU.

The chapter opens with a discussion of different approaches to labour market flexibility before proceeding to an analysis of recent trends in the European labour market which provides the context for later sections on policy. The chapter then traces the evolution of labour market policy from its beginnings to its post-Amsterdam Treaty phase, concluding with analysis of policy proposals for the new century.

APPROACHES TO LABOUR MARKET FLEXIBILITY

Labour market flexibility can be defined in several ways but in broad terms it can be categorised as arising from:

- highly deregulated labour markets in which competition is based on low wage costs and highly mobile global capital, or;
- 'flexible specialisation' in which a skilled workforce is viewed as a major resource: the key to competitiveness in this model resides in labour market co-operation and 'trust' between employers and employees.

The former model is based on the neo-classical approach which regards regulation as an unjustifiable interference in the operation of the market. Its proponents support only the most minimal forms of regulation, notably in the realm of health and safety. Non-intervention, they argue, facilitates efficiency and enables employers to pay a market clearing wage and to compete with low cost suppliers, particularly from Asia, who are placing severe competitive pressures on European businesses. Many supporters of this view also argue for the roll back of the welfare state and social security benefits which they claim raises the 'reservation wage', that is, the wage below which the unemployed will not seek employment. On the other hand, the deregulation approach also relies on wage flexibility, including downward flexibility, and the assumption that the social security system will subsidise low wage employment – the role played by the system of family credit in the United Kingdom. This model gives employers a high degree of flexibility in terms of hiring, dismissals and wages and is suitable for low wage economies, encourages adversarial industrial relations and discourages internal organisational flexibility based on multi-skilling, goodwill and the higher levels of productivity resulting from greater investment in the workforce.

The term 'flexible specialisation' was coined by Piore and Sabel (1984) as a reaction to the shift away from 'Fordist' production methods and 'Taylorist' traditions of work organisation which were too inflexible for the new demands for customised and high quality products (see Box 13.1). The intensification of competition arising from globalisation also encouraged rapid changes in consumer tastes and necessitated more frequent product adaptations and shorter production runs, resulting in leaner production and greater emphasis on teamwork, multi-skilling, flexible deployment of labour and closer links between production and marketing. In other words, the new production techniques require a co-operative, skilled labour force which is both prepared and able to respond to rapidly changing consumer demands.

These changes in the workplace imply a variant of labour market flexibility which does not view regulation as inhibiting adjustment to changing markets but as providing opportunities to reconcile the legitimate claims of labour with efficiency. According to this view, labour market regulation exists to protect the workforce in terms of health and safety, job security and working conditions. Respect for workers' rights and welfare generates greater workplace flexibility by reducing the disillusion and alienation which is frequently present in the first model and by encouraging worker identification with the long term well-being of the firm and generating trust between employer and employee. An emphasis on worker information and consultation and ongoing workplace training also accompanies this approach. Any rigidities in the model, it is claimed, are outweighed by long run gains in terms of greater technical and organisational innovation. One of the downsides of this approach is its potential exclusion of the low skilled, long term unemployed.

It is the flexible specialisation approach which is currently exerting the greatest influence on EU labour market policy. This view of flexibility is very different from the crude 'regulation equals increased cost' approach propounded by the British Conservatives and leads to a set of policy prescriptions based on active labour market policies and the creation of a more co-operative, less adversarial system of industrial relations. The extent to which flexibility can be introduced into Europe's labour markets is at the heart of the current debate about the future of the EU's labour market policy.

BOX 13.1 KEY LABOUR MARKET CONCEPTS

Taylorism and Fordism

Frederick Taylor was an engineer who aimed to improve the efficiency of production by breaking each task into small, repetitive stages. This approach was incorporated into mass car production by Henry Ford. Taylorism, or 'scientific management', dominated industrial production until the 1980s. It lent itself to long production runs but was inherently inflexible and relied heavily on a relatively unskilled, plentiful labour force and remains popular in developing countries where capital is scarce but labour is plentiful.

Passive and active labour market policies

Passive labour market policies are directed towards management of the unemployment problem via income support to the unemployed rather than to job creation or moving the unemployed into employment. Active labour market policies are more concerned with job creation and improving labour market flexibility. Such policies include measures to improve employability through emphasis on the acquisition of skills through education and vocational training programmes. The EU's current concentration on employability, entrepreneurship and adaptability represent a renewed and increased commitment to active labour market policies.

Social dumping

The practice of relocating to regions with lower costs as a result of disparities in labour market regulations, the origin in part of differences in labour costs. In a frontier-free world, it is feared that, in the absence of common standards, member states with high standards might be pressured to lower their standards in order to compete, resulting in a downward spiralling of the standards of social provision. In practice, it is very difficult to attribute relocation decisions to social dumping. In 1993, Hoover decided to move its factory from Dijon in France to near Glasgow in Scotland: 600 French jobs were lost and 400 jobs were gained in Scotland. This is often quoted as a clear example of social dumping in action and of the competitive distortions created by the UK's failure to sign the Social Charter. Different labour conditions were a factor in Hoover's decision to move, but it is not all clear that they were the decisive factor nor that social dumping has occurred in any systematic or widespread way. Shortly after the Hoover decision, Rowntree made the reverse move, resulting in a net loss of jobs in Glasgow and a net gain in Dijon but without the same political fallout or comment. Relocation decisions take place all the time and an emphasis on labour costs ignores the key dimension of productivity. In reality, high levels of social protection in Europe are generally associated with high per capita income, the result of high productivity, and other competitive advantages.

TRENDS IN EU LABOUR MARKETS

One of the key drivers in thinking about the labour markets has been the evolution of unemployment (see Table 13.1). In the 1970s, with perhaps the exception of Ireland and Italy, unemployment was not a problem for current EU members for whom rates of below 3 per cent were the norm. Such low unemployment rates are commonly regarded as representing full employment: at such levels, unemployment is frictional and represents the unemployed who are between jobs. All this changed in the 1970s following the collapse of the Bretton Woods system and the oil price shocks which gave rise to a period

Table 13.1 Evolution of unemployment rates by member states, 1970–98 (% of labour force)

	1970	1980	1985	1991	1992	1993	1994	1995	1996	1997	1998
Austria			3.6	3.5	3.6	4.3	3.8	3.9	4.3	4.4	4.5
Belgium	2.2	9.1	13.6	6.6	7.3	8.9	10.0	9.9	9.7	9.2	9.0
Denmark	1.0	6.7	8.7	8.4	9.2	10.1	8.2	7.2	6.9	6.1	4.8
Finland			5.1	7.6	13.1	17.9	17.4	16.3	15.4	14.0	12.5
France	1.3	6.4	10.3	9.5	10.4	11.7	12.3	11.7	12.4	12.4	12.0
Germany	0.6	3.4	8.4	5.6	6.6	7.9	8.4	8.2	8.8	9.7	10.0
Greece			7.8	7.7	7.8	8.6	8.9	9.2	9.6	9.6	n.a.
Ireland	5.3	8.2	18.0	14.8	15.4	15.6	14.3	12.3	11.6	10.2	9.4
Italy	4.4	7.2	12.9	8.8	9.0	10.3	11.4	11.9	12.0	12.1	12.0
Luxembourg	0.0	0.7	1.7	1.7	2.1	2.7	3.2	2.9	3.3	3.7	2.2
Netherlands	1.0	6.2	13.3	5.8	5.6	6.6	7.1	6.9	6.3	5.2	4.6
Portugal	2.8	8.4	8.6	4.0	4.2	5.7	7.0	7.3	7.3	6.8	6.5
Spain	1.2	12.0	21.9	16.4	18.5	22.8	24.1	22.9	22.1	20.8	19.5
Sweden				3.3	5.8	9.5	9.8	9.2	10.0	10.2	8.3
UK	2.5	6.0	12.0	8.8	10.1	10.4	9.6	8.7	8.2	7.1	6.5
EU (15)				8.2	9.3	10.7	11.1	10.7	10.8	10.6	10.3
Japan	1.1	2.0	2.6	2.1	2.2	2.5	2.9	3.1	3.1	3.2	3.8
US	4.9	7.0	7.2	6.7	7.4	6.8	6.1	5.6	5.5	5.2	4.7

Source: Eurostat

Notes: All figures are seasonally adjusted annual averages, apart from those for 1998 which are seasonally adjusted rates for March, except for Spain, Finland, Netherlands and the United Kingdom which are for February of high inflation and unemployment and resulted in the breakdown of the widely prevailing consensus about economic management. By 1980, unemployment was several times higher than in 1970 in many member states. By 1985, as Europe approached the end of a deep recession, jobless levels were even higher. Although cyclical fluctuations have taken place since then, levels have persisted around this higher trend. Consequently unemployment has moved up the policy agenda as policy makers try to tackle the structural aspects of unemployment.

The structure of EU labour markets and employment have undergone massive changes since the formation of the Community. As a consequence of the relative decline in the importance of agriculture and of the deindustrialisation which has taken place within Europe since the 1960s, services now form the EU's dominant economic sector. This is reflected in shifts in the structure of the labour force. In the mid-1960s, agricultural employment as a share of total employment in present member states ranged from 3 per cent in the United Kingdom to 47 per cent in Greece. Thirty years later, agriculture's share of employment in the EU(15) was 5 per cent, ranging from 2 per cent in the United Kingdom to 21 per cent in Greece.

The service sector already provided most employment in many current member states in the mid-1960s but its lead over industrial employment, which ranged from 24 per cent of all jobs in Greece to 48 per cent in Germany, was marginal in most cases. In the United Kingdom, for example, 50 per cent of all jobs were in the service sector compared to 47 per cent in industry. The service sector was also the leading employer in Belgium, Denmark, Finland, France, Greece, Ireland, the Netherlands, Portugal and Sweden. By the mid-1990s, however, the dominance of service sector employment was unambiguous, accounting for almost two-thirds of all jobs compared to about 30 per cent in the industrial sector. The share of service sector employment ranged from 56 per cent in Greece and Portugal to over 70 per cent in Luxembourg, the Netherlands, Sweden and the United Kingdom. The development of the service sector, in conjunction with the rise of the information society (see Chapter 12), is also changing the skills mix required by employers and contributing to the growing trend for active labour market policies to ensure Europe's labour force is more responsive to the competitive pressures from globalisation. These factors require a highly skilled and educated workforce to ensure commercial success.

This trend has helped transform Europe's labour force: no longer is it typically composed predominantly of male full-time workers employed in the manufacturing sector but it is increasingly made up of female, part-time and short-term workers engaged in service sector activity. The feminisation of Europe's workforce is demonstrated by Table 13.2: female activity rates increased throughout the Community between the mid-1980s and mid-1990s, continuing a trend which began at least two decades before in some member states. Female activity rates are highest in Finland and Sweden where the gap between male and female activity rates is only about five percentage points. The lowest female activity rates are in Greece, Ireland, Spain, Italy and Luxembourg. The increase in activity rates has been particularly marked in Germany, Austria, Ireland, the Netherlands, Portugal and Spain.

Although these trends are not so clear-cut for employees on fixed term contracts, there has been a tendency for an increase in such work since the early 1980s. Indeed many of the new jobs which have been created in recent years have been either of limited duration or part-time in nature and involve the employment of women. Table 13.2 shows that over 80 per cent of the EU's part-time workers are women. On the one hand, this offers flexibility to female workers who frequently bear the main burden of family commitments and to employers who can break away from traditional work organisation. On the other hand, this trend raises questions regarding the rights of part-time workers who historically

Table 13.2 Feminisation of Europe's labour force

Activity rates of women aged 15–64 (%)

	1985	1995		1985	1995
Austria	50.8	58.6	Italy	39.7	42.5
Belgium	45.1	51.7	Luxembourg	41.5	44.1
Denmark	74.6	73.3	Netherlands	41.1	58.9
Finland	73.2	70.0	Portugal	49.4	59.1
France	56.7	60.6	Spain	33.7	44.9
Germany	51.7	61.3	Sweden	79.2	76.1
Greece	41.0	44.3	UK	61.0	66.0
Ireland	39.1	46.7			

Emergence of non-standard employment contracts

	% of employees with fixed term contracts		Part-timers as a % of employees	Women's share of part-time employment
	1983	1996	1996	1995
Austria	n.a.[1]	8.0	14	88.3[2]
Belgium	5.4	5.9	16	87.5
Denmark	n.a.	11.2	22	73.3
Finland	n.a.	17.3	11	65.1
France	3.3	12.5	17	82.0
Germany	n.a.	11.0	17	87.4
Greece	16.2	11.0	4	62.7
Ireland	6.1	9.2	13	71.5[3]
Italy	6.6	7.5	7	70.6
Luxembourg	3.2	2.6	8	91.1
Netherlands	5.8	12.0	38	73.6
Portugal	n.a.	10.4	5	69.1
Spain	n.a.	33.6	8	76.3
Sweden	n.a.	11.6	25	80.1
United Kingdom	5.5	6.9	25	82.3
EU (15)	n.a.	n.a.	n.a.	81.1

Source: Eurostat
Note: [1] n.a. = not available; [2] Austria = 1993; [3] Ireland = 1994

have not been accorded the same benefits as their full-time colleagues and which, unless addressed, will perpetuate inequality between the sexes.

A side-effect of the demise of manufacturing and the rise of service industries, the feminisation of the workforce and changes in the organisation of work has been a general reduction in trade union membership as a percentage of Europe's workforce (see Table 13.3). Numbers alone can, however, belie the strengths of the union movement. France, for example, despite one of the lowest levels of trade union membership in the EU, remains subject to highly effective strikes, particularly in the public sector. Also, the International Labour Organisation's (ILO) 1997–8 *World Labour Report: Industrial Relations – democracy and social stability* claims that Europe's unions 'have also sought to represent the workers as a whole [and] present themselves as mass social and labour movements rather than just as trade unions'. Given the European Commission's commitment to the social dialogue and involvement of the social partners in the formulation of social and employment policy, the importance of Europe's unions, despite their relative decline, remains high.

Table 13.3 Trade union membership as a % of wage and salary earners

	1995	1985–95 (% change)		1995	1985–95 (% change)
Austria	41.2	−19.2	Italy	44.1	−7.4
Denmark	80.1	2.3	Netherlands	25.6	−11.0
Finland	79.3	16.1	Portugal	25.6	−50.2
France	9.1	−37.2	Spain	18.6	62.1
Germany	28.9	−17.6	Sweden	91.1	8.7
Greece	24.3	−33.8	UK	32.9	−27.7

Source: ILO

EVOLUTION OF EU LABOUR MARKET POLICY

Although it is commonplace to argue that the European social dimension has been weak, the Treaty of Rome contained an extensive range of social policy provisions (see Box 13.2) which facilitated future developments. The recitals and preamble included broad social objectives, speaking of 'economic and social progress' and 'an accelerated raising of the standard of living'. Some aspects of the Treaty were ahead of their time, particularly Article 119 which established the principle 'that men and women should receive equal pay for equal work' – a seemingly remarkable inclusion in the Treaty for the 1950s but which occurred because of French concerns about competitiveness.

BOX 13.2 SOCIAL POLICY PROVISIONS OF THE TREATY OF ROME

Article

48–51 Free movement of workers to be achieved by the abolition of discrimination on the grounds of nationality regarding employment, pay and other employment conditions

52–58 Right of establishment for nationals, agencies, branches and subsidiaries of one member state in the territory of another

59–66 Freedom to provide a service by nationals established in a member state different from the recipient of the service

117–22 *General social provisions, including*:
   117 Recognition of the need to improve working conditions and living standards. This will occur as a result of the operation of the common market and from provisions in the Treaty
   118 Powers for the Commission to promote co-operation between member states in matters of employment, labour law and working conditions; training; social security; health and safety; occupational hygiene and the right of association and collective bargaining
   119 Men and women should receive equal pay for equal work
   120 The requirement for member states to maintain existing equivalences between paid holiday schemes
   121 Powers for the Council to assign the Commission tasks relating to common measures, especially regarding social security for migrant workers (linked with Articles 48–51)
123–8 Establishment of the European Social Fund

The buoyant economic growth and low unemployment of the 1960s resulted in a Community social policy which was not concerned with job creation but with measures directed towards the correction of mismatches between labour supply and demand such as the promotion of labour mobility; the mutual recognition of qualifications and the transferability of social security rights for migrant workers. Some health and safety measures were also introduced during this period.

In the 1970s, social policy was given a fresh impetus with the adoption of the 1974 Social Action Programme which launched initiatives in the field of employment law, equal opportunities, industrial democracy, workplace health and safety and further development of the European Social Fund (ESF). The 1970s was an important decade in Europe for equal opportunities legislation: in 1975, the equal pay directive required member states to abolish pay discrimination and applied the principle of equal pay for work of equal value; the 1976 equal treatment directive gave equal access for men and women to employment, promotion, vocational training and working conditions and in 1978 a directive on equal treatment for men and women in state social security systems was adopted. A substantial body of case law on workplace gender issues has subsequently evolved.

BOX 13.3 MILESTONES IN EU LABOUR MARKET POLICY

1957 Treaty of Rome contains several articles relating to the labour market (see Box 13.2)
1974 Social Action Programme directed towards attainment of full employment, industrial democracy, health and safety, equal opportunities and a greater role for the ESF
1987 Single European Act introduced qualified majority voting for health and safety measures and incorporates Social Dialogue into the Treaties
1989 Framework Health and Safety Directive
1989 Social Charter signed by eleven out of twelve member states (excluding the United Kingdom)
1989 Commission adopts Second Social Action Programme to implement Social Charter and to develop social aspects of the SEM
1993 Social Protocol annexed to the Treaty on European Union. UK social opt-out results in two legal bases for social policy
1993 White Paper *Growth, Competitiveness, Employment* published

1993	Social Policy Green Paper published
1994	Social Policy White Paper published
1994	European Works Council directive adopted – first directive adopted under Social Protocol
1995–7	Third Social Action Programme initiated
1996	Parental Leave Directive adopted – second directive adopted under Social Protocol, first legislation adopted by Council on basis of collective agreement by European Social Partners
1997	Following Labour election victory, United Kingdom abandons Social Protocol opt-out
1997	Amsterdam Treaty: Social Protocol brought into main body of treaties and Employment Chapter included in the Treaties for the first time
1997	Employment Summit leads to Employment Guidelines based on employability, entrepreneurship, adaptability and equal opportunities
1998	Social Action Programme 1998–2000 confirms commitment to flexible specialisation and active labour market policies

The 1980s began with further progress on a number of health and safety issues and equal treatment for men and women, but measures relating to worker information and consultation (the Fifth Company Law Directive and the Vredeling Directive) and to part-time and temporary work reached stalemate. However, fresh impetus was given to social policy via the campaign to create a Single European Market (SEM). Although not explicitly included in the 1985 Single Market White Paper, social policy was regarded as a 'flanking policy' of the SEM, that is, it was intended to provide support to broad SEM aims. The Commission had become increasingly concerned that the SEM was widely perceived as a programme to benefit business but that its success required the support of both employers and employees. Without a widening of its appeal, Commission President Jacques Delors believed the SEM programme would lose support.

Social policy received a major boost from the Single European Act (SEA) which confirmed the basic social and political rights of citizens in its preamble, thereby strengthening future claims of the Community to work in this area. From the point of view of the labour markets, the key feature of the SEA related to the introduction of Article 118A which required member states to pay particular attention to harmonisation of workplace health and safety standards whilst maintaining improvements which had already been made and taking care that such harmonisation measures did not damage the development of SMEs. In other words, member states were not to use the drive towards harmonisation of standards as an opportunity to reduce standards. At this time, differences in labour market regulations were regarded by many as equivalent in effect to the other non-tariff barriers scheduled for removal under the SEM. The wording of 118A, reinforced by 100A, ensured that the SEM would not result in a general lowering of workplace health and safety standards. Member states with higher labour market standards (and not only in relation to health and safety) were fearful that in a single market, companies would relocate to regions of the Community with lower standards and thus lower costs – the phenomenon of 'social dumping' (see Box 13.1). In this scenario, such member states would be faced with the choice of losing a significant number of jobs or giving in to pressure to reduce standards.

Article 118A also introduced qualified majority voting for health and safety measures. This assumed great significance when the Commission put forward a number of labour market provisions under the guise of health and safety measures following the UK's opt out from the Social Protocol, a tactic which was spectacularly successful for the Working

Time Directive (see Case Study 13.1). Unanimity was still required for other measures relating to labour market policy, including free movement and other employment rights. Article 118B gave the Commission responsibility for encouraging dialogue between employers and employees at European level which it hoped would lead to formal agreements between both sides of industry.

The changes brought about by the SEA were insufficient to dispel fears of social dumping. The Commission chose to combat such concerns via the Community Charter of the Fundamental Social Rights of Workers, signed by eleven out of the then twelve member states (the exception being the United Kingdom) in December 1989. The Charter was not a legally binding document but a 'solemn declaration' which established basic minimum rights in the workplace. These minimum rights served both as a defence against alleged social dumping and responded to concerns about an over-preoccupation with the priorities of business. In order to implement the principles of the Social Charter, the Commission introduced a Social Action Programme containing forty-seven proposals for directives and regulations.

BOX 13.4　KEY FEATURES OF THE SOCIAL CHARTER

Freedom of movement

- free movement rights for all EC workers subject to public health, security and health considerations
- all EC workers to enjoy same treatment as host nation nationals regarding access to employment, working conditions and social protection
- harmonisation of conditions of residence, especially concerning family reunification,
- elimination of obstacles arising from non-recognition of qualifications
- improvements in the living and working conditions of frontier workers

Employment and remuneration

- all employment to be fairly remunerated – i.e. wages sufficient for a decent standard of living
- equitable reference wage to be established for workers not on open-ended, full-time contracts
- all individuals to have access to free public placement services

Improvement of living and working conditions

- improvements in living and working conditions via upward approximation, particularly of duration and organisation of working time, atypical work contracts and collective redundancy and bankruptcy laws
- all workers entitled to a weekly rest period and annual paid leave

Social protection

- all citizens entitled to adequate social protection

Freedom of association and collective bargaining

- all workers have the right to belong to professional organisation or trade union of their choice and the right to refuse to join without penalty

- employer and employee organisations have the right to negotiate collective agreements according to national legislation and practice
- the right to strike subject to national regulations and collective agreements

Training

- access for all EC workers to vocational training throughout their working lives

Equal treatment for men and women

- equal treatment guaranteed and equal opportunities to be developed, especially regarding employment access, pay, working conditions, social protection, education and training and career development
- measures to allow men and women to reconcile their occupational and family obligations

Worker participation, information and consultation

- must take into account national practices and take place in 'due time', especially regarding introduction of technological changes affecting work organisation; restructuring or mergers with employment effects; and collective redundancy procedures.

Workplace health and safety

- all workers must enjoy satisfactory health and safety conditions – further harmonisation will take place

Protection of children and adolescents

- establishment of a minimum employment age
- young people to receive equitable wage and appropriate vocational training in working hours

The elderly

- all retired workers must have sufficient resources to guarantee a decent standard of living
- all EC citizens without pension or other support entitled to minimum income and medical assistance

The disabled

- additional measures to be taken to ensure the social and professional integration of disabled people, especially in relation to training, ergonomics, accessibility, mobility, transport and housing

Although many aspects of the Social Charter were largely symbolic (which employer, for example, would admit to paying their workforce 'unfair remuneration?), the Social Charter gave rise to fierce opposition from the United Kingdom. In the early 1980s, Mrs Thatcher's government prided itself on limiting trade union powers and on reducing the number of controls over business in industrial relations – the labour market flexibility argument. Mrs Thatcher was anxious that her government's reforms were not reversed by the actions of the European Community and vigorously opposed the Social Charter. British opposition to the Social Charter was partly a reflection of a more voluntarist approach to labour market regulation than prevailed elsewhere in Europe. Although the majority of employers in the United Kingdom already met most, if not all, of the requirements of the Social Charter, there was no legal requirement on them to do so, unlike in other member states where many of the rights were already enshrined in law and, in some cases, in the constitution. In short, implementation of the Social Charter implied big changes in UK law, although not necessarily in the practices of all UK businesses. Moreover, given the unanimous and indeed enthusiastic support of all other member states, several of whom had centre-right governments, it is also difficult to give credence to Mrs Thatcher's argument that the Social Charter represented 'socialism through the back door'.

The debate over the Social Charter cut across the key labour market debate identified above – over the need for and the nature of labour market flexibility. The United Kingdom argued vehemently that the Social Charter would inevitably lead to increased cost burdens on business with resultant losses in competitiveness. Exaggerated claims were made that the Social Charter would lead to harmonisation of social protection and to the introduction of a minimum wage, for example. In fact, at no time has there been any suggestion that the EU would harmonise social protection schemes (EU action in this area has been limited to facilitation of free movement of workers), nor is there any intention to introduce European legislation on a minimum wage – which is only one, very restrictive, interpretation of the phrase 'fair remuneration'. However, that is not to say that implementation of the Social Charter's principles is costless, but rather that the alleged costs were frequently over-estimated.

CASE STUDY 13.1 THE WORKING TIME DIRECTIVE

The main features of the Working Time Directive (WTD), which was adopted in 1993, are:

- a minimum rest period of eleven consecutive hours a day;
- a rest break where the working day is longer than six hours;
- a minimum rest period of one day a week;
- an average maximum working week of forty-eight hours including overtime;
- four weeks annual paid holiday (three weeks in an initial transition period);
- a restriction on night working of no more than eight hours on average.

Although drawing its inspiration from the principles of the Social Charter (that is, the approximation of conditions in relation to the duration and organisation of work; the right of every worker to a weekly rest period and to annual paid leave and the right of all workers to satisfactory workplace health and safety) to which the United Kingdom was not a signatory, the WTD itself was based on the health and safety provisions of Article 118A which were outside the procedures of the Social Protocol and therefore applicable to the United Kingdom.

The United Kingdom opposed the directive in its entirety, maintaining that it represented an unwarranted interference in business activities and would increase costs and reduce competitiveness – a view which was in accord with its free market philosophy. It was perhaps also significant that British workers work longer hours than those in other member states, implying that UK employers would have to make the greatest adjustments to comply with the directive. In addition, the directive represented a major change in practice in the United Kingdom where, unlike most other member states, working hours were not regulated by law, and where during the period of the Conservative government there had been a steady decline in collective sector agreements – the main source of working time regulation.

Average working hours for full time employees in 1996

Belgium	38.3	Germany	40.0
Italy	38.6	Sweden	40.0
Denmark	38.7	Greece	40.4
Finland	38.7	Ireland	40.4
Netherlands	39.4	EU	40.4
Luxembourg	39.5	Spain	40.6
France	39.8	Portugal	41.2
Austria	40.0	UK	43.9

Source: Eurostat

These factors resulted in a challenge by the UK government to the directive's legality in the European Court of Justice (ECJ). Its main argument was that the appropriate legal base was Articles 100 and 235, which relate to the rights of employees and the integrity of the single market, both of which require unanimity at the Council of Ministers and which would have allowed the United Kingdom to exercise a veto. In November 1996, the ECJ rejected the UK's case almost in its entirety. However, the Court did recommend annulment of the sentence which said that the weekly rest period in principle should include Sunday as the Council had failed to establish why Sunday was more closely associated with workplace health and safety than other days. As a result, the United Kingdom was required to take measures to implement the Directive, provoking fierce denunciations from the UK's ruling Conservative Party and threats from Prime Minister Major to block the intergovernmental conference (which was due to conclude in Amsterdam in June 1997) if the United Kingdom did not obtain an exemption from the WTD. The May 1997 general election intervened to prevent this threat becoming reality.

Estimates of the numbers of UK workers affected by the ECJ decision vary. However, figures from the House of Commons Library suggest that the number of UK workers without paid holiday entitlement rose by almost 20 per cent between 1992–6, from 1,975,000 to 2,358, 000, representing over 10 per cent of the workforce. Moreover, over half of the UK's four million plus part-time workers had no paid holiday entitlement whatsoever. In addition, another three million workers had paid holiday entitlement of between zero and three weeks. A Warwick University Study estimated that 3.5 million workers worked longer than forty-eight hours. The directive itself was actively opposed by many British companies even if, as was the case with many, they complied with its provisions. Many of them opposed the additional bureaucracy required by the directive to demonstrate compliance and many under-estimated the degree of flexibility which was contained in the directive via a series of derogations for all but its paid leave provisions. For example, the average forty-eight working week can be based on reference periods of up to six months in cases where derogations are allowed and up to twelve months in the case of collective

continued . . .

agreements or agreements between both sides of industry. In other words, workers can work longer than forty-eight hours a week for several weeks at a time providing they do not exceed the forty-eight hour average in the long term, allowing employers to organise working time in relation to busy and slack periods.

Almost immediately following the ECJ decision, a sector-wide agreement between the MSF (the technician's union) and the Heating and Ventilating Contractors' Association was reached to use a twelve month reference period to calculate the weekly forty-eight hour average. Proposals were also put forward for significant pay increases for UK construction workers, who average 44–46 hours per week if their unions agreed to operate a derogation.

The directive was originally intended to apply to all economic sectors and activities but the Council of Ministers decided to exclude certain sectors, namely 'air, rail, road, sea, inland waterway and lake transport, sea fishing, other work at sea and the activities of doctors in training'. The Commission estimates this effectively excluded about 5,630,000 employees from the scope of the directive. Apart from trainee doctors, a common feature of all the excluded sectors is that key workers spend time away from home as an integral part of their duties. In many cases, the directive has been interpreted to imply that all workers in the above sectors are excluded from the directive even when they are non-mobile. The Commission maintains that there is no reason why non-mobile workers should be treated differently from those workers carrying out similar tasks in other industries and that the exclusion should apply to the nature of the activity and not to the sector. Accordingly, in 1997 the Commission published a White Paper on the excluded sectors in which it proposed to:

- extend the full provisions of the directive to all non-mobile workers;
- extend to all mobile workers and those engaged in 'other work at sea' the directive's provisions on four weeks' annual paid leave and health assessments for night work and to provide a guarantee of adequate rest and a maximum number of annual working hours;
- introduce or modify legislation for each sector or activity concerning working time and rest periods for mobile workers, preferably by reference to social partners.

The Social Charter debate spilled over into negotiations over the Treaty on European Union during which the eleven Charter signatories clearly stated their wish to incorporate the principles of the Charter into the treaties (the eleven later became fourteen following the 1995 enlargement). This proved impossible in view of UK opposition and led to a unique compromise which resulted in the annexation of an Agreement and Protocol on social policy to the Treaty, effectively enabling the Charter signatories to act without Britain. The Social Protocol resulted in two legal bases for social policy action within the EU. The first related to social policy provisions emanating from the Treaty of Rome and the SEA which applied to the United Kingdom as much as to other member states. Wherever possible, new social policy initiatives were introduced under this heading in order to encompass all member states. The second related to the Social Agreement which set out social policy objectives largely along the lines of those in the Social Charter.

One of the first acts of the new Labour government following the UK election in May 1997 was to abandon the British opt-out. This move was welcomed by the other fourteen member states and facilitated the incorporation of the Social Protocol within the main body of the Treaty at the Amsterdam Council. In practice, only two pieces of legislation were passed under the Social Protocol during the short life of the opt-out – the 1994 Works Council Directive and the Parental Leave Directive which was adopted in 1996.

The former required the establishment of works councils to act as a formal channel for information and consultation of employees in companies with over 1,000 workers or employing over 150 in two or more member states. In practice, many large UK companies with a presence in other member states chose to comply with the directive. The Parental Leave Directive entitled employees to three months unpaid leave to look after children aged eight years or under, the first legislation adopted by the Council on the basis of collective agreement by the social partners. In 1997, the social partners announced a European-wide collective agreement on part-time work which is due to be turned into a formal directive.

The early 1990s saw recession throughout Europe with a consequent increase in unemployment and a shift of policy emphasis from rights to employment creation. Attempts to resolve the unemployment issue coupled with increasing recognition of the need to reduce the budgetary burden of generous social welfare provision, which would become increasingly unsustainable in the light of ageing populations, began to dominate policy making. In addition, Europe experienced a crisis of confidence arising from globalisation and the fear that Europe will increasingly have to compete with low labour cost countries, particularly from the Far East. Table 13.4 identifies the high level of indirect costs (that is, statutory social security contributions, collectively agreed, contractual and voluntary social security contributions, direct social benefits, vocational training and other social costs) which in many European countries represent one-quarter to one-third of total employment costs – levels which are high compared to Europe's competitors, adding to the burden on enterprises and also damaging Europe's competitiveness.

In response, the European Commission published its 1993 White Paper *Growth, Competitiveness, Employment* which placed job creation at the top of the EU policy agenda. In order to deal more specifically with these challenges, it issued a Green Paper on Social

Table 13.4 Indirect costs as a % of labour costs in industry

	1984	1988	1992	1995
Austria	24.2	24.7	24.5	25.2
Belgium	24.9	30.6	32.1	34.4
Denmark	7.6	3.8	6.8	n.a.
Finland	n.a.[2]	24.1	24.1	27.3
France	31.9	32.0	31.4	n.a.
Germany[1]	23.3	23.7	22.2	23.0
Greece	19.0	20.0	21.0	22.9
Ireland	17.5	17.8	17.3	17.4
Italy	27.4	30.0	29.6	n.a.
Luxembourg	16.3	16.8	15.9	15.0
Netherlands	27.1	27.1	25.1	24.6
Portugal	25.5	25.8	25.9	25.9
Spain	n.a.	25.1	26.4	n.a.
Sweden	n.a.	30.2	31.3	28.3
UK	25.1	14.5	15.4	16.0

Source: Eurostat

Notes:
[1] German figures for 1984 and 1998 do not include the new länder; [2] n.a. = not available

Policy – the basis for the 1994 Social Policy White Paper which set out the main guidelines for future EU social policy. The Green and White Papers were based on the assumptions that member states face growing demographic, technological, fiscal, human and industrial pressures which require significant adaptation of existing policies. Technological change is causing shifts in employment patterns and the role of work in society as witnessed by the growth of part-time and temporary work contracts. Unemployment, the ageing of populations, changes in family structure and growing poverty are placing the welfare state under extreme pressure and increasing demands for health care. Issues of social justice, equality of opportunity, the role of education and training, changing workplace relationships and workers' and women's rights also figured highly in the policy deliberations. These issues are closely intertwined with questions of socio-economic co-operation and competition on an international level.

The outcome of this debate was a greater concentration on the issues of labour market flexibility, albeit not necessarily in terms which would be understood by British Conservatives. The thrust of policy has moved away from a focus on workers' rights, which have not been abandoned, towards measures which are intended to:

- improve workplace adaptability;
- shift the burden of taxes away from labour (see Box 14.6);
- increase the quantity and quality of training;
- develop new areas of employment (see Box 14.1);
- encourage the development of self-employment and SMEs, considered an important source of new jobs;
- develop local job creation initiatives.

AMSTERDAM AND BEYOND

This debate culminated in the inclusion of an Employment Chapter and the incorporation of the Social Protocol and Social Agreement into the Amsterdam Treaty (see Box 13.5). Although of great symbolic importance, it is difficult to see how these changes, which confirm the importance of employment and social policy but do not confer major new powers on the European Union, will make a major difference to the EU's employment situation. However, the non-discrimination provisions relating to age, religion and sexual orientation could lead to important changes in practice and the greater use of qualified majority voting may make it easier to reach agreement in some areas.

Part of the rationale for the intergovernmental conference and the negotiation of the Amsterdam Treaty was to review the workings of the Maastricht Treaty. In this respect, the incorporation of the Social Agreement into the Treaties represents one of the biggest successes of Amsterdam, ending an anomalous and unsatisfactory situation for most member states. That is not to say that the worst fears of Prime Minister Thatcher and her successor John Major about increasing regulation of the labour market will be realised. Both the Employment and Social Chapters contain elements of a more flexible approach to labour market policy, speaking of the need for an 'adaptable workforce' and 'labour markets responsive to economic change'.

In addition, although the new British government was anxious to sign up to the full European social acquis, it does not support further extension of workers' rights, preferring instead to encourage labour market flexibility to promote competitiveness, albeit more in line with the flexible specialisation approach than the old full-blooded free market, deregulatory model. This position is increasingly shared by other member states, including Germany, and is reflected in various EU policy documents.

BOX 13.5 SOCIAL AND EMPLOYMENT INITIATIVES IN THE AMSTERDAM TREATY

Article

Preamble	A new recital confirms the EU's commitment to the principles of the Social Charter – made possible by the 1997 UK election and the end of the British opt-out
6A	Affirms the principle of non-discrimination and gives the Council of Ministers, acting unanimously, power to take action against discrimination based on gender, racial or ethnic origin, religion or belief, disability, age or sexual orientation. This Article has implications for the United Kingdom and other member states where religion, age and sexuality do not figure in domestic legal regimes. The unanimity requirement could inhibit the use of this Article for legislative purposes but the ECJ and the CFI will face an increased case load from alleged victims of such discrimination.
2 and 3	Gender equality is mainstreamed by insertion of the words 'equality between men and women' to the list of general principles to be promoted by the EU and an addition to Article 3 which states 'In all the activities referred to in the Article, the Community shall aim to eliminate inequalities, and to promote equality, between men and women.'

Employment policy – Article B TEU and Title VIA Employment, Articles 109N–109S

B TEU	This Article has been extended to include 'a high level of employment' in the Union's objectives and additions to Article 3 establish a co-ordinated employment strategy as a Community objective (see new Title VIA for details)

Title VIA	
109N	Member states and the Community required to develop 'a co-ordinated strategy for employment and particularly for promoting a skilled, trained and adaptable workforce and labour markets responsive to economic change'
109O	Employment promotion – a matter of common concern and to take national practice into account
109P	Incorporates the high employment objective into the treaties
109Q	Sets out the process for the submission of national and Community reports on employment
109R	Empowers the Council, following consultation, to adopt incentives to encourage co-operation between member states and to support their employment action
109S	The Council will establish an Employment Committee to advise on the promotion of co-ordination between member states on employment and labour market policies

Social policy

Following the end of the UK opt-out, the Social Protocol and Social Agreement are integrated into the Treaty (with a few amendments) in the form of a new Chapter on Social Policy.

117	Similar to Article 1 of the Social Agreement: also social policy measures must take into account the diversity of national practices and the need to retain competitiveness
118	Corresponds to Article 2 of the Social Agreement with the addition of provisions enabling the Council to adopt measures to encourage the exchange of information and best practice on how to tackle social exclusion
	Article 118(2) seeks to ensure that health and safety legislation does not discriminate against SMEs
118C	Extends Article 5 of the Social Agreement to list matters where the Commission will encourage member states to co-ordinate their actions, including employment, labour law and working conditions, basic and advanced vocational training, social security, prevention of occupational accidents and disease, and the rights of association and collective bargaining between employers and workers
119	A new paragraph is added, allowing use of the co-decision procedure to adopt measures to ensure the application of the principle of equal opportunities, including the principle for equal pay for equal work or work of equal value

Procedural changes

Co-decision	The co-decision procedure is extended to employment incentive measures and equal opportunities and treatment
QMV	Qualified Majority Voting is extended to the employment guidelines and incentive measures in the Employment Chapter and to social exclusion and equality of opportunity and treatment of men and women

Following the June 1997 Amsterdam Summit, a special Employment Summit was held in Luxembourg in November 1997 which set about implementing and operationalising the employment and social policy principles incorporated into the treaties at Amsterdam. In reality, the Summit, the subsequent Employment Guidelines and the Social Action Programme (SAP), published in spring 1998, contain nothing startling or new but represent a codifying, consolidation and stronger articulation of themes which had been increasingly stressed since the 1993 Competitiveness White Paper, the 1994 Essen Summit and the Green and White Papers on Social Policy. The SAP summarises current thinking on labour markets and takes as its main themes the need to enhance labour market flexibility and the need to place greater emphasis on active labour market measures. In order to promote these aspirations, the SAP has identified four key areas for EU activity:

- job, skills and mobility;
- the changing world of work;
- an inclusive society;
- the external dimension.

Jobs, skills and mobility

The EU's employment policy aims to create the conditions for prosperity and sustained long term growth. As such, labour market policies cannot be separated from other policy initiatives, such as the creation of the SEM or the convergence process leading to EMU. Overall, the process of creating jobs and preventing unemployment is shared between the

EU and member states. The Employment Guidelines, for example, require member states to draw up national plans to implement the employment strategy in relation to the following four pillars:

1 *Employability*: member states are to ensure that all unemployed young people are offered training, retraining, work practice, a job or other employability measures before they have been unemployed six months with similar opportunities to adults before they have been unemployed a year. Benefits and training schemes are to be adapted, to ensure they support employability and provide incentives for the unemployed to seek work or training opportunities. The social partners are also encouraged to promote possibilities for training, work experience, traineeships and other employability measures and are to work with member states to promote lifelong learning. The EU will contribute via increased investment in human resource development and lifelong learning through the ESF and by a new generation of education and training programmes.

2 *Entrepreneurship*: SMEs are a potentially important source of new jobs and it is to be made easier to start up and run businesses via improved conditions for setting up risk capital markets, lower administrative and tax burdens on SMEs and reduced obstacles to self-employment. Member states are also to investigate job creation possibilities at local level and to reverse the long term trend towards high taxes and charges on labour.

3 *Adaptability*: member states are urged to promote the modernisation of work organisation, particularly by incorporating into law more adaptable forms of contract which recognise the increasing diversity of employment and the need for employee security. The social partners are invited to negotiate agreements which include flexible working arrangements and achieve a balance between flexibility for the firm and security for the employee. These agreements could cover part-time working, lifelong training, career breaks and the expression of working time as an annual figure.

4 *Equal opportunities*: member states are to support the increased employment of women and to act to reverse the under representation of women in certain economic sectors and occupations and their over-representation in others. Efforts are to be made to ensure there is adequate provision for good quality care for children and other dependants. Member states are also to investigate ways of facilitating the return of workers to the workforce and to give special attention to problems encountered by disabled people in the workforce.

The changing world of work

Technological change, rapidly changing markets and the growth of services impose a need for speedy adaptation to new circumstances if enterprises are to compete in a global marketplace. The Commission proposes to take action in the following areas, which complement the adaptability pillar of the Employment Guidelines discussed above, to facilitate this process.

• *Modernisation of working organisation*: the Commission will present a Communication on work organisation which will identify measures needed at EU level to adapt legal frameworks to encourage more flexible contractual arrangements. The Commission will also consult on the need for EU action to protect teleworkers, bring forward guidelines on state aids for training and present a Communication on ways to adapt and promote social dialogue.

• *Anticipating industrial change*: given that many enterprises are undergoing a period of fundamental restructuring, the European Commission will continue to encourage adequate information and consultation of workers on decisions which affect them, particularly by pursuing the adoption of minimum standards for national information and consultation and by reporting on the operation of the European Works Council Directive.

- *Seizing the opportunities of the information society*: the growth of the information society offers opportunities to improve the way Europeans live and work and in 1997, the Commission presented a Communication on the social and labour market dimension of the information society. The Commission intends to develop this work by maximising the contribution of the information society to the promotion of employment, training, equal opportunities and social inclusion (for example, by considering the opportunities for disabled people) and by raising awareness of the social and labour market implications of the information society.
- *Creating a safe and healthy workplace*: since the late 1980s a legislative framework for minimum workplace health and safety standards has been in place. Emphasis is shifting towards effective implementation and operation of this framework and on adapting standards to new workplace risks and to technological change and scientific advances.

An inclusive society

In line with the 'European social model', EU social policy seeks to secure a cohesive and inclusive society which provides appropriate social protection and fights inequality and discrimination. In the face of demographic changes and the need to restrain costs, there is pressure to modernise and reform the Community's social protection systems to make them 'more employment friendly' (to widen the gap between unemployment benefit and wages to make employment more attractive?); to adapt the systems to the consequences of ageing populations; to adjust to the shifting gender balance in the workforce; and to reform social security co-ordination for individuals moving within the EU.

Despite Europe's success in securing improvements in living and working conditions, poverty and social exclusion remain problems. Accordingly, the Commission intends to present a communication on social inclusion; to propose incentive measures to combat social exclusion and to develop a programme for the integration of refugees. In addition, new Treaty articles enable the Community to take measures to fight discrimination on the grounds of gender, race, ethnic origin, religion or belief and sexual orientation. The Commission therefore intends to ensure that equal opportunities becomes a mainstream element of all relevant Community policies and will develop specific actions to improve the situation of women, including measures to combat workplace sexual harassment. Legislation to combat racial and all forms of discrimination will also be considered.

The external dimension

Social and employment policy tends to be inward looking but it also has an external dimension and is increasingly on the agenda in the EU's bilateral relations with third countries and in multilateral negotiations. Enlargement offers the most immediate example of this and in order to smooth the transition, the Commission intends to gradually involve all the applicant countries in its social policy programmes and the social dialogue. It will use the Accession Partnerships (see Chapter 15) to ensure full adoption and implementation of the social acquis and use PHARE assistance to help the development of the social infrastructure.

In the wider international sphere, social policy is gradually appearing on the agenda as advanced industrial nations fear their industries will be unable to compete against the low labour costs of third countries (much of the initial concern is focused on the issue of child labour) – an internationalisation of the social dumping argument which was prevalent within the European Union in the 1980s. The Commission intends to clarify its position on the external dimension of European social policy through a Communication. In addition, it intends to work through the International Labour Organisation (ILO) to promote internationally recognised core labour standards.

In order to implement the SAP, the Commission intends to use a balance of instruments. First, it intends to develop the social dialogue and involve the social partners more in the formation of policy. This approach is based on the philosophy of consensus and collaboration and has been a theme of Commission action for some time, seeing concrete results in the Parental Leave Directive and in the part-time work proposals.

Second, the Structural Funds, particularly the ESF, enable the Community to provide financial support and incentives for the modernisation and adaptation of employment and education and training. Proposed ESF reforms make an explicit link with the employment plans of member states drawn up under Europe's employment strategy. Mainstream Structural Fund spending will continue to promote human resource spending. In addition, a Community Initiative will be developed with a focus on the fight against discrimination and inequalities in the labour markets and a small number of innovative projects will be funded to develop and test new approaches. Moreover, the Amsterdam Treaty provides incentive measures for employment and combating social exclusion. These will be brought forward once ratification is complete.

Third, the Commission intends to continue to use legislation to encourage fair and decent living and working standards; to ensure full implementation and enforcement of legislation to provide a level playing field of minimum standards and to introduce new or updated rules where necessary. The list of pending proposals in the SAP is modest and tends to represent amendments to existing legislation. In other words, there are no plans for further controversial pieces of social or employment legislation. Employment policy has certainly become more high profile but there is more consensus among member states about policy direction – and not simply because of the election of a new British government, the position of other member states has also shifted.

CONCLUSION

As part of a trend towards a growing consensus around modified economic liberalism, there has been a subtle but perceptible shift in the EU's social policy since the debates of the late 1980s and early 1990s which arose from the Social Charter and efforts to achieve minimum rights and standards for workers in Europe. However, there is no move to remove those standards (indeed, it is proposed to extend the Working Time Directive to cover excluded workers) which are, in any case, relatively modest by the standards of most member states. Rather, there is recognition of the importance of labour market flexibility. However, the vision of flexibility which has been accepted is not one of total labour market deregulation and unfettered capitalism but of flexible specialisation. This recognises the need to introduce supply-side measures to improve the quality of the workforce so that Europe can compete in an increasingly technological and knowledge-rich age and explains the emphasis on adaptability and employability. This approach does not require an extensive legislative programme but a range of active labour market measures (and here the Commission can act as a broker of best practice), a co-operative system of industrial relations and a greater involvement of all workers in strategic planning.

The stakes for getting this policy right are high. Employment has moved to the top of the EU agenda and is likely to remain there. Although unemployment is falling as Europe enters the new millennium, the EU fears that structural problems will keep unemployment stubbornly high by historical standards, even at the peak of the economic cycle. However, employment policy is increasingly an issue of quality as well as quantity. High levels of unemployment cause social problems and increase the burden on the public purse. The need for flexibility and more employment is also increased by the demands of EMU, both from the point of view of limiting public expenditure and of improving factor mobility which will assist in the adjustment of countries within the Eurozone to internal economic pressures. The long term solution to labour market problems, in this view, is in line with the needs of enterprises which, given increasing global competition and the changing demands placed on the workforce, require highly trained and adaptable workers. The pure market forces position sees low wages as the key to competition and ignores the contribution of productivity to competitiveness which will be higher with skilled and committed workers. Depriving them of even minimum rights and paying low wages is unlikely to result in the type of workforce which Europe needs in order to compete.

↘ KEY POINTS

- **The emphasis of labour market policy has shifted from a concern for workers' rights to the battle against unemployment.**

- **Europe's labour market can no longer be characterised as being composed of predominantly male full-time workers employed in the service sector but is increasingly made up of female workers on atypical contracts in the service sector.**

- **Labour market flexibility is increasingly important as globalisation develops. However the concept is open to divergent interpretations and has crystallised around the market forces view of the labour market in which low wages and other labour costs enable firms to compete and the 'flexible specialisation' model.**

- **The European Union favours flexible specialisation, incorporating a vision of highly trained and motivated workers prepared to involve themselves in a variety of work organisations into its formulation of policy.**

- **Employability, entrepreneurship, adaptability and equal opportunities are key themes in the EU's current labour market policy**

SUGGESTED FURTHER READING

Addison, J., and Siebert, W.S. (eds) (1997) *Labour Markets in Europe: Issues of Harmonisation and Regulation*, Dryden.

Adnett, N. (1995) 'Social Dumping and European Economic Integration', *Journal of European Social Policy*, Vol. 5, No. 1, 1–12.

European Commission (1993) *European Social Policy: Options for the Union*, Green Paper, COM(93) 551.

European Commission (1993) *Growth, Competitiveness, Employment: the Challenges and Way Forward into the 21st Century*, COM (93) 700.

European Commission (1994) *European Social Policy: A Way Forward for the Union*, White Paper, COM (94) 333.

European Commission (1997) *Partnership for a New Organisation of Work*, Green Paper, COM (97) 128.

European Commission (1998) *Social Action Programme 1998–2000*, COM (98) 259.

Hantrais, L. (1995) *Social Policy in the European Union*, Macmillan.

Marsden, D. (1997) *Management Practices and Unemployment*, OECD Jobs Study: Working Paper Series No. 2., OECD, Paris.

Piore, M.J., and Sabel, C.F. (1984) *The Second Industrial Divide*, Basic Books.

Van Ruysseveldt, J. and Visser, J. (eds) (1996) *Industrial Relations in Europe: Traditions and Transitions*, Sage.

14

ENVIRONMENT POLICY – A GREEN LIGHT FOR COMPETITIVENESS?

Since the early 1970s, when environmental issues made their first tentative steps into the political mainstream, conceptualisation of the relationship between economic growth and environmental protection has changed radically. This change has given rise to a broader range of environmental policy instruments and to a more complex and positive attitude on the part of policy makers and business to environmental protection. In the early days of environmental awareness, there was a general assumption of incompatibility between continuing economic growth and environmental protection. This was symbolised in the title of the Club of Rome's influential 1972 report *Limits to Growth* which warned that mankind could not afford to exploit the earth's resources indefinitely without dire consequences. Such an underlying philosophy resulted in inflexible command-and-control policies which sought to regulate and constrain the activities of business. Increasing knowledge about the environment and the growing complexity and depth of the environmental debate have challenged this conventional wisdom and caused a reassessment of the link between economic growth and the environment. This is symbolised by the phrase 'sustainable development', the main theme of the European Union's Fifth Environmental Action Programme (Fifth EAP), which has been incorporated into the Amsterdam Treaty as a fundamental objective of the EU and which has become a common theme in environmental debate in many countries and international institutions like the OECD and the United Nations.

This chapter commences by examining the debate on the link between environmental policy and competitiveness, paying particular attention to the ideology of ecological modernisation which is increasingly permeating EU environmental policy. The following sections trace the evolution of EU environment policy and examine attempts to widen the range of policy instruments to include environment taxes and other economic instruments, before briefly examining the international dimension of environmental policy. The chapter concludes by examining the corporate response to environment issues.

ENVIRONMENT POLICY AND COMPETITIVENESS: COSTS VERSUS ECOLOGICAL MODERNISATION

The concept of sustainable development implies that environmental protection need not be a burden but can be a source of economic growth. This is termed 'ecological modernisation' and is implicit in much contemporary debate about the environment. This philosophy generates a more pro-active approach to environmental policy management and was typified in a 1995 speech in Helsinki by European Environment Commissioner Ritt Bjerregaard who urged that 'respect for the environment must not be seen as a burden for industry, but as an opportunity to stimulate innovation and to reduce inefficiencies'. In other words for business, ecological modernisation represents a shift away from the perception of environmental policy as a threat in terms of increased compliance costs and reduced competitiveness to providing opportunities for future growth.

The most direct manifestation of this is the growth of eco-industries (see Box 14.1) which have developed as a response to the growing market for environmental goods and services and which have generated billions of ECU in revenue and thousands of new jobs, both in large companies and in SMEs. For example, the proliferation of recycling legislation which occurred from the 1980s, stimulated research, development and investment in recycling technology and created new markets. This was the case in the plastics sector which faced problems in the sorting and separation of individual resins, a process which is crucial to the economic viability of plastics recycling as the greater the homogeneity and purity of the resin which is recovered, the more suitable is the resulting recyclate for higher value-added applications. Development of this technology to deal with a wider range of plastic resins and products at greater speed requires substantial initial investment, but the potential returns for the companies which manage to establish themselves in this market are significant. It is in markets where recycling legislation is strongest that the incentive to develop such technology is greatest and participants can gain first mover advantages.

BOX 14.1 THE EUROPEAN ENVIRONMENT INDUSTRY

The global market for environmental equipment and services was estimated at around ECU 246 billion in 1992 and is forecast to increase to ECU 300 billion by 2000 and ECU 572 billion by 2010. Demand for environmental equipment and services has traditionally been limited to the advanced industrialised countries of the US, Japan and Europe, which accounts for one-third of the world market. Greater interest is anticipated in the coming years from the rapidly developing countries of south and east Asia and from Latin America. The EU industry will be in a favourable position to benefit from this growth.

The European market has grown, in part, out of the need to implement EU pollution control directives and in 1994 amounted to ECU 90 billion, of which ECU 35 billion was spent on investment goods and ECU 55 billion on services. Over 90 per cent of this market was in activities linked to waste water treatment (42 per cent); control of air pollution (19 per cent) and waste management (29 per cent). The German market constituted over one-third of demand but the relative significance of eco-industries was greatest in Austria and the Netherlands where they were equivalent to 2.3 per cent of GDP (as opposed to 1.4 per cent for the EU as a whole) and where per capita spend on environmental goods and services was equal to ECU 430 in Austria and ECU 450 in the Netherlands, compared to ECU 240 for the EU. Expenditure on eco-goods and services is below ECU 100 per head in Greece, Portugal and Spain, but the gap between the southern countries and the rest of the EU is anticipated to decline as the impact of the Cohesion Fund, which has a strong environmental dimension, starts to emerge.

The Europe environmental industry employs an estimated one million people in 20–30,000 firms: roughly 70 per cent are engaged in operating environmental installations or in providing services and the rest are employed in producing the environmental goods or the infrastructure to provide the service. In addition, environmental expenditure also leads to investment in sectors outside the environmental industry (such as construction, services and intermediate goods), resulting in an estimated additional half a million jobs.

Estimates of the size of the EU's eco-industries exclude renewable energy technologies and markets which, even if the EU's renewable energy strategy is only partially successful, could represent a cumulative market of between ECU 78 billion (assuming a contribution of renewable energy to total energy demand of 6.8 per cent by 2020) and ECU 226 billion (a 12.9 per cent renewable energy contribution). Furthermore, the EU has a technological lead in some renewable technologies, particularly wind power, photovoltaics and advanced biomass which, with supportive policy, could result in the EU becoming a leading world supplier of renewable goods and services, with further positive knock-on effects for jobs and investment.

Source: EU Database of Eco-Industries

In short, it is increasingly perceived that possession of the proven technical and production capability to produce low polluting goods acts as a significant competitive advantage. This manifests itself, for example, in the motor sector's attempts to develop cars with high levels of fuel efficiency and component recyclability. Not only does this generate marketing advantages in relation to increasingly environmentally sophisticated consumers (although the extent to which consumers will pay extra for less environmentally damaging products is probably limited), the constant effort to gain an environmental edge encourages innovation and can help companies build up important technological leads in increasingly competitive markets. In this respect, ecological modernisation is more appropriate to higher value-added sectors with a high technological content. Its application is likely to be less relevant to resource intensive and commodity-based activities. In addition, the negative competitive impact of environmental regulations can be offset in part by the promotion of incentives for research and development, support for infrastructure and a generally more favourable business environment.

In addition, as environmental protection legislation becomes more widespread throughout the advanced industrial world, there is a strong view that product standards will increasingly be determined by those countries with the strongest pollution control. Enterprises located in these countries and which have been obliged to adapt to the more stringent controls will profit from significant 'first mover' advantages. This view is not uncontested and contrasts strongly with the 'pollution havens' hypothesis that high environmental standards encourage firms to relocate to regions with fewer and laxer controls – a phenomenon which is discussed in the later section on the international dimension of environmental policy.

Although ecological modernisation is an important factor in changing the nature of contemporary environmental debate, resistance to environmental legislation on the grounds that it increases costs and therefore decreases competitiveness retains strong resonance (for example, see later section on environmental taxes). The challenge to the EU and to other environmental policy makers is to formulate policy in such a way that it meets environmental goals without damaging the EU's competitiveness at a time when unemployment is the dominant economic and political issue. In other words, there is a need to operationalise the principles of ecological modernisation. This can, for example involve the use of a wider range of policy instruments and co-ordination of policy at international level, both of which the EU is trying to do with varying degrees of success.

EVOLUTION OF EU ENVIRONMENT POLICY

The Treaty of Rome contains no direct reference to environmental issues. The preamble did speak of 'the constant improvement of living and working conditions'. This can be interpreted not only as a commitment to boost real incomes but also to improve the quality of life. Article 2 refers to a 'harmonious development of economic activities' which is also open to a wide interpretation to include environmental issues. However, there is little evidence that this was the intention of the drafters of the Treaty. Indeed, given the rudimentary level of environmental awareness in the 1950s, it would have been remarkable if the environment had been incorporated into the treaties.

BOX 14.2 MILESTONES IN EU ENVIRONMENT POLICY

1972	United Nations Conference on the Human Environment, Stockholm
1972	Paris Summit instructs the European Commission to develop an environmental policy
1973–6	First Environmental Action Programme
1977–81	Second Environmental Action Programme
1982–6	Third Environmental Action Programme
1987	Single European Act explicitly incorporates the environment into the Treaty
1987–92	Fourth Environmental Action Programme
1992	Rio Earth Summit commits industrial countries to return CO_2 emissions to 1990 levels by 2000
1993	Maastricht Treaty extends qualified majority voting to most aspects of environmental policy
1993–2000	Fifth Environmental Action Programme
1997	Amsterdam Treaty consolidates environmental gains of Maastricht
1997	Kyoto summit agrees an average 5.2 per cent reduction by 2010 in six greenhouse gases compared to 1990 levels in the major industrialised countries: The EU assigned a target of an 8 per cent reduction, compared to 7 per cent for the United States and 6 per cent for Japan.

By the late 1960s, there was an upsurge in environmental debate, culminating in the influential United Nations Conference on the Human Environment in Stockholm in 1972. The themes of the Stockholm conference were taken up by the Paris Summit of EC Heads of State and Government in October 1972 and were reinforced by growing environmental concerns within the Netherlands and West Germany. The result was a communiqué which instructed the European Commission to draw up a Community environmental policy. The ensuing First Environmental Action Programme ran from 1973 to 1976 and identified three key areas of activity:

- reduction and prevention of pollution and nuisances;
- improvement of the environment and quality of life;
- common environmental action, either by the Community on behalf of member states or by member states themselves within international organisations.

Early Community environmental policy used two Treaty articles as a legal base:

- Article 100 which empowers the Council to pass directives to approximate laws which 'directly affect the establishment or functioning of the common market';
- Article 235 – a useful catch-all article which enables the Council to take actions which prove necessary to meet Community objectives where the 'Treaty has not provided the necessary powers.'

The rationale for EU environmental policy grew as the campaign to develop the single market gathered pace during the 1980s. This arose from the possibility that differences in national environmental regulation would perpetuate market fragmentation by allowing discrimination against goods from member states with less strict or simply different environmental regulation. The possibility was also raised that persistence of different environmental standards would result in downward pressure on standards as higher standard countries strove to prevent migration of investment to member states with lower standards.

Articles 130r–t of the Single European Act gave the Community explicit powers in the environmental field for the first time, establishing that Community action on the environment should aim to preserve, protect and improve environmental quality; contribute towards human health; and ensure a prudent and rational use of natural resources. Community action was to be based on:

- the prevention principle;
- the rectification of environmental damage at source;
- policy integration – the incorporation of environmental protection requirements into other Community policies;
- the 'polluter pays' principle.

BOX 14.3 KEY ENVIRONMENT POLICY PRINCIPLES

The 'polluter pays' principle stipulates that those who generate pollution should pay for it and the costs of environmental damage should not be relieved by subsidies or be left to public authorities. This principle is closely linked to the concept of internalisation of external costs. Environmental costs are often referred to as 'externalities' (for example, damage to health, rivers, the air, etc. arising from economic activity) which are not incorporated into the market price of a good. The purpose of internalisation of external costs, which is an explicit aim of a number of EU environmental policies, is to ensure that these externalities are included in the market price of a product.

The prevention principle implies changes to products and processes to prevent the occurrence of environmental damage rather than reliance on pollution control or end-of-pipe solutions which only come into operation once damage has actually occurred. This implies the development of 'clean technologies', including minimal use of natural resources such as energy and raw materials; minimal releases into the atmosphere, water and soil; and maximisation of the recyclability and lifespan of products.

The precautionary principle requires that the absence of full scientific certainty about the causes of an environmental problem should not be used to justify delays in the introduction of measures believed necessary to prevent further environmental degradation. Scientific inquiry is a continuing process and absolute certainty is not usually attainable. Therefore, in one sense, the introduction of environmental protection measures can be regarded as an example of risk containment and management. In practice there can be significant differences about the degree of potential threat needed before policy action should be taken: Germany, for example, tends to come down on the side of caution whereas, in recent years, the United Kingdom has frequently argued for greater scientific information before committing itself to a particular course of action. In fact it was the British government which insisted that the Community should consider 'available scientific and technical data' when introducing environmental measures. This followed the UK's long-standing rejection of suggestions that sulphur dioxide from British power stations was responsible for acid rain in Scandinavia.

It was in relation to the environment that the principle of subsidiarity was introduced into the treaties for the first time (a principle which was granted much wider application in the Maastricht Treaty). Article 130r of the SEA authorises the Community to take action when its environmental objectives 'can be attained better at Community level than at the level of the individual Member States'. In practice, it can be argued that many environmental problems may be more appropriately dealt with at a supranational level as pollution is no respecter of borders. The ongoing discharge of waste into the river system and incidents such as the 1986 Chernobyl accident demonstrate the trans-national, trans-continental and, in the case of global warming, the global nature of many environmental problems. This same Article also acknowledges the competence of the Community to co-operate with third countries and international organisations in certain environmental matters whilst acknowledging the continuing scope for member state action in this field.

Most importantly for member states in northern Europe, particularly Denmark, Germany and the Netherlands, the SEA allows member states to take stronger environmental measures than those advocated at Community level, provided they are compatible with other aspects of the Treaty such as the SEM and competition rules. This inhibits potential levelling down of the higher standards of 'green' countries. Despite the safeguards about compatibility with the Treaty, this provision increases the possibility of a 'two speed' Europe and continuing fragmentation of the market.

The Maastricht Treaty took Community policy further. It confirmed the 'preventive', 'polluter pays' and 'rectification at source' principles and added another – the 'precautionary principle' (see Box 14.3). The Treaty also made the promotion of 'measures at international level to deal with regional or world-wide environmental problems' an explicit Community objective and committed the Community to aim for a 'high level of protection.' However, the potentially most important change to the development of Community environment policy, however, was the extension of qualified majority voting to most environmental matters with the exception of measures:

- 'primarily of a fiscal nature': governments guard their taxation responsibilities fiercely and it is the continuing unanimity requirement which is largely responsible for limited progress on approximation of excises on mineral oils and for failure to agree carbon taxes and an extension of excise duties to all energy products (see below);
- relating to town and country planning, land use (but not waste management and measures of a general nature) and water resource management;
- significantly affecting the choice between energy resources for member states and the general structure of their energy supply.

The Amsterdam Treaty consolidated the environmental gains of the Maastricht Treaty by giving them greater prominence. The commitment to sustainable development became a core EU objective, having previously ambiguously been represented as 'the constant improvement of living and working conditions' and of 'harmonious development of economic activities'. As such, it was incorporated into the preamble and Article 2 of the Treaty and the integration of environmental policy into all aspects of Community policy was moved from the environmental title to Article 3c. The net result was to give environmental policy greater prominence and status. The Commission also attached a declaration to the Treaty committing it to incorporate environmental impact assessments into all proposals with significant environmental implications and in the month following the Amsterdam Council (that is, in July 1997), the Commission tabled a proposal to improve its own internal procedures for the integration of environmental considerations into policy.

Amsterdam also extended the co-decision procedure to all environmental measures, thereby increasing the role of the European Parliament, the Community institution which has shown the greatest appetite for enhancing the Community's environmental role. However, proposals to extend qualified majority to all aspects of environmental policy, proposals which were strongly supported by Denmark, DGXI and environmental pressure groups, were not accepted.

THE EXPANDING RANGE OF ENVIRONMENT POLICY

During the 1970s and 1980s, European environmental policy largely took the form of 'command-and-control' legislation – that is, a series of directives which aimed to limit the amount of emissions of particular pollutants from motor vehicles, industrial plant and agriculture, for example. Such standards were imposed in reaction to environmental problems and fall into the following categories:

- *Process standards*: such standards are designed to control the production process and are intended to protect the health of workers and to minimise pollution from production. Their direct effects are purely domestic and do not have an impact on intra-Community trade nor cause friction with trade policy generally. However, process standards can act as an incentive for manufacturers to relocate where regulations are less strict.
- *Product standards*: these standards are concerned with the composition and performance characteristics of a product. Examples include the directive on lawnmower noise or vehicle emission standards. The implementation of product standards which are stricter than normal Community product standards can fragment the single market as failure to meet stricter national environmental standards can keep products from another member state out of that market.
- *Environmental quality standards*: such standards establish the maximum amount of polluting substances which can be permitted in a particular environmental medium such as the soil, water or air. These standards allow a certain leeway to local conditions: identical behaviour in different eco-systems can result in substantially different outcomes, requiring different technological responses for the purposes of environmental control.

National and Community environmental thinking has gradually become more sophisticated. The broad parameters, principles and ambitions of European environmental policy were set out in a series of environmental action programmes which, as knowledge about and commitment to environmental objectives increased, have progressively become more complex. The action programmes themselves do not comprise a list of proposed initiatives, as their name suggests, but rather provide a framework for action. Each action

BOX 14.4 RANGE OF EU ENVIRONMENT MEASURES

Water

Several directives have been passed to protect the environmental quality of different types of water, including surface and underground water, bathing water, drinking water and fish and shellfish water. Legislation also covers discharge of toxic substances into water. Implementation and enforcement of these directives has been problematic and several member states have appeared before the European Court of Justice on non-compliance charges. The Community also participates in international conventions to control pollution in important international waterways such as the Mediterranean, the North Sea and the Rhine.

Air

Several directives exist to limit emissions from large combustion plants, particularly power stations and from motor vehicles – directives which are constantly being amended and upgraded. The Community has also embarked upon a strategy to limit acid rain and in 1996 put forward an action plan to reduce methane emissions from oil and natural gas production. Given the global nature of atmospheric pollution, the Community has been active in international initiatives to combat these problems.

Noise

Directives are in place to establish maximum noise levels for cars, lorries, motorcycles, tractors, aircraft, lawnmowers and construction machinery. Similar proposals for other items are in the pipeline.

Chemicals

The 1977 Seveso incident in which a large area was contaminated with highly toxic dioxin resulted in a range of measures relating to the classification, packaging and labelling of dangerous substances. A 1982 directive requires manufacturers to inform the authorities about substances, plants and the possible location of accidents and since 1986, a European Inventory of Existing Chemical Substances has listed all chemical products on the market, enabling them to be subject to procedures for notification, evaluation and control.

Waste

Several directives govern the collection, disposal, recycling and processing of various categories of waste and attempt to control transboundary waste shipments and particular types of waste, such as waste from the titanium dioxide industry, waste oil, radioactive waste and the dumping of waste at sea.

Horizontal legislation

This refers to directives and regulations which govern environmental management across sectors and includes directives on Environmental Impact Assessment, access to environmental informa-tion and the implementation of environmental directives. The establishment of the European Environment Agency, whose purpose is to provide information on the state of Europe's environ-ment and the LIFE regulation, the first Community financial instrument for environmental actions also fall within the category of horizontal measures.

programme has built upon the previous one and the principles laid down in them have often been ahead of actual achievements. The First Action Programme, for example, acknowledged the 'polluter pays principle' and the concept that decisions should be taken at the most appropriate geographical level, a forerunner of the subsidiarity debate referred to above. By the time the Fifth Action Programme came into force in 1992, the Community's approach towards the environment had become more integrated and programmatic, focusing on sectors such as transport and energy (see Box 14.5) rather than on environmental media such as water and the air.

The Commission has claimed that the Fifth EAP marks a turning point in the development of European environmental policy, particularly in its attempts to take an integrated view of environmental problems and to incorporate environmental issues into the Community's wider political and economic priorities. In many senses though, the Fifth EAP rather than representing a new departure builds on and develops themes which had been evolving for the previous twenty years. Nevertheless, although environmental pressure and activism at Community level (at least measured in terms of the number of pieces of legislation) have slackened since the Fifth EAP was drafted, its introduction coincided with a number of factors which gave it a higher profile than its predecessors, including:

- heightened awareness of environmental issues at local, regional and global levels;
- the Maastricht Treaty negotiations which, among other things, strengthened the environmental provisions of the treaties by extending the amount of qualified majority voting on environmental matters;
- the Rio Earth Summit where developed and developing countries formulated a strategy (known as 'Agenda 21') for environmental problems which could only be tackled on a global level;
- the early stages of the economic transition in Central and Eastern Europe which faces monumental environmental problems which will complicate the enlargement negotiations.

BOX 14.5 THE FIFTH ENVIRONMENTAL ACTION PROGRAMME (1992–2000): TOWARDS SUSTAINABILITY

The Fifth EAP's sub-title is *Towards Sustainability*. Sustainable development is open to various interpretations, but from the perspective of the European Union it refers to a strategy which enables the current generation to meet their own needs without preventing future generations from meeting theirs. The key features of the Fifth EAP are:

- a commitment to maintaining the overall quality of life;
- continuing access to natural resources;
- the avoidance of long term environmental damage;
- development which meets the needs of current generations without adversely affecting the ability of future generations to meet theirs.

The programme differed from its predecessors by covering eight years instead of five – a reflection of the long term nature of many environmental problems and the solutions required in turn. It also envisaged the use of a wider range of instruments to combat environmental problems; placed a greater emphasis on the need to monitor and research environmental problems; established a Financial Instrument for the Environment (LIFE) to complement other environmental actions and identified greater co-operation with third countries as a priority.

In order to achieve the sustainability goal, the fifth EAP addresses problems of climate change, acidification and air quality, the protection of nature and bio-diversity, the management of water resources; the urban environment, coastal zones and waste management and is based on the following principles:

The targeting of key sectors

The following five sectors have been selected for special attention under the fifth EAP: these are sectors which exercise a significant influence on the environment and in which, according to Commission claims, the Community has a unique role to play and where the Community approach is the most effective.

- *Industry*: the fifth EAP represents a shift away from regulation towards strengthening dialogue with industry to find solutions to environmental problems and encouraging, where appropriate, voluntary agreements and other forms of self-regulation. The Community's strategy is to be based on rational resource use; the use of information to improve consumer choice and public confidence in industrial activity; and Community standards for production processes and products. Special consideration is to be given to the position of SMEs and to international competitiveness.
- *Energy*: the challenge is to manage the simultaneous attainment of economic growth, reliable and secure energy supplies and environmental integrity. During the fifth EAP, environmental efforts will be directed towards improving energy efficiency and the development of technology to facilitate moves towards less carbon-intensive energy consumption, with a particular emphasis on renewable energies.
- *Transport*: present transport trends create congestion, pollution, inefficiency, wasted time, health and safety risks and general economic inefficiency. The strategy for sustainable development in terms of mobility will require improved land use and economic development planning; improved planning and management of transport infrastructures and facilities, including the incorporation of the real costs of infrastructure and environmental impact in investment decisions and user costs; the development of public transport; the continued improvement of vehicles and fuels; and the promotion of a more environmentally rational use of the private car.
- *Agriculture*: changes in farming practices, in part encouraged by the logic of the Common Agricultural Policy (CAP), have led to environmental degradation of the soil, water and air and difficulties in terms of over production, rural problems, the Community finances and international trade. The fifth EAP builds on the proposals for CAP reform.
- Tourism: tourism can both facilitate the economic development of regions and bring environmental degradation which will ultimately destroy the tourism industry. In order to develop sustainable tourism, the fifth EAP proposes diversification of tourist activity; improved quality of tourist services; and campaigns to change tourist behaviour. The Community's main role is to support investment in tourist infrastructures: in practice, the main focus of attempts to resolve the tourism-environmental problem will occur at national, regional and local levels in line with the principles of subsidiarity.

The integration of the environment into all policy areas

Environmental policy does not exist in a vacuum: most other EU policies have an environmental dimension to a greater or lesser degree. The Fifth EAP recognised this by calling for the integration of the environmental dimension into all policy areas – a commitment which was reinforced in 1996 by the mid-term review. The June 1997 Treaty revisions agreed at Amsterdam also strengthened the requirement to integrate environmental issues into other Community policies. Accordingly, in July 1997 the Commission adopted measures to improve its internal procedures for integration of environmental considerations into its policy making, including, among other things, the evaluation of the environmental impact of all policy proposals at an early stage in their development by the appropriate Directorate-General (DG).

The use of a broad range of instruments

Previous EAPs concentrated almost entirely on legal instruments (that is, centralised environmental regulation) to achieve their objectives. These will remain important to maintain fundamental levels of public health and environmental protection, especially within a wider international context, and for ensuring that environmental measures do not conflict with the SEM. However, the fifth EAP proposed use of a much wider range of policy instruments, including:

- market-based instruments, including environmental charges designed to avoid pollution and waste via the internalisation of external costs (through fiscal incentives and disincentives, the application of the concept of environmental liability, voluntary agreements; fiscal reforms and environmental accounting, etc.);
- the development of supporting, horizontal measures, including improved base-line statistical data (an area in which the European Environmental Agency has played a significant part), scientific research and technological development, improved sectoral and spatial planning, and better public/consumer information and education and training.
- financial support mechanisms as a way of promoting sustainable development: the fifth EAP itself created the LIFE fund, the first Community financial mechanism specifically devised for environmental protection and also aimed to improve the integration of environmental considerations into the Structural and Cohesion Funds.

The introduction of a broader range of environmental instruments has the greatest potential to transform EU environmental policy. However, as confirmed by the mid-term review, this aspect of the fifth EAP has been disappointing, particularly in relation to economic instruments (see Box 14.5).

Implementation and enforcement of legislation

The implementation and enforcement of legislation has been more of a problem in the environmental field than in any other. The Commission proposes consideration of a number of measures to rectify the situation, including an enhanced role for reporting requirements under Community legislation; greater co-operation between the bodies responsible for the implementation and enforcement of environment policies and possible sanctions for non-compliance.

International co-operation

The Community intends to reinforce its international role in environmental policy, both in bilateral (for example, with the countries of Central and Eastern Europe and the Mediterranean Basin) and multilateral negotiations, including contributions to United Nations initiatives, and the greater integration of the sustainable development dimension into the Lomé Convention.

ECONOMIC INSTRUMENTS: THE CASE OF ENVIRONMENT TAXES

There are two broad approaches to environmental policy. The first involves regulations such as licences, standards or bans – instruments which, as discussed above, were favoured by the Community in the early years of environmental policy. The second entails economic instruments, including environmental taxes, charges, tradable permits, deposit refunds and subsidies. These instruments aim to use market forces and the price mechanism to encourage consumers and producers to restrain their polluting behaviour and to avoid degradation of resources. Economic instruments have increasingly found favour over the more traditional command-and-control measures as they allow for greater flexibility in meeting environmental objectives. Economic instruments act as an incentive to producers and consumers: an energy tax could, for example, encourage greater investment in energy efficiency technology; restrain energy consumption altogether; promote a switch to fuels which incur less tax or lead to consumption of the same amount of energy and higher tax revenue. In this scenario, energy users can choose to respond to the market signals sent out by the tax in the way which is most appropriate to their needs. A more regulatory approach tends to impose the same solution on all parties regardless of their circumstances.

Since the mid-1980s, economic instruments have increasingly been adopted in advanced industrial economies. The fifth EAP advocated use of a much broader range of environmental measures, including market-based instruments. However, in practice, at EU level at least, progress on the use of economic instruments has been extremely limited. Whether attempts are made to introduce environmental taxes at member state or EU level, policy makers have to deal with a number of barriers to implementation.

Competitiveness

The impact of any environmental tax on competitiveness depends not only on the size of the tax itself but also on the prevailing market situation: in a tight market experiencing fierce competition and narrow profit margins, even small tax-induced cost increases can have negative impacts on individual firms and sectors. Furthermore, if a tax results in the relocation of production to a country where such a tax is not levied, the environment-ally damaging behaviour simply shifts elsewhere. However, in certain circumstances, the competitiveness argument centres not upon the question of cost but on the possible improvements to innovation and efficiency in the ecological modernisation debate referred to above. The technological innovations stimulated by the environmental charges would result in 'first mover' advantages if stricter environment policies spread to other countries and regions. In other words, countries or regions which lead moves towards environmental charges could develop a significant technological edge in a world in which fiscal incentives encourage a search for less environmentally damaging production solutions. In practice, however, countries which have introduced carbon-energy taxes, for example, have responded to the competitiveness problem by exempting their more energy intensive industries from the tax (a possibility also catered for in the Commission's carbon energy tax proposals – see Box 14.6), thereby negating some of the potentially beneficial effects of such taxes. However, the more countries introduce environmental taxes, the less is the temptation to grant these exemptions.

BOX 14.6 EU ATTEMPTS TO INTRODUCE ENVIRONMENT TAXES

Despite the Community's promotion of fiscal incentives in environmental policy, the number of such initiatives which have actually been adopted is small and includes a 1970 directive recommending the use of fiscal incentives by member states to control noise nuisance; a 1978 directive allowing taxes on waste oils and toxic waste and a 1992 directive establishing differentiation in relation to minimum excise duties for leaded and unleaded petrol. Attempts to introduce more ambitious environmental taxes have come to nothing.

In 1991, the European Commission proposed a tax on carbon dioxide emissions and the use of energy, often referred to as the 'carbon/energy tax'. The proposal was for the introduction from 1 January 1993 of a tax of $3 per barrel of oil equivalent (world market prices of oil at that stage were approximately $19) to be split equally between the carbon and energy content. This would rise by $1 per annum until 2000, leading to a tax of $10 per barrel on all energy products except renewables and feedstocks in industrial processes. The tax rate for each product would vary according to its energy and carbon content. The Commission proposed tax neutrality: in other words, the overall tax burden would remain unchanged, a target to be achieved by reducing other taxes. The proposal also contained a strong conditionality clause: that is, in order not to disadvantage energy intensive sectors, the proposal would not be applied until the Community's main OECD competitors introduced a similar tax or measures which had an equivalent effect. The proposal also envisaged tax reductions for energy intensive firms in circumstances in which the conditionality clause was not sufficient to preserve their competitiveness, for example if competitors were located in countries at which the conditionality clause was not aimed. Although the proposal was amended and received support from countries with strong environmental policies like the Netherlands and Denmark, the requirement for unanimity on fiscal measures, the fervour with which member states protect their tax raising prerogatives and the conditionality clause were enough to sink the proposal.

Nevertheless, the Commission has not given up on energy taxes and in 1997 proposed to extend the scope of excise duties to cover all energy products, to include not only mineral oils as at present but also natural gas, electricity and solid fuels. The rationale given for this radical proposal is that the present excise system distorts competition between different energy supplies. Moreover, in addition to single market, fiscal harmonisation reasons, the proposal promotes the objectives of the stalled carbon energy tax. Broader justifications stem from the 1993 White Paper *Growth, Competitiveness, Employment* and the Commission's 1995 *Confidence Pact for Employment* which stressed job creation as the prime objective of the EU (reinforced by the June 1997 Amsterdam Council) and urged a refocusing of fiscal policy to reduce statutory charges on labour whilst maintaining overall revenue levels by introducing a new, more comprehensive system of taxing energy products. In May 1997, the Environment Commissioner Ritt Bjerregaard claimed that the proposed energy tax could create 145,000 jobs by 2002.

The proposals themselves set minimum rates of excise duty which are significantly higher than existing rates. Subject to approval by the Council (the difficult part), the uprating was to take place in stages, beginning on 1 January 1998, continuing on 1 January 2000 and further amended from 2002 (the 2002 rates are targets). Tax refunds are proposed for energy intensive firms who may encounter competitiveness problems with a negative effect on jobs and for firms who embark upon investment aimed at reducing energy efficiency.

Current and proposed minimum excise duties on energy products

	Current	1.1.98	1.1.2000	Target: 1.1.2002
Motor fuels				
Petrol (ECU per 1,000 l)	337	417	450	500
Unleaded petrol (ECU per 1,000 l)	287			

Gas oil (ECU per 1,000 l)	245	310	343	393
Kerosene (ECU per 1,000 l)[1]	245	310	343	393
LPG(ECU per 1,000 kg)	100	141	174	224
Natural gas (ECU per gigajoule)	n.a.[2]	2.9	3.5	4.5
Heating fuels and electricity				
Heating gas oil (ECU per 1,000 litres)	18	21	23	26
Heavy fuel oil CN code 27100074 (ECU per 1,000 litres)	13	18	23	28
Other heavy fuel oil CN code 2710 (ECU per 1,000 litres)	13	22	28	34
Kerosene (ECU per 1,000 litres)	0	7	16	25
LPG (ECU per kg)	0	10	22	34
Natural gas (ECU per gigajoule)	n.a.	0.2	0.45	0.7
Solid fuels (ECU per gigajoule)	n.a.	0.2	0.45	0.7
Electricity (ECU per MW)	n.a.	1	2	3

Note: [1]Jet fuel kerosene is exempt until an international agreement is reached; [2]n.a. = not applicable

Reaction to these proposals has been less than enthusiastic and the continuing requirement for unanimity on tax measures (unchanged at Amsterdam) is unlikely to progress these proposals further than the carbon energy proposals. Implementation of the taxes would force Spain and Greece, among others, to increase their excises substantially and they are opposed to it. Reaction to the proposals has been more favourable in the Nordic states where use of taxation to support environmental objectives is more common. Other member states have expressed a variety of reservations. Germany and industry is concerned about fiscal neutrality. The Commission intends that the overall tax burden should not rise as a result of implementation of the proposals: this will occur as other taxes, especially statutory taxes on labour, are reduced to compensate for increased energy taxes. However, even if there is no overall increase in the tax burden, it is extremely unlikely that the proposals will be fiscally neutral in terms of individual companies or sectors, especially as the more energy intensive industries are not necessarily the same industries which will benefit from reduction in labour taxes.

The reaction of European industry to the tax proposals has been uniformly hostile. UNICE, the European employers' confederation, argues that improved competitiveness is much more important than harmonisation of energy taxes and that tax harmonisation should be achieved by reduction of the highest taxes rather than by increases in the lowest. For UNICE, and other trade associations such as the chemical manufacturer's association, CEFIC, the proposals represent an overall increase in the tax burden for European companies and significant increases in production and distribution costs, thereby damaging competitiveness.

On the other hand, the Green group in the European Parliament believes the proposals do not go far enough and will result in minor reductions only in CO^2 emissions. They are particularly opposed to proposed exemptions for the use of kerosene as aviation fuel – one of the main contributors to greenhouse gas emissions.

Distributional effects

Concern has been expressed about the equity of environmental taxes as they have the greatest impact on low income households. This is particularly true of energy taxes as energy accounts for a proportionally larger share of the expenditure of poor households. Such concerns lay behind the unpopular, and unsuccessful, attempts of the UK government to raise VAT on domestic fuel from 8 per cent to 17.5 per cent in 1994. Various techniques can be used to overcome adverse distributional effects: the Dutch small energy users' tax introduces a tax-free threshold of energy use according to which households get tax relief so that the average energy user in four different categories of household income are not made worse off by the energy tax: below and above average energy consumers in each group are made better and worse off respectively. Such thresholds can and have been used for taxation on other essentials: in many parts of Portugal, for example, a progressive sliding scale is used for water consumption and treatment of waste water.

Legal and administrative obstacles

Policies pursued on behalf of another objective may have adverse effects on the environment which may render environmental taxes ineffective: in the EU context, for example, the Common Agricultural Policy's concentration on production incentives (albeit lessened by the 1992 reforms to switch support from prices to income) will work to offset, partially or fully, the environmental impact of certain environmental taxes. In short, environmental taxes, if they are to achieve their objectives, must be introduced as part of a package and other policies must not work in conflict with them.

Article 130S of the Maastricht Treaty specifies the maintenance of unanimous voting on taxation matters – a situation which was not changed by the Amsterdam Treaty. Member states guard their rights to tax jealousy and are extremely reluctant to cede this right to the European Commission (see Chapter 4). Furthermore, the possibility of gaining the agreement of fifteen member states to introduce tax EU level tax measures is remote.

Although the introduction of environmental taxes has not been so successful at EU level, there has, particularly during the 1990s, been a big increase in environmental taxes introduced by member states. Table 14.1 gives a brief overview of the incidence of the main environmental taxes in member states. From this, it is clear that Denmark, Sweden and Finland have adopted environmental taxes as a method of pollution containment in a major way. Others have adopted them in specific areas. Germany, France, the Netherlands and Portugal, for example, clearly see the use of water and waste charges as an important way of minimising water usage and the production of waste. Even the United Kingdom, which has been among the less enthusiastic users of environmental taxes, has seen fit to introduce a landfill levy resulting from the dominance of landfill as a source of waste disposal in the UK and the resulting pressure on existing landfill sites and difficulties in developing new ones. The one tax which has been universally adopted by member states is the introduction of a differential between taxation on leaded and unleaded gasoline – a tax which resulted in a rapid and major shift in consumption from the former to the latter.

The Commission generally supports the use of environmental taxes by member states: such instruments are an example of the 'polluter pays' principle at work and act as incentives to guide both producers and consumers to more economically sustainable behaviour. However, the Commission is concerned to ensure that member states do not use such instruments to discriminate against products and services from other member states, thereby fragmenting the SEM. The Commission is also concerned about the use of revenue from such levies: if revenues accrue to the general state budget, then there is unlikely to be any negative impact on the SEM. However, if the revenue is allocated for a special purpose, it could come under the remit of the EU's state aids policy.

Table 14.1 Overview of EU environmental taxes and charges (Oct. 1996)

	Aust.	Belg.	Dk	Fin.	Fran.	Ger.	Gree.	Ire.	Italy	Lux.	Neth.	Port.	Spain	Swed.	UK
Motor fuels and vehicles															
Sales/excise/registration	✓	✓	✓	✓				✓	✓		✓	✓	✓	✓	
Road/registration tax)	✓	✓	✓	✓		✓	✓	✓	✓	✓	✓	✓	✓	✓	✓
Lead/unleaded gasoline	✓		✓	✓	✓	✓				✓			✓	✓	✓
Diesel (quality)			✓	✓										✓	
Carbon/energy tax			✓	✓										✓	
Other excise taxes	✓	✓	✓	✓	✓	✓	✓	✓	✓	✓	✓	✓	✓	✓	✓
Gasoline (quality)			✓	✓										✓	
Other energy products															
Other excise taxes	✓	✓	✓	✓	✓	✓	✓	✓	✓	✓	✓	✓	✓	✓	✓
Carbon/energy tax	✓		✓	✓	✓								✓	✓	
Sulphur tax			✓		✓									✓	
No$_x$ charge					✓									✓	
Agricultural inputs															
Fertilisers	✓													✓	
Pesticides		✓	✓	✓										✓	
Other goods															
Batteries		✓	✓												
Plastic carrier bags															
Disposable containers		✓	✓	✓											
Tyres			✓												
CFCs and/or halons			✓												
Disposable razors/cameras		✓													
Air transport															
Noise charges	✓	✓			✓	✓					✓				
Other charges					✓										
Water and waste															
Water charges			✓	✓	✓	✓					✓	✓		✓	✓
Sewage charges			✓	✓	✓	✓					✓	✓		✓	✓
Water effluent charges					✓	✓					✓				
Groundwater extraction					✓	✓					✓	✓			
Municipal waste water				✓		✓					✓	✓			
Waste disposal charge	✓	✓	✓	✓	✓	✓		✓	✓		✓	✓	✓	✓	✓
Hazardous waste charge	✓	✓	✓	✓	✓								✓	✓	
Landfill tax or charge									✓						✓

Source: European Commission, *Environmental Taxes and Charges in the Single Market*, COM (97) 9

THE INTERNATIONAL DIMENSION OF ENVIRONMENT POLICY

Environmental issues have increasingly taken on an international perspective and feature prominently on the agenda of international organisations like the United Nations, the World Trade Organisation and the OECD. This is both because of growing awareness of the transboundary and even global nature of much pollution and because of trade liberalisation and the greater interdependence of the world economy which increases the relative importance of remaining regulatory differences, such as environmental policy. This focus on the environment stems from concern over the implications of the potential competitive disadvantage, particularly in relation to high compliance costs, experienced by firms located in countries which aim for higher levels of environmental protection.

This concern manifests itself in a number of ways. A common fear is that the existence of countries with lower process standards will act as 'pollution havens' – that is, in order to avoid the costs of complying with these standards in their current location, firms will relocate to countries where they do not incur such costs with consequent loss of jobs and investment in the country with higher standards. These higher standards would then, ironically, lead to greater environmental damage as firms are free from constraints in their new location. These developments will also lead to pressure to lower standards to prevent such migration occurring. Although these arguments have a certain logic, reality is more complex. The pull of pollution havens depends to a large extent on the overall share of environmental compliance costs in total costs. In general, such costs tend to be no more than 1 to 2 per cent of total costs and as such are only a relatively minor factor in a whole host of other locational factors. That is not to say, that in certain sectors such as chemicals, for example, the additional costs incurred as a result of environmental regulation may be a determining factor in relocation or casting around more widely for location for new investment. The environmental cost factor will become more influential when profit margins are tight and the economic environment is generally unfavourable. Nevertheless, although there are examples of the pollution haven hypothesis in action, research by the OECD and others has not revealed its existence in any systematic way.

Responses to these concerns range from studies into the link between trade and the environment through to debate about the possibility of the use of trade barriers to offset the negative competitive impact of some environmental measures and of the formulation of international approaches to global environmental problems. Case Study 11.1 summarises the evolution of international environmental policy in relation to one of the biggest global environmental challenges of all – climate change. Increasing convergence and harmonisation of environmental policy would appear to be the most promising environmental approach to dealing with cross-border pollution issues. However, there are important environmental and economic limits to this approach arising from legitimate differences in process standards which stem from a diversity of environmental conditions and which themselves could be argued to be part of a country's comparative advantage.

Trade liberalisation, if carried out against a background of an effective environmental policy, particularly one which provides for full internalisation of external costs, could make a positive contribution to the environment by facilitating a more efficient allocation of resources. The stimulus which trade liberalisation gives to growth can release resources which can be used to promote environmental technology and, again in line with the philosophy of ecological modernisation, countries with high levels of environmental protection can benefit in terms of greater technological change and promote the development of new markets. Assuming the pressure for stronger environmental protection spreads throughout the trading world, companies operating with high environmental standards will have a competitive advantage, not only in the market for environmental technology but also in the practice of adapting to stronger environmental requirements and in promoting its own environmental expertise as a marketing asset. Without effective environmental policies, trade liberalisation can accentuate environmental problems, depending on the prevailing circumstances and characteristics of individual countries and companies. There could, for example, be an uncontrolled increase in toxic chemicals or waste – a problem which must be tackled through multilateral agreement or an appropriate international framework. In these circumstances, pressures could arise to impose barriers against countries which have a more relaxed attitude to environmental matters.

CONCLUSION: THE CORPORATE SECTOR AND ENVIRONMENT POLICY

For many years, companies complained about the cost and other burdens placed upon them by the growth of environmental regulation. These complaints were often accompanied by warnings of reduced employment and loss of investment. However, the movement of environmental measures into the policy mainstream, both at member state and at EU level, has meant that resistance to the principle of environmental regulation has become pointless. The real challenge for business is to secure policies which meet environmental objectives in a flexible manner. Environmental planning, therefore, has become an important part of corporate strategy and most major corporations now produce regular environmental reports and action plans, both to demonstrate their commitment to environmental goals, a commitment which will do them no harm in marketing terms provided the commitment is not seen as hollow, and to help them to contend with the changing regulatory framework. Case Study 14.1 demonstrates German chemical giant BASF's response to the challenge.

CASE STUDY 14.1 BASF AND THE ENVIRONMENT

Between 1991–6, BASF estimates it spent DM 1.85 bn world-wide on environmental protection facilities. Given that the integration of the environmental features into processes is increasingly being done as a matter of course, BASF claims this figure underestimates the amount being spent on environmental protection. In 1996, the net operating costs of the group's environmental protection facilities were DM 1.6 bn and DM 223 m was spent on capital expenditure for environmental protection. These figures do not include the amounts spent on research into eco-friendly products and processes.

The BASF board have formulated environmental policy guidelines, which are reviewed regularly and which are implemented according to local directives and procedures. The company supports the chemical industry's Responsible Care initiative and has committed itself to a process of continuous improvement in safety, health and environmental protection on all its sites world-wide and on-site audits are carried out to check on implementation. The company has committed itself to a range of good practice measures, including an undertaking that 'regardless of commercial interests, we will restrict or discontinue commercialisation and manufacture of products if the results of a risk assessment require this to prevent health and environmental hazards'. In addition, the company has a policy of making its expertise and experience available to help in the development of laws, regulations and standards to protect the environment.

The company's annual environmental report publishes statistics about the company's environmental performance in line with industry guidelines and, in a relatively new departure, sets out environmental objectives. Future reports will enable judgements to be made about how the company is meeting its objectives. Targets in the 1996 Environmental Report included:

- *Antwerp*: the introduction of a safety and quality evaluation scheme for the shipment of NH_3 and naphtha by sea by 2000;
- *Ludwigshafen, Germany*: the reduction of atmospheric emissions of nitrous oxides by at least 90 per cent by 2000;
- *Schwarzheide, Germany*: the updating and review of the risk prevention plan by mid-1999;
- *Schwarzheide, Germany*: the reduction of the nitrogen load in wastewater by 50 per cent by 2000;
- *Seal Sands, UK*: a reduction of VOC and CO_2 emissions by 90 per cent by 2000;
- *Tarragona, Spain*: a study in the reuse of elutriation wastewaters from the cooling towers by 1998;
- *Tarragona, Spain*: installation of a flare/muffle for offgas purification in a dispersion plant by 1999.

The company is also taking part in the EU's voluntary eco-audit scheme. In 1996, the company's Schwarzheide plant was the first site to be certified as meeting and exceeding legal requirements. A declaration was signed by the company and independent experts which explained the company's objectives for improving environmental protection, including a reduction in the nitrogen load of the waste water treatment plant outfall by 50 per cent, a 10 per cent reduction in waste volumes and a drop in NOx emissions from residue incineration to fifty metric tons per annum.

In addition to requiring compliance with environmental regulations, the European Union is trying to develop a sense of shared responsibility between industry and the regulators. Auto-Oil, a long term programme designed to reduce emissions from road transport and involving extensive collaboration between the European Commission and the EU's oil and automobile industries, is an example of this shared responsibility in action. The programme gives companies an opportunity to shape legislation, ideally to make it more flexible, and in theory moves policy making away from a confrontational framework. So far Auto-Oil has focused on emission reduction via improvements in fuel quality and vehicle technology (resulting in the tabling of draft directives) and the extension of vehicle maintenance and inspection schedules. The initiative has not been without its problems or critics: the European Parliament, which has been the most vociferous EU institution in support of a stronger environment policy, has criticised Auto-Oil for appeasing motor and oil interests and for failing to consult independent experts, resulting in unambitious proposals. In addition, the two industries involved in the collaboration have competed rather than co-operated with each other, with the motor sector complaining that the burden of implementing Auto-Oil would be borne substantially by it.

Notwithstanding these problems, it is likely that attempts will be made to extend the Auto-Oil approach to other areas and industry generally will became more pro-active in developing more environmentally benign policies.

⌖ KEY POINTS

- **Conflict persists between those who view environmental policy as increasing cost burdens on industry and those who see environmental policy as providing opportunities to promote competitiveness. EU policies are increasingly reflecting the latter approach of 'ecological modernism'.**

- **As scientific knowledge improves and environmental awareness increases, the range of policy instruments has expanded.**

- **Member states, although introducing national environmental taxes, are loathe to do so at EU level.**

- **The trade–environment policy link is increasingly appearing on the agenda of international institutions and can be expected to take on greater prominence within future multilateral talks.**

- **In recent years, most major companies have developed their own environmental strategies. These developments and efforts to encourage greater industrial participation in policy formation will intensify.**

SUGGESTED FURTHER READING

European Environmental Agency (1996) *Environmental Taxes: Implementation and Environmental Effectiveness*, Copenhagen.

Lévêque, F. (1996) *Environmental Policy in Europe*, Edward Elgar.

Turner, K., Pearce, D., and Bateman, I. (1994) *Environmental Economics: an Elementary Introduction*, Harvester Wheatsheaf.

Weale, A. (1992) 'The Politics of Ecological Modernisation', in *The New Politics of Pollution*, Chapter 3, Manchester University Press.

Welford, R. (1995) *Environmental Strategy and Sustainable Development: the Corporate Challenge for the 21st Century*, Routledge.

European Commission documents

Environmental Taxes and Charges in the Single Market, COM (97) 9.

Guide to the Approximation of European Union Environmental Legislation, SEC (97) 1608.

15

CENTRAL AND EASTERN EUROPE: TRANSITION TO A STABLE BUSINESS ENVIRONMENT

As the new century unfolds, the European Union faces two of its biggest ever challenges in the form of EMU (see Chapter 16) and eastward enlargement. The accession of Central and Eastern European (CEE) countries will expand the EU's total area by one-third and increase its population by over one hundred million with an average GDP per head estimated at 32 per cent of the EU average. Taken together, these developments will fundamentally transform the European Union and radically alter the business environment, creating threats and opportunities for both Western and Eastern European enterprises.

In order to clarify the extent of the transition challenge facing the CEE countries, the chapter commences by examining the legacy of the Communist period. It then discusses the strategies developed to assist in the process of transition and enlargement and makes initial assessments of the progress made to date towards satisfying these strategies within Central and Eastern Europe. The chapter then examines the potential impact of eastward enlargement on the EU before concluding with analysis of the corporate response to the changes in Central and Eastern Europe.

THE LEGACY OF THE PAST

Although still incomplete and not without severe problems, the extent of the transformation which has taken place in a relatively short period of time within Central and Eastern Europe and in its relations with the European Union is remarkable. The old East–West divisions had inhibited the development of meaningful trade and commercial co-operation between the two blocs and limited formal contact to the bare minimum despite their proximity. It was not until the joint June 1988 declaration between the EC and the Council for Mutual Economic Assistance (CMEA), the organisation which provided the framework for trade and economic relations among the CEE countries and the Soviet Union, that official relations between the countries of eastern and western Europe were established. Only ten years later, in 1998, negotiations opened between the

EU and four CEE states (Poland, Hungary, the Czech Republic and Slovenia) and one Baltic state (Estonia) with a view to their eventual full membership of the European Union. In the interim, the applicant countries have embarked upon radical reform of their political and economic systems to bring them into line with the western model and as a pre-requisite for EU membership.

The period between the end of the Second World War and 1989 in Central and Eastern Europe was one of Communist experiment in which the USSR imposed its own political and economic system upon the countries of the region. The chief characteristics of this period were:

- *Soviet domination*: political and economic systems were formally modelled on those of the USSR and the CEE countries were also obliged to follow the USSR's foreign policy, resulting in extremely limited contacts with the West. The only exception was Romania which, under Nikolae Ceaucescu, was allowed to pursue a relatively independent foreign policy, largely because it followed a hard-line Communist régime at home. Soviet domination also extended to military matters: the CEE countries were united through the Warsaw Pact in a unified military command structure under the guidance and control of the Soviet Union.

- *Authoritarian, one-party political systems*: the CEE Communist parties were under the influence of the Communist Party of the Soviet Union and were formally committed to Marxism-Leninism. These parties wielded ultimate power via their tight control of the organs of the state and were inseparable from the state machinery. This control extended to national, regional and local bureaucracies, trade unions, the media and enterprise management. There was, in short, an absence of democratic institutions and processes, such as elections or a credible opposition, as normally understood in the West.

- *Command or planned economies*: in a command system, allocation of resources is undertaken by the state, which also owns the means of production. The command system is thus the complete antithesis of a market economy and of the underlying philosophy of the Single European Market (SEM) where the allocative role of competition and the price mechanism is pre-eminent. The command system by-passes the price mechanism and the basic laws of supply and demand: enterprises decide what and how much to produce according to targets established by state planning agencies. The pre-transition plans followed by the CEE countries were closely aligned to the preferences and interests of the USSR, resulting in neglect of the consumer sector and an economic structure skewed towards heavy industry and ill-prepared for integration into the SEM and the global economy. The rigid planning and isolation of the CEE economies from the rigours of the market resulted in uncompetitive enterprises with obsolete, decaying capital stock and from which the concepts of entrepreneurship and incentives for greater efficiency or innovation were almost completely absent. This was the case throughout Central and Eastern Europe, although the New Economic Mechanism had introduced limited elements of the market into Hungary before 1989 and some private agriculture had been allowed in Poland and elsewhere.

The Soviet hegemony in Central and Eastern Europe looked complete: the Soviet bloc presented a united face to the rest of the world and the Cold War resulted in a permanent state of antagonism between East and West. This antagonism was derived from competition between the different political and economic systems – competition which affected all aspects of the international economic and political system. Indeed, part of the rationale for the creation of the European Community was to establish a political and economic framework in Western Europe to act as a counterweight to and a defence against the Soviet bloc. The status of the Soviet Union as one of the world's two 'super powers' ensured that the Soviet bloc, with its alien ideology, was treated with a circumspection which further increased the psychological distance between eastern and western Europe.

However, the Soviet bloc was not without its problems. These came in particular from the build up of economic problems within the command system and became acute in the 1980s when economic stagnation and falling living standards took hold and the credibility of the regimes themselves was questioned. This is not the place to analyse the reasons and events behind the collapse of the Soviet system. However, once the process of change began, it became unstoppable. Change became possible under the regime of Soviet President Gorbachev who, faced with a stagnant economy, embarked upon limited market reform and restructuring ('perestroika'), accompanied by political reform under the heading of openness ('glasnost'), and a more positive relationship with the West. In Central and Eastern Europe, the catalyst for change was the September 1989 opening of the border between Austria and Hungary. This was followed in November 1989 by the symbolic breaching of the Berlin Wall. The collapse of the Communist regimes of Central and Eastern Europe was bloodless (almost), sudden, rapid and complete and by 1990, free elections had been held in all CEE countries.

RAPPROCHEMENT BETWEEN EAST AND WEST EUROPE

Faced with the disintegration of the political and economic system in Central and Eastern Europe, countries on both sides of the Iron Curtain suddenly had to reassess their basic assumptions about the internal and external policies of the CEE countries. For the CEE countries themselves, the events of 1989–90 represented total rejection of the previous past four decades and a reorientation towards the western model of liberal democracy and market economics. The key consideration for them was not what they wanted to achieve (the goals of a free market and liberal democracy were taken for granted) but how they could achieve it and was largely framed in terms of the pace of reform – rapid and immediate with short term pain but with long term benefits, the 'big bang' approach as followed in Poland, or a more measured, gradual approach as adopted in Hungary.

Each CEE country quickly came to view membership of the European Union as immensely desirable and as a crucial part of their transition. The economic imperatives, which reinforced and were reinforced by political imperatives, assumed particular importance. Once the CEE countries decided they wanted re-integration into an all-encompassing European economic and political space, they also had to develop strategies to engage with the internationalisation of markets which poses key questions for European competitiveness generally. In other words, the CEE states, previously isolated behind the walls of CMEA, suddenly lost not only the security of belonging to a regional bloc, but were also immediately opened to strong international competitive forces. Membership of the EU, which is itself striving to respond to this competitive challenge, will provide a better platform for the CEE states to respond both to the new global marketplace and to their own internal challenges. Moreover, the EU, as the dominant regional framework in Europe, also provides challenges for states remaining outside those structures.

BOX 15.1 MILESTONES IN THE EU–CEE RELATIONSHIP

1985	Gorbachev becomes General Secretary of the Soviet Communist Party and effective leader of the USSR
June 1988	Joint EC–CMEA Declaration on mutual recognition

Nov. 1988	EC and Hungary sign ten year trade and economic co-operation agreement
June 1989	G7 Paris Summit decides European Commission to act as PHARE co-ordinator
Sep. 1989	EC and Poland sign five year trade and economic co-operation agreement
Sep. 1989	Hungary allows GDR citizens to emigrate via Austria
Nov. 89	Berlin Wall breached
Dec. 89	Romanian uprising and execution of the Ceaucescus
1990–95	PHARE supports projects in CEE countries to tune of ECU 5.42 bn
1990	Free elections throughout Central and Eastern Europe
Jan. 1990	Poland implements shock reform therapy
Jan. 1990	PHARE begins operations (Poland and Hungary only), extended later in 1990 to Bulgaria, Czechoslovakia and former East Germany
3.10.90	German unification
1991	CMEA and Warsaw Pact formally dissolved
1991	Inauguration of European Bank of Reconstruction and Development (EBRD)
1991	PHARE extended to Romania, Albania, Estonia, Latvia and Lithuania
26.12.91	USSR formally dissolved following Gorbachev's resignation the previous day
1992	Slovenia recognised by EC
1992	EC interim trade agreements with Czech Republic, Hungary and Poland
1992	Trade and economic co-operation agreement with Albania in force
1993	Interim trade agreements between EC and Bulgaria and Romania
1993	Trade and economic co-operation agreements with Latvia, Estonia and Lithuania in force
1.1.93	Czechoslovakia split into Czech and Slovak republics
March 93	Central European Free Trade Area (CEFTA) (Visegrad 4) in force
June 1993	Copenhagen Council sets out conditions for CEE membership of EU and speeds up trade liberalisation
1.9.93	Co-operation agreement with Slovenia in force
1.2.94	Europe Agreements with Poland and Hungary in force – within two months, both countries apply for EU membership
Dec. 1994	Essen Council adopts pre-accession strategy – Europe agreements, 'structured dialogue', development of PHARE and alignment of single market legislation
1995–9	PHARE budget of ECU 6.7 bn
1995	Slovakia, Bulgaria, Romania, Estonia, Latvia and Lithuania apply for EU membership
1.1.95	Free trade agreements with Estonia, Latvia and Lithuania in force
1.2.95	Europe Agreements with Czech and Slovak Republics, Romania and Bulgaria in force
May 1995	White Paper on alignment of CEE states with SEM legislation
12.6.95	Europe Association Agreements signed with Estonia, Latvia and Lithuania
15.6.95	Europe Agreement with Slovenia initialised
July 1995	PHARE extended to Slovenia
1996	Czech Republic and Slovenia apply for EU membership
July 1997	Agenda 2000 published, includes Commission Opinions on membership applications and recommends Czech Republic, Poland, Hungary, Slovenia, Estonia and Cyprus for first wave of next enlargement
31.3.98	Enlargement negotiations begin with Czech Republic, Poland, Hungary, Slovenia, Estonia and Cyprus
1998–9	Screening of 31 chapters of the acquis communitaire to ascertain readiness, ability and willingness of applicant states to comply with the acquis

The disintegration of the conventional wisdom about relationships between East and West extracted a complex reaction from the EU. Although the triumph of the democratic, liberal economic model on which the EU itself was firmly based and the end of the Cold War security problems were welcome, the transition of Central and Eastern Europe created a number of other problems and dilemmas which, given their proximity to the EU, could not be ignored. The Communist regimes had, for example, kept tight control over their populations, enabling them to contain centuries old ethnic rivalries. The consequences of the re-emergence of old rivalries became only too tragically apparent in former Yugoslavia (a country outside the Soviet bloc for most of the post-war period but which had maintained its own form of command economy). The Slovak Republics, Bulgaria and Romania also contain sizeable ethnic minorities which have the potential at least to create significant political instability. In short, the possibility of superpower conflict as a result of East–West divisions gave way to fears about the possibility of balkanisation on the Union's eastern borders.

The EU's reassessment of its relationship with CEE countries extended beyond security issues. Although economic links had been minimal between the two for decades and real personal disposable income was low in CEE countries, the size and long term potential of CEE markets was significant. Furthermore, the European Union and its members had to decide precisely how close relationships with the CEE countries should become. There is, for example, serious concern that enlargement on such an unprecedented scale and with countries with incomes so significantly below those of existing members will place an intolerable financial burden on the European Union and jeopardise further integration within the Union itself. In light of the magnitude and suddenness of the transformations, the EU's initial reaction to the CEE changes was, unsurprisingly, piecemeal and ad hoc. Development of a commitment to CEE accession and a systematic accession strategy took longer to devise.

THE ENLARGEMENT TRIANGLE

Figure 15.1 highlights the three main, highly interdependent factors in the process of successful integration of Eastern and Western Europe – transition, accession and the corporate response. Transition is defined as the transformation of the CEE countries into democratic, market economies. Membership of the European Union is only open to democratic countries with market economies. The requirements of bringing the CEE countries into line with the acquis communitaire, an essential part of the enlargement process, coincide with the tasks which are central to the transition process. In other words, enlargement requires successful transition which is driven by the timetable and steps set out in the pre-accession strategy (see below).

The third, frequently ignored but essential component is a positive response from the corporate sector, both from within the CEE countries themselves and from third country enterprises, particularly but not only in the form of foreign direct investment. Transition and accession are primarily about putting in place the conditions in which the private sector can prosper – an essential pre-requisite of a successful market economy. However, corporate support will only be fully forthcoming when key aspects of transition are in place, namely the appropriate legal and institutional framework of a market economy. Similarly, enlargement necessitates a competitive market economy which implies a dynamic corporate sector able to benefit from the extension of the single market to cover Central and Eastern Europe.

In short, although enlargement is not in itself a necessary condition for a successful transition, in practice, the linking of the two has raised the stakes and made these processes highly interdependent on each other. The emergence of a strong CEE private

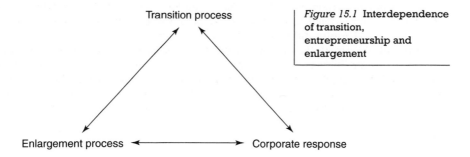

Transition process

Enlargement process ← → Corporate response

Figure 15.1 Interdependence of transition, entrepreneurship and enlargement

sector runs parallel to both objectives, neither of which can be achieved without it. Not only, therefore, do transition and enlargement involve the creation of an environment in which the private sector can flourish, either in the form of indigenous or foreign-owned companies, but also one in which these companies can take advantage of these opportunities to ensure the success of transition and enlargement.

THE PRE-ACCESSION STRATEGY

The initial reaction of the EU to the changes in the CEE countries was to negotiate bilateral trade and co-operation agreements with them and by October 1990, such agreements had been reached with all CMEA's European members. These 'first generation' agreements were important, not so much for their substance as they soon proved overly modest and unambitious in view of the rapid changes taking place, but as symbols of the political support from the EU for these changes. This support was reinforced by the establishment of the PHARE programme, initially set up by the G7 countries in 1989 to provide financial and technical assistance to Poland and Hungary. The European Commission was given the task of co-ordinating this aid which was rapidly extended to other CEE states as the dynamics of change spread across the region.

It quickly became apparent that these conventional forms of assistance would not suffice in the unprecedented circumstances and the EU quickly moved to negotiate 'Association' or 'Europe' agreements with the CEE countries. These agreements were more far-reaching than traditional trade agreements, although they were still criticised for being unduly restrictive in crisis-ridden sectors such as steel and textiles. In addition to enhanced trading arrangements, the Europe Agreements included a political dialogue via regular high level meetings and consultation on issues of common interest; provisions on supply of services and movement of capital and a commitment by the Associate states to render their legislation compatible with EU laws, especially in the areas of competition policy, non-discriminatory procurement policy and intellectual property rights. The Europe Agreements also covered economic, cultural and financial co-operation and established an Association Council which meets at least once a year to supervise the Agreement's implementation and an Association Committee to assist the work of the Association Council. The first Europe Agreements were in force with Poland and Hungary by February 1994. Although forming some of the most extensive agreements the European Union had ever reached with third countries, and formal links between the two groups has only begun six years previously, the Agreements themselves fell short of making a direct link between Associate status and accession. However, they did acknowledge accession as the ultimate objective of the Associate states, an objective which was confirmed by Poland and Hungary who both applied for full membership less than two months after their agreements came into force.

The European Union was thus coming under increased pressure from the CEE countries to commit itself to further enlargement and preferably to establish a timetable for the process. Despite differing views on enlargement within member states, a major breakthrough was made at the June 1993 Copenhagen Council which, in addition to speeding up trade liberalisation, concluded that 'the associated countries in Central and Eastern Europe that so desire shall become members of the European Union. Accession will take place as soon as an associated country is able to assume the obligations of membership by satisfying the economic and political conditions required'. The Council then set out four conditions which CEE associates must satisfy before accession can proceed. They are:

- stable institutions which guarantee democracy, the rule of law, human rights and respect for and protection of minorities;
- a functioning market economy;
- the capacity to cope with competitive pressure and market forces within the Union;
- the ability to take on the obligations of membership including political, economic and monetary union.

In addition, the Council added a fifth condition which applied to the European Union, stipulating that 'the Union's capacity to absorb new members while maintaining the momentum of European integration, is also an important consideration in the general interest of both the Union and the candidate countries'.

The December 1994 Essen Council took the process a stage further and drew up the outline of what became known as the 'pre-accession strategy', which included:

- implementation of the Europe Agreements;
- PHARE;
- the 'structured dialogue'.

The 'structured dialogue', originally outlined at Copenhagen, envisaged regular meetings between EU ministers and their CEE counterparts on issues of common interest within a multilateral framework. Essen determined how this should work in practice, setting out the frequency of meetings and issues to be discussed as well as providing a schedule for such meetings at the beginning of each year.

The Essen Summit also identified preparations of the CEE countries for integration into the internal market as 'the key element in the strategy to narrow the gap [between Western and Central and Eastern Europe]' and resulted in May 1995 in the publication of a White Paper which specified measures which needed to be taken in each sector to align the CEE countries with the SEM. The White Paper went further, suggesting the sequence in which the approximation of measures should take place and included competition, social and environmental policies – measures central to the workings of the SEM. The White Paper is at pains to point out that the main responsibility for alignment lies with the CEE countries themselves but offers technical assistance for the process through PHARE.

The White Paper is a detailed, technocratic document whose importance lies in the extent to which it provides guidance for aspiring EU entrants regarding the steps which need to be taken to comply with the acquis communitaire. Compared to previous enlargements, the extent of preparation and discussion about the requirements of accession are unprecedented. However, never before has the EU faced such a challenging enlargement. The White Paper also links the process of reform and the pre-accession strategy, stating 'progressive alignment with the Union's internal market policies will reinforce the competitiveness of the CEE economies and increase the benefits of transition thus contributing to the achievement and consolidation of macro-economic stability'.

The pre-accession strategy also identifies other policies to promote the integration of the CEE countries into the EU. These include infrastructural developments and the implementation of policies to extend trans-European networks to CEE states, the promotion of environmental co-operation, the Common Foreign and Security Policy, and co-operation in judicial and home affairs, culture, education and training.

The pre-accession strategy agreed at Essen was only the first phase of the immensely complex process of enlargement. The intergovernmental conference (IGC) which culminated in the Amsterdam Treaty in 1997 was intended, in part, to reform the Union's institutions in preparation for the first eastward enlargement. At best, progress in this area was partial (see Chapter 2) and the Commission has suggested that a new IGC should take place at least one year before Union membership exceeds twenty. The conclusion of the Amsterdam Treaty acted as the catalyst for the July 1997 publication of 'Agenda 2000' which sets out the broad perspectives for the development of the EU into the twenty-first century, including the financial perspective for the years to 2006, the Commission Opinions on the accession applications and the impact of enlargement on EU policies.

Agenda 2000 also set out the basic principles of the reinforced pre-accession strategy which builds on the existing strategy and adds two new elements:

1 *Accession partnerships*: these partnerships encompass the priorities for each applicant in meeting the acquis and the financial resources which are to be made available for that purpose. Each partnership's priorities are based on analysis contained in the Commission's opinion on membership and are intended to guide applicants in their membership preparations. The accession partnerships also contain a conditionality clause making assistance dependent on fulfilment of obligations under the Europe Agreements and the Copenhagen criteria. Monitoring of the accession partnerships will assist the Commission's regular reviews of progress.
2 *Extension of the participation of the applicants in Community programmes and mechanisms to apply the acquis*: this element of the reinforced pre-accession strategy provides for increased EU assistance for the approximation of laws and for the involvement of applicant countries in EU programmes, such as education, training, culture, research, environment, SMEs and the single market, prior to accession. This has already been provided for, in principle, by the Europe Agreements and will facilitate the accession process by familiarising the applicant countries with the policies of the EU and the way it operates.

PROGRESS IN CENTRAL AND EASTERN EUROPE

The Copenhagen conditions provide an appropriate framework for assessment of the readiness of the CEE countries for EU accession and of the progress of transition. The Essen pre-accession strategy and the developments arising out of Agenda 2000 are designed, in part, to facilitate the movement of these countries towards EU membership and fulfilment of these conditions. Progress so far has been impressive but uneven. Indeed as the countries emerge from their period of Communist conformity, their long suppressed distinctiveness is becoming more apparent as reflected in the Commission's Opinions on their membership applications and its identification of five of them for the first wave of enlargement.

The creation of stable democratic institutions which protect basic freedoms constitutes the first Copenhagen condition. Elections took place in all CEE countries soon after the transition process got underway. The real test of whether democracy and democratic institutions were truly embedded in the fabric of political life was the robustness of the political systems once the initial euphoria, which had accompanied the overturning of the former regimes, had passed and the actual scale of the problems facing these countries became apparent.

In the early years of reform, in particular, economic growth plummeted as the command systems disintegrated and before reforms began to take effect. This resulted in severe falls in living standards and an increase in social problems, which could have imperilled the whole reform process. In practice, although individual countries had experienced several changes of government in the interim, including the return in several cases of key personnel from pre-reform days, the countries have retained a strong commitment to democracy and the reform process. Poland, for example, has experienced six governments in almost as many years; Slovenia has been able to develop a prolonged and consistent reform strategy despite the need to maintain a fine balancing act in the face of a multi-party coalition and Estonia has seen several changes of government whilst keeping the reform process moving. In fact, in several instances, economic crises have strengthened the political processes by reaffirming the commitment to reform and demonstrate the growing maturity of the region's new democracies by the willingness of its governments to take difficult political decisions, as witnessed by events in 1997 in the Czech Republic and, more significantly, in both Bulgaria and Romania, two countries which have been lagging in the reform process. In general, the legitimacy of the democratic governments in the CEE countries remains unchallenged – a factor which has been assisted by the reform process which has given a stake in the success of reform to a range of interests and which has helped prevent large shifts in policy. As the reforms start to show more positive results and the countries become more deeply integrated not just into the European Union but also into the world economy generally, both the democratic and economic reform processes become more deeply rooted. The European Commission has acknowledged the success of political reforms in its opinions, with the sole exception of Slovakia which remains outside the first wave of countries embarking upon membership negotiations, primarily because of its failure to satisfy the political criteria. In particular, the Commission cited concerns about the independence of the Slovak judiciary, the role of both the police and the security forces, the disregarding of the opposition and regard for the rights of the Hungarian minority.

The second Copenhagen condition, the creation of a functioning market economy, is a complex, long term process requiring macro-economic stability, changes in ownership and legal reform to liberalise and open the CEE economies to competition. Success will result in an environment in which the private sector and entrepreneurship can flourish – a pre-condition for attainment of Copenhagen condition three. Transition to a market economy does not imply the total disappearance of the state sector but a significant diminution of it and a change in its role from producer to creator and regulator of the appropriate legal framework governing enterprise behaviour. Significant progress has been made on these fronts already and further progress is anticipated before accession takes place.

Macroeconomic stability is a necessary but not sufficient condition for transition to a market economy. Stabilisation and recovery are essential for establishing confidence in potential domestic and foreign investors; for providing a suitable economic environment and market for the nurturing of new businesses and, above all, for retaining popular support for reform. However, policy-induced supply-side shocks inevitably sent the CEE economies into apparent freefall in the first phase of reform: real GDP plummeted (see Figures 15.2 and 15.3); unemployment soared; inflation rocketed, exceeding 200 per cent in six of the applicant countries by 1991; and industrial and agricultural output collapsed

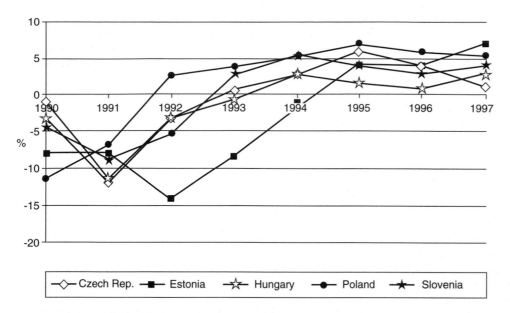

Figure 15.2 Real GDP growth in first wave applicants

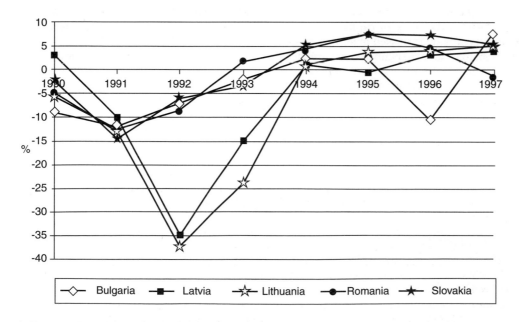

Figure 15.3 Real GDP growth in second wave applicants

as inefficient state enterprises were unable to keep going. These developments, plus pent up demand for imported consumer goods, contributed to a deterioration in the current account and a worsening of fiscal deficits and external indebtedness. The perilous macro-economic situation combined to create severe social and economic hardship across the region.

By 1993, growth was beginning to return to the region, albeit unevenly and a state of chronic recession persisted in the Baltic states in particular. By 1994, growth was more widespread and by 1997, most applicant countries had experienced three or four years of growth. Bulgaria was an exception, plunging into its own severe crisis in 1996 when GDP fell by over 10 per cent and hyperinflation took hold. The pace of growth has been varied and irregular throughout the region with economic performance generally more positive in the CEE countries identified for the first wave of enlargement. Poland's economy has consistently grown at over 5 per cent per annum since 1994 whereas the Czech Republic, where growth appeared to be accelerating, suffered a setback arising from currency instability and weaknesses in its financial sector. Inevitably the pace of growth has been less rapid than the decline which took pace in the early 1990s with the result that by 1997, Poland was the only applicant nation whose real GDP exceeded 1989 levels (see Table 15.1). In practice, however, the size of the unofficial economies, widely estimated as significantly larger than those in Western Europe, results in real GDP somewhat higher than the official statistics indicate.

Inflation generally has been brought under control, in most cases to within the 10 to 20 per cent range. Further reductions in inflation are only likely to occur when full price liberalisation and the process of relative price adjustment have taken place. Public finances, a key indicator if the applicant countries are eventually to join a single currency area, are vulnerable. A number of countries have struggled to introduce effective tax systems and are experiencing low levels of tax collection, a situation which has not been helped by years of low economic activity. External balances have deteriorated in several countries. In part, this is an inevitable consequence of the return of growth and the rapid increase in consumption and investment spending which has boosted the growth of imports, particularly of capital goods, and diverted output from export markets which were generally depressed in any case.

Changes in ownership and governance have proceeded rapidly. Table 15.2 shows that, according to EBRD estimates, the share of private sector in GDP is 60 per cent or above in all but two of the applicant countries. The transfer of a substantial proportion of economic activity from the public to the private sector is central to the establishment of a market economy, opening up the possibility that competition, the main force behind inno-vation and increased efficiency, regulates markets. Small scale privatisation in the first wave of applicant countries at least has been completed to levels equivalent to those in

Table 15.1 Projected level of real GDP of EU applicants in 1997 (1989 = 100)

First wave		Second wave	
Czech Republic	90	Bulgaria	63
Estonia	76	Latvia	54
Hungary	89	Lithuania	44
Poland	110	Romania	87
Slovenia	99	Slovak Republic	94

Source: European Bank of Reconstruction and Development

Table 15.2 1997 transition indicators in applicant countries

(a) Ownership and governance

	Private sector % GDP	Large scale privatisation	Small scale privatisation	Governance and restructuring
First wave				
Czech Rep.	75	4	4+	3
Estonia	70	4	4+	3
Hungary	75	4	4+	3
Poland	65	3+	4+	3
Slovenia	50	3+	4+	3–
Second wave				
Bulgaria	50	3	3	2+
Latvia	60	3	4	3–
Lithuania	70	3	4	3–
Romania	60	3–	3	2
Slovak Rep.	70	4	4+	3–

(b) Liberalisation and competition

	Price liberalisation	Trade/foreign exchange	Competition policy	Banking reform and interest rates	Securities and non-financial intermediaries
First wave					
Czech Rep.	3	4+	3	3	3
Estonia	3	4	3–	3+	3
Hungary	3+	4+	3	4	3+
Poland	3	4+	3	3	3+
Slovenia	3	4+	2	3	3
Second wave					
Bulgaria	3	4	2	3–	2
Latvia	3	4	3–	3	2+
Lithuania	3	4	2+	3	2+
Romania	3	4	2	3–	2
Slovak Rep.	3	4	3	3–	2+

Source: Adapted from Transition Report 1997: Enterprise growth and performance, EBRD (1997)
Note: 1= little progress → 4+ (most advanced industrialised countries)

advanced industrialised nations. Large scale privatisation has inevitably proceeded more slowly. In the Czech Republic, Estonia, Hungary and the Slovak Republic, the EBRD estimates that over 50 per cent of large state enterprises and farms have passed into private hands. In the other applicants, the figure falls to between 25 per cent and 50 per cent.

In terms of raw statistics, the privatisation process has resulted in a share of the private sector in the economies of most applicant countries which is similar to that of many EU member states. However, the applicant countries still need to make significant progress in corporate discipline and governance. Although budgetary subsidies to enterprises have been substantially reduced in most countries, the impact on competitiveness and efficiency has often been offset by increases in off-budget subsidies (such as soft bank loans and continuing energy tariff arrears), weak tax collection and ineffective bankruptcy laws. State procurement at non-market prices has largely ceased and substantial advances have also been made in price liberalisation although further progress is needed still in liberalisation of utility prices, especially those in the energy sector.

Commencement of economic reform precipitated the collapse of well-developed intra-regional trading relationships. CEE states have rapidly redirected themselves towards western European markets and EU exports to the CEE have been growing at about 20 per cent per annum since the mid-1990s. These changes resulted in part from the Europe Agreements but mostly came from the transition process which opened up previously closed trade opportunities and created significant demand for western consumer and investment goods. The framework in which the trade of the CEE countries takes place has been radically reformed so that, for all but Estonia among the first wave applicants, most tariff barriers have been removed and the countries are operating in line with the standards and norms of the advanced industrialised countries, enabling them to become members of the WTO. Second wave applicant countries are not far behind.

The opening of the economy to competition is not so well developed. Competition policy and institutions have been set up in all CEE states, largely in line with the competition principles of the Treaty of Rome. However, enforcement of these principles is often not yet fully developed and substantial restrictions on market entry can remain.

A successful market economy requires a robust banking and financial sector to provide the capital for enterprise. This has proved a particularly difficult challenge for the transition economies, several of which have experienced banking crises which have resulted in the liquidation of some banks. Bank lending is small in relation to the size of the economy and confidence in the soundness of loans is limited. In short, the basic legal and institutional framework to support a buoyant banking system does not exist and sufficient time has not yet passed to develop the experience, skills and practices which are vital for a successful financial sector. The banks, however, are more well developed than the securities markets and other non-banking finance institutions which exist only in the most basic forms in most CEE countries and which are not yet able to act as a serious source of debt and equity finance for the private sector or as a means of extending corporate ownership.

Success in the third Copenhagen condition – the capacity to cope with competitive pressures and market forces within the European Union – depends to a large extent on success in the second condition – the creation of a functioning market economy. Assessment of this criterion is forward looking. Nevertheless, Agenda 2000 concludes that 'provided they stay on their present course', Hungary and Poland should meet this condition. The Czech Republic, Slovakia and Slovenia should also be able to do so provided they 'strengthen their efforts and avoid policy reversals'. Estonia comes close but large external imbalances give cause for concern. The remaining Baltic states and Romania need to consolidate their efforts further. Bulgaria appears to be pulling out of its severe crisis of 1996 and 1997 and 'is on course to join the others during the next decade'.

The final Copenhagen condition for the applicant states – the ability to take on the obligations of membership – is a major task and one which all applicants have had to complete since the 1973 enlargement. The CEE applicants however face the biggest ever challenge in this respect, in part because of the significant extension in scope and depth of the acquis in recent years and in part because of the transition process itself and from their own low economic starting point. The transition indicators in Table 15.2 correspond to some extent to the type of measures the candidate countries need to take to meet the requirements of the acquis. In addition to transposing EU legislation into national law (the 1995 White Paper is one example of how the candidate countries are being helped in this process), Agenda 2000 maintains that modernisation of the applicants' administrative capacities is essential so that the acquis can be implemented and enforced – a process in which PHARE is deemed to play a key role. Agenda 2000 concludes that Poland, Hungary and the Czech republic should be able to take on the major part of the acquis and establish the requisite administrative structure in the medium term. The Baltic states and Slovenia and Slovakia are adjudged only to be in a position to do so if they substantially increase their efforts.

IMPLICATIONS FOR THE EUROPEAN UNION

The fifth Copenhagen condition refers to the requirement for the European Union to absorb new members whilst continuing the momentum of integration. This requirement has, for example, placed additional urgency on the need to avoid delays to the implementation of EMU, which would become even more complex if it was entangled in the process of enlargement. Enlargement has also created a need to reform the Union's institutions to make them responsive to the demands of a much bigger organisation – a process which was only partially carried out by the Amsterdam Treaty. Agenda 2000 sets out the principles which will guide reform of the policies most deeply affected by enlargement – the budget, the Common Agricultural Policy and the Structural Funds (see Chapter 7). All three policies are inter-related and would be undergoing fundamental scrutiny in any case – although enlargement adds an extra dimension and urgency to the process by virtue of the extent to which incomes in Central and Eastern Europe lag behind those in the European Union (see Table 15.3).

Table 15.3 GDP per capita in PPS

Bulgaria	4,210	Lithuania	4,129
Czech Republic	9,857	Poland	5,318
Estonia	3,876	Romania	4,159
Hungary	6,390	Slovenia	10,199
Latvia	3,144	Slovakia	7,036
EU (15)	17,264		

Source: Eurostat

However, in addition to the budget, CAP and Structural Funds, which are most often quoted as requiring reform as a result of enlargement, the accession of the CEE states will place pressure on and have profound implications for virtually all European policies. Box 15.2 highlights briefly some of the implications for business of enlargement in key policy areas.

BOX 15.2 ENLARGEMENT, EU POLICIES AND THE IMPLICATIONS FOR BUSINESS

Internal market

Enlarged market, enhanced economic activity, greater competition and more consumer choice but:

- some sectoral/regional tensions resulting from need to adjust
- infrastructure inadequacies reduce enlargement benefits
- need to ensure compliance with single market acquis.

Free movement of goods and services

- Adjustment problems in existing and new members, especially in sensitive sectors – for example, textiles and steel
- Enforcement and compliance essential in financial services in particular.

Free movement of capital

- Capital liberalisation requires solid financial system and economic stability.

Free movement of people

Migration likely to increase[1] – driven by east–west labour differential. Could lead to:

- more flexible labour markets in western Europe
- greater unemployment and strains on social systems in western Europe
- relief of some skills shortages in western Europe.

Competition policy

- Substance of policy not affected by enlargement but enforcement could be a problem as a result of heavier and more complex administrative burden.
- Candidates in process of approximating their competition laws – the next challenge is the creation of a 'competition culture'.

Social policy

- Adoption of acquis requires major financial and legislative effort, especially in health and safety. Failure to do so will undermine the SEM.
- Enlargement creates risk that support for broad social policy could be weakened if candidate countries adoption of social policy is inadequate.

Environment policy

Applicants suffer severe environmental degradation in most spheres. Some improvements but gap likely to remain wide for some time, especially in water and energy. Possible outcomes:

- new market for environmental products in CEE countries?
- cross-border environmental problems with or without accession but enlargement should facilitate their solution

- scale of CEE environmental problems could lead to inward looking EU policy and neglect of global issues
- persistence of environmental gap → distortion of competition. Long term strategy based on lower standards therefore not acceptable.

Research and development

- R&D declined in applicant countries since transition began
- EU programmes open to CEE states. Enlargement increases scientific potential.

Information society and telecommunications

- CEE – one of the world's most promising information and communication technology markets.

Transport

- CTP involves application of SEM to transport, harmonisation of competition conditions and development of infrastructure
- Urgent need in candidate countries for investment and improvements in infrastructure (quality and quantity), safety and environment to enable full benefits of enlargement and SEM to be realised
- Opportunities for construction firms, equipment manufacturers and related activities.

Energy

- Enlargement increases EU dependence on imports from former Soviet Union
- EU energy policy needs to take into account need for network investment, nuclear safety, energy efficiency measures and environmental standards.

Industrial policy

- Candidate countries combine low labour costs and good skill and technical levels with overcapacity, outdated industrial sectors → low productivity, poor quality polluting products
- Enlargement will encourage better allocation of resources and could initially lead to use of new members as low cost production locations
- Horizontal approach of EU industrial policy could help competitiveness problem of CEE countries but regional and sectional adjustment problems likely to receive much attention.

SMEs

- EU enterprise policy characterised by high degree of subsidiarity
- Accession and exposure to competition will put great pressure on CEE SMEs which will need support but they will also benefit from increased economic activity brought about by enlargement.

Economic and monetary union

- New members unlikely to adopt Euro immediately but they must be prepared to endorse aim

continued . . .

of EMU and meet requirements of non-participant members in EMU. Otherwise could endanger integrity of SEM (this threat, however, is not great given the relatively small economic weight of the new members). Loss of exchange rate flexibility may cause problems while transition still underway. Participation in EMU will require compliance with convergence criteria – unlikely to be the focus of policy for some time.

Note: [1] Expectations of labour migration in earlier enlargements were greater than outturn

CONCLUSION: CORPORATE OPPORTUNITIES AND RESPONSES

The combined impact of the transition process and the preparations for accession is intended to create an environment in which business can flourish and in turn contribute to the success of the transition process. In the short term, the most promising way of encouraging private sector activity in the region is by attracting foreign investment. In the longer term, the challenge is to develop a competitive, flourishing indigenous business sector.

An obvious attraction of the CEE countries for foreign investors is the existence of a large, relatively untapped market for consumer and industrial goods. However, given the low levels of GDP per head and the currently limited disposable income in these countries, profitable exploitation of these markets in many sectors will take time. However, these countries have other attractions to potential investors: their geographical proximity to western European markets plus the access to these markets which is being developed through the pre-accession strategy, makes these countries attractive investment destinations. In addition, these countries have a level of education and skills which is much higher and more diversified than that of other countries at a similar level of development. Although existing skills are not necessarily the most appropriate for the development of a market economy, an educated workforce knows how to gain knowledge and adapt key skills in a rapidly changing environment.

CEE governments have sought to attract foreign indirect investment (FDI) as a way not only of increasing the quantity of their capital stock but also of increasing productivity, technology levels and improved quality and environmental standards. Their capital requirements, however, are huge: in its 1993 Annual Report, the EBRD quoted a range of estimates for the annual investment needed, with $100 billion at the bottom of the range and with estimates several times higher at the upper end. To put this into perspective, at the time of German reunification, estimates of capital transfer requirements of $90 billion per annum for a decade were quoted as needed to bring former East Germany up to West German standards, making the EBRD estimates appear modest. However, the East German example is not directly transferable and accession can be achieved without attempting to bring the CEE countries up to the standards of the most prosperous EU member, as happened in the case of Germany.

Table 15.4 summarises the flows of FDI into the applicant countries to the end of 1996, by which time over $30 billion had been invested there – a significant amount but below the levels anticipated and hoped for in the early days of transition. Over $25 billion or 85 per cent of the total of FDI into the region had been directed towards the three most advanced transition countries, the Czech Republic, Hungary and Poland. Hungary, in particular, has been popular with foreign investors, a reflection of Hungary's longer experience of elements of market economics; confidence in the reform programme; a

Table 15.4 Foreign direct investment in Central and Eastern Europe

	1996 (US$ m)	Cumulative FDI (1989–96, US$ m)	Cumulative FDI per capita (1989–96, US$ m)
First wave applicants			
Czech Rep.	1,264	7,120	692
Estonia	110	735	477
Hungary	1,986	13,260	1,300
Poland	2,741	5,398	140
Slovenia	186	743	372
Second wave applicants			
Bulgaria	100	425	51
Latvia	230	644	258
Lithuania*	152	285	76
Romania	210	1,186	52
Slovak Rep.	177	623	117
Total	7,156	30,419	

Source: EBRD
Note: * Figures for Lithuania are incomplete and are only available from 1993

skilled and educated labour force; proximity to Western European markets and the nature of the privatisation process, which emphasised the need to attract capital rather than to spread share ownership.

Success in attracting foreign investment requires a favourable legal framework and political and economic stability. Even in Hungary, reports persist of arbitrary bureaucratic interference in the activities of joint ventures involving foreign investors. Such reports create a reputation for a difficult investment climate, deter potential investors and give weight to EBRD's concerns that improvements in corporate and institutional governance remain a priority. In short, the more successful the transition, the more likely it is that investment will be directed towards Central and Eastern Europe.

Other factors also intervene to deter FDI. In the early days of transition, the advanced industrialised countries were hit by an economic downturn and their companies were not in a strong position to invest abroad. Since then, the situation has improved in Western Europe and the US but the crisis in the Far East continues to place question marks about the likelihood of significant investment from that quarter. Competition for foreign investment is also intense: in the early days of transition, the East Asian region and the region of Latin America and the Caribbean each received about five times the amount of FDI of Central and Eastern Europe. Latin America remains a relatively attractive home for such investment but the attractiveness of the Far East, for the time being at least, has diminished. Such developments may work to the advantage of the CEE countries who, notwithstanding all their problems, have demonstrated their commitment to transition and the market economy. Approaching EU membership could also give a fillip to foreign investment.

CASE STUDY 15.1 THE GENERAL ELECTRIC-TUNGSRAM EXPERIENCE

In 1989, US multinational General Electric bought a controlling interest in Hungarian light bulb manufacturer, Tungsram, consolidating its position in 1994 by increasing its stake to 100 per cent. Tungsram has proved to be an important element in General Electric's strategy of building a lighting base outside the US and has become the centrepiece of General Electric's European lighting activities and the focus of its European lighting research and development.

In the early years, the success of this venture was in the balance. Tungsram had been an attractive acquisition for General Electric: it appeared to be a sound, albeit rundown, business with a good reputation and brand name, high technology standards for the region, a lowly paid workforce and a friendly government, which gave General Electric a five-year tax break – later extended in return for investment pledges. However, performance was sub-standard in several key areas and many products failed to meet international standards. Production line breakages, for example, were as high as 50 per cent and there was a ninety day interval between order and delivery – a gap which was reduced to thirty days by 1994, in part by slashing manufacturing cycle times.

On taking control, General Electric divested itself of Tungsram's non-lighting activities, cut costs and invested heavily in infrastructure, new products, training, meeting environmental standards and research. Tungsram's management was also totally reorganised away from a rigid hierarchy towards a more team-based structure and the labour force has been reduced from almost 18,000 in 1989 to 10,000 in 1998. Tungsram's research and development was judged uncommercial, run down and restarted more or less from scratch.

Nevertheless, it took some time to turn the company around and Tungsram suffered heavy losses in 1991 and 1992 before turning in a small profit in 1993. In 1996, sales reached $376 million and Tungsram had the tenth largest turnover in Hungary and exported over 90 per cent of its output, mostly to western Europe. The company also uses about 2,000 local firms as suppliers. Production volumes have increased by more than 50 per cent since 1989 and the product mix has shifted towards modern, energy efficient lighting and diversification into lighting fixtures is under consideration. By 1998, General Electric had invested about $800 million in Tungsram and in the spring of 1998 announced further investments which will take place in the years to 2002. These will fund the establishment of new production facilities in eastern Hungary and the expansion of existing plants in Vac and Budapest, resulting in the creation of 500 new jobs.

General Electric's eastern European venture can be considered a success but it has taken a number of years, large amounts of money and a fundamental reappraisal of all aspects of the business. Given the amount of effort that had to be expended on a company which was one of the most successful and highly regarded in pre-transition Hungary, and Central and Eastern Europe generally, the Tungsram experience demonstrates clearly the extent to which CEE enterprises in general were ill-prepared to meet the new business environment and the scale of the transition challenge. Without the General Electric intervention or similar, Tungsram probably would not have survived in view of its precarious financial situation, its inability to cope with full exposure to competitive forces without substantial investment and the absence of a commercially oriented management.

The form in which foreign investors have managed the entry into the CEE market has varied, including acquisition through privatisation, conventional acquisition, licensing deals, joint ventures and greenfield developments. Each method brings its own problems. Licensing agreements are common in Eastern Europe and are used for the production of a range of items including textiles, clothing, footwear, beer, cigarettes, food products, chemicals and electrical equipment and appliances among others. These agreements allow western companies to establish brand loyalty without absorbing large amounts of upfront capital or management resources and can yield relatively quick returns with less risk than other forms of involvement. Licensing agreements can facilitate deeper involvement in a market via transformation into joint ventures, subsidiaries, etc. They also require a thorough investigation into the background and capabilities of the new partner to avoid the production of substandard products and subsequent damage to brand reputation. In view of the unique situation in Central and Eastern Europe, several western companies tried to overcome the problems of entering upon such arrangements in the region by greater involvement in management and production than is normal in the West.

Cross-border acquisitions are always complex but particularly so in Central and Eastern Europe where legal frameworks are not always firmly established and where the transition process is still underway. The experience of General Electric during and following its acquisition of Tungsram, one of Hungary's best known and run companies under the former regime, demonstrates some of the challenges which need to be overcome (see Case Study 15.1). One way of trying to avoid some of the problems arising from licensing agreements or acquisitions is to embark upon greenfield development. Obstacles encountered here can include the difficulties of finding suitable local suppliers or local staff.

Notwithstanding all these problems, the countries of Central and Eastern Europe have travelled a long way in a relatively short period of time. The transition challenge facing these countries was huge and progress has been steady, albeit not without its temporary reversals. What is clear is that that transition and enlargement have become linked and their success in turn depends on a positive response from the corporate sector.

✎ KEY POINTS

- **Although much remains to be done, economic and political transformation in Central and Eastern Europe has progressed a long way in a relatively short time.**

- **Transition and enlargement are interdependent. Both depend on the emergence of a strong private sector.**

- **Levels of FDI in Central and Eastern Europe have been disappointing and foreign investors have generally found life difficult in the region.**

- **The Copenhagen conditions provide a valuable framework for assessing the readiness of CEE states for EU membership.**

- **Enlargement will have a profound effect on most EU policies and on the European economy with significant knock-on effects for the business community.**

SUGGESTED FURTHER READING

Crampton, R.J. (1997) *Eastern Europe in the Twentieth Century and After*, second edition, Routledge.

European Bank for Reconstruction and Development (1996) *Transition Report 1996: Infrastructure and Savings*.

European Bank for Reconstruction and Development (1997) *Transition Report 1997: Enterprise Growth and Performance*.

European Commission (1995) *Preparation of the Associated Countries of Central and Eastern Europe for Integration into the Internal Market of the Union*, White Paper COM (95) 163.

Grabbe, H. and Hughes, K. (1998) *Enlarging the EU Eastwards*, Pinter.

Preston, C. (1997) *Enlargement and Integration in the European Union*, Routledge.

16

ECONOMIC AND MONETARY UNION: THE CHALLENGES FOR THE EUROPEAN BUSINESS ENVIRONMENT

Of all the events, both within and external to the European business environment, occuring over the coming years, none is likely to have as great an impact as the move towards Economic and Monetary Union (EMU). EMU is essentially about creating the conditions under which a single currency, the Euro, can be established and ultimately sustained within the EU's borders. EMU's establishment generally needs to be based upon four core facilitatory factors, namely:

- an evident need for EMU;
- the willingness and ability of states to accept the economic implications of EMU;
- the willingness of states to accept the political commitments implied by EMU;
- the acceptance by all users of the new currency system.

EMU has been justified as a solution to the problems facing European economies in terms of enhancing their strength and positioning within the global economy – initially through its ability to enhance the effects of the SEM. Longer term benefits will be realised if EMU delivers the anticipated lower inflation across the EU thereby stimulating higher levels of investment and economic growth.

In the era before the introduction of the Euro, there has been concerted action to create the conditions within which EMU can be established and sustained. This provides the initial focus of this chapter. It then goes on to examine the practical implications of the introduction of the Euro for business both in generic and sectorally specific terms. Finally, the chapter examines the broader implications of the EMU, initially in terms of EU non-members (especially the UK) and for non-EU states in general.

BOX 16.1 HISTORICAL PROGRESS TOWARDS EMU

October 1970:   Werner Report proposes establishment of EMU by 1980.
March 1972:   European 'Snake' established to keep intra-EU stable within narrow limits of fluctuation.
April 1973:   European Monetary Co-operation Fund established to provide financial support to keep exchange rates stable.
March 1979:   European Monetary System (EMS) founded.
February 1986: Signing of Single European Act which includes provisions for a single capital market.
April 1989:   Delors Committee on EMU published promoting a three stage approach to EMU.
June 1989:   European Council agrees that Stage One of EMU to start July 1990.
October 1990:   European Council agrees Stage Two to start January 1994.
December 1991: European Council adopts Treaty upon European Union (came into force 1 November 1993).

Note: See also Table 16.2

EMU AND THE EUROPEAN BUSINESS ENVIRONMENT

The European business environment has been dominated in recent years by preparation for the shift towards EMU. Fiscal and monetary policy measures taken to fulfil the terms of EMU membership have had a generally negative short term influence upon enterprise performance as they have tended to limit economic growth. These short term negative effects are expected to be overcome in the medium to long term as the anticipated ability of the EMU to deliver and sustain price stability will create a more stable and predictable business environment within Europe.

The move towards EMU highlights new challenges for policy makers in complementing the competitiveness of indigenous enterprises. The option of a competitive devaluation to secure competitiveness in foreign markets is explicitly ruled out in terms of trade with other EU states. This places emphasis upon firms to alter costs and exhibit greater flexibility if they are to compete successfully in both European and global markets. Flexibility requires governments to free up market forces within the European economy in both factor and product markets (see Chapter 13).

The dual, but interlinked, processes of economic and monetary unification have been a long term objective of EU states. The former has been more prominent with policies such as the Structural Funds and the SEM contributing to the process. Monetary unification has arguably been more reactive: only emerging as progressive economic unification necessitated macro-economic co-ordination and currency stability. Current moves towards EMU emerged from the development of the Exchange Rate Mechanism (ERM) and other aspects of the European Monetary System (EMS) which was established in 1979 and formed the backbone of monetary arrangements in the EU until the creation of the EMU. The ERM sought to maintain exchange rate stability between EU states within agreed limits of fluctuation around pre-established central rates. The permitted limits of fluctuation (prior to August 1993 when they were widened to 15 per cent) were normally 2.25 per cent – although higher inflation states (like Italy and Spain) were permitted wider variations. Every currency had an agreed central rate against all other participating currencies around which the agreed limits of fluctuation operated. The need to sustain stability against all currencies within the system implied that the allowed flexibility was more apparent than real.

The initial phases of the development of the ERM (between 1979–87) were not particularly effective as states persistently devalued within the system. Thus the ability of the ERM to act as a disciplinary device to promote convergence in terms of key monetary indicators (that is, inflation and interest rates) was severely curtailed. In the mid to late 1980s, the ERM became much more credible as a means of delivering convergence as member states showed a greater commitment to its rules and procedures (see Steinherr and Gros, 1994). Consequently, through the mid-1980s to early 1990s, inflation and interest rates converged and membership of the ERM expanded to include all EU states bar Greece. However as the ERM expanded, differentials between the participating states (both in terms of policy performance and preference) grew. This meant that as the effects of the early-1990s recession and German reunification took hold, the policy requirements and preferences of states started to diverge. Typically some states had unemployment problems whereas others had inflationary difficulties. Such differences could not be sustained within the ERM framework and contributed to the instability within the system in 1992 and 1993.

The crisis had unfortunate timing for the EU as it had just committed itself, within the Treaty upon European Union, to a progressive move to EMU by the end of the decade. These economic problems were compounded by the political uncertainty arising from the rejection of the Treaty by the Danish referendum. The response of states to these difficulties was markedly different. For the more sceptical states, the crisis reinforced a belief that moves towards EMU were premature whereas, for the more Europhile states, the crisis highlighted that, in a world of free capital movements, a single currency was the only way to achieve the desired currency stability. Importantly, the events indicated to financial markets those states that were able to deliver both the necessary political commitment and economic conditions needed to participate in the EMU project, thereby differentiating between those states that were likely to be in the first moves to EMU and those that were likely to fall behind in the process.

The Treaty upon European Union advocated a three stage approach to the transition towards EMU.

- *Stage one* is based upon moves to free capital flows and the integration of capital markets linked to the SEM programme.
- *Stage two* centres upon the creation of the European Monetary Institute (EMI), a transitional institute designed to prepare the EU for stage three when the EMI would be replaced by the European Central Bank (ECB).
- *Stage three* is when the ECB takes over responsibility for monetary and exchange rate policy. Plans for stage three are outlined in Table 16.2.

Table 16.1 indicates some of the main costs and benefits associated with the move towards EMU. Many of these are difficult to quantify and thus make it rather difficult to assess the relative merits of EMU. Where they have been assessed, as they have in the case of transactions costs (for which it is estimated EMU will save some 0.5 per cent of the EU's GDP), the gains do not appear to be particularly great. Such benefits as there are, will be unevenly spread with smaller states, who have a higher dependence upon intra-EU trade, benefiting the most. In practice, many of the gains may be unquantifiable as many of the benefits of the single currency will only be realised over the medium to long term (for example, through greater price stability stimulating higher levels of investment).

The positive effects will also be unevenly spread across businesses. The biggest beneficiaries will be those enterprises which derive the highest proportion of their revenues from foreign markets. Thus larger enterprises are expected to benefit more from EMU. These benefits will extend to large non-EU companies with extensive investments

Table 16.1 The costs and benefits of EMU

Costs	Benefits
• The loss of the exchange rate as a tool of domestic economic policy • The short term deflationary impact of the convergence process • Potential problems related to a lack of 'real' convergence and potential policy conflicts	• Elimination of transaction costs in intra-EU trade • Lower interest rates across the EU • Removal exchange rate uncertainty in intra-EMU trade • Aid development of a true SEM by increasing price transparency and removing option of competitive devaluations between EU states • Create new international currency to represent the EU's combined economic weight (see below)

throughout the EU. However not all large companies will benefit. Enterprises with a strong domestic market (such as utilities) will seemingly gain little until their markets start to exhibit a greater degree of internationalisation. For SMEs, the impact is difficult to predict. Although many SMEs have a strong tendency to serve local markets, there are a number with a high export focus (such as IT companies) which can expect to benefit from the introduction of the Euro.

It is widely expected that the Euro will provide impetus towards greater price/cost transparency. This transparency will extend to wages (and other labour costs) as firms will be more able to assess differentials and alter operations accordingly. This could lead, so many unions hope, to EU-wide collective bargaining. Price transparency should also lead to price harmonisation within sectors such as banking, financial services, cars, chemicals and pharmaceuticals. Despite nearly a decade of the SEM, there still remain large price differentials for many products between states (see Chapter 3). For many businesses, EMU is likely to speed up the convergence of prices through greater freedoms for consumers and an ability to compare prices across member states (through enhanced transparency). However, uniformity is unlikely because of differences between regions in terms of transport costs, spatial variations in tastes and preferences, the costs of cross-border shopping, local cost differences and different competitive situations. This has been borne out by the experiences of most other EMUs. Overall, the EU market will start to exhibit less fragmentation with internationalisation of markets affecting an ever increasing number of enterprises (regardless of size) as each is more able to sell its goods to a more geographically dispersed market. This process is likely to be enhanced as inter-state direct mail and electronic commerce become more widespread.

In practice, many of the positive and negative aspects of EMU will only manifest themselves over the medium to long term. Advocates of the process will play up the fact that the benefits of EMU are directly linked to its size. As EMU membership expands, so the benefits to European business will grow. Opponents regard EMU as primarily a political exercise with negligible benefits. However, the core concern has to come down to whether the states are sufficiently similar for them to co-exist with a common currency.

BOX 16.2 THE PRE-REQUISITE FOR EMU: THE PROCESS OF CONVERGENCE

The success of EMU depends upon convergence between EU states in terms of economic development and performance to the extent that the objective of economic and monetary unification is both realistic and credible. The end point of the convergence process is a state of 'cohesion' between states. This does not imply uniform economic development and performance, merely harmonious economic conditions. Convergence comprises three distinct yet ultimately related processes.

- *Nominal convergence*. This is convergence in terms of macro-economic performance as indicated by a number of core fiscal and monetary variables and is the form of convergence referred to within the Maastricht Treaty. Thus for entry into EMU, states must have converged in terms of budget deficits (which must be at most 3 per cent of a state's GDP), government debt (which must be at most 60 per cent of a state's GDP), interest rates (which must be no more than 2 per cent above the three 'best' performing states), inflation rates (which must be no more than 1.5 per cent above the three best performing states). Finally, all states must have been able to sustain exchange rate stability within the framework of the ERM for at least two years prior to entry.
- *Real convergence*. This is convergence in terms of economic development and implies that levels of unemployment and industrial and economic development between states should broadly approximate (see Chapter 7). Whilst there are no set criteria, certain core indicators need to converge to ensure that harmony can be established within the management of a single currency. For example, vast differences in unemployment between states could imply differing policy priorities between constituent parts of the EMU. The EU sought to strengthen real convergence by including provisions for a Cohesion Fund within the Treaty upon European Union.
- *Institutional convergence*. The move towards EMU also implies increasing uniformity in terms of economic management. The most obvious form is to achieve a consensus between states around the priorities of economic policy (namely, low and stable inflation). As part of the commitment towards this policy objective, potential members have to guarantee the independence of the national central bank. There are broader implications, for example, in terms of the behaviour of labour markets within the EMU. Some commentators stress that EMU requires more flexibility across Europe's factor markets, particularly labour markets (see Chapter 13).

Over the short term, the core benchmarks for membership of the EMU are the nominal criteria. In practice, there is little economic rationale for these other than to prove that states can live with, and are committed to, what are essentially criteria for sustaining price stability. These criteria also underline that convergence is a long term process which has merely been reconfigured and re-focused within the Maastricht Agenda for EMU: many other policies (notably the ERM and Structural Funds) have proved longer term devices for the process of convergence between EU states.

Meeting the nominal convergence criteria by 1999 has proved to be a core political objective for many member states. The monetary conditions have not posed much of a problem as many of these were already well on the way to being achieved (if they had not already done so) within the existing framework provided by the ERM. The fiscal policy criteria have proved more difficult to meet as fiscal retrenchment has come at a time when the opposite policy prescriptions were probably called for. There can be little doubt that in the short term, this fiscal tightening has magnified Europe's unemployment problem and created a fear that the nominal convergence criteria could lock Europe into permanent mass unemployment.

SUSTAINING CONVERGENCE

As mentioned above, the move to EMU is based around a consensus upon low inflation as the primary goal of economic policy. To ensure this priority is not diluted within EMU (and thus that states keep to pre-EMU commitments), there has been an agreement to sustain the Maastricht nominal convergence criteria after EMU is in place. In practice, the primary focus of this 'stability pact' is to ensure that states keep to the public financing targets specified within the Treaty. This pact asserts that if a state contravenes the nominal convergence criteria, it will face heavy financial penalties. The fear is that excessive borrowing by one state will not only weaken the Euro but will also allow that state to expand debt at the expense of other states if its actions prompt the ECB to raise the EMU-wide interest rate (in practice, there is little evidence to support this fear). The pact also outlines that if extra tax revenues start to flow as economic growth resumes, national bodies are prohibited from spending it. This may prove difficult for some governments who promised business and unions that fiscal retrenchment was temporary and that once tax revenues started flowing again they would be directed towards job creation.

Many members of the EMU feel that they should be allowed to vary government borrowing as a percentage of GDP throughout the stages of the trade cycle. In EMU, fiscal policy is the one macro-economic weapon left to states to manage their economies. If constraints are imposed upon this, then the automatic stabilisers (that is, unemployment benefits, etc.) could be severely affected. Such problems can only really be countered by a stronger central fiscal policy: something which states will clearly not countenance. Thus, in short, the stability pact has the ability to undermine the effectiveness of the Euro to function and of the Eurozone to respond flexibly to cyclical downturns. It, therefore, represents an unnecessary and unwarranted degree of central control over the one instrument of macro-policy left available to states to manage their domestic economy. Such features have the potential to turn EMU's members against one another. In practice, the political capital locked up by respective member states in the process may be sufficient to sustain convergence.

Further problems could limit the ability to sustain convergence, including the perception that not all EMU states are at the same stage of the trade cycle – a major reason given for the UK's delayed entry into the EMU (see Case Study 16.2). A classic example is Ireland which has experienced relatively rapid economic growth whilst many other EMU states were either in recession or experiencing sluggish expansion. The implication is, that with a single monetary policy, some states will have the 'wrong' interest rate. In practice, this is unavoidable as interest rates do not have uniform effects either within or between economies. Thus, the concern is more of how economies respond to these challenges in terms of factor mobility to balance out such differences and how closer integration may bring these cycles into closer alignment.

A lack of real convergence between states potentially represents the most serious of the problems facing the fledgling EMU. If there is insufficient real convergence between states, EMU will be subject to asymmetric shocks whereby different parts of the zone will be affected by external shocks in markedly different ways (for example, some states could see unemployment rise, others could see inflation increase). If this is the case, a single monetary and exchange rate policy becomes impossible to sustain. Only if shocks are symmetric or if there is an adequate response mechanism (in terms of fiscal transfers or resource mobility and flexibility) to compensate for such effects will an EMU work. As none of these conditions exist in the EU, EMU should, in theory, be a non-starter for this group of states. Despite this being a theoretical extreme (individual states are themselves subject to asymmetric shocks or have inadequate resource mobility or flexibility to compensate for such effects: for example, most states have regional variations in unemployment), it does imply that EMU needs to be accompanied by structural reform of labour markets.

THE TRANSITION TO EMU

As highlighted in Table 16.2, the process of introducing the Euro is multi-staged. In May 1998, amid some degree of cynicism and accusations of creative accounting, the European Commission recommended that eleven states had met the necessary conditions to adopt the Euro on the 1 January 1999. It was clear that not all states were going to strictly meet the nominal criteria outlined within the Treaty. However, the Commission decided that as long as the criteria, especially those for public finances, were moving into alignment, then membership was valid. Only one of the states remaining outside the Eurozone (Greece) was excluded for economic reasons. The others (Denmark, the UK and Sweden) remained outside EMU largely for political reasons.

Table 16.2 EMU changeover timetable

Date	Stage	Associated Actions
1998	Decisions upon which countries will participate. (In May 1998, the Commission decided that Belgium, Germany, Spain, France, Ireland, Italy, Luxembourg, the Netherlands, Austria, Portugal and Finland were able to participate in EMU.)	• Establish European Central Bank (ECB) and the European System of Central Banks (ECSB) and make them operational • Prepare ECB/ECSB to conduct monetary policy in stage three • Set date for introduction of Euro banknotes and coins • Start production of Euro banknotes and coins • Conversion rates into EMU fixed (December)
1 January 1999	Start of full EMU	• Irrevocable fixing of conversion rates between participating currencies and the Euro • Euro introduced in non-cash form • Entry into force of legislation for the introduction of the Euro • Single monetary and foreign exchange policy to be conducted in the Euro by the ESCB • Issue new tradable public debt in Euro • Private sector to change to use of Euro on basis of 'no compulsion, no prohibition'
From start of 2002	Euro notes and coins introduced	• Withdraw national banknotes and coins (by 1 July at latest) • Implement the complete changeover of public administration • Monitor the complete changeover of the private sector

The decision to maximise the number of states within the initial moves towards EMU, despite their apparent deviation from the Maastricht targets, derives largely from political expediency (notably so in the case of Italy) and a recognition that the level of benefits from EMU are directly linked to the size of membership. In addition, an improving general economic environment would, according to the Commission's calculations, eventually eliminate deviations from the set targets.

Despite the introduction of EMU in 1999, Euro notes and coins will not come into circulation until 2002. It is important to distinguish between the Euro as a currency and its existence in cash form. After 1999, different currencies will still exist in EMU states but they will not be separate currencies. They will be 'non-decimal denominations' (which means that national currencies will be expressions of the Euro locked in at permanent conversion rates) freely convertible to the Euro and with each other according to fixed exchange rates. Thus before 2002, the Euro will exist only as book money in bank accounts with Euro payments made only by bank transfers, cheques, credit cards etc.

As a complement to the transition process, the European Council of December 1996 established a legal framework for the introduction of the Euro, notably with regard to:

- *contractual issues*: all contracts will remain unaffected by the changeover and as such no party will be permitted to terminate or alter a contract on the basis of the shift to the Euro;
- *conversion issues*: as of 1 January 2002, all contracts have to be quoted in Euros and any contracts negotiated in national currencies will be converted into Euros at the official rate.

Public administrations have a vital role in facilitating the efficient changeover to the Euro. In this context, the European Commission has launched communication campaigns to inform citizens and business of the practical aspects of the introduction of the Euro. Banks and businesses (as highlighted below) will participate actively in the introduction of the Euro by altering their internal organisation, products and services as well as educating staff and customers. Eventually the process of adoption of the Euro by businesses should take on its own dynamism as the use of the new currency starts to exhibit greater maturity.

To date, there is little evidence of demand from individuals or SMEs for Euro-denominated financial products (credit cards, cheques, etc.) before the introduction of notes and coins in 2002; although many larger enterprises have indicated that they will be using the Euro for some transactions from 1999 (see below). Additionally, existing government securities will be re-denominated to reflect the change in currency over their lifespan.

THE IMPACT UPON BUSINESS OPERATIONS AND FUNCTIONS

EMU will have a profound effect upon the strategies and operations of enterprises. Right across the European economy, the introduction of the Euro requires major changes for commerce including:

- major modifications to national and international payment and settlement systems;
- the transition of all banking transactions to the Euro;
- the pricing of all goods and services in Euros;
- the conversion of financial contracts to Euros;
- the auditing, consolidation and reporting of company accounts in Euros.

The complexity of its effects across business operations mean that its total impact will be difficult to foretell. In stages one and two of EMU, a great deal of uncertainty over whether EMU would occur or not led to many companies delaying strategies to initiate actions to integrate the Euro into their internal operations and functions. Thus, when the timetable and membership were finally agreed, many enterprises found themselves with a lot of work to do within a relatively short timespan. Their core problems were related to the sheer scale of the exercise and uncertainty over the nature of the link between the old and new currencies.

Planning for EMU

The move towards EMU requires intensive preparation to ensure business systems are adjusted to reflect its implications. In moving towards EMU, enterprises:

- need to define how they will operate in the Euro environment;
- need to understand the differential impact of the Euro across the enterprise;
- need to establish how they would handle the transition process.

Core concerns arising from the introduction of the Euro across an enterprise's functions are outlined in Table 16.3.

Overall, there are as many as five cross-functional areas affected by EMU which will require special attention:

- *information technology*: all sections of the enterprise involved in the changeover will use the computer system;
- *communication*: information needs to be passed throughout the company as well as customers and suppliers;
- *general support services*: such as stationery etc. will be an area where EMU will have cross-functional impact;
- *human resources*: to implement the chosen strategy and be trained in the use of the Euro;
- *management strategy*: responsible for drawing up plans and processes for all segments of the enterprise.

The main losers from the introduction of the Euro are expected to be SMEs. These are among the least prepared enterprises for whom the switchover to the Euro will involve the greatest cost relative to total turnover. Many SMEs will find their pace of adoption of the Euro forced by their need to sustain smooth commercial relations with larger enterprises. To assist in this process, banks and public administrations are performing a broad educative function to make SMEs aware of the need to adopt and adapt to the Euro. This process also needs to extend to customers and suppliers to ensure both are aware of their partner's Euro strategy.

Despite firm commitments and dates for the introduction of the Euro, many companies faced uncertainty over when they should convert internal and external accounting systems to the new currency. In the period up to 2002, companies have the right to use the Euro under the 'no compulsion, no prohibition' principle. Some companies such as Daimler–Benz, Marks & Spencer and Siemens (see Case Study 16.1) introduced the Euro as the in-house currency from 1 January 1999. In the case of Daimler–Benz, suppliers will have to quote prices in Euros, Mercedes Cars will be priced in Euros and it is possible employees could be paid in Euros from this date. Other companies are less radical. Avis Europe is operating dual accounting and IBM has pencilled in 2001 as its conversion date (though technically it already reports in a single currency – the dollar). Saint-Gobain, the

Table 16.3 Business functions and EMU

Business function	Concerns
Marketing and pricing	Enterprises need to assess the impact of EMU upon each of their markets. This is important in terms of their integration and restructuring. Pricing strategies need to be reassessed especially if there are differentials between national markets. Firms need to assess the requirements of suppliers for Euro pricing. The Euro requires new pricing lists, catalogues and a review of distribution channels.
Production management	As EMU will make exporting to the EU easier, it is likely to offer both opportunities and challenges for business to which the production process needs to respond in terms of areas such as product modifications.
Systems and IT	Operational systems need to be assessed to identify where the Euro will have an impact. Equipment and systems need to be identified to aid the transition process and adoption of the Euro. IT systems need to be flexible enough to deal with old and new currencies and convert between the two.
Finance and payroll	Internal accounting procedures need to be altered.
Purchasing	Purchasing practices will be affected by EMU either because they are part of a new market strategy or it creates opportunities for savings via new sourcing.
Training	Staff need to be able to implement the strategy for the changeover and carry out the operational changes needed.
Treasury and banking	There will be an impact upon developing banking relationships within the Eurozone and opportunities for saving in terms of treasury operations. The Euro will also alter balance sheets, corporate finance, cash flow management and currency management.
Legal issues	Contract continuity will need to be assessed over the transition period. In addition, staff employment contracts and pension arrangements will all need to be altered to Euros.
Potential longer term issues	EMU could have a long term impact upon location decisions as firms seek to minimise costs. Other operational factors could also be affected such as the rationalisation of the supply chain.

French glass and ceramics group, is also planning a phased approach with the Euro being used for consolidated accounts from 1 January 1999 with subsidiaries retaining the freedom to determine as and when they decide to move to the Euro provided they do so by 2001. These preparations are also being developed within companies who are based in states outside the initial Eurozone. Leading Swedish multinationals are already planning to switch assorted business functions quickly to the Euro.

Enterprises planning a rapid transition period could face obstacles from national tax authorities and public administrations. For example, the German tax authorities will not accept the Euro until the end of the official transition process (that is, 2002). Rapid enterprise transition is also likely to be inhibited by the assorted social security funds which are likely to stick with the national currency for as long as they can. The rapidity of the transition process will be demand led. Thus once a critical mass of large companies starts to move over to the Euro, pressure will increase for the removal of these and other impediments sooner rather than later. However such a critical mass is likely to remain elusive until Euro notes and coins are issued in 2002.

CASE STUDY 16.1   PREPARING FOR EMU: THE CASE OF SIEMENS

Siemens has prepared for rapid conversion to the Euro from its very beginning in January 1999 and used the currency for all its external business from this date. On 1 October 1999, the first fiscal year after the introduction of the Euro, Siemens converted its accounts and records into Euros. Its readiness for the rapid introduction has had a two-year lead time across the numerous affected business functions. The rapid introduction is designed to give Siemens a head start in exploiting the integrated market that is expected to emerge as a result of EMU. Currently, more than half of Siemens business is generated in currencies within the Euro area and the enterprise therefore expects savings equivalent to tens of millions of German marks. Siemens anticipates that such savings will emerge from no longer having to hedge against interest and exchange rate movements, from smaller differences in interest rates, from the requirement for fewer bank accounts and from more efficient and effective cash pooling within the Euro area.

These benefits will be offset by the costs associated with the transition which the firm expects to be around DM 100 million, although these costs will be offset by savings within three years. When Siemens converts to Euros, its internal transfer prices (used to price intra-company trade) will all be quoted in the new currency. The strategy of Siemens does not merely apply to itself; it asked all its suppliers to convert to Euros by 1999, including companies located both inside and outside the Eurozone. Indeed, more than 14,000 UK companies are expected to be affected by this decision. To aid this process, Siemens has been advising its suppliers (many of which are SMEs) of its Euro requirements notably with regard to changes in payments systems and banking. This insistence by Siemens is designed to deliver better price transparency from its suppliers, enabling it to pick and choose its suppliers on a lowest cost basis and to switch accordingly. This could create difficulties for non-Eurozone suppliers who may be prone to swings in their exchange rate with the Euro.

The sectoral impact

The impact upon individual sectors will depend upon the extent to which they thrive with fragmented markets. The main beneficiaries will be those most exposed to intra-EU trade, and the biggest costs will fall upon those companies that deal in cash with a large number of customers, notably retail stores and banks (see below). Overall, a number of sectors will be particularly affected, both in terms of costs and commercial opportunities, by the introduction of the Euro.

Vending machines

Makers of these machines are expecting a surge in orders as existing equipment is converted to accept Euros. For operators, the introduction of the Euro means nothing more than increased investment. In the EU, there are nearly four million vending machines (in addition to millions of service machines such as parking meters and launderettes) which dispense a range of goods and which are mainly (some 90 per cent) coin operated. The EU has worked with the industry to design Euro coins in a manner to minimise transition and conversion costs.

Retailers

This is a group which faces substantial costs from the introduction of the Euro. It is estimated that the transition will cost it some ECU 28 billion – a figure derived from staff training costs, labelling in two currencies and adjustment of software. Generally, the longer the period of transition, the higher the costs incurred by the enterprise. Different retailers have developed differing strategies for its introduction. Marks & Spencer is planning for a prolonged transition period over two to three years and has invested in a new electronic point of sale system to enable it to accept foreign currency notes for Eurozone members before the introduction of Euro notes and coins in 2002. Others, such as the Kingfisher Group, believe a prolonged strategy is more troublesome and are planning a shorter introduction over six months or so. On the whole, retailers prefer a 'big bang' introduction whereas consumers favour a prolonged transition, not only to deny enterprises the opportunity of hiding price increases within the conversion process but, and probably more importantly, to give them time to accustom themselves to its use in everyday transactions. Retailers estimate that a six month dual circulation will cost 2.6 per cent of annual revenue compared to 1.3 per cent if the move took place overnight, reflecting the fact that they need to run two parallel accounting systems for a longer period of time. There are, of course, longer term benefits as opportunities for better sourcing emerge and as the whole process of trade is made easier: aided no doubt by the emergence of electronic commerce (see Case Study 12.2). It is already apparent that mail-order companies will be expected to exploit price differentials between national retail markets and can be counted on to act as price arbitrageurs to exploit overpricing by incumbent retailers.

IT companies

These companies can expect large benefits from the introduction of the Euro. Software changes need to be made to enable firms to account in Euros. Many in the industry feel that the changeover, if not done correctly, will create turmoil. The software must have the ability to report in the Euro and national currency over the 1999–2001 period. There is the possibility of further gain for IT companies as the introduction of the Euro causes firms to rethink their computer systems. The cost of the changeover to the Euro is estimated at ECU 4.6 billion. IT companies have expanded the scale of the issues, warning that a severe shortage of skills could jeopardise the ability of banks etc. to meet the challenge, ultimately leading to some business failures. Banks dispute this, maintaining that existing systems can cope and a mere 15 per cent have set money aside to cope with the changes.

Banks

Over the short term, most banks will be losers as they bear the cost of the transition. It is estimated that this changeover will cost European banks some ECU 10 billion in staff training and adapting IT systems: a process that is expected to take two years. The biggest losers in the transition will be banks within smaller states who will face the greatest challenges to profitability and will prove (and are indeed proving to be) the most vulnerable to takeover. Longer term implications are more dramatic as banks find that their revenue from retail and corporate currency exchange transactions is slashed. This, coupled with increased competition between banks within the Eurozone, is predicted to lead to consolidation within the European banking sector as well as to new opportunities within investment banking. The role of the banks is also important in advising customers of how they should switch to the Euro. For banks in states which will remain, initially at least, outside the Eurozone, preparations are less intense especially on the retail side but they will still need to adjust operations within their wholesale business. There are further predictions that EMU will challenge the primacy of the financial industry via securities markets as a stronger Euro bond market emerges and there is a consolidation amongst Europe's stock markets. This will be driven by improvements in capital allocations and lower capital costs as EMU facilitates a more integrated EU-wide capital market. The fragmentation of Europe's capital markets (and its consequences for the price of capital) is blamed by many for the persistently high levels of unemployment within the EU.

The impact of the introduction of the Euro upon consumers is difficult to predict. There can be little doubt that they will benefit from the anticipated reductions in interest rates (especially for long term debts such as mortgages) and from increased levels of price transparency. This analysis must be qualified if EMU leads to concentration or rationalisation within those sectors particularly affected by the introduction of the Euro. The Euro will also have a big impact upon wholesalers. Greater price transparency will enable wholesalers to compare prices more readily across-borders and to switch to low cost suppliers. To exploit these opportunities, many wholesalers are developing electronic commerce systems to enable them to check prices across-borders. The development of such systems will be assisted by an accompanying fall in the cost of inter-bank payment systems. Suppliers will be particularly affected by the move towards price harmonisation especially companies which operate across-borders and where price differentials are sizeable (such as car component manufacturers).

THE EXTERNAL IMPLICATIONS OF EMU

Any state, and enterprises therein, outside EMU but which have trade links with or investments within it must develop a strategy to adjust to the Euro. Broadly, the external implications of the Euro can be categorised according to:

- its impact upon non-Euro EU states;
- its impact upon the broader international arena.

Non-Eurozone EU states

Those EU states that for political and/or economic reasons have decided not to participate in the initial moves towards EMU need to define how they are to co-exist with the single currency. Greece has already stated that it will take the necessary steps to ensure that it is able to join EMU by 1 January 2001. For the Scandinavian states, the issue remains largely undefined. Denmark and the UK have a legal right to opt out of EMU under the

Treaty on European Union. Sweden has no such right but was excluded from the Euro on the basis that it was not a member of the ERM. This was politically expedient as the Swedish government felt its population was not ready for EMU.

Ultimately the effects of the Eurozone upon these states are linked to the size of EMU. Overall, the larger than expected size of the Eurozone suggests a greater inward focus than if it had been smaller. The creation of a successor to the ERM (ERM2), with stability against the Euro being the focus of policy, will also determine the impact upon these economies. Within the ERM2, participants will have to prove their anti-inflationary credentials by pursuing cautious macro-economic policies if they are to sustain a stable exchange rate link with the Euro. It is already likely that current ERM members (Denmark and Greece) as well as new members of the EU from Central and Eastern Europe (CEE) will use a new framework based around the Euro as a monetary anchor to guide exchange rate policy. The UK is unlikely to join such an arrangement, believing that the events of 1992–3 have tarnished the credibility of any such framework. In addition, any instability or uncertainty within the Eurozone is likely to spill over into these states whether they are part of ERM2 or not.

CASE STUDY 16.2   OPTING OUT OF EMU: THE CASE OF THE UK

The UK's decision to opt out of the initial moves to EMU is significant due to its relative economic importance within the EU. The UK is not only the headquarters and primary EU location for many major multinational companies but is also, through the City of London, the major European financial centre. That the UK opted out of EMU came as little surprise to anyone. The primary reason for such action was political and driven by public opinion. Thus any move to EMU would lack popular support. There are other more practical reasons for the UK's exclusion, notably that its economic cycle is out of step with much of the rest of the EU. This difference is driven by four factors:

- Trade: the UK has a lower level of intra-EU trade than other member states so is more vulnerable to external shocks;
- Personal sector: mortgage debt in the UK is equivalent to 57 per cent of GDP; compared to an average of 33 per cent in the rest of the EU, making the UK more susceptible to changes in interest rates than other EU states;
- Corporate sector: UK companies rely more upon the stock market than banks for finance;
- Oil: the UK is affected differently by oil price movements than other EU states.

Business may force the Euro issue by developing a Euro strategy out of commercial need. External pressure upon UK suppliers from firms in the Eurozone is driving this pattern whereas others recognise that ignoring the Euro would be commercially disastrous. Across all sectors and sizes of firms, there is a growing consensus, now that EMU is certain, that there needs to be an acceptance of the Euro if they are to exploit the advantages of integrated markets and a growing belief that EMU will enter the UK via the 'back door'. A number of big EU groups active in the UK, as well as top UK enterprises (such as ICI, Unilever, Shell, BP and Marks & Spencer), have indicated that they intend to shift accounting towards the Euro from 1999. This list is likely to grow as EMU is realised and becomes a feature within major UK export markets. Indeed once large multinationals alter their business methods to account for the Euro so the pressures upon SMEs to alter their processes will also grow. Despite the fact that operating dual currency systems will be expensive, this cost is more than outweighed by potential losses from ignoring the Euro. Whatever their opinions upon EMU as a policy measure, UK business cannot ignore it as non-membership will act as a constraint upon their competitiveness within core EU markets. UK minds were focused upon the economic cost of non-membership when the head of Toyota mentioned that it may have to re-consider future investments in the UK if it remained outside EMU fearing that its exclusion could put its UK production at a competitive disadvantage.

Further concerns were highlighted about the potential relative decline of the position of the City of London as Europe's main financial centre if the UK decides to sustain its exclusion from the Euro. The impact upon employment within the City depends upon its ability to capture a share of the market for Euro securities. The fear is that new investment and the focus of banks could shift towards Frankfurt at the expense of London. Others doubt this, noting that the UK is a centre for international, not just European, business. Thus global, rather than intra-European, competition is more of a threat. Some feel that the ability of the City of London to be innovative and exist in 'unofficial markets' as well as global markets will mean that the move to EMU may deliver more benefits than costs especially if it is able to successfully enter Euro markets. However, this could be undermined by the desire of some states to keep UK banks out of the Euro payments system; TARGET (Trans-European Automated Real-time Settlement Express Transfer). The City of London feels its pre-eminence in the European market is linked to its ability to access TARGET and has been developing alliances with Europe's other major stockmarkets to help secure its position.

Business planning has been assisted by a commitment by the Labour government to consider entry into EMU in 2002 or 2003. The government expects there will have been sufficient convergence within EMU states by then to make acceptance of the EMU more practical and popular. In preparation, the government is not only adopting measures to promote convergence in areas such as market flexibility but has also introduced an active awareness campaign to inform businesses of the need to adjust corporate strategy and operations to prepare for the Euro. This campaign will gradually be extended to consumers. It is this awareness campaign which is key to public acceptance of the practical necessity of EMU for the UK. In addition to the five aforementioned convergence criteria, the UK has set five tests in judging a move to EMU:

1 business cycles must converge;
2 more flexible labour markets across the EU;
3 EMU must benefit UK investment;
4 EMU must benefit the UK's financial sector;
5 there must be a positive impact upon the real economy (growth and employment).

These are qualitative criteria to highlight to an otherwise sceptical public that there are obvious advantages from membership. In early 1999, the government clearly stated its intention to join the Eurozone (subject to a referendum) when it announced its 'National Changeover Plan'.

THE IMPACT OF THE EURO UPON THE BROADER INTERNATIONAL ENVIRONMENT

The broader international impact of EMU is very mixed and depends upon levels of trade undertaken with the Eurozone and the possible emergence of the Euro as an international currency. As the Euro is created, all states will inevitably develop exchange rate policies *vis-à-vis* the currency (as typified by the ERM2). On the whole, the Eurozone will only conduct around 10 per cent of its trade with non-members. In its uncertain initial years, the Euro is expected to be a volatile currency and enterprises trading outside the Euro-zone may have to hedge against exchange rate risks. Additionally, there is an argument that the Euro may increase exchange rate volatility, because only a small proportion of trade will be done with states outside the Eurozone, which means that the states can afford to ignore Euro exchange rate policy. The implications of this may require renewed currency co-ordination between the major players in the international monetary system.

States expected to be particularly affected will be those in CEE and the CFA Franc-zone (a group of French, largely African, ex-colonies who use the CFA Franc as a trading currency). Both of these groups tend to peg their exchange rates to EU currencies but pay their contractual financial obligations in dollars. Consequently, they will face problems as any depreciation in the Euro *vis-à-vis* the dollar could increase levels of debt. CEE currencies pegged to the DM or the ECU basket are likely to switch to the Euro (Bulgaria and Estonia were quick to state their intention). The CEE states will benefit if EMU is a success as they will experience growth within their primary export market and benefit from lower interest rates that will aid the financing of their restructuring. For the CFA states, who do a lot more trade with non-Euro states, there will be the potential for worsening terms of trade as the Euro varies against other currencies.

The issue for CEEs is more pertinent given that they are prospective members of the EU (see Chapter 15). As yet, there has been no decision upon when CEE states will be ready for EMU. Poland has explicitly said that it is putting into place reforms that should enable it to be part of EMU between 2006 and 2008. Until then, the CEE states have to decide how to cope with the Eurozone. Most CEE states are likely to peg their currencies to the Euro which should result in increased monetary stability and lower exchange rate risk. This depends upon these states aligning policies alongside those of the EU and implies a radical overhaul of their financial sectors and a strengthening of the public administrations needed to implement the necessary changes. The process towards membership could be via an ERM-like framework which would allow member states wide fluctuations around established agreed central rates against the Euro. However, some feel that such a framework may be inappropriate and too strict as it is designed for western not eastern economies.

The direct effect on advanced economies (such as Japan and the US) of the introduction of the Euro will be mild but they may be affected by the emergence of the Euro as a reserve currency which could lower the prominence of both the dollar and the Yen in international markets (see below). Japanese and US investments in the EU are also likely to be swayed by the shift to Euro. Toyota (as mentioned) has already signalled that any new EU investment is likely to be within not outside the Eurozone. Subsidiaries of the US and Japanese companies will all have to change internal practices and procedures if they are to sustain their competitive positioning within EU markets. It has already been indicated that cars, electronics and banking (key areas of multinational investment in the EU) are among those sectors that are likely to be particularly affected by the advent of the Euro. Indeed Nissan and Sony moved to the Euro for EU operations from 1999.

The Euro as an international currency

One of the major attractions of EMU for EU states is that they can escape the implications of the US administration's attitude of 'benign neglect' towards the Dollar. Because the US is a largely self-contained single market and the source of many of its own raw materials, swings in the value of the dollar have little impact on US inflation (whereas rapid changes in smaller EU currencies tend to have a much more marked effect upon output). Whether the EU can escape this depends upon the ability of the Euro to emerge as an international currency to rival the dollar.

The growth of the unified capital market within the EU and the reputation for stability of the Euro, should lead to its use as a reserve currency (that is, it will be used widely to finance international trade and other international currency transactions). The emergence of the Euro as an international reserve currency is not expected to be rapid due to the lead of the dollar in this area. Nearly half of the world's foreign-held bank deposits are in dollars and half of global trade is invoiced in this currency. That this will be challenged by the Euro cannot be questioned, but it is unclear how quickly the hegemony of the dollar can be overcome. In part, this will be determined by the pegging strategies of third countries. Many in the CFA zone and CEE states will shadow the Euro. Many Asian states, despite recent crises, continue to shadow the dollar. The large economic base of the Euro and the elimination of transaction costs (associated with multiple exchange rates) will no doubt increase the use of the Euro as a unit of account in international trade flows, especially with developing and transition states.

There can be little doubt that the emergence of the Euro is going to signal a big change within the international monetary system. In terms of its international weight, the Euro will be second only to the dollar; the combined GDP of the eleven Euro members is roughly the same as that of the US but their share of international trade is larger (30 per cent as opposed to 27 per cent for the US). The Euro's status as a popular and widely used reserve currency will depend upon its ability to gain the confidence of global capital markets. This depends upon its ability to present itself as a risk-free currency. If the ECB (via attaining anti-inflationary credibility) can achieve this, then it will inspire markets to adopt the Euro. However this has to be balanced against the fact that the Euro, as an international reserve currency, is untested. Therefore capital markets may be hesitant to use it especially where they are accustomed to using the dollar.

One of the reasons for the creation of the Euro was that many of the privileges that the US gets from dollar hegemony would be enjoyed by EU states. These benefits include the ability to borrow without limit in its own currency (enabling it to run unlimited current account deficits) and leadership of the international monetary system. However there is a fear that the emergence of two rival currencies could destabilise the international monetary system if both operate policies that ignore the value of the exchange rate in favour of domestic objectives. The result could be competitive depreciations between these currencies leading to trade disputes. Additionally, if both the US and EU's Eurozone members do operate a benign neglect policy in relation to exchange rates, this could spell turmoil for other states whose policies are based upon shadowing one or other of these currencies. In practice, such a scenario is unlikely as no state (or states) can afford to ignore exchange rate policy totally. However to avoid the possibility of such problems occurring within the international monetary system, renewed international co-ordination will clearly be needed.

CONCLUSION

Whilst there may be ambiguities over whether EMU will deliver the anticipated benefits to the European economy that are expected of it, EMU will happen and enterprises have to respond. Few business functions will be unaffected by its development. In the years, leading up to 2002, many of Europe's leading enterprises are developing strategies to adopt the new currency. Importantly the interdependence between EU states means that those enterprises within states that are not part of the initial moves towards EMU must also develop appropriate strategies. Consolidation of the economic power of European business reflected within the moves towards EMU should enable greater non-tangible benefits for EU business in terms of leverage within global markets. This is important, for the true impact of EMU upon European business will be felt in terms of its ability to enhance internal competition as a precursor for enterprises to operate more successfully within global markets.

↘ KEY POINTS

- **EMU represents the biggest challenge facing European business over the coming years.**

- **States, to qualify for membership, have had to meet certain specified convergence criteria.**

- **Most aspects of an enterprise's operation are going to be affected by the advent of the Euro.**

- **The advent of the Euro is also going to challenge the Dollar as the cornerstone of the international monetary system.**

SUGGESTED FURTHER READING

Britton, A. and Mayes, D. (1992) *Achieving Monetary Union in Europe*, Sage.

The Economist (1998) 'An Awfully Big Adventure: a Survey of EMU', 11 April.

European Commission/DG II (1997) *Round Table upon the Practical Aspects of the Changeover to the Euro*, Workshop, 11 June.

Financial Times (1997) 'Economic and Monetary Union: Europe Prepares', 21 November.

Financial Times (1998) 'Economic and Monetary Union: a Survey', 23 March.

Funke, N. and Kennedy, M. (1997) *The International Implications of European Economic and Monetary Union*, Economics Departments, Working paper No. 174, OECD, Paris.

Steinherr, A. and Gros, D. (1994) *From EMS to EMU*, Longman.

Note: Details upon the practical aspects of the transition to EMU can be found upon a number of Internet sites, notably the Association for Monetary Union In Europe at
http://www.aume.if.net

17

EUROPEAN BUSINESS IN
A GLOBAL CONTEXT

European firms encounter a multitude of obstacles abroad of a very different nature. There-fore, in addition to carrying out adequate policies to promote the international competitiveness of European industry, the Community must strive to achieve improved market access in third countries in parallel to the continued progressive opening of its own market, both by ensuring the full implementation by its partners of their Uruguay Round obligations and through other market access actions.

(The Global Challenge of International Trade: A Market Access Strategy for the
European Union, COM (96) 53)

Although practice has not always matched the rhetoric, the thrust of trade policy within multilateral negotiations since the end of the Second World War has been to free up the trading system. Successive rounds of tariff reductions have isolated and highlighted other obstacles to trade and have given rise to moves to extend the liberalisation of trade in goods to services, agriculture and a range of non-tariff barriers. In turn, this opening up of cross-border exchange is in the process of spilling over into a range of new issues demanding attention at an international level, such as the link between trade and the environment and the difficulty of regulating competition when companies are increasingly operating across the boundaries of both national and European competition authorities. The European Union continues to be one of the prime movers behind freer trade and more open economies, a tendency which is completely in line with the currently dominant neo-liberal economic philosophy, and which also parallels developments in the EU's domestic market and is fuelling the trend towards greater interdependence of global markets (see Chapter 1).

  This chapter addresses these issues by first highlighting the main features of the EU's strategy for improving the access of European business to third country markets, a strategy which was first explicitly articulated in 1996 and which is having a marked effect on the direction and focus of EU external economic policy, both bilaterally and multilaterally. The following section outlines the EU's position as an economic actor in global terms and the changing structure of its external economic ties. This analysis provides both an explanatory framework for subsequent discussion of EU external economic policy and a snapshot of the external environment in which European business must develop its strategy. The next section highlights the main external policy instruments at the EU's disposal. A central plank of EU policy is the complex range of bilateral arrangements it maintains with third parties. These arrangements and their implications are examined in general terms, followed by a more in-depth discussion of one set of preferential arrangements – the evolving partnership between the European Union and twelve Mediterranean countries. This is followed by an example of a key non-preferential link – that with the United States, one of the EU's most important external economic partners and one with which there is a history of disputes. The chapter then examines the EU's role within the multilateral framework provided first by the General Agreement on Tariffs and Trade (GATT) and later by its successor body, the World Trade Organisation (WTO) and how the latter's agenda is evolving. The chapter concludes by drawing together these separate strands and by assessing their impact on European business.

OPENING MARKETS FOR EUROPEAN BUSINESS

Greater openness in the global trading system has exposed European firms to more competition than ever before in their domestic market and is creating opportunities for them to compete more effectively in overseas markets. The goals of internal and external EU policy are converging as external policy increasingly focuses on improving market access for EU firms in third countries, including traditional SEM issues such as technical standards and service liberalisation.

In 1996, the Commission announced its new Market Access Strategy (MAS) which explicitly reflects these trends. The MAS does not represent a major change in the underlying approach of the EU's external economic policy, but it does imply a more systematic and co-ordinated use of existing policy instruments and resources. The guiding principles of the MAS are to concentrate the EU's international economic relations efforts on improving the climate in which European firms operate – principles which are entirely consistent with general EU economic policy and with the objectives of the SEM. This is to be achieved by creating opportunities for Community firms to compete in third country markets on equal terms with other businesses. The benefits of open markets arise, according to the Commission, from increased competition, which in turn boosts competitiveness and generates additional growth and jobs. This additional liberalisation, interdependence and competition requires constant adjustments from business in terms of strategies for investment, networking, sourcing, financing, etc. – adjustments which were also necessitated on a less global scale by the SEM and related policies.

The MAS is based on the assumption that European firms face many and various obstacles in third country markets. Its overall objectives, therefore are to adopt a 'more systematic, coherent and pro-active approach' to the negotiation and enforcement of trade deals and rules and to place greater emphasis on the aim of opening third country markets. More specifically, the MAS will pursue the following goals:

- the compliance of trading partners with their obligations arising out of WTO agreements. Implementation and enforcement of WTO obligations extends beyond tariff reductions into issues such as service liberalisation and intellectual property rights. Successful achievement of this goal also requires strict compliance of the EU with its WTO obligations;
- the full exploitation of existing market opening instruments. Subsequent sections demonstrate the role that the Trade Barriers Regulation (TBR) and bilateral relations can play in this respect;

- action against other barriers to cross-border economic flows which do not fall into the traditional category of 'trade barrier'. These barriers include discriminatory national investment or competition laws. The Community is actively promoting the introduction of rules to reduce and eliminate such barriers;
- the provision of information to businesses about the possibilities offered by existing instruments to press for greater market opening.

The Commission can choose to pursue its market opening objectives bilaterally or multilaterally. In view of its role as the world's largest trading partner, the EU has a strong interest in strengthening multilateral provisions. However, this is complex and can be extremely time-consuming, leading to a role for bilateral actions in the interim. Bilateral actions can take the form of ad hoc country and country–sector specific negotiations, visits, more comprehensive agreements with individual countries or regional trade group-ings and use of the TBR. More specifically, the bilateral agenda includes:

- the identification of trade barriers: the Commission has set up an on-line Market Access Database which contains details of known trade barriers and which relies on information provided by European business. This information is then used as a resource in determining where and how market access initiatives should occur. The maintenance and availability of the database is part of a broader Commission strategy of creating closer co-operation with industry;
- identification of the most coherent opportunities for the elimination of trade barriers, including the establishment of priorities and selection of appropriate instruments;
- improved coherence between bilateral and multilateral approaches and their co-ordination with other initiatives such as the promotion of industrial co-operation and technical assistance;
- improved co-ordination of market opening activities by the Commission, member states, business and Commission delegations.

The main multilateral forum is the WTO, but others, such as the OECD, the Energy Charter Treaty, the International Maritime Organisation, the International Civil Aviation Organisation, etc. also provide opportunities for further market opening. Specific multilateral objectives include:

- consolidation of the Uruguay Round acquis and its implementation;
- more extensive market opening in areas already subject to multilateral rules and the identification of new areas suitable for market opening: sectors regarded as ripe for such action include financial services, basic telecommunications, maritime transport, services generally and government procurement;
- responses to the challenges raised by globalisation, particularly in the areas of cross-border investment, regulation of competition and the links between trade and the environment and trade and labour conditions.

As noted, the MAS does not represent a radical new departure for EU external economic policy but it does herald a consolidation and intensification of existing efforts and codifies them within a consistent framework. As a result of the early operations of MAS, the Commission intends to draw up detailed reports, using its market access data base, on particular types of barriers, including those relating to intellectual property rights, stan-dards and certification and trade-related investment measures with a view to developing strategies to reduce and eventually eliminate them.

THE EU AS A GLOBAL ECONOMIC ACTOR

Recent figures both demonstrate the extent of the EU's economic power and emphasise the importance to European traders of effective bilateral and multilateral negotiation on their behalf by the European Commission. Despite containing only 6.5 per cent of the world's population, in 1997 the EU accounted for 28 per cent of world GDP, 19.7 per cent of world merchandise exports and 17.8 per cent of world merchandise imports (see Table 17.1). The inclusion of intra-EU trade in world trade figures raises the share of EU trade in the world total to 40 per cent for exports and almost 38 per cent for imports.

Table 17.1 also shows a significant decline in the EU (15)'s share in both exports and imports between 1960 and 1997. This fall represents both a steady increase in intra-EU trade (intra-EU exports grew from almost 50 per cent to 63 per cent of total EU exports between 1960 and 1996 and intra-EU imports grew from 46 per cent to almost 64 per cent over the same period) as European integration has widened and deepened and a stronger trade performance by several Asian countries has taken place.

One of the major changes in the economic structures of the advanced industrial economies during recent decades has been the relative decline of the manufacturing sector and the growing strength of the service sector which accounted for two-thirds of the EU's

Table 17.1 World's top 20 merchandise traders in 1997, excluding intra-EU trade

Share of world exports (%)

	1960	1997		1960	1997
European Union (15)	29.3	19.7	United States	18.0	20.8
United States	24.9	16.5	European Union (15)	31.1	17.8
Japan	4.7	10.1	Japan	4.6	7.8
Canada	7.1	5.1	Hong Kong, China	1.1	4.8
Hong Kong, China	0.8	4.5	Canada	6.5	4.7
China	—	4.4	South Korea	0.3	3.3
South Korea	0.0	3.3	China	—	3.3
Singapore	0.2	3.0	Singapore	0.5	3.1
Taiwan	n.a.	2.9	Taiwan	n.a.	2.6
Mexico	0.9	2.6	Mexico	1.2	2.6
Malaysia	—	1.9	Malaysia	—	1.8
Switzerland	2.3	1.8	Switzerland	2.5	1.8
Russia	—	1.6	Australia	2.5	1.5
Australia	2.4	1.5	Brazil	1.6	1.5
Thailand	0.4	1.4	Thailand	0.5	1.5
Saudi Arabia	—	1.3	Russia	—	1.1
Indonesia	0.7	1.3	Turkey	0.5	1.1
Brazil	1.5	1.3	Poland	—	1.0
Norway	1.1	1.1	Indonesia	0.7	1.0
India	1.6	0.8	India	2.5	0.9
Total top 20		86.1	Total top 20		84.0

Source: World Trade Organisation and Eurostat

GDP by the mid-1990s. The increasing importance of services is also reflected in trade figures: in 1997, world exports of commercial services totalled $1.3 trillion in 1997, compared to $5.3 trillion for merchandise exports. EU service exports comprised 38.6 per cent of the total (that is, just over $500 billion) and four out of the world's top five service exporters were EU members (see Table 17.2). These factors help explain why the European Union has been at the forefront of efforts to promote the liberalisation of services within the framework of multilateral organisations.

Since the EU's formation, trade with other industrialised nations has remained strong, reflecting the growth of intra-industry trade, and is represented in Table 17.3 by trade with NAFTA, the destination for about 20 per cent of EU exports in both 1960 and 1996, and EFTA. In recent years, there has been a significant increase in both exports to and imports from Central and Eastern European countries – a result of the transition process and the re-direction of trade towards the west. Increases in trade shares have also occurred with the rapidly growing economies of Japan and Asia which, from being also-rans in 1960, were not far behind North America as a destination for EU exports and a

Table 17.2 World's top 20 traders in commercial services, 1997

Share of world exports (%)		Share of world imports (%)	
United States	17.8	United States	12.0
United Kingdom	6.5	Japan	9.7
France	6.3	Germany	9.2
Germany	5.6	United Kingdom	5.5
Italy	5.5	Italy	5.5
Japan	5.3	France	4.9
Netherlands	3.7	Netherlands	3.4
Spain	3.4	Canada	2.8
Hong Kong, China	2.9	South Korea	2.6
Belgium–Luxembourg	2.6	Belgium–Luxembourg	2.5
Austria	2.4	Austria	2.1
Singapore	2.3	Taiwan	1.9
Canada	2.3	Spain	1.9
South Korea	2.2	China	1.9
Switzerland	1.8	Hong Kong, China	1.8
China	1.8	Sweden	1.6
Australia	1.5	Australia	1.5
Sweden	1.3	Singapore	1.5
Taiwan	1.3	Russia	1.4
Denmark	1.3	Thailand	1.4
EU* (intra and extra exports)	38.6	EU* (intra and extra imports)	36.6
Total top 20	77.8	Total top 20	75.1

Source: World Trade Organisation

Note: * EU figures slightly under-estimate EU's actual shares as only EU service providers inside the top 20 are included

Table 17.3 Extra-EU export and import shares by main trading partners, 1960–96 (%)

	Exports				Imports		
	1960	*1980*	*1996*		*1960*	*1980*	*1996*
ACP	10.2	8.5	3.0	ACP	10.3	7.7	3.8
Mediterranean Basin	12.5	12.3	11.6	Mediterranean Basin	6.3	7.9	8.5
DAE*	4.4	6.4	16.9	DAE*	4.3	10.4	18.9
OPEC	11.9	19.5	6.9	OPEC	15.2	29.0	7.8
NAFTA	20.5	17.1	20.9	NAFTA	29.3	21.2	21.9
EFTA	11.6	15.5	11.6	EFTA	6.5	9.8	12.9
CEE	5.2	7.1	11.3	CEE	4.2	4.3	8.6
Latin America	10.0	7.0	5.7	Latin America	11.0	6.5	5.2
Rest of world	13.7	6.6	12.1	Rest of world	12.9	3.2	12.4

Source: Eurostat

Note: * DAE = Dynamic Asian Economies, including Japan and the Asian tigers

source of EU imports in 1996. However, in view of the Asian economic crisis, it is unlikely Asia will overtake North America as Europe's leading trade partner in the short term at least.

The gains in trade share by Central and Eastern European and Asian countries were largely at the expense of raw material producers, many of which are among the poorest of the developing countries and are highly vulnerable to sudden shifts in commodity prices. The African Caribbean Pacific countries (largely ex-colonies of EU member states) the major beneficiaries of EU development policy, have declined significantly as a source of EU imports, both as a percentage of EU imports and in real terms, raising questions about the long term effectiveness of current development policies, including the EU's preferential trade regime. Latin American countries have also not fared well. OPEC's declining trade share is a reflection of the ups and more recently downs of the oil markets. In 1980, at the time of high real oil prices, OPEC accounted for 29 per cent of extra-EU imports and nearly 20 per cent of EU exports as the oil producers pushed ahead with heavy capital spending to fuel ambitious development plans. By 1996, when oil prices had returned to historically low real levels and oil production was spread more widely throughout the globe, OPEC's share in EU trade dropped massively.

The power of commodity prices is also shown in the structure of EU trade by product (see Table 17.4). The EU is traditionally an exporter of manufactured products and an importer of raw materials. However, specialisation in manufactures has intensified, both in imports and exports, partly as a result of growth in intra-industry trade. This trend is particularly pronounced on the import side, where raw materials accounted for only 28 per cent of EU imports in 1996, compared to 53 per cent in 1980, a fall which was once more largely attributable to lower oil prices.

As discussed in Chapter 1, flows of foreign direct investment (FDI) have increased more rapidly than trade in recent decades. Much of this activity is concentrated within OECD countries and a handful of Asian economies. Indeed, much of the FDI within the European Union is intra-EU in nature as firms seek to adjust to the opportunities and challenges of the SEM. However, that is not the whole story. Significant amounts of FDI by EU members takes place in third countries, a factor which underpins pressure to

Table 17.4 Extra-EU import and export shares by product (%)

	Export		Import		1996 trade balance (ECU bn)
	1980	*1996*	*1980*	*1996*	
Raw materials	14.6	11.2	53.1	28.0	−92.6
Food	7.9	6.6	9.3	7.9	−4.5
Raw materials (excl. fuel)	1.8	2.1	9.6	6.4	−23.9
Fuel products	4.9	2.5	34.3	13.7	−64.2
Manufactures	71.0	87.5	32.1	69.3	143.5
Chemicals	9.3	12.9	3.8	7.7	35.7
Machinery, transport	33.5	45.2	11.6	32.3	94.6
Other manufactures	28.1	29.4	16.7	29.3	13.2
Not elsewhere specified	14.4	1.3	14.8	2.7	−7.5

Source: Eurostat

develop investment protection rules at international level. EU FDI is mostly focused in developed countries, reflecting their greater stability which helps explain why EU FDI assets in 1995 were greater in Australia than in Central and Eastern Europe (see Table 17.5) where instability and risk resulted in increasing, but nonetheless disappointing, levels of FDI (see Chapter 15).

PRINCIPLES AND INSTRUMENTS OF EU TRADE POLICY

Articles 110–116 of the Treaty of Rome set out the principles of the Common Commercial Policy (CCP) and provide the starting point for analysis of the EU's external economic relations. Their aim was to establish the principles and provide the legal base for the formulation of a common trade policy and their presence in the Treaty was essential to the attainment of the objectives of creating a customs union and ultimately a common market. Article 110 set out the basic principles of the CCP:

> By establishing a customs union between themselves Member States aim to contribute, in the common interest, to the harmonious development of world trade, the progressive abolition of restrictions on international trade and the lowering of customs barriers.
>
> The common commercial policy shall take into account the favourable effect which the abolition of customs duties between Member States may have on the increase in the competitive strength of undertakings in those States.

Article 110 encapsulates key features of subsequent Community policy, in both internal and external integration. It highlights the impact of the creation of the customs union on the competitive strength of enterprises in member states, foreshadowing many of the arguments surrounding the creation of the SEM in the 1980s (see Chapters 2 and 3). Moreover, it embodies the fundamental principles of a liberal free trade system, emphasising the principles of 'harmonious development', 'the progressive abolition of restrictions on international trade' and 'the lowering of customs barriers' – principles which have permeated the development of GATT and subsequently the WTO.

Table 17.5 Portrait of FDI

1 1985–95 top 20 host economies for FDI, cumulative inflows ($ billion)

United States	477.5	Singapore	40.8
United Kingdom	199.6	Sweden	37.7
France	138.0	Italy	36.3
China	130.2	Malaysia	30.7
Spain	90.9	Germany	25.9
Belgium-Luxembourg	72.4	Switzerland	25.2
Netherlands	68.1	Argentina	23.5
Australia	62.6	Brazil	20.3
Canada	60.9	Hong Kong	17.9
Mexico	44.1	Denmark	15.7

2 EU FDI assets and liabilities by key partners, 1995

	Assets	*Liabilities*	*Net*
Extra-EU	417.91	366.87	105.04
United States	207.18	188.31	18.87
Switzerland	45.41	72.35	−26.94
Australia	20.97	9.88	11.09
Brazil	17.06	0.88	16.18
Canada	17.02	11.13	5.89
Japan	11.05	28.16	−17.11

3 EU FDI assets in emerging markets, 1995

	Central and Eastern Europe	*MERCOSUR*	*ASEAN*
EU	14.75	24.10	20.58
Denmark	0.36	n.a.	0.57
Germany	5.43	n.a.	2.76
France	1.18	4.13	1.27
Netherlands	1.25	2.69	4.20
Austria	2.53	n.a.	0.05
Finland	0.07	0.09	0.09
United Kingdom	0.60	3.57	10.52

: not available

Source: Eurostat and World Trade Organisation

Article 113 sets out the broad guiding rule that:

the common commercial policy shall be based on uniform principles, particularly in regard to changes in tariff rates, the conclusion of tariff and trade agreements, the achievement of uniformity in measures of liberalisation, export policy and measures to protect trade such as those to be taken in case of dumping or subsidies.

Uniformity of approach is necessary to preserve the integrity of the customs union and the single market. It also gives the Community, as the world's biggest trading bloc, much greater bargaining power in international trade negotiations than if individual member states were acting independently.

Article 113 also provides a good example of the continuing struggle between the centralisation of European institutions and member states. The European Commission's competence and pre-eminence in the formulation of trade policy relating to goods and the negotiation of trade agreements with third parties, has generally been accepted by member states who nevertheless, subject to strong pressure from national interest groups, argue their own points vociferously within the Council of Ministers when debating the terms of negotiating mandates to be given to the Commission. A 1994 decision by the European Court of Justice confirmed the exclusive competence of the Commission to negotiate agreements relating to trade in goods in matters of both tariffs and non-tariff barriers but determined that competence was shared between member states and Community institutions in negotiations relating to services and intellectual property. In practice, member states accepted the Commission as sole negotiator at the Uruguay Round in issues of mixed competence but without prejudice on the competence issue.

Efforts to extend formal Community competence in external commercial negotiations in line with the lengthening of the external economic agenda have met with limited success. Chapter 10 discusses the resistance encountered by the Commission in its so far unsuccessful attempts to persuade member states to grant it exclusive competence in the negotiation of airline agreements with third countries. The Commission's strong arguments about the need for a unified approach to protect the integrity of the single aviation market have so far taken second place to the wish of member states to retain competence in this area. Similarly, efforts to grant the EU exclusive competence in services and intellectual property within the Amsterdam Treaty were unsuccessful and the status quo set out in the 1994 ECJ decision was confirmed.

The Common External Tariff

The Common External Tariff (CET) lies at the heart of the CCP and is its most well-established and visible element. A customs union, as opposed to a looser free trade area arrangement, requires its members to adopt common tariffs. Without common tariffs, third countries would be able to by-pass the higher tariffs involved in exporting to certain parts of the union by exporting to the lowest tariff member and then re-exporting the goods within the customs union area, where internal trade is tariff-free, to the final destination.

Eight successive rounds of trade liberalisation talks within the GATT framework have systematically reduced the MFN average tariff on industrial imports into the European Union to 4.9 per cent in 1997. The 1997 WTO interim review of EU trade policy anticipates a further fall in such tariffs to below 3 per cent by 2000. Average figures, however, hide many variations in the tariffs levelled against EU imports. Many goods, especially raw materials and semi-manufactures, enter the European Union duty-free and are relatively free of non-tariff barriers. In addition, a further significant proportion of imports enter the European Union duty-free under the terms of preferential trading agreements (see below). Other more sensitive products where EU producers are particularly vulnerable to competition from overseas producers (for example, clothing, cars, footwear, consumer electronics and iron and steel) attract tariffs of 10 per cent, 20 per cent or more and also tend to be the subject of other measures such as anti-dumping duties and are excluded from the preferential elements of trade agreements.

Agricultural products fall under the remit of the Common Agricultural Policy (CAP) which operates on the principle of Community preference, resulting in high tariffs and other import restricting measures on food products. This approach was strongly attacked during the Uruguay Round, resulting in tariffication of non-tariff barriers to agricultural trade with a view to progressive removal of such tariffs. In 1995, EU agricultural tariffs averaged 25 per cent, falling to 20.8 per cent in 1997. Multilateral talks on trade in agricultural products are scheduled to recommence by the turn of the century and further tariff cuts can be expected as a result.

Anti-dumping duties

Dumping occurs when goods are sold in an export market below a 'normal value' (usually interpreted as the price at which the good is sold on the home market), giving exporters an unfair competitive advantage and causing damage to producers located in the export market. In order to combat such irregularities, the EU has devised its own rules and procedures, in line with the WTO Anti-Dumping code, which enable it to impose anti-dumping duties for up to five years on dumped imports which cause significant injury to Community producers.

Anti-dumping duties have proved to be a popular defence against imports for EU companies, particularly in the sectors of process materials, chemicals, textile yarns and fabrics and electronic and electrical products. At any one time since the late 1980s, between 135 and 150 EU anti-dumping duties have been in force, largely aimed at high tech producers from Japan and the Newly Industrialising Countries and against low cost producers in the rest of Asia. The 1997 WTO interim review of EU trade policy noted an increase in the number of measures in force during the preceding two years, affecting textile products in particular, but also noted a trend towards fewer initiations of investigations. Although developed as a device to ensure fair trading practices, anti-dumping duties themselves are open to abuse, particularly in the way dumping margins are determined – a charge which has been levelled at the Commission on occasion.

Voluntary export restraints

A voluntary export restraint (VER) occurs when an exporter 'voluntarily' agrees to limit its exports to the importing country. Such measures have been used extensively within the Community against Japanese and other Asian products such as ball bearings, forklift trucks, machine tools, machinery products, video recorders and, most notably, on Japanese cars. Such measures are incompatible with WTO rules and are to be phased out. Since national car quotas were replaced by an EU-level VER in the early 1990s, the European market situation and the attitude of European car manufacturers have changed. Japanese car production in Europe has expanded dramatically and, with Toyota's 1997 announcement that it intends to build a second European plant in northern France, looks set to continue to rise. European car manufacturers, although mindful of the European market situation, are pressing not so much for an extension of limits on Japanese car imports but for access to overseas markets, particularly in Asia.

The Trade Barriers Regulation

The TBR, which came into effect on 1 January 1995, empowers EU companies and industries to take action through EU institutions against trade measures which adversely affect their access to third country markets. The TBR offers more possibilities than its predecessor, the New Commercial Policy Instrument (NCPI) which was introduced in 1984 to match Section 301 of the US Trade Act (see below) but which was rarely invoked and which suffered from the weakness of the GATT dispute settlement machinery. Early indications are that the TBR will be much more widely used and influential than the NCPI. Case Study 17.1 gives examples of utilisation of the TBR mechanism.

The TBR is intended to ensure that European business benefits from the rights which it has gained through international and bilateral agreements. It also applies to what are commonly referred to as 'non-violations', that is, practices which are not strictly illegal but which nevertheless constitute barriers to trade. Unlike other trade policy instruments such as anti-dumping duties or VERs, the TBR is not confined to defence of the EU's domestic market but is intended to help Europe's enterprises exploit market opportunities outside its borders and as such is a key component of the Market Access Strategy.

Two types of complaint are possible. The first occurs when a firm, group of firms or industry association submit a complaint to the European Commission on the grounds that their trading activities in a third country are suffering as a result of trade obstacles or that there is a threat of future damage. In addition to injuring a company, the trade effects must also have a negative impact on the Union's economy or on one of its regions or industrial sectors to justify action. The second complaint cannot be made by an individual company but must be lodged by a trade association or equivalent and relate to a situation in which the trade barrier affects trade on the EU's home market, leading to financial loss, redundancies, lack of investment or a surge in imports or fall in exports. Member states can lodge a complaint in both cases.

Upon receipt of the complaint, the Commission has forty-five days to determine whether there are sufficient grounds to mount a full investigation. If so, the Commission will report on the result of its inquiries within five to seven months. Upon establishing the existence of a trade barrier contrary to international rules and that injury or adverse effects have been experienced by a Community company or industry, the Commission first opens talks with the country concerned to try to find an amicable resolution of the problem. If this proves impossible, the Commission will probably bring a case under the WTO dispute settlement procedure or other appropriate mechanism. If the dispute settlement body finds in the EU's favour but the country concerned fails to comply with the decision, the Union can take retaliatory measures.

CASE STUDY 17.1   THE TRADE BARRIERS REGULATION IN ACTION

Chile and fish

July 1998: the Commission announces it is to investigate whether Chile's treatment of fish imports is in line with the WTO Agreement on Sanitary and Phytosanitary Measures. This follows complaints from Spanish fishermen that Chile discriminates against foreign trawlers unloading fish in its ports and imposes burdensome certification procedures on all fish products entering its customs territory, even if they are not for sale in the Chilean market. This forces trawlers to make a six day journey to unload in Peruvian ports which raises costs and reduces the competitiveness of the catches of Spanish vessels in the Community and third country markets.

South Korea and cosmetics

May 1998: the Commission decided there are sufficient grounds to launch an inquiry into Korean import restrictions on cosmetic products following a complaint by Colipa, the European cosmetic industry trade association, relating to certification and advertising rules that are more binding on foreign than on local products. Colipa is also considering filing a complaint against China which it believes is planning to exclude cosmetics from the chemicals customs classification when it joins the WTO, enabling China to impose higher tariffs on cosmetics than those negotiated for chemicals.

US: 1916 US Anti-dumping Act

1997–8: following complaints by Eurofer, Europe's iron and steel lobby, in response to a law suit filed in Utah by US company Geneva Steel Corporation against Thyssen Steel Corporation under the 1916 US Anti-dumping Act, the Commission announced that it intends to lodge a formal complaint against the Act at the WTO on the grounds that it infringes the WTO Anti-dumping Agreement.

Brazil: textiles and clothing

March 1998: the Commission launches an investigation into trade obstacles facing EU exports of textiles and clothing to Brazil following complaints about Brazil's textile import licensing procedures, especially compulsory import payment terms and minimum import prices. The Commission is already using the TBR to investigate complaints against trade obstacles facing European exports of cognac and flat steel to Brazil.

US rules of origin for textile products

1997: the Commission challenged the US within the WTO over rules that classified Italian scarves, German furnishings or British cotton goods as 'Made in China' or 'Made in India' on the grounds that the raw material came from these countries, even if the articles in question had been cut, bleached, dyed, printed, etc. in Europe. The Commission feared the rules could damage European designers by resulting in the imposition of quotas or by undermining the marketability of top European labels. The WTO complaint was withdrawn by the EU following agreement by the US to change the rules.

PREFERENTIAL AGREEMENTS

The EU maintains a complex and changing hierarchy of preferential trading agreements with third countries (see Box 17.1). The choice of partners has usually been determined by proximity and mutual benefits in terms of growth and economic stability (for example, free trade agreements with EFTA members, the Europe Agreements with countries in Central and Eastern Europe and the Euro-Mediterranean Partnership) or by long-standing ties with former colonies. Since 1990, many assumptions about external relations have been overturned, forcing the EU to refashion its relationships: three former EFTA countries, for example, have become EU members, leaving only Iceland, Norway and Liechtenstein within the European Economic Area. The changes in Central and

Eastern Europe following the disintegration of the former Soviet Union resulted in a total overhaul of EU relations with these countries and the negotiation of extensive agreements which range far beyond trade issues in recognition of the mutual interest of both sides in a flourishing Central and Eastern Europe and in preparation for eventual EU enlargement.

BOX 17.1 MAIN EU PREFERENTIAL AGREEMENTS

European Economic Area (EEA): Norway, Ireland, Liechtenstein

Free trade area (FTA); from 1 January 1994 most benefits of SEM extended to EEA.

Turkey

1963 EC–Turkey Association agreement (but shortly afterwards suspended). From 1996, customs union for industrial products and limited agricultural concessions.

Switzerland

FTA signed in 1972. 1992 referendum turned down membership of EEA. Negotiations with EU on transit, agricultural trade, public procurement, labour markets, etc.

Europe agreements: Bulgaria, Czech Republic, Estonia, Hungary, Latvia, Lithuania, Poland, Romania, Slovak Republic and Slovenia

Associate status: abolition of EU tariffs and quotas on most industrial goods – those on sensitive sectors (steel, textiles, clothing) removed by end 1997. Some concessions for agricultural trade. CEE countries have up to ten years to remove their barriers. Also covers political co-operation in many other areas of economic relations (see Chapter 15) and are part of the pre-accession strategy.

Mediterranean countries: Algeria, Cyprus, Egypt, Israel, Jordan, Lebanon, Malta, Morocco, Palestine, Syria, Tunisia, Turkey

For all above except Israel (FTA with EU since 1975) and Turkey, Cyprus and Malta (customs unions with EU), non-reciprocal free access to EU for raw materials, most industrial products and some agricultural trade. Also trade, economic, financial and technical co-operation. Relaunch of EU relations with above Mediterranean (12) under the umbrella of the Euro-Mediterranean Partnership: FTA planned by 2010 with closer political co-operation and financial assistance.

Partnership and co-operation agreements: Russia and the CIS – Ukraine, Moldova, Kyrygystan, Belarus, Kazakhstan, Georgia, Armenia and Azerbaijan

Economic concessions and political dialogue. TACIS assistance.

Lomé IV (1990–2000): seventy developing countries from Africa, the Caribbean and the Pacific

Non-reciprocal tariff-free access for industrial products and agricultural products outside the Common Agricultural Policy (CAP). Limited preferential access for goods within the CAP. Commodity stabilisation schemes – Sysmin and Stabex. Financial aid. EU receives non-preferential, non-discriminatory MFN treatment. Negotiations for renewal/reform of Lomé IV began in late 1998.

Generalised System of Preferences (GSP): 145 developing countries

Autonomous preferences (renewed multi-annually): preferences limited for sensitive products but free access for many industrial products and some agricultural products from the least developed countries. GSP preferences withdrawn when beneficiaries exports exceed 25 per cent of EU imports in specified sectors.

The Euro-Mediterranean partnership

After its initial and understandable preoccupation with its links with the countries of Central and Eastern Europe following the disintegration of the USSR (see Chapter 15), the European Union has begun to pay greater attention to its relationship with the countries of the southern and eastern Mediterranean, namely Algeria, Cyprus, Egypt, Israel, Jordan, Lebanon, Malta, Morocco, Syria, Tunisia, Turkey and the Palestinian Autonomous Territories. The Community is motivated by an assumption that the Mediterranean is of crucial strategic economic and political importance to it and that consolidation of peace and security in the region is a priority.

Co-operation, free trade area and association agreements have long been at the heart of links between the European Union and its Mediterranean neighbours. In October 1994 the Commission relaunched its Mediterranean policy through the creation of the 'Euro-Mediterranean Partnership' (EMP) which is designed to foster free trade, economic integration and closer political and security co-operation between the EU (15) and the Mediterranean (12). Subsequently, there have been extensive discussions between the two sides. The Barcelona Declaration of November 1995 made a commitment to build a free trade area among all twenty-seven nations by 2010 and pledged increased co-operation across a wide range of social, political and economic issues. Support for economic and social reform to promote sustained growth and higher living standards in the Mediterranean region, so the reasoning goes, will help defuse political instability and extremism and decrease pressure for large-scale migration to the European Union. A successful strategy will also create investment and trade opportunities for EU companies, creating a combined market of an estimated 700 million people by the year 2010. Table 17.6 sets out the bilateral trade position.

The financial and economic aspects of the EMP are based around three key, inter-related principles (see Figure 17.1):

- creation of a free trade area by 2010;
- EU support for the economic transition of its Mediterranean partners;
- the need to boost private investment in the Mediterranean Basin.

Trade liberalisation will help improve competitiveness in the region and consequently the process of macro-economic reform and structural adjustment in the Mediterranean

Table 17.6 1997 trade between the EU and the Mediterranean (12)

1 By partner (ECU million)

	EU imports	EU exports		EU imports	EU exports
Algeria	8,370	4,339	Syria	1,995	13,443
Morocco	4,739	5,308	Israel	6,255	11,418
Tunisia	4,005	5,272	Gaza and Jericho	1	37
Egypt	2,575	6,750	Turkey	11,842	22,267
Jordan	172	1,192	Cyprus	373	1,932
Lebanon	151	3,085	Malta	701	1,993
Total	41,181	64,936			

2 By product

	EU Imports		EU Exports	
	ECU million	% of total	ECU million	% of total
Agricultural products	3,896	9.5	4,543	7.0
Fuel products	9,667	23.4	1,516	2.3
Manufactures	23,555	57.2	54,039	83.2
Raw materials and other unspecified goods	4,063	9.9	4,838	7.5
Total	41,181	100.0	64, 936	100

Source: Eurostat

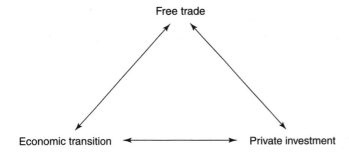

Figure 17.1 The EMP dynamics

countries. Sectoral reforms and technical support from the European Union will help the Mediterranean countries take advantage of the opportunities in the more open trading environment. Open markets will also encourage greater levels of private sector investment, both from within the Mediterranean countries themselves and from the

European corporate sector. To be forthcoming in significant amounts, however, private investors will require the reduction of risk through the negotiation of a suitable legislative and administrative environment and more progress on political stability and security. More private investment will facilitate the process of transition and modernisation which, in turn, will set off a virtual circle, drawing forth more private sector investment.

A key element of the process is the negotiation of new Euro-Mediterranean Association Agreements, EMAs, which go further than the existing agreements with the Maghreb and Mashraq countries which were essentially non-reciprocal (that is, the EU offered these countries access to its markets but did not require them to open their markets in return). The EMAs are reciprocal and extend far beyond purely trade. The precise details of the EMAs vary from partner to partner, but they will all contain certain key common aspects:

- a free trade area, fully compatible with WTO obligations and which will be completed over a transitional period of up to twelve years;
- gradual reduction of customs duties on EU industrial product exports to the Mediterranean partners – the region's industrial exports already benefit from duty-free access to the EU market;
- gradual liberalisation of agricultural trade through the application of preferential access;
- a high level of intellectual property rights;
- gradual liberalisation of trade in services;
- gradual liberalisation of public procurement;
- the inclusion of competition provisions: EMAs negotiated so far, for example, include elements which parallel Articles 85, 86 and 92 of the EU treaties.

In addition a number of cross-regional sectoral initiatives relating to industrial co-operation, the information society, energy and water management have been taken.

The gap between ambitions and achievement in the EMP has so far proved to be wide. The initiative has been dogged with problems and has proved to be a first-rate example of how the formulation and limits of external economic policy are frequently dependent on politics. The second Euro-Mediterranean Ministerial Conference in Malta in April 1997 was effectively paralysed by the stalling of the Middle East peace process. Israel also objects to European Commission proposals to exclude the products of Jewish settlers in Palestinian territory from the Europe–Israel free trade agreement. Continuing tension between Ankara and Athens is holding up some initiatives and the disbursement of funds from the EMP's financial package, MEDA, has been criticised as overly bureaucratic and slow. The result was a relaunch of the EMP at an informal ministerial meeting in Palermo in June 1998 when the participants reasserted their commitment to the original goals of the EMP. The success of this relaunch is by no means assured and will rely on political will and must be judged by its achievements rather than by political declarations. However, both sides have a strong economic interest at least in ensuring the success of the Partnership.

EU-US economic relations

Central as the EU's preferential trading arrangements are to its external economic relations, the EU's links with its single most important economic partner, the United States, are on a non-preferential basis, apart from the granting of each other Most Favoured Nation (MFN) status. In 1996, EU exports and imports to the US totalled ECU 114 billion (18.3 per cent of extra-EU exports) and ECU 112.5 billion respectively (19.4 per cent of extra-EU imports). Similarly, the European Union accounted for 21.2 per cent of US exports and 17.7 per cent of US imports in 1995.

The structure of this trade is dominated by machinery, transport equipment and other manufactured products which alone account for 76 per cent of EU exports to the US and nearly 68 per cent of its imports from the US (see Table 17.7). These figures reflect the increasing importance of intra-industry trade which, according to WTO estimates grew from 39 per cent of EU-US trade in 1980 to 57 per cent in 1995. The growth in intra-industry trade represents specialisation within product categories as producers take advantage of economies of scale and is also partly a result of the stock of FDI each partner maintains in the other's territory. In 1995, the EU had FDI assets of ECU 418 billion in the United States and FDI liabilities of ECU 188 billion – the world's most important bilateral investment relationship.

In view of these figures, the European Union and the United States clearly have a mutual interest in fostering a favourable bilateral trading environment for their enterprises and in creating a benign multilateral trading environment. This process is facilitated by the absence of any long term structural imbalance in the relationship: in 1996, the EU ran a small trade surplus with the United States following a small deficit the year before. This contrasts with the trade relationship with Japan with whom the EU has systematically run large-scale deficits for many years, raising questions about the access of EU companies to the Japanese markets. Nevertheless, despite their common ground, official contacts between the EU and US administrations have been spasmodic and informal with the two sides coming together to resolve numerous trade disputes. In the 1990s initiatives took place to regularise and promote the relationship in a positive manner. Nevertheless, the tensions in the relationship are strong and include, among others, the following concerns:

- *US unilateralism*: the European Union has repeatedly complained about what it regards as the unilateralist trend in US trade policy. Section 301 of the US Trade Act (and the subsequent 'Super 301' and 'Special 301' on intellectual property) authorises the US government to combat practices by foreign governments which the US government deems discriminatory, unjustifiable and burdensome or restrictive on US business. According to the EU, such measures are unilateral in that they rely exclusively on a US interpretation of the trade practices of other countries and cast doubts about the extent of the US commitment to a multilateral system. In addition, the economic power of the

Table 17.7 1996 EU trade with the US as a share of extra-EU trade, by product (%)

	Exports	Imports
Raw materials		
Food	4.4	4.7
Raw materials (excl fuel)	1.1	6.1
Fuel products	3.0	2.1
Manufactures		
Chemicals	12.0	12.6
Machinery, transport	47.9	47.3
Other manufactures	28.0	21.3

Source: Eurostat

US exposes it to criticism of bullying by its trading partners. The EU acknowledges that since the Uruguay Round, the US has resorted more frequently to use of the WTO trade dispute settlement system but, whilst Section 301 remains on the statute books, potential remains for the United States to take unilateral measures which undermines the multilateral trading system. The EU's parallel policy instrument, the TBR, differs from Section 301 in that rather than bilaterally imposing penalties on trading partners for restricting the market access of EU companies, the EU uses the TBR to prise open markets within the multilateral system through making maximum use of the WTO's dispute procedure.

- *Extra-territoriality*: the EU is implacably opposed to the increasing extra-territoriality of US laws (see Case Study 17.2) which manifests itself in a number of fields, including the environment, banking, taxation, export control and economic sanctions directed towards political objectives. The European Union opposes in principle the practice of forcing EU citizens and companies incorporated in the European Union to follow US laws or policies outside US territory. In EU eyes, such practices infringe the sovereignty of partner countries and once more represent an abuse of US power and undermine multilateralism.

- *Public procurement*: the 1933 Buy America Act establishes the general principle of a national purchasing policy, thereby restricting third country exports to the United States. Bilateral negotiations between the EU and the US, the outcome of which has been integrated into the WTO Government Purchasing Agreement, have extended the range of non-discriminatory purchasing but on the US side sub-federal coverage remains incomplete and several sectoral pieces of legislation retain discriminatory purchasing practices. Rows about telecommunications purchasing practices on both sides of the Atlantic have also fuelled procurement disputes.

- *Subsidies*: disputes over subsidies have dogged the EU-US relationship. US allegations of European subsidies to its aerospace industry have been high profile whereas the EU maintains that the US does not comply with WTO rules on the transparency of subsidies by failing to notify all federal schemes and by refusing to notify sub-federal schemes as a matter of principle.

- *Anti-dumping and countervailing duties*: the EU argues that the US 1916 Anti-dumping Act runs counter to the WTO Anti-dumping Agreement and initiated proceedings against it at the WTO Anti-dumping Committee following a complaint under the TBR (see Case Study 17.1).

- *Agriculture*: disagreements about the trade regime for agricultural products almost derailed the Uruguay Round. The US and other agricultural exporters objected to the EU's variable import levies, which effectively restricted access to the European market, and to the EU subsidies granted to its agricultural exports. This practice disrupts world agricultural product markets and was necessitated by the Community's system of price support which encouraged the generation of food surpluses.

- *Tariffs*: despite successive rounds of tariff reduction and low weighted average tariff levels, both the United States and the European Union (see section on policy instruments) retain significant tariffs on selected items. Peak tariffs which the EU would like to see lowered persist in the US food products, textiles, footwear, leather goods, jewellery, ceramics, glass, trucks, watches and clocks and medical and pharmaceutical product sectors.

- *Tax discrimination*: the EU maintains that a number of tax practices at federal and state level discriminate against foreign-owned corporations.

- *Standards*: the US's relatively low use and awareness of international standards and the complexity of standards arrangements in the United States amount to a de facto restriction on market access, argues the European Union. In addition to the WTO

Agreement on Technical Barriers to Trade, the EU and US have also concluded a Mutual Recognition Agreement (covering medical devices, pharmaceuticals telecommunications equipment, electrical safety, electromagnetic compatibility and recreational craft) which is intended to provide some solution to these problems. The partners are also working on regulatory co-operation and on agreements in individual sectors.

A breakthrough in EU-US relations occurred at the EU-US summit in Madrid in 1995 when the New Transatlantic Agenda (NTA) was signed. Rather than the ad hoc arrangements which prevailed previously, this agreement provided a framework for consultation and policy formulation in the following general areas:

- the promotion of peace and stability, democracy and development throughout the world;
- response to global challenges;
- closer economic relations and the expansion of world trade.

The NTA was accompanied by an Action Plan containing 150 actions, ranging from political and economic initiatives to measures to combat AIDS. The Agenda also provided for six monthly summits which bring together the President of the Commission, the President of the Council of Ministers and the US President to discuss progress and set the future agenda.

Working in parallel with the NTA and feeding into the NTA is the Transatlantic Business Dialogue (TABD), a forum in which business representatives from both sides of the Atlantic and EU and US officials discuss issues of common concern. This initiative is essentially business-driven and has the guiding objective of working towards a transatlantic regulatory model based on the principle 'approved once and accepted everywhere'. The TABD provides an opportunity for business to work on detailed technical resolutions to knotty sectoral disputes, to feed into the policy formulation process and to contribute to the process of removing barriers to trade and investment. To date, it has made recommendations on issues such as common standards and mutual recognition agreements, the elimination of tariffs in information technology products, adding to or accelerating tariff cuts and anti-bribery and corruption laws.

A potentially important outcome of the May 1998 EU-US Summit was the agreement on the Transatlantic Economic Partnership (TEP), itself a less ambitious version of a Commission proposal for a New Transatlantic Marketplace that was blocked by France who objected, among other things, to proposals to reduce industrial tariffs to zero by 2010 unless a critical mass of trading partners do the same. The TEP contains both multilateral and bilateral elements, committing the two partners to work together to secure broadly based liberalisation within the WTO and to focus on the removal of bilateral trade barriers, particularly in the following areas:

- technical barriers to trade in goods;
- services;
- agriculture, especially stronger co-operation in human, plant and animal health issues, biotechnology and improved scientific co-operation;
- government procurement via enhanced compatibility of procurement information and government contracting systems;
- intellectual property.

Although closer, more formal ties between the EU and the US are welcome, particularly if they facilitate resolution of damaging bilateral disputes and contribute to the furtherance of multilateralism, there is a danger that their combined economic power and joint actions will ignore or override the legitimate interests of third countries.

CASE STUDY 17.2 TRADE DISPUTE: EXTRA-TERRITORIALITY AND THE HELMS–BURTON AND D'AMATO ACTS

In recent years, there has been a large increase in US sanctions legislation with an extra-territorial reach, both at federal and at state level. Indeed, during the period 1993–6, sixty-one US laws and executive actions involving unilateral economic sanctions for foreign policy purposes aimed at thirty-five different countries were placed on the statute books. Texas, California and Massachusetts, for example, are planning sanctions against Burma. Such actions have created major tensions between the United States and its trading partners. The European Union is leading opposition to two acts with a strong extra-territorial dimension:

- the 1996 Cuba Liberty and Democratic and Solidarity Act, more commonly known as the Helms–Burton Act, which:
  - allows US citizens to sue foreign corporations and individuals using property confiscated by the Castro regime (Title III);
  - requires denial of entry to the United States to individuals and their families who have business dealings in Cuba involving expropriated property subject to a claim by a US citizen. This requirement also applies to individuals working for companies engaged in similar activities (Title IV).
- the 1996 Iran and Libya Sanctions Act (ISLA), also known as the D'Amato Act, which requires the US President to impose penalties on companies which invest more than $20 million in the oil and gas sectors of Iran or Libya.

Critics of Helms–Burton also argue that unilateral sanctions have been in force against Cuba for almost forty years and have proved ineffective in their aim of ousting the Castro regime and have damaged business interests with little effect on anything else. The mere existence of such legislation can modify behaviour: a survey carried out by the European–American Business Council in 1997 concluded that 60 per cent of the European firms surveyed claimed that they had been affected by US sanctions, causing them to reconsider existing activities or shelf plans to explore opportunities in Cuba for fear that their executives would be banned from entering the United States, that their firms would be banned from receiving US imports or that they would be denied licences to export to the United States. Companies participating in the survey identified eighteen cases in which US sanctions had forced them to miss out on business opportunities worth $1.9 billion.

The European Union has actively opposed both acts, regarding them as an unwarranted interference by the United States in the EU's rights to legislate over its own citizens and companies and as against all principles of international law. Accordingly, it has introduced a Regulation which prohibits EU individuals and companies from complying with the Helms–Burton Act and other US legislation with extra-territorial effect. This Regulation places firms in an invidious position, forcing them to choose which law it will be least damaging for them to ignore. A similar act exists in Canada and created a dilemma for Wal-Mart Canada which sold Cuban-made pyjamas in its stores. Faced with a possible $1 million fine under the Helms–Burton Act, the US parent decided to withdraw these garments from its Canadian stores. However, Canada also has a law which forbids companies to comply with the economic laws of other governments and within a short period of time, faced with a fine of over $1 million, Wal-Mart restarted sales of these goods in Canada.

The second element of the EU's opposition involved the filing of a formal complaint with the WTO that Helms–Burton imposes US law upon US trading partners. The potential for the dispute to damage the credibility of the WTO's new dispute settlement system was high following US indications that it did not consider the panel competent to act in a matter which it claimed was primarily one of national security. However, this outcome was diverted by an agreement, firmed up at the May 1998 EU–US Summit, which resulted in the EU suspending its complaint at the WTO provided no actions are taken against EU companies or individuals under this or the D'Amato Act. This agreement was timely given French oil company TOTAL's involvement in a $2 billion deal with Russia's Gazprom and Malaysia's Petronas to develop Iran's massive South Pars gasfield. The removal of the threat of sanctions opens up the possibility of major investment in Iran (which possesses the world's second largest gas reserves and is the third largest global oil exporter) by other European-based oil and gas multinationals who had earlier placed investment decisions in Iran on hold. The stability of this compromise relies particularly on the absence of any major international terrorist incidents which could feasibly be linked to Iran and Libya and the internal dynamics of US politics in terms of a powerful Cuban exile lobby and frequent elections.

THE EUROPEAN UNION AND ITS INTERNATIONAL OBLIGATIONS

The European Union and its member states are members of the WTO and subject to all its agreements. As international economic interdependence and European integration unfolds, so it appears that the European Union is playing a more positive leadership role within the WTO. It has, for example, been leading the calls for a more general round of multilateral trade talks to accompany agriculture and services negotiations scheduled for the end of the century and has been lobbying hard for the consideration of competition policy within the WTO framework.

Although the Community has been committed since its earliest days to a liberal, free trade system, the EU's present positive stance cannot be taken for granted. The architects of the GATT were concerned about potential clashes between regionalism and multi-lateralism. Article XXIV of the GATT set out the regulations which governed the creation of free trade areas and customs unions to limit incompatibilities with a liberal free trade system. These could arise, for example, through trade diversion and the exclusion of erstwhile partners from a particular market as the result of the formation of a customs union or the negotiation of a preferential agreement.

This debate over regionalism and preferential arrangements divides economists. Some argue that regional blocs are discriminatory, offering preferential access to each others' markets while excluding third countries. Moreover, the most powerful participant in an agreement can often impose conditions on their less powerful partners. Supporters of regional and preferential agreements argue that the negotiation of multilateral barrier reductions, although important, is also very complex and time consuming, often resulting in a lowest common denominator outcome. Regional integration and preferential agreements offer the possibility of more rapid liberalisation and attract more members when the benefits of greater openness become apparent. The expanding European Union is an example of this process in action.

Precise assessments of regionalism and preferential agreements are difficult because of the wide variation in their scope and make up. It is perfectly feasible that regionalism could degenerate into clashing groups which undermine the integrity of the multilateral system which has been painstakingly built up over five decades. The benefits of regional integration depend on the extent to which regional blocs become inward looking. If they do so, they could have a generally negative impact upon globalisation. However, from the EU perspective at least, the experience of regional integration and preferential agreements with third countries demonstrates the power of greater market opening. This feature is reinforced as the process of integration spreads and spills over into globalisation.

BOX 17.2 MAIN URUGUAY ROUND OUTCOMES

World Trade Organisation (WTO)

WTO established as successor body to the General Agreement on Tariffs and Trade (GATT) to provide a single, permanent world trade body.

Industrial tariffs

- average tariff cuts by industrial countries of one-third

Agriculture

- tariffication of non-tariff barriers with a view to the eventual reduction of these tariffs
- reduction of domestic farm support, production and export subsidies and import barriers

Textiles and clothing

- incorporation of the Multi-fibre Arrangement into the GATT system by 2005 through the abolition of quotas and reduction of tariffs and non-tariff barriers

Services: General Agreement on Trade in Services (GATS)

- introduction of basic fair trade principles like non-discrimination
- further negotiations on financial services (concluded December 1997)
- restrictive provisions for air transport, labour movement, financial services and tele-communications

Public procurement

- Tokyo Round agreement extended to public utilities, services and procurement by local and regional governments

Investment: trade-related investment measures (TRIMS)

- governments not to make the operation of a foreign company within its borders conditional

Intellectual property rights: trade-related aspects of intellectual property rights (TRIPS)

- measures to protect copyrights, patents and trademarks with longer transition periods for developing countries

Technical barriers

- information exchange regarding technical regulations

Anti-dumping and safeguard measures

- new rules relating to the determination of dumping, the establishment of 'injury' and the dumping investigations themselves and time limits on the use of anti-dumping duties

Subsidies

- agreed list of prohibited subsidies: excludes agriculture, aircraft, regional aid and research and development
- developing countries allowed longer to phase out export subsidies

Dispute settlement

- general tightening up of procedures, including removing of consensual voting, the introduction of stricter time limits and tighter procedures regarding appeals and binding arbitration
- restrictions on unilateral decisions to seek trade remedies outside the multilateral system; for example, Section 301 of the US Trade Act (see above)

It has been noted in several previous chapters that as the global environment has become more interdependent, the rationale behind European integration in specific policy areas is changing to reflect the requirements of internationalising markets. Conversely, as globalisation proceeds, so the drivers behind European integration appear to be replicating themselves in an international context, albeit to a lesser degree given the greater complexity and heterogeneity at world level. This is reflected in the extension of the agenda of the WTO which now goes far beyond its original tariff cutting remit (see Box 17.2). Since the conclusion of the Uruguay Round, new multilateral agreements have been negotiated in telecommunications, information technology and financial services.

Pressure is building for the incorporation of new issues into the WTO framework with the blurring of the demarcation line between trade policy and other economic and social policies – as happened in Europe. Lobbying is taking place for the inclusion of the following issues, in particular, on the WTO agenda:

- *Competition policy*: the pressure for greater WTO action on competition policy is coming from the European Union which views inadequate competition policy in some trading partners as thwarting its market access strategy. In addition, as companies operate increasingly across borders, it is becoming impossible in some cases for traditional competition authorities to exercise appropriate control over potentially damaging practices (see Chapter 6).
- *Environment policy*: the use of environmental protection as a pretext to introduce trade

protecting measures under the guise of environmental protection is causing concern. The link between trade and the environment is receiving attention in a number of fora in an attempt to find ways of incorporating genuine environmental concerns into the world trading system.

- *Labour policy*: the United States has been leading the push to include respect for core labour standards in trade agreements, especially in relation to child and forced labour. Fears over low cost competition have certainly played a role in these campaigns and some developing countries are concerned that labour policy will be used to justify protection.
- *Investment*: OECD efforts to devise tougher rules for the protection of FDI have run into problems and attention has shifted to the WTO as the most appropriate forum for developing such rules.

CONCLUSION

The launch of the single market initiative raised fears among Europe's trading partners of the creation of a 'Fortress Europe'. These fears proved unfounded. The intention of the SEM was not to exclude third countries from the Community's market but to provide a platform for European business to compete in a wider world. Indeed, given the range of initiatives included in it, the original single market programme initially ignored its external implications, not out of design but more as an oversight. In fact there were no precedents for regulating the external dimension of such a huge economic integration programme and the Commission was somewhat taken aback by the response of its trading partners.

However, the persistence of internal obstacles to trade within the European Union occurs more because of the incompleteness of the SEM than because of any protectionist element within the programme itself. This conclusion has been confirmed by successive GATT and WTO reports on the EU's trade policy. The 1997 WTO interim review of EU trade policy highlighted the synergy between the SEM and multilateral liberalisation, claiming:

> the European Union's single market programme and liberalisation under the WTO have generally improved access conditions for the EU's trading partners and increased exposure of the EU economy to international competition and structural change . . . in an increasing number of areas such as the liberalisation of services trade or the harmonisation of standards, the single market process and multilateral liberalisation have been mutually supportive, resulting in improved market access for non-EU suppliers.

The blurring of the distinction between the internal market and the external world has, in some ways, made the SEM an unintentional, and unacknowledged blueprint for changes underway in multilateral talks. This has enabled the European Union to become in many ways the driving force behind the multilateral agenda. The SEM has shown the scope for integrating policy in non-traditional areas such as mutual recognition of standards and liberalisation of the service sectors, both within the EU's preferential agreements and multilateral trade talks.

Globalisation is extending economic interdependence beyond trade into services, investment and creating the rationale for extending the reach of the CCP and for the introduction of cross-border regulation of issues which were previously regulated solely within national borders, such as competition policy. In this respect, European regional integration can be regarded as only one aspect of a much broader process of increased economic interdependence.

⬦ KEY POINTS

- **Although trade remains important, external economic relations now cover a much broader range of issues both bilaterally and multilaterally.**

- **EU external policy objectives increasingly mirror its main internal policy objective – the creation of the optimal operating environment for European firms.**

- **External economic relations frequently inextricably mixed with politics.**

- **Greater international economic interdependence and integration is pushing many new issues onto the multilateral agenda, including issues with which the EU has had to contend as part of its integration process such as competition policy and technical standards.**

SUGGESTED FURTHER READING

European Commission (1996) *The Global Challenge of International Trade: a Market Access Strategy for the European Union*, COM (96) 53.

European Commission (1996) *On Relations Between the European Union and the ACP Countries on the Eve of the 21st century*, Green Paper, COM (96) 570.

European Commission (1996) *WTO Aspects of EU Preferential Trade Agreements with Third Countries*, COM (96) 2168.

European Commission (1997) *The Single Market Review: Foreign Direct Investment*, Vol. IV/1.

European Commission (1997) *The Single Market Review: External Access to European Markets*, Vol. IV/4.

European Commission (1997) *Guidelines for the Negotiation of New Co-operation Agreements with the African, Caribbean and Pacific (ACP) Countries*, COM (97) 537.

Hanson, B. (1998) 'What happened to Fortress Europe? External Trade Policy Liberalization in the European Union', *International Organization*, 52(1), Winter, pp. 55–85.

Heidensohn, K. (1995) *Europe and World Trade*, Pinter.

Keohane, R.O. (1998) 'International Institutions: Can Interdependence Work?', *Foreign Policy*, No. 110, spring, 82–96.

18

EUROPEAN BUSINESS POLICY AND ITS CHANGING ENVIRONMENT

The European business environment combines commercial activities within three, increasingly interdependent domains; the national, the European and the global. It is our central contention that it is increasingly difficult to separate one environment from another: frequently policy actions or commercial strategies within one of these arenas will be justified by or have a direct impact upon enterprise performance in the others. Notably national actions can frequently be expressed in terms of securing success within European or global markets.

Such a broad definition of the European business environment needs to reflect all the pressures which exist upon business within this arena. European business, particularly, within a globalising economy, is not merely about indigenously owned and operated businesses nor about the operations of these enterprises in foreign markets. The European business environment is about the activities of all enterprises (whether indigenously owned or not) in all markets (both European and non-European) insofar as they affect Europe's commercial and socio-economic well-being. This inevitably broad definition encompasses the need to reflect international integration and emerging global inter-dependence as key determinants upon the performance of European business.

Throughout this text we have examined core policies and events within Europe that have affected and will continue to affect the performance of enterprises within the European economy. In line with the definition of the European business environment offered above these policies and events are explored within the national, European and global context on the basis that actions within each arena will affect the performance and corporate strategies within the respective markets within which enterprises operate. In each chapter, the aim is to encourage the reader to consider how policies have impacted upon business performance and/or strategy. This underlines a core theme for each of the policies and processes explored within this text: that is, how do they contribute to the success of business, whether on a sectoral or generic basis, within increasingly international markets. This concern was at the heart of each chapter and was provided to enable the reader to understand why policy has developed in the way that it has. Consequently, the aim of this chapter is to explore these three dimensions of the

European business environment within the context of the policies and themes explored within this text. and to draw some tentative conclusions.

THE NATIONAL LEVEL

The increasing irrelevance of national boundaries in terms of policy issues and the formulation of corporate strategy has created a feeling of unease and lack of control among some EU citizens and particularly among representatives in national parliaments, leading to questioning of the continuing relevance of national policy and influence in areas which affect business. These fears are heightened particularly by the introduction of EMU and the constraints on national policies which it appears to impose.

The Treaties acknowledge the role of member states in a number of ways. First, the concept of subsidiarity (see Chapter 2), which was introduced in relation to environment policy in the Single European Act and given a more general application and extended in the Maastricht and Amsterdam Treaties, is an attempt to clarify the division of labour between European and sub-European entities and to ensure that only decisions which need to be taken at European level are taken there.

Second, unanimity in the Council of Ministers, although declining as a requirement, remains in a number of policy areas, including taxation. In relation to policies subject to qualified majority voting, member states can still halt the passage of a particular policy, provided they can persuade sufficient other states of the wisdom of this course of action. If a member state makes known its dislike of a particular piece of legislation, the Community's inclusive approach to policy making frequently results in amendments to try to bring the member state on board. This occurred in the case of the Working Time Directive, for example: the United Kingdom made known its strong opposition to the Directive and many of its provisions were effectively watered down to try to gain UK support. These attempts were to no avail as the UK challenged the legal base of the directive in the ECJ – and lost (see Chapter 13).

Third, multi-speed Europe, although no longer applicable to the social policy area since the change in UK policy in 1997, still applies to EMU and the Schengen Agreement and could be developed further in relation to Central and Eastern Europe. The Amsterdam Treaty formalised the notion of flexibility: that is, allowing member states, subject to certain conditions (see Box 2.4), to push ahead with common policies without having to move in the words of Chancellor Kohl at 'the speed of the slowest ship in the convoy'. In other words, flexibility enables member states who wish to do so to push ahead with integration. Conversely, it enables member states to opt out of such initiatives.

Fourth, in relation to directives, member states have discretion on how they implement directives in national law. This discretion is constrained in the sense that they must ensure that their actions comply with the objectives of the directive but nevertheless there can in some cases be considerable scope for the implementation of directives in ways which respect national traditions and conditions. This can be particularly important in the areas of environment and social policy.

Fifth, although EU decisions are sovereign in areas defined by the Treaties (Treaties which the representatives of member states and, in states where referenda are held as part of the ratification process, EU citizens themselves have agreed to), there are many areas in which the EU has no role or only a limited role to play such as health, education and welfare. Even in areas where the EU does have a formal role, member states policy remains important where policies do not have cross-border implications.

These formal acknowledgements of the continuing role of member states do not tell the whole story. Chapter 1 argued that there was some degree of convergence among the various models of capitalism in existence within Europe as those member states with a strong social market economy tradition are adopting a more liberal economic approach and being forced to rein back some of their welfare spending in view of budget constraints and demographic changes. There is some evidence that the Labour government elected in the United Kingdom in 1997, although firmly wedded to the market economy, may mitigate the more extreme free market stance of its predecessors. If this convergence proves real, then genuine consensus at European level is more likely and complaints about policies being passed which are against the interests of individual states will be less forceful.

None of these arguments, however, address the real issue of how much sovereignty and influence individual member states can realistically expect to exercise in an increasingly interdependent world. Opponents of EMU, for example, are concerned that a single currency removes potent instruments of macro-economic control (that is, exchange and interest rates) from national governments. These concerns presuppose that governments have been able to use these instruments effectively and independently. The reality is that currency devaluations, for example, although occasionally bringing short term benefits, have tended to be inflationary and therefore largely ineffective over the medium to long term and have disguised the impact of other factors which can have a fundamental impact on long run competitiveness. Furthermore, governments, even those outside the Exchange Rate Mechanism, have for a long time not had free rein to determine their own interest rates without serious consideration of rates in other countries. In short, claims for loss of sovereignty as a result of EMU are exaggerated as this sovereignty was, to some extent, already illusory. EMU, although open to criticism on a number of grounds, does offer member states the possibility of pooling their sovereignty in economic matters and reclaiming some degree of their lost influence. In a more interdependent world, arguments about the benefits of pooled sovereignty also apply in other areas, particularly those which are the subject of international policy initiatives such as trade and increasingly the environment and competition policy.

THE EUROPEAN LEVEL

The key themes at this level are the consequences for business of the process of integration. This has proved to be an evolutionary process in which the scope and influence of integration have expanded since the formative years of the European Community. It is important to distinguish between the high profile policy measures (such as EMU) and the day-to-day commercial transactions which offer a more complete justification for the measures proposed by Europe's political élites and which underline the important role that business has played in the integration process. Policy decisions are often reactive to the needs created by the everyday interactions of business which by seeking new markets and in developing trans-national networks stimulate, albeit passively, the integration process. Alongside this reactive element, there are aspects of policy making which tend to be more pro-active to commercial operations (such as those measures associated with the SEM).

These facets underline a core aspect that must be reflected within the integration process and the policies that accompany it: that is, the process must be user-led. If measures are put into place which do not facilitate commercial actions, then their impact upon the integration process will be minimal. This is important. Many of the current moves towards enhancing the potency of policy (such as competition policy and the components of industrial policy) and towards deepening integration (through moves to the SEM, for example) need to be based on an evident need either to simplify commercial operations/strategy or to appreciate that there are tangible competitive benefits to the European economy from the process (such as in the case of EMU). Thus the 'policy creep' (the gradual extension of the policy competencies of the EU institutions) which has been a feature of EU integration must be justified by offering tangible benefits to the European economy, such as the synergistic gains from changes in production/logistical systems or because spillover between national policy domains means that interdependence develops sufficiently to justify common policy (a notable feature across many of the EU's expanding portfolio of policies such as environment or infrastructure). This latter feature is further justified by the recognition that common problems (such as competitiveness, the environment, etc.) are best solved commonly rather than independently and that in seeking to mould the global agenda to reflect the EU's interests, the representation of member states interests through a common, mutually agreed position is the most effective method of achieving their objectives.

This highlights a core point underpinning the European integration process: that is, the fundamental motives behind its progress have altered as the political and economic landscape of Europe has changed. The original intention of the founding fathers of European integration was to create a situation of mutual reliance and interdependence between member states which rendered war in Europe impossible. As the Cold War appeared and disappeared and as globalisation became a major theme of policy debate, the rationale behind the pursuit of integration has been tacitly re-assessed. In the late twentieth century integration is increasingly justified as necessary to create conditions within which European business has a chance to be successful within the global marketplace. Policy makers, no doubt under the influence of business, were persuaded that fragmented markets, disparate solutions to common problems and a multitude of regulatory structures were impeding the attainment of this objective. Thus, 'policy creep' and new pushes towards deeper integration were often increasingly justified on the grounds that such measures were beneficial for the performance of European business on a global scale. Consequently, clarity over rules (in areas such as competition and factor markets) and measures to stimulate efficiency within the indigenous, integrated market are regarded as the necessary pre-requisite for the success of European business in the global marketplace.

The efficiency derived from overcoming socio-economic fragmentation within Europe has become a driving theme in the strengthening of the integration process and in ensuring that the process can obtain mass support. The desire to overcome fragmentation inevitability meant that a new range of policies became integral to the objectives of the integration process. For example, the freer mobility and access associated with the SEM created a need for a supporting set of infrastructures to complement these freedoms. Indeed as firms exploited the opportunities of freer mobility, this movement started to place pressure upon governments to extend competition in otherwise protected business services (such as transport, energy and telecommunications) as further necessary complements to this process. Thus the message from business was that if Europe was committed to overcoming fragmentation and achieving efficiency within its businesses, then no tradable sector (notably the aforementioned network sectors) could be excluded from the implications of market integration nor could any competitive distortion (such as state aids or national monopolies) be tolerated or justified on anything but exceptional grounds. Though of course there are some areas where states appeared willing to sustain fragmentation either under political duress (such as airline state aids) or through sovereignty arguments (such as taxation). How long such distortions can last, especially when they run counter to commercial desires for market integration and fair competition, is an issue which is open to conjecture.

In many policy areas, the notion of overcoming fragmentation was also driven by the desire to address the common concerns of EU member states (for example, in stimulating sustainable employment). Whilst member states seek to create conditions, via mutual agreement, where the enterprises of each state can compete fairly there is a recognition that different national actions in areas of pre-competitive initiatives (that is, developments in commercially distant product markets) are a waste of resources and could ultimately damage Europe's commercial success. These concerns are particularly important in areas in which the EU needs to sustain its global competitive positioning. This has led to active trans-national collaboration in areas such as research and development and the information society. These are domains where the demand for products and services is immature and where common action is unlikely to lead to competitive distortion in the integrated marketplace. However once this support has reached a sufficient degree of maturity, firms will need a level playing field to compete fairly in products that result from this collaboration (the EU is attempting to achieve this in the emerging market for information society services and technologies – see Chapters 5 and 12). Thus EU business finds itself in the somewhat paradoxical situation in which firms need to collaborate with each other in order to compete with each other. This collaboration is not merely linked to those products which are some way from commercial reality. Where there is a global market for a product, collaboration (and often rationalisation) in production (or other parts of the logistical chain) often takes place to allow synergies to realise greater efficiency as a means of enabling these companies to compete successfully globally (such as the Airbus consortium) – which may not be possible on an independent basis. Indeed the trans-national rationalisation of production is one of the major outcomes of attempts to overcome fragmentation in EU markets.

As Europe develops a common commercial/economic front in relation to the rest of the world, so there is growing pressure for this to be accompanied by a common political front. Indeed if European states have the same economic concerns, there is a genuine case for greater political collaboration to enable member states to exercise greater collective influences over issues that are of direct concern to them than they would if they continue to act independently. However this raises real fears among national élites who do not necessarily acknowledge the links between political and economic unification or, if they do, argue (as the UK's Conservative Party does) that deeper economic unification explicitly requires a deep political union and should be resisted. This argument depends upon the degree to which EMU, for example, transfers power away from member states towards central supranational institutions. EU institutions have tended to develop in a reactive manner to the integration process. Supranational European institutions have grown gradually in power over the last five decades or so – a process which has been carefully monitored and controlled by member states. The key issue is how much power needs to be ceded to European institutions within a framework of balancing the need for market unification with national sovereignty. Business clearly requires regulations to enable it to operate successfully across the EU: these can frequently be achieved most effectively by a single body which avoids duplication of effort or uncertainty over market rules. Most member states now agree on a role for these institutions in performing the commercially desirable (though albeit limited in power) 'one-stop shop' approach for economic and commercial management. At the end of the twentieth century, there is very little commercial/economic decision making that is not influenced to some degree by central institutions. The issue which must be confronted is how the political dimension of these bodies is represented *vis-à-vis* the global economy. Any agreement on this issue is either likely to be protracted or even ultimately elusive.

THE GLOBAL LEVEL

European integration in one sense is merely a more intense form of the interdependence which is occurring as a result of globalisation. This is reflected in the increasing need of the EU to take heed of the international dimension in the majority of its policies. This is a relatively recent but unsurprising phenomenon. Competition policy, for example, is increasingly having to contend with extraterritorial issues (see Chapter 6) and, once the basic instruments of TENs policy were established, greater emphasis was quickly placed on improving infrastructure links with third countries. The SEM itself was introduced to improve Europe's competitiveness in relation to major global economic operators. In the process of preparing its companies to compete more effectively in third country markets, the SEM also eased the access of third country enterprises to its own markets. That is, once these companies had gained access to Europe's marketplace, their products were legally able to cross Europe's internal borders in the same way as Europe's own domestic companies. It is not surprising therefore, that one of the developing themes of the EU's external commercial policy is its attempts to gain access to the markets of third countries through measures such as the Trade Barriers Regulation and its Market Access Strategy (see Chapter 17).

The parallels between the SEM and what is currently happening in the global marketplace are striking. In the same way as the SEM created the need for flanking policies and the extension of the scope of existing policies, so the interdependence which has been created by reduced barriers to trade globally has pushed many new items onto the agenda of international organisations such as the WTO, the UN and the OECD. Labour market, competition and environment policies are leading the way in this area as policy makers strive to ensure that these policies are not used as trade barriers once other obstacles have been negotiated away.

This 'policy spread' is more than a reaction to the post-war policy of barrier reduction. In many cases, it is a result of the intrinsic nature of the policy or sector itself. For example, many aspects of environment protection, particularly (but not only) in the area of climate change, are most effectively tackled at a global level. Markets too are often truly global: the success of European airlines, for example, is not only dependent on their performance within Europe but also on the well-being of their long-haul business. This explains their current urgency in trying to develop strategic alliances to gain access to routes world-wide (see Case Study 10.2) and also why the European Commission is anxious to negotiate airline agreements on behalf of the Community rather than the currently fragmented situation in which each member state negotiates its own bilateral deals.

Energy markets are also intrinsically international. This stems from the fact that energy resources tend to be located in parts of the world where energy consumption is relatively low and consumed in regions, like Europe, where indigenous resources are limited. With current consumption trends, Europe will need to import an ever greater share of its energy needs from outside its borders. To address this concern the EU has gradually been developing its own forms of energy diplomacy to cultivate good relations with major suppliers and to help countries whose consumption threatens to rocket, as in North Africa, to develop more efficient energy consumption, thereby taking pressure off energy markets. Significantly the Commission has not encountered the same type of resistance in this area as it has in its attempts to gain a mandate for airline negotiations. In the latter case, the Commission is seeking to perform a role currently played by member states whereas in the case of energy the Commission is breaking new ground rather than encroaching on the territory of member states.

Market characteristics are not the only factors adding to policy spread. Technology too plays its part. Indeed some commentators regard the development of telecommunications and related technologies as responsible for the globalisation phenomenon. This is not the place to debate this. However, it is certainly the case that technology developments have not only made certain business functions easier but have also enabled businesses to do things which were not previously possible. The ease with which finance is transferred across the globe is one example of how technologically induced changes impact on the business environment: as well as bringing efficiencies, it also makes businesses and economies more vulnerable to the effects of crises taking place elsewhere. Technology also underpins the emergence of the information society (see Chapter 12) which not only has the potential to alter radically the way we live and work but also is no respecter of national boundaries.

The upshot of this growing interdependence is a requirement on the part of EU member states and European institutions to reconsider their traditional attitudes to policy making. In many senses, businesses have shown themselves to be more in tune with the changes taking place in the national, European and international environments than politicians who, with the current dominance of the ideology of economic liberalism, have shown themselves willing to transfer sovereignty to the market but have not proved quite so ready to endorse the necessary regulation of this market power at an appropriate level by engaging positively at European or international level. This is demonstrated clearly at European level by the delay in reforming European institutions so that they can deal more democratically and efficiently with the new realities. The Amsterdam Treaty was initially intended to prepare the European Union to deal with the major challenges of the twenty-first century. Although some progress was made, in many senses the outcome was disappointing and necessitates the holding of a further IGC before enlargement can take place. That reforms to institutions and policies will have to take place is incontrovertible (enlargement can be delayed only so long whilst the EU puts its house in order) but it appears that it is only the existence of an imminent deadline and the need to avoid crisis which will lead to major breakthroughs. This was not always the case as the negotiation of the Single European Act shows and may not always be the case in the future.

CONCLUSION

At the signing of the Single Europe Act, the Chairman of Fiat noted that the core challenge was about establishing a new order for the old world. The global influence of European commerce was centuries old as a result of Europe's imperial past and colonialism which gave it a strong international trading position. Yet as the twentieth century neared its conclusion, it was clear that Europe's position was being challenged by rising globalisation and by an indigenous economic system that inhibited commercial efficiency. Consequently since the Single European Act, the traditional national based order is being replaced as the common commercial paradigm as enterprises reorganise themselves on a trans-national basis to take the opportunity of more open international markets. This shift, however, produced a backlash from the member states as they saw the conventional unit of political management, the nation state, come under attack as national sovereignty became more loosely defined as a consequence of internationalising markets. Internationalising markets meant that national policy was no longer, in some cases, the most effective and efficient way to manage and regulate the activity of business. Consequently, states sought to re-impose sovereignty through co-operative forums to establish the necessary policy framework at the supranational level. The policy framework at this level has shifted over time to reflect the changing environment of business. The central theme of the state providing direction and help to industry is changing and shifting towards a belief that the entrepreneur knows what is best and that this is broadly guided by the market. Thus Europe is shifting (albeit at varying speeds) towards a liberal, pro-market agenda to facilitate the success of European business on a global stage with the expectation that successful European enterprises will ultimately benefit Europe's citizens.

INDEX